BATTLES

OF

NEW

REPUBLIC

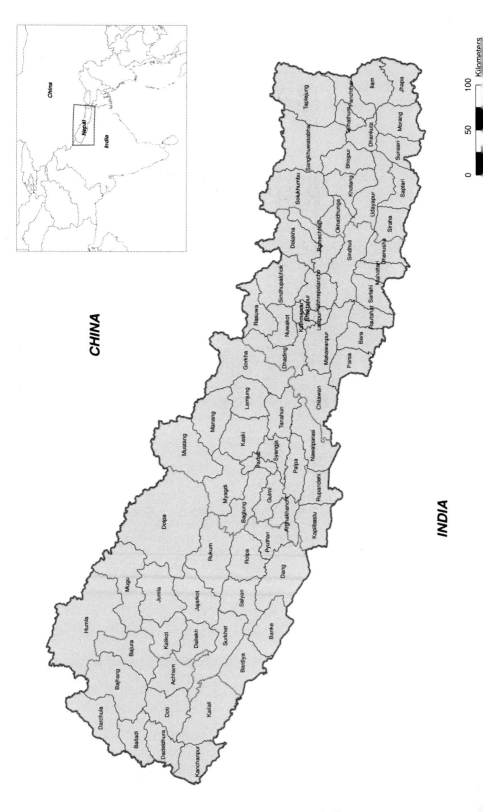

BATTLES
OF THE
NEW
REPUBLIC

A
CONTEMPORARY
HISTORY OF NEPAL

PRASHANT JHA

HURST & COMPANY, LONDON

First published in the United Kingdom in 2014 by
C. Hurst & Co. (Publishers) Ltd.,
41 Great Russell Street, London, WC1B 3PL
© Prashant Jha, 2014
All rights reserved.

Printed in India

Distributed in the United States, Canada and Latin America by
Oxford University Press, 198 Madison Avenue, New York, NY 10016,
United States of America

The right of Prashant Jha to be identified as the author
of this publication is asserted by him in accordance with
the Copyright, Designs and Patents Act, 1988.

A Cataloguing-in-Publication data record for this book
is available from the British Library.

ISBN: 978-1-84904-459-2

This book is printed using paper from registered sustainable
and managed sources.

www.hurstpublishers.com

To Tatta,
for making the journey;
to Papa,
for fighting it out, being so brave;
and to Mummy,
for being the pillar, and for holding us together

Contents

List of Illustrations

Page ii: The map showing the districts of Nepal has been reproduced here courtesy the United Nations Resident Coordinator's Office, Nepal. The boundaries and names shown and the designations used on this map do not imply official endorsement or acceptance by the United Nations.

Page 7: Gyanendra Shah addresses a press conference on 11 June 2008—his first and last—before driving out of the Narayanhiti Durbar, marking the end of the monarchy. (Copyright © AFP)

Page 22: A bearded Baburam Bhattarai gives an interview five days before the start of the People's War in 1996. In 2011, after being elected prime minister, a radically transformed Bhattarai receives garlands and greetings. (Copyright © Bikas Rauniar)

Page 27: One of the two rifles used by the Maoists to launch the People's War. This weapon was originally air-dropped by the Central Intelligence Agency for use by Tibetan rebels who were battling China in the early 1960s, and was picked up by Prachanda, nearly three decades later, from Manang in the upper Himalayas. (Copyright © Dinesh Shrestha)

Page 47: Prachanda (centre), Baburam Bhattarai (to his left), and Mohan Vaidya 'Kiran' (to his right) at the first meeting of the People's Liberation Army (PLA) in 2002. (Copyright © Dinesh Shrestha)

Page 59: Deputy commander of the PLA, Barshaman Pun 'Ananta', chalks out strategy for a planned assault on Bandipur in the mid-hills of Nepal in 2005. (Copyright © Dinesh Shrestha)

Page 64: A state against its people. A photograph from the nineteen-day Janandolan of April 2006, which forced King Gyanendra Shah to concede that sovereignty lay with the people, and not with the Palace. (Copyright © Bikas Rauniar)

Page 98: (left to right) Sita Dahal, Prachanda's wife; Prachanda; Baburam Bhattarai; and Hisila Yami, Bhattarai's wife, pose for a group portrait in Rukum district at the end of 2004. Soon after this picture was taken, Prachanda and Bhattarai disagreed on the approach the Maoist party should take with India and the Palace, and made up only after the monarch's coup in 2005. (Copyright © Dinesh Shrestha)

Page 104: Special envoy from India, Karan Singh, arrives at the Palace to counsel King Gyanendra at the peak of the Janandolan. The Nepali Street rejected Singh's compromise formula, which allowed the Palace to retain authority. (Copyright © Bikas Rauniar)

Page 135: Girija Prasad Koirala, the veteran democratic leader, died in March 2010, leaving a gaping hole in the peace process. The citizens of Kathmandu turned out in the thousands to mourn his passing. (Copyright © Bikas Rauniar)

Page 141: Special envoy from India, Shyam Saran, arrives in Kathmandu in August 2011 to issue a stern message to the Maoists and to deter Madhesi parties from supporting Prachanda's bid for the prime ministership. Behind Saran, to his left, stands Ambassador Rakesh Sood. (This picture is reproduced here via special arrangement.)

Page 211: Former prime minister of India, Chandra Shekhar, firmly supported the movement for democracy in Nepal. The speech he gave in 1990 inspired many to rise up against the monarch's autocracy. Chandra Shekhar is seen here with Ganesh Man Singh (to his left), G. P. Koirala (to his immediate right), and Krishna Prasad Bhattarai (further along to Chandra Shekhar's right). (Copyright © Bikas Rauniar)

Page 218: Tula Narayan Sah (sitting cross-legged on the bed) speaks to Madhesi villagers in the Tarai. (Photograph courtesy the Nepal Madhes Foundation.)

Page 243: A garlanded Ram Baran Yadav, wearing a daura-saluwar, takes oath as the first President of the republic in Nepali. To his right, vice-president Parmanand Jha, wearing a kurta, takes oath in Hindi. To his left, G. P. Koirala, the man who expected to be President, looks on. (Copyright © Bikas Rauniar)

Page 272: Prachanda and Baburam Bhattarai embrace warmly after the latter is elected prime minister in August 2011. The Maoists won with the support of the Madhesi parties. (Copyright © AFP)

Page 286: Deepak Chand, a PLA combatant, in the Kailali cantonment in far-west Nepal, plays with his daughter. Chand and his wife, who were both once warriors, were grappling with their future as a final peace agreement was signed in November 2011. (Photograph courtesy the author.)

Page 329: On 27 May 2012, the last day of the current term of the Constituent Assembly (CA), members of the Brahmin and Chhetri Samaj congregate outside the complex which houses the CA, protesting against identity-based federalism. The backlash from the conservative elements of Nepali society, among other reasons, led to the collapse of the CA without a Constitution having been drafted. (Copyright © Bikas Rauniar)

A Timeline of the Transition

1951: The year marks the end of the 104-year-old, autocratic Rana oligarchy. King Tribhuvan Shah, the Nepali Congress (NC) and Rana rulers arrive at a compromise in Delhi, mediated by Jawaharlal Nehru, and agree to hold elections for a Constituent Assembly (CA).

1959: Parliamentary elections are held under a Constitution granted by King Mahendra Shah. The NC wins two-thirds majority.

15 December 1960: Mahendra Shah dismisses Nepal's first democratically elected government, headed by Prime Minister Bishweshwor Prasad Koirala.

1962: The monarch promulgates a Constitution which institutionalizes a party-less framework and centralizes power in the Palace. This is known as the Panchayat system.

1972: Mahendra Shah dies at fifty-two and Birendra Shah takes over as the new king.

1979-80: Student protests force the king to call a referendum on the nature of the polity. The party-less framework defeats the multiparty system amid suspicions of electoral fraud.

1990: A People's Movement, the Janandolan, leads to the restoration of multiparty democracy. A new Constitution limits the monarchy's role, retains Nepal as a Hindu kingdom, paves the way for a parliamentary system, and grants fundamental rights. Radical Left forces reject the Constitution.

1991: Elections are held. The NC wins and Girija Prasad Koirala is elected prime minister.

1994: An internal rift in the NC leads to mid-term polls; the Communist Party of Nepal (Unified Marxist Leninist) [UML] emerges as the single largest party. Veteran Left leader Manmohan Adhikari becomes prime minister.

1995: NC leader Sher Bahadur Deuba becomes prime minister with the support of a pro-monarchy outfit, the Rastriya Prajatantra Party.

1996: The Communist Party of Nepal (Maoist) launches a 'People's War'.

1996-99: Nepal's run with instability continues, with three different prime ministers in as many years. The third parliamentary poll results in a victory for the NC. Krishna Prasad Bhattarai is elected prime minister.

2000: Prime Minister Bhattarai initiates back-channel talks with the Maoists, but is replaced by G. P. Koirala, who advocates a more belligerent, security-based approach.

2001

June: King Birendra and his immediate family are massacred. The official investigation indicts Crown Prince Dipendra, amid widespread perception of a conspiracy. Birendra's younger brother, Gyanendra, takes over as monarch.

July-November: Ceasefire talks are held between the government, now led by Sher Bahadur Deuba, and the Maoists.

23 November: The Maoists attack a barracks of the Royal Nepalese Army (RNA). The ceasefire collapses, the government declares an emergency and deploys the RNA. The civil war intensifies.

2002

May: As NC president, G. P. Koirala, opposes the extension of the emergency, Prime Minister Deuba dissolves Parliament with the support of the Palace and the RNA. The NC splits.

4 October: King Gyanendra dismisses Prime Minister Deuba, assumes a more direct political role, and appoints a loyalist, Lokendra Bahadur Chand, as prime minister.

2003

February: A second ceasefire is signed between the Nepal government and the Maoists.

August: The RNA executes seventeen unarmed Maoists in Doramba. The civil war resumes.

2005

1 February: King Gyanendra assumes direct executive power, arrests political leaders, stifles civil liberties and declares a state of emergency.

October: A Maoist party conclave in Chunbang declares that the party's immediate political objective is to make Nepal a 'democratic republic'; monarchy and feudalism are categorized as the principal enemies.

22 November: A 12-point Understanding is signed between the Seven Party Alliance and the Maoists in Delhi to fight 'autocratic monarchy'.

2006

April: A nineteen-day People's Movement, the second Janandolan, succeeds. King Gyanendra concedes that sovereignty rests with the people. The Parliament, dissolved in 2002, is reinstated. A ceasefire is declared and G. P. Koirala takes oath as prime minister.

May: The Parliament clips royal privileges, brings the RNA under direct civilian rule, declares Nepal a secular state and abolishes untouchability.

16 June: Maoist chairman Prachanda appears over ground, escorted by Nepal's home minister, Krishna Prasad Sitaula. Peace talks begin at Prime Minister Koirala's residence.

21 November: The Comprehensive Peace Agreement declares the end of the civil war and creates a roadmap for elections to a CA.

2007

15 January: An interim Parliament is constituted with participation by the Maoists. An interim Constitution is also promulgated, which replaces the Constitution of 1990.

16 January: Upendra Yadav of the Madhesi Janadhikar Forum is arrested in Kathmandu after he sets fire to a copy of the interim Constitution.

17 January: A young protestor, Ramesh Mahato, is killed in Lahan. The Madhes movement erupts across Nepal's southern plains.

7 February: Prime Minister Koirala promises federalism and an equitable electoral system.

1 April: An interim government, with ministers from the Maoist party, is constituted.

December: Parties agree to institutionalize a mixed electoral system and to abolish the monarchy by the time the CA holds its first meeting.

2008

February: The Second Madhes movement breaks out. An 8-point agreement, hammered out between the government and Madhesi parties, commits to a Madhes province, the group entry of Madhesis into the Nepal Army (NA), and to ensuring the proportionate and inclusive representation of Madhesis in organs of the state.

March: 'Free Tibet' protests erupt in Kathmandu. China asks the Nepal government to crack down on the protesters.

10 April: Elections are held. In a surprise result, the Maoists emerge as the single-largest party.

28 May: The CA holds its first sitting. The monarchy is abolished and it is decided that Nepal will have a Federal Democratic Republican Constitution.

July: The NC general secretary, Ram Baran Yadav, is elected Nepal's first-ever President.

August: The Maoist chairman, Pushpa Kamal Dahal 'Prachanda', is elected the first prime minister of the new republic. He visits Beijing to attend the concluding ceremony of the Olympics.

September: Prime Minister Prachanda visits Delhi.

November: The Maoist party holds a conclave in Kharipati; the party's ideology takes a radical, confrontational turn against India and the NC.

2009

3 May: The Maoist-led government dismisses the army chief, General Rukmangad Katawal. President Yadav asks him to stay on.

4 May: Prime Minister Prachanda resigns from office, terming the President's move 'unconstitutional', and blames 'foreign forces' for conspiring against the Maoists.

25 May: The UML leader, Madhav Kumar Nepal, is elected the new prime minister.

2010

1-7 May: The Maoists call for an indefinite, nationwide strike, demanding Prime Minister Nepal's resignation. The strike fails and middle-class defiance forces the Maoists to withdraw.

28 May: The CA's two-year term is extended by another year. Prime Minister Nepal agrees to resign and make way for a national unity government.

July onwards: A prime minister cannot be elected even after repeated rounds of voting in Parliament.

2011

February: Jhalanath Khanal is elected prime minister on the basis of a secret, 7-point pact between the Maoists and the UML.

May: As the CA's term lapses for the second time, parties agree on a three-month extension. Prime Minister Khanal agrees to resign to make way for a unity government.

June: A tactical alliance between Maoist leaders, Mohan Vaidya 'Kiran' and Baburam Bhattarai, forces Chairman Prachanda to nominate Bhattarai as the party's prime ministerial candidate.

28 August: Baburam Bhattarai is elected Nepal's thirty-fifth prime minister, with the support of Madhesi parties, and on the basis of a 4-point agreement.

1 November: A 7-point agreement is signed. Parties agree to integrate a maximum of 6,500 former Maoist combatants into a specially created NA directorate. Combatants start to ponder their options for the future.

2012

10 April: Dissent breaks out in the People's Liberation Army (PLA) ranks. The Maoist-led government sends the NA to take over PLA cantonments. The peace process is now declared to be 'irreversible'.

15 May: Parties arrive at a pact on constitutional issues, including a mixed form of government and eleven federal provinces.

16 May: The Mohan Vaidya 'Kiran' faction of the Maoists, the Upendra Yadav-led Madhesi alliance, MPs belonging to ethnic minority groups, and second-rung leaders of the Madhesi front oppose the pact.

17 May: The Maoists and the Madhesi parties seek a revision of the earlier agreement. The NC and the UML reject it.

18-20 May: A three-day strike called by an umbrella ethnic organization paralyses the country.

22 May: Law minister and NC leader, Krishna Prasad Sitaula, registers an amendment bill in Parliament to extend the CA's term by three months. Party president Sushil Koirala opposes the extension.

24 May: NC ministers resign from the government, bowing to pressure from within the party to disallow further extensions to the CA's term of operation.

25 May: The Supreme Court forbids any further extensions to the CA's term.

27 May, 10.45 p.m.: Negotiations fail. The Cabinet calls for elections to a new CA to be held on 21 November.

27 May, midnight: The term of Nepal's first elected CA runs out, without a Constitution having been written.

29 May: President Ram Baran Yadav terms the Prime Minister Bhattarai-led government a 'caretaker' government and restricts its role.

June: The Unified Communist Party of Nepal (Maoist) splits. Mohan Vaidya 'Kiran' splinters off to form the Communist Party of Nepal-Maoist and accuses Prachanda of 'Right-wing revisionism'.

June-November: The NC and the UML refuse to participate in elections under a government led by the Maoists. Prime Minister Bhattarai fails to hold polls on 21 November.

2013

February: The Maoists, led by Prachanda, hold a party convention and reiterate their commitment to peaceful political change, a new Constitution, a moderate stance on India as well as to formally drop the protracted People's War line.

March: An interim election government is constituted under Chief Justice Khila Raj Regmi to hold polls to elect a second CA. Members of the Council of Ministers include former bureaucrats.

19 November: Nepal holds elections for a second CA. The NC emerges as the single-largest party and the Maoists and the Madhesi parties face a severe electoral rout.

2014

February: NC President Sushil Koirala is elected prime minister with the support of the UML.

Prologue

It should not have come as a surprise.

I was attending a morning class on problems in international relations at the Jawaharlal Nehru University (JNU) in Delhi. As the professor began his lecture on Francis Fukuyama's end-of-history thesis and the victory of liberal capitalism, my cellphone beeped. A text from Hari Roka, a senior at the university, announced crisply: 'The king has taken over.'

A month earlier, friends in Kathmandu had said that it was just a question of time—when, not if. Old loyalists of the Narayanhiti Durbar, the Palace, had sniggered about how they would clean up the mess created by mainstream political parties in the previous decade of democratic rule. We will also finish off the Maoist insurgency in six months, senior army generals itching to exercise direct control had told me gleefully.

During that winter break, I interned at a research organization which also doubled up as a hub for democratic activists. Human rights defenders, journalists, Left sympathizers and academics used to drop by the office located right next to Singha Durbar, the government secretariat. Over endless cups of tea, they would worry about how the wrong Durbar—Narayanhiti—was once again emerging as the centre of power.

A royal coup had abruptly ended the country's brief experiment with democracy in 1960. After thirty years of autocratic royal rule, a popular movement, the Janandolan, had led to the restoration of multiparty democracy. But the new Constitution was a document of compromise. Tensions between democratically elected governments and the king continued to simmer and, in recent years, the Palace had misinterpreted constitutional provisions to expand political control.

Here was an ambitious monarch, egged on by an aristocracy and an army contemptuous of popular representatives, smug in the belief that only he had the right answers. Political observers in Kathmandu, warring with each other at the best of times, had now arrived at a rare, haunting consensus. His Majesty King Gyanendra Bir Bikram Shah Dev was about to trample on the remaining traces of the democratic Constitution of 1990 and assume absolute power.

Hari's message left me with a sinking feeling.

The sanitized academic lecture suddenly seemed irrelevant to the political reality I inhabited—where a dogmatic far-Left, a discredited democratic Centre and a lunatic far-Right were fighting each other in a militarized set-up; where liberalism had become a cover for perpetuating the status quo while a revolution devoured those in whose name it was being fought; where violence had become a legitimate tool to push one's politics; where a toxic mix of economic deprivation and the fury of marginalized minorities had led to massive resistance against a crippled state; and where successive generations of Nepali citizens—ever since the early twentieth century—had to fight oppressive regimes for freedom, only to see it reversed within a short span of time.

I sneaked out of class and walked down to the Indian socialist activist, Vijay Pratap's house near the Brahmaputra hostel inside JNU.

Nepali political activists in Delhi were huddled together, watching the television channel, Nepal 1. It showed footage of King Gyanendra making a televised address, sacking Prime Minister Sher Bahadur Deuba and taking over power in order to 'restore democracy'. The Royal Nepalese Army (RNA) was on the streets and politicians were under arrest. The anchor announced that the phone network had been cut off. Internet was unavailable and sites hosted from Nepali servers could not be accessed. And there were rumours that flight connections may be terminated.

Nepal was being pushed back to its isolationist days.

'It will not work,' said Pradeep Giri. Giri was a senior ideologue of the Nepali Congress (NC)—the party which had ruled Nepal for most of its democratic period since 1990 and had, from most accounts, not been very good at its job. He belonged to a political family from the Siraha district in the country's southern plains, the Tarai. His uncle, Tulsi Giri, was an ardent monarchist who had been appointed prime minister by Gyanendra's father, Mahendra, in the 1960s when the king had dismissed the elected government. Gyanendra would soon pull the same man out of retirement, which he had been spending as a Jehovah's Witness in Bangalore, and make him the vice-chairman of his Council of Ministers.

But Pradeep Giri was himself a long-standing socialist. He counted the late Indian veterans, Ram Manohar Lohia and Jayaprakash Narayan, as mentors, and continued to share intimate ties with the current generation of democratic and Left leaders in Delhi, Patna and Lucknow. Widely admired for his erudition and commitment to radical non-violent politics, Giri was also seen as a bit of a maverick for his utter frankness—a delight for journalists, but a quality not much appreciated by colleagues.

Giri was often in Delhi and made it a point to visit JNU, his alma mater. He said, 'His father did exactly this. He thinks he can repeat the act. The world has changed. This is the final nail in the monarchy's coffin.'

On a day when the king looked invincible with military support, when party leaders were in the dock, and when the Maoists were still in the jungles, this seemed exactly like the wishful thinking politicians engage in for public consumption. I nodded politely, but was unconvinced, little knowing how prophetic Giri's words were.

Giri then threw up his ace. He had been in touch with sections of the Indian government when the rumours of the coup had picked up. He announced, 'They have told me this does not have Delhi's green signal.'

The mood in the room seemed to change. We all stared at Giri. It was difficult to believe that the king would take such a step without the consent of what Nepalis often call the Dilli Durbar. South Block, which houses both the Prime Minister's Office and the Ministry of External Affairs, had been supporting the 'twin pillar' policy of constitutional monarchy and multiparty democracy in

Nepal in public. Privately, it had backed the king's de facto rule since 2002 when Gyanendra first dismissed an elected prime minister while maintaining a facade of democracy by appointing prime ministers from political parties.

Hari Roka jumped in and said, 'This is our chance.' Roka was a Left activist who had spent more than seven years in jail for opposing the Palace's dictatorship before 1990. After swinging between various Left parties, he had decided to become an independent analyst and wrote prolifically in the Nepali press. At that time, he was working on his doctoral thesis on Nepal's political economy at JNU.

Along with others, he had been arguing that the two pillars of monarchy and democracy were antithetical to each other. This school believed that the political parties and the Maoists had to get together against the king, reversing the conventional wisdom of the day among pundits in Kathmandu and Delhi that 'constitutional forces'—the parties and the king—should unite against the Maoists.

Those present—Giri, Roka, Nepali student activists and Indian socialists—realized the need to quickly generate pressure in Delhi. This would fill in for the vacuum in Nepal where a total clampdown had made dissent impossible, as well as send a message to the foreign policy mandarins of the Indian capital.

Nepali migrant organizations were tapped. The JNU Students' Union jumped in, promising to provide people for demonstrations. Sympathizers of the Maoists were contacted to initiate channels of communication with the rebels. Indian political leaders gave appointments readily—and expressed solidarity. A loose coalition called the Anti-Monarchy Front was immediately formed and a big rally was called for the next day in front of the Nepal embassy on Barakhamba Road in central Delhi.

The date was 1 February 2005.

~

After eight years of studying and working in Delhi, I returned home in early 2007.

While I was attending high school, finishing university, forging friendships, having late-night, alcohol-fuelled debates on politics in hostel rooms, interning in Indian newsrooms, and falling in love, Nepal had changed. A royal massacre which left everyone stunned, a brutal civil war, the monarch's coup, an alliance between democratic forces and the Maoists, and a People's Movement, had transformed the country.

The Janandolan of 2006, a mass upsurge for democracy, had forced King Gyanendra Shah to accept that sovereignty lay with the people, not the Palace. The monarchy was in a suspended state. The partnership between the Maoists and other political parties had become institutionalized. Nepal's decade-long civil war had ended on 21 November 2006 with a peace pact being struck between erstwhile warring forces. The RNA was now just the Nepal Army (NA)—in law, and in nomenclature, it had been brought under democratic control. Ethnic groups, long excluded from the power structure, had begun asserting themselves. The promise of an elected Constituent Assembly (CA), which would draft a new social contract, held popular appeal.

For the next six years, I travelled across the country, talked to a wide range of politicians and ordinary citizens, and reported on the internal and external dimensions of Nepali politics.

From war to peace, from monarchy to republicanism, from being a Hindu kingdom to secularism, from being unitary to a potentially federal state, and from a narrow hill-centric notion of nationalism to an inclusive sense of citizenship—Nepal's transformation was, and is, among the most ambitious political experiments in recent years in South Asia.

Battles of the New Republic: A Contemporary History of Nepal is a personal attempt to explore the underlying processes that are at the heart of this transition. The decade-long People's War waged by the Maoists and the nineteen-day long People's Movement are striking and powerful instances of mass political mobilization. They provide different templates of how society can be re-engineered and power structures shaken up. But this is an attempt to not merely look at wars and movements, but what happens after them.

After the crowds return home, after the frenzy which accompanies a moment of political victory dissipates, after the camera lights shift and reporters move on to the next story, the hard work of politics begins. In the last six years, the promise of a new Nepal has collided with the entrenched power structures and the decadent political culture of the old Nepal. Instability has remained the norm, with a government changing every nine months. A multi-class, multiparty alliance enabled Nepal to defeat the monarchy and restore democracy. But the broad consensus broke, natural social and economic cleavages widened, and political polarization sharpened when it came to attaining the goals of justice, inclusion, rights, dignity and state restructuring.

This is a story of the politics of gradual revolution, where former rebels attempt to change the mainstream even as the mainstream co-opts and changes them; of partial sovereignty where domestic political actors have to grapple with the role of a regional power in a complex international environment; of inclusive nationalism where marginalized social groups struggle for dignity and power and challenge long-held notions of what constitutes being a citizen; and of institutionalizing shanti and sambidhan, peace and the Constitution, in a polity governed by a fragile balance of power, with no outright victors or losers.

This is a story of how managing political change is always more difficult than the act of bringing it about. This is a story of war and peace, of the fate of a revolution, of popular aspirations, of weak and strong men and their ambitions and vulnerabilities, of the deepening of democracy, and of the death of a dream. Ultimately, it is a story of a society and a nation grappling with the fundamental political question of who ought to exercise power, to what end, and for whose benefit.

BOOK 1

POLITICS OF GRADUAL REVOLUTION

'Hami Rato Manche [We, the Red People]'

We can swallow fire, we can drain the ocean
We are the people who were created from the martyrs' blood
We are the people who will destroy all the enemies' forts
We, the red people, of the People's Liberation

We are the people who keep hunting for the people's enemies
We make the earth and the sky tremble, cause the wind and storms to blow
We chew up the hearts of feudalists and imperialists
We, the red people, of the People's Liberation

—A Maoist revolutionary song used by the People's Liberation Army
during training, battle marches, and for propaganda.

Walking into the Sunset

Kings do not hold press conferences.

But when a king is no longer king; when a 240-years-old dynasty crumbles; when a man is spending his last night in what has been his ancestral home for decades, where he was born, and where his brothers died, established protocol ceases to matter.

The Narayanhiti Durbar was crowded on 11 June 2008. Journalists had lined up and had surrounded the Palace's southern gate. Guards carefully scrutinized identity cards before allowing entry. After a short walk over unkempt, open lawns, and up steep stairs, we entered a big hall. Glittering chandeliers were hanging from high ceilings, but if one was looking for signs of grandeur, that was about it. Rickety chairs and benches had been set out. Television cameramen jostled for space up front, waiting for the occupant of the house to arrive.

Fifteen days earlier, in its first sitting, Nepal's elected Constituent Assembly (CA) had abolished the monarchy. Close to midnight, Krishna Prasad Sitaula, home minister in the interim government, had moved a resolution declaring Nepal an 'independent, indivisible, sovereign, secular, and inclusive democratic republican nation'. The motion had been passed with a resounding majority.

The CA's declaration was a logical outcome of the nineteen-day People's Movement of 2006. Slogans such as 'Gyane chor, desh chod! [Thief Gyane, leave the country!]'; and 'Loktantrik ganatantra jindabad! [Long live the democratic republic!]', marked the popular protests.

With his coup of 1 February, King Gyanendra Shah had opened up multiple fronts simultaneously. A broad alliance—supporters of older parliamentary parties, Maoists, businessmen, civil society organizations, academics, journalists, workers, peasants, the middle class, as well as women's groups and people from different castes and ethnicities—had taken over the streets and had forced the king to make that fundamental declaration which distinguished a monarchy from a democracy: that sovereignty lay with the people and not with the Palace.

Nepali democrats had consistently remained committed to the idea of a constitutional monarchy, but monarchs had repeatedly betrayed their promise to stay within limits prescribed by statutes and sought greater power. This time, the political class—and their supporters—had decided that it had had enough. Monarchy and democracy could not coexist. The king's actions had also intensified the violence. Killings had shot up, and the civil war showed no sign of resolution, shattering the monarch's promise that he would usher in peace. The brutalities of the Royal Nepalese Army (RNA)—of which Gyanendra Shah was the supreme commander—had alienated citizens from the state. The king was increasingly seen as being a part of the problem rather than the solution. The impulses for full democracy and peace had guided the movement.

Anthropologists went beyond the immediate political triggers. A generational transformation, the dismantling of the older networks of patronage, the emergence of a new economic order and middle class, and the shattering of the laughable myth that the king was an incarnation of god slowly eroded the traditional legitimacy of the institution. The unconstitutional takeover had removed whatever little political legitimacy the monarchy was left with.

Republicanism was the guiding spirit of the partnership between the Maoists and the democratic political parties—the latter had given up support for constitutional monarchy and the former accepted the logic of a peaceful movement to achieve the goal. If there was any doubt left about popular sentiment, the April 2008 elections cleared it—parties with a republican platform won overwhelmingly, with the Maoists leading the charge. The openly pro-monarchy Rastriya Prajatantra Party (Nepal) bagged only four out of the 601 seats in the CA.

Home Minister Sitaula had met the monarch, whose position

was officially 'suspended' by the interim Constitution, soon after the poll results became clear. The king had a list of demands, chief among which was a desire that his stepmother, in her late eighties, be allowed to stay on in a building inside the palace complex. The government provided him accommodation in the capital's outskirts, in Nagarjun, and continued minimal security arrangements. Palace insiders later confided to me that the king was hoping that his old ally, the army, would step in to rescue him. But the military had accepted the regime change and had put in its lot with the civilian government. It had realized that the Palace was a sinking ship and there was little to gain by being on the wrong side of history.

~

As Gyanendra Shah walked into the room, he was accosted by the mob of cameramen. In his trademark daura-saluwar, looking calm, he sat down and began reading out from a document in Nepali.

The country, which had been founded by 'our ancestor, Prithvi Narayan Shah', 240 years ago, was going through 'serious and sensitive upheaval'. Shah highlighted 'unification, preservation of nationalism, democratization and modernization' as the contribution of the Nepali monarchy. Admitting that his 'efforts' to ensure peace and prosperity had not been successful, Shah reiterated that he had noble objectives when he had taken over 'seven years ago', as a result of an 'unnatural, unexpected and tragic incident'.

This was a direct, and surprising, reference to the massacre of 1 June 2001 in which Gyanendra's brother and the then king, Birendra, and his immediate family, were killed. A report filed by a commission, as well as eyewitness accounts, blamed the massacre on the then crown prince, Dipendra, who had been upset with his parents for not allowing him to marry the girl of his choice. But the Nepali Street never bought the official version. Many blamed Gyanendra and his son, the notorious prince Paras who was known for drunken brawls and hit-and-run vehicular assaults, of having engineered the killings to take over the throne. The fact that Gyanendra was out of town on the night of the massacre, and Paras escaped unscathed, added to the conspiracy theories. While there is no evidence to prove this thesis, it still gained traction, eroding the monarchy's appeal. When Gyanendra finally took over power, many connected the dots and suspected that assuming absolute power had been his intention all along.

Now, the Shah dynasty's final monarch had brought up the massacre—for the first time—himself.

'I would like to express, with god as my witness, certain things which I couldn't express earlier because of my official responsibilities but which have been troubling my inner heart all the time.' He added that he had not been able to shed tears, and lighten the burden of pain at the 'gruesome destruction of my relatives'. At that time, some people had accused him of 'great indiscretion and cruelty', but he had had no choice but to tolerate it. The former monarch pointed out that bullet fragments were still in the body of his wife, 'who was also wounded and survived'.

Gyanendra had been a businessman before becoming king in 2001, with interests in hotels, tea estates, tobacco and real estate. During the royal dictatorship, speculation about royal wealth had intensified, with rumours of money stashed away in foreign accounts and property amassed across the world regularly doing the rounds. The Maoists had, in their political narrative, often juxtaposed the monarch as representing the rich feudals, as opposed to the poor, starving, toiling Nepali masses. At the press conference that day, the former king categorically stated that he had no 'movable or immovable' property outside Nepal.

The clincher came with Shah declaring that he would abide by the decision of the CA. Dispelling the rumour that he may flee the country, Shah said he would stay on in his 'motherland' and continue to contribute in whatever way he could. He handed over the 'crown and scepter used by the kings of the Shah dynasty' to the government of Nepal for 'safekeeping and protection for ages to come'. He ended the Shah monarchy's first and last press conference in the Narayanhiti Durbar with the customary prayer to Pashupatinath to bless Nepal.

It was a sight laden with symbolism. A man who had always stayed insulated from the crowds, who had always been protected by

layers and layers of security, who was used to being respectfully addressed as 'sarkar', who would decide when others in his presence could speak, now had to confront a mob of journalists who asked him questions and wanted him to stay on at the press meet, and only reluctantly made way for him when he refused to add to the statement that he had made. Hierarchies were breaking down, no one was beyond scrutiny, and even those at the pinnacle of the political system had realized that they could not remain unaccountable. If Gyanendra Shah had imbibed these lessons a little earlier, history might have taken a different course.

I was at the back of the hall. The drizzle outside had become a downpour and, as we walked out, Sudheer Sharma, then editor of the *Nepal* weekly and a veteran Palace-watcher, told me, 'He won't give up so easily. He will stay in politics in some form.'

But that day, Gyanendra Shah displayed an uncharacteristic trait—he walked away. He converted what was a compulsion into virtue by his grace. Two hours later, Gyanendra, his wife sitting next to him, drove out of Narayanhiti Durbar for the final time. The twelfth king of Nepal would go down in history as an accidental monarch, and one who had failed in the ultimate duties of a king—retaining the trust of his subjects and preserving the dynasty. Nepal's monarchy was dead. The Palace would soon become a museum. The old had gone, but the new was yet to be born.

The new republic would move on to newer political battles, dominated by the political force which had been at the forefront of the endeavour to abolish the feudal monarchy—the Communist Party of Nepal (Maoist). But the end of the monarchy did not mean the end of the old order. The battle between new forces born out of popular movements and those which derived strength from established social structures would be long and hard. That battle would define the course of the rocky, volatile, unstable, non-linear and, ultimately, disheartening transition in Nepal. But how did the Kingdom of Nepal transform into the Federal Democratic Republic of Nepal in the first place?

Waging War and Peace

The Shah dynasty was originally from Gorkha district in the mid-hills of central Nepal. It was ironic that the man who could justifiably take a large part of the credit for ensuring the end of the monarchy also happened to be from Gorkha.

Baburam Bhattarai was born in 1954 in Khoplang village in a peasant family which traced its lineage back to the Gorkha kingdom's priestly clan. Three years earlier, Nepal's first democratic revolution had seen King Tribhuvan and democratic activists come together to topple the 104-year-old oligarchic regime of the Rana aristocracy. Through this period, the Rana family had treated the country like a private fiefdom. The king had remained locked up inside the palace.

Internally, the Rana rulers maintained an extractive relationship with the populace. Family members and administrators took ownership of huge tracts of land, where the poorest worked in the most exploitative of circumstances. There was nothing by way of representative government, and incremental political reform was an alien concept. Next door in India, even the British had—gradually—introduced constitutionalism and sought to accommodate emerging voices through token legislative mechanisms. Unlike the colonial power, the Nepali rulers had made no investment in improving the country's infrastructure and communication networks.

Externally, they maintained a subservient relationship with British India. Men from the hills of Nepal served as cheap mercenaries in the British Indian Army, killing and dying for imperial masters even as Orientalists created the myth of the 'brave Gorkha' to romanticize, and legitimize, the practice. When the Sepoy Revolt broke out in 1857, the then Nepali ruler, Jung Bahadur Rana, personally led troops to north India as a gesture of loyalty to help the British out. The Empire, in return, gifted the area that is today Nepal's western Tarai to the Ranas. The quid pro quo was simple— the Ranas would help secure key British interests in Nepal and the region, and London would allow Kathmandu to remain notionally independent.

With the Indian independence struggle picking up steam, stirrings of change had engulfed the neighbourhood. Nepali exiles in India had formed the Nepali Congress (NC), modelled on the lines of the Indian National Congress, while Left activists had drawn inspiration from the Indian communists to set up the Communist Party of Nepal in the late 1940s. Nepali activists participated in the Quit India Movement, calculating that until India was free, Nepal would not be able to oust the Ranas—who derived support from the British.

In 1950, the NC began an armed rebellion against the Ranas, while the king took refuge in the Indian embassy and flew to Delhi as a mark of protest against the regime. After the British had left, the new Indian government inherited the imperial legacy of influencing Nepal affairs. Unlike the British, though, the new nationalist regime in Delhi was more sympathetic to accommodating forces of freedom. In 1951, the Delhi Compromise—mediated by Prime Minister Jawaharlal Nehru—saw the end of the Rana aristocracy, a new power-sharing arrangement between the political forces, and the promise of an elected CA to draft Nepal's social contract.

1

In 1954, the year Baburam Bhattarai was born, the capital was a hotbed of intrigue. Tribhuvan was dying and his son, Mahendra, was about to take over. The uneasy pact between the Palace, the old Rana regime, and the NC, mediated in Delhi, had all but crumbled. The monarch had begun shuffling prime ministers at regular intervals. The political landscape was fragmented, with several factions jostling for power and lobbying with the Palace for patronage. Instead of making way for popular democracy, the Shah reign had slowly replaced the Rana aristocracy. The promise of elections to constitute a CA had remained just that, a mere promise, and, in another five years, the new king would go back on the pledge. Mahendra unilaterally declared a Constitution and held elections for a Parliament in 1959. The NC won a resounding majority in the polls, but Prime Minister Bishweshwor Prasad Koirala's tenure was short-lived.

In 1960, Mahendra Shah sacked and arrested the elected prime minister. He used the army to crack down on political activity, banned political parties, and assumed absolute control. Castigating basic liberal democratic precepts and practices as a Western import, monarchists introduced what they termed the Panchayat system. The nomenclature was a bid to project it as a new form of 'grassroots democracy suited to the soil'. But like experiments of 'guided democracy' in Indonesia and Pakistan around the time, this essentially meant centralized control with token elections, the curtailing of fundamental rights and the stifling of freedom.

Baburam had begun school when the short-lived experiment with democracy failed. But he was too young, and his family too distant from the capital, to be aware of the machinations underway. Life for him entailed walking several miles to a primary school in a nearby village, and helping at home and in the fields. Baburam was lucky that the district had the infrastructure to meet his family's emphasis on learning. Missionaries, led by teachers from the US and Kerala, ran the Amar Jyoti Janata School, which was also known as the Luintel School, in Palungtar village. Baburam enrolled in the new school in Class 3 at the age of seven. In 1970, he was to rise to national prominence when he topped the national School Leaving Certificate examination with distinction. At sixteen, Baburam had become a 'Board First', a prelude to successive academic achievements and a label that would remain with him for the rest of his life.

The success enabled his shift to Kathmandu, where he joined the Amrit Science College. Baburam recalls that this was where he received his initial political education. He developed an instinctive dislike for the monarchy, which was running a dictatorship under the garb of localized democracy. He was not alone. A new generation was now emerging, which had grown up during the 1960s, which had been exposed to at least a high-school education, had read and heard about democracy, communism, social change and revolutions elsewhere in the world, and wondered why Nepal had to live under an absolutist king. Baburam once again stood first in intermediate exams in 1972, the year Mahendra died and made way for his son, Birendra, as Nepal's king. Baburam then received a scholarship under the Colombo Plan to study architecture in Chandigarh and left Nepal.

~

The bus had broken down on the rough gravel road.

'It would be quicker to just walk down,' said the Maoist leader Hisila Yami. Her husband, Baburam Bhattarai, the elected Member of the Constituent Assembly from Gorkha, had kept up his promise of visiting his home district at least once every month. As finance minister in 2008, he had sanctioned money for the construction of the road on which we were now stranded. A year later, he was in the opposition, travelling across the country and mounting a popular campaign against the government of the day.

Aditya Adhikari—a writer and a close friend—and I had accompanied Baburam as he spoke at public meetings in the western Tarai. That morning, we had driven up from Nawalparasi in the plains and stopped over to eat at the highway junction, Mugling. Locals came over to greet the Maoist leader as he ate a spartan meal of one roti and a little daal. A short distance later, we had walked up from the highway and climbed on to a ramshackle bus to travel to a village school. Here, Baburam had narrated the achievements of the short-lived Maoist-led government, and the measures he had introduced in a popular budget. The event was replete with Maoist cultural performances, an integral component of their politics ever since the war.

It was on the way down that the bus had broken down. Hisila said, 'The locals won't have a problem. It is those of us too used to the cities.' Looking at Aditya and me, she asked, 'Are you sure the two of you can walk?' We nodded enthusiastically, hoping to snatch more time with the senior leaders, even though a twelve-kilometre hike was not a particularly attractive proposition.

The couple had met while studying in India.

In Chandigarh, and later in Delhi where he first studied at the School of Planning and Architecture and later enrolled for a PhD in Regional Development at the Jawaharlal Nehru University (JNU), Baburam had begun to be increasingly influenced by Marxism. He had seen the plight of Nepali workers in India, and this made him both angry and reflective. Baburam began asking himself a range of questions—why did the Nepali poor have to leave their own country and work in circumstances without dignity elsewhere? Why were Nepalis soldiers serving in foreign armies as mercenaries? Why was it that they worked so hard, yet remained poverty-stricken? Why did Nepal not take care of its citizens? What was the way out?

Baburam set up the All India Nepalese Students' Association, his first formal foray into political activism. He may have turned to communism, but he remained open to all political currents of democratic thinking in Nepal. He would often visit B. P. Koirala, the NC patriarch, who spent time in Delhi during visits in the late 1970s. Here, he met Shekhar Koirala, B. P. Koirala's nephew and then a student at the All India Institute of Medical Sciences, who would go on to become an interlocutor in peace negotiations with the Maoists over two decades later.

In 2009, over breakfast at the Shangrila Hotel in Lazimpat in Kathmandu, Shekhar Koirala recalled those times and told me, 'Chandra Shekharji [who would go on to become India's prime minister in 1990] had arranged a house for BP in South Extension in Delhi. Baburam used to come and visit BP in that house. He had already become a hardcore republican. I got to know him well, and we even had regular fortnightly discussions.' With a glint in his eye, the NC leader added, 'I remember an incident after the Soviets invaded Afghanistan. Baburam sent a message saying there is a solidarity meeting in JNU. Many Nepali speakers addressed it, and they all supported the invasion. The solidarity was with the Soviets! One of them even went on to say he wanted to see a Soviet tank in Kathmandu's New Road. That was the political climate of the times.'

Baburam, groomed in such an ideological worldview, thought that the NC's prescription of liberal democracy with constitutional monarchy would not address Nepal's complex socio-economic problems. He had seen the 'bourgeoisie democracy' of India and, like the Indian radical communists who were waging a war against their own state, felt that it did not benefit the poorest citizens of the country.

It was under Baburam's spell that Hisila had turned to Marxism. This was unusual for a woman of her background. She was from a privileged ethnic family of Kathmandu and her father had served as a minister in the 1950s. As Baburam struggled to manage both a PhD programme and his political activism, Hisila became his pillar of support. Baburam, an introvert with few friends, was certain that he would not marry; politics and books would remain the passions of his life. But Hisila broke his resolve—'It just happened,' he was to tell me years later. The two decided to marry in a simple Arya Samaj ceremony conducted by Swami Agnivesh—who himself became a prominent Indian activist in the following decades.

In the mid-1980s, after finishing their education, both returned home. They had joined the Communist Party of Nepal (Masal), led by a stalwart of the communist movement, Mohan Bikram Singh. Hisila began teaching at a local college while Baburam took up assignments in urban planning. Like in Delhi, he made it a point to meet people of all political persuasions, from Rishikesh Shah, a royalist foreign minister of the 1960s who had become a critic of the regime and had set up a human rights organization, to Devendra Raj Panday, a former bureaucrat who quit the Panchayat system and was an active supporter of the movement for democracy.

Panday was then close to the NC, but his home and office were open to activists of all hues. Panday would go on to become a voice of conscience in the movement for democracy and then a finance minister. Twenty years later, during one of our regular conversations at his cosy residence in Kathmandu's Bishal Nagar, over cups of black coffee, Panday looked back at the Baburam of those years as a sincere young man, keen to learn, but firm in his communist convictions.

It was a time of enormous turbulence in Nepali politics. When

Baburam had last been in Kathmandu in the early 1970s, he had only slowly begun to see the dark side of the monarchy. In the mid-1980s, he had returned to Nepal a Marxist, clear in his wider conception of the world—as one divided between the haves and the have-nots, locked into a perennial class conflict; as one where the proletariat and the oppressed had to be inculcated with revolutionary consciousness to rise up and smash the existing system; as one where society would move from feudalism to capitalism to socialism and, ultimately, communism.

Among the different Left factions of the Nepali polity, he had chosen one of the more extreme variants—which called for an armed revolution against the system. But there was another faction, called the Mashal, which was even more radical. Many of Baburam's future colleagues—Pushpa Kamal Dahal 'Prachanda' and Mohan Vaidya 'Kiran'—were in Mashal. Mashal advocated immediate revolution, and had even launched a failed bid to foment an armed rebellion in Kathmandu under Kiran's leadership. This failure eventually cost Kiran his position as general secretary of the party and catapulted Prachanda as the new leader. Masal, Baburam's party, was more circumspect, and argued that they must wait for the 'objective conditions' to ripen before launching the rebellion.

~

By the end of the 1980s, the NC and different factions of the moderate Left—which went on to form Communist Party of Nepal (Unified Marxist Leninist) [UML]—had allied on a common platform against the Palace.

This was a remarkable achievement, since the two sides had viewed each other with suspicion all along, to the benefit of the king. The NC saw communists as Palace agents, darbarias, who had damaged the cause of the democracy with their radical-sounding slogans and had ignored the fact that the basic fight was about restoring the multiparty system. The communists saw the NC as Indian agents and an anti-national element, arashtra tatva, since its leaders were inspired by the Indian-style parliamentary system, maintained close links with socialists in India, and had spent time across the border in exile.

B. P. Koirala's deep aversion to the communists had prevented any possible unity or collaboration between the two forces. But he had died of cancer, and NC's other founder-leader, Ganesh Man Singh, had now taken charge. A Newar of Kathmandu, he was not a deep thinker like Koirala, but was known for his sense of integrity, his spirit of sacrifice, his simplicity and his pragmatism. Singh managed to bridge the trust deficit with the moderate Left forces, which, too, had shed some of their baggage. He was acknowledged as the supreme commander of a joint movement for democracy. A nascent civil society, led by figures like Devendra Raj Panday, supported the andolan and mobilized the capital's professional classes. Kathmandu's streets now rose up against the Panchayat, and the resounding cry was for democracy.

King Birendra resisted. Hardliners in the Narayanhiti Durbar—particularly his wife, Queen Aishwarya, and his brother, Prince Gyanendra—were opposed to any concession being granted to democratic parties and insisted on retaining control. Street protests, and even violence, intensified.

I was only six when the Janandolan of 1990 took place. There is little I remember of the period, except being conscious that something big, something beyond the control of my parents, something outside the confines of our comfortable, protected home in the Babar Mahal area of the capital was occurring. In the evenings, responding to the call of the demonstrators, my parents, too, switched off the lights at home. I only later understood that they did it not out of fear but out of solidarity. My grandfather was partial to the regime, though, and appeared unhappy. He would tune in to his radio set and attentively watch the news on television, besides spending a lot of time on the telephone. We would occasionally hear people shouting slogans outside during the day.

'Curfew,' my father told me, 'means if you go out, you will be caught or shot.' That caused such fear that we dared not step out of the house to collect the cricket balls which we hit outside the compound. When curfew hours were relaxed, my father's colleagues would visit and relay news of what was happening outside. One of them—a bearded man we knew as Sitaram Uncle—was a part of the protests and I remember others greeting him effusively. Then, late one night, my mother woke me up so that I could watch the king—who I recognized—announce something on television.

My father took us all out the next morning in his green Toyota van for an ice cream, which indicated that something really good must have happened the previous night. I still remember crowds on the roads, people walking, waving, even as he tried to navigate his way through the Baneshwor crossing and the Tinkune triangle. It was a moment of victory, of happiness, that has remained etched in my memory. We went back to our routine—playing cricket, fetching the ball from outside the compound, resuming school, and keeping the lights on during the evenings.

That night, in April 1990, King Birendra had read the writing on the wall. At the cost of being labelled weak by members of his own family and by palace sycophants who dreaded losing power and privileges, he had lifted the ban on political parties. This was an act of both wisdom and shrewdness—wisdom, because it allowed the Palace to come across as respecting popular wishes and the king to emerge as a statesman; shrewdness, because it prevented the movement from assuming a more radical tone, and gave the royalists a seat at the negotiating table in devising the future political system. A constitutional commission, which included candidates nominated by the king, representatives of the NC, and moderate Left leaders, was set up to draft a new Constitution. An interim government, led by NC veteran Krishna Prasad Bhattarai, was constituted. And Nepal, like much of the world, joined in the wave of democratization with elections in 1991.

~

The radical Left, including both Masal and Mashal, had contributed to the struggle for democracy, but maintained a separate identity. They also insisted that only the long-promised CA, and not a Constitution granted by the king in precisely the same manner as his father had granted Constitutions, would be acceptable. Baburam and Hisila had, by then, quit Masal and merged with their more dynamic ultra-Left comrades, led by Prachanda, to form the

Communist Party of Nepal (Unity Centre). While the party would remain underground, it took a conscious decision to participate in the first elections under the new Constitution in 1991, in order to expose the system from within. The party's over-ground avatar, Samyukta Janamorcha, emerged as the third-largest party with nine seats. Baburam was its head, and a regular at the capital's political meetings and seminars. But the legislature was merely a tactical tool. Both Prachanda and Baburam had little faith in the Constitution, in Parliament, in pluralism, and in what they dismissed as 'bourgeoisie freedoms'. They were merely waiting for the right time to launch an armed rebellion.

The Girija Prasad Koirala-led NC government lasted three years. For the first time, Nepalis were free to speak, to organize, to oppose and rally around causes legitimately. The polity opened up and pluralism was to slowly become a norm. The first democratic government took a rapid turn towards free-market economic policies. Certain liberalization measures benefited the emerging middle class; investor sentiment was high and macro-economic indicators improved. But other policies—the cutting out of fertilizer subsidies and the privatization of public sector units—hurt peasants and workers.

If the Palace had been the sole source of crony capitalism until then, the NC leadership soon learnt the tricks of the trade. The Koirala family itself was implicated in the loot of public institutions. The government collapsed due to intra-party dissent and mid-term polls were held in 1994, throwing up UML as the single-largest party. In its nine-month tenure, the minority moderate Left government, led by communist stalwart Manmohan Adhikari, restored some balance to economic policies. It initiated welfare measures such as old-age pensions and began giving out more funds to grassroots structures. But its term was too short. Its decision to dissolve Parliament was overturned by the Supreme Court, and a new NC government—supported by Right-wing parties loyal to the monarch—came to power. It lasted for a year before UML, now allied with another Right-wing faction, toppled the government.

Ideology was now dead, political categories became meaningless, horse-trading was rampant in Parliament, the state was merely an instrument to extract rent and dispense patronage, and power for its own sake became the ultimate objective. It had taken less than five years for the warriors of democracy to practise the most degenerate form of democracy, with governments replacing each other in rapid succession.

All of this sharpened the debate within the Unity Centre about the logic and timing of an armed revolt. One faction argued that there must be more preparation and that 'objective conditions' were not yet ripe enough, while others—led by Prachanda and Baburam—decided that it was time to take the plunge. The party split on the issue and the Communist Party of Nepal (Maoist) was born.

Five years after communism had been declared dead in the rest of the world, as Nepali democracy struggled to find its feet, Maoists—deriving inspiration from Marx, Lenin, Mao, Stalin, Peru's Shining Path and the Indian Naxalite tradition—were ready to challenge the system. Baburam Bhattarai submitted a 40-point demand to the then prime minister, Sher Bahadur Deuba, on issues as varied as nationalism, livelihood and democracy. Their demands included abrogating royal privileges, having popularly elected representatives write a new Constitution, overhauling the 'semi-colonial' relationship with India, and the 'semi-feudal' nature of the economy.

Neither did the Maoists expect the government to respond to the demands, nor did the government think much of the Maoists' revolutionary rhetoric.

~

We had continued trekking down to the main highway in Gorkha. Baburam was walking briskly, a stick in his hand. Hisila and Aditya had moved a little ahead, and Aditya later told me that they were speaking about the couple's only trip to the US in the late 1980s, when the two had driven around the East Coast, meeting Nepali academics and the diaspora. Hisila had really liked the country.

Exposure to the pinnacle of capitalism had only convinced Baburam further that Nepal needed to get out of the feudal rut. It is ironic that a revolutionary Maoist's belief was reinforced by a visit to the citadel of the 'free world'. But it is also a reflection that, contrary to widespread perception, Nepal's Marxist ideologues were not necessarily fighting for a communist utopia. True to the original scriptures of their religion, they only hoped to overhaul the existing 'relations of production' of Nepal and enable a shift to the next stage of development.

Nepal's classical liberal democrats continue to ask a fundamental question. Did society—in the mid-1990s—need an insurgency to bring about the stated goal of 'socio-economic transformation'? Irrespective of whether the Maoists' prescription was correct or not, why was the path of violence chosen? After all, Nepal had just become a democracy. There were non-violent political methods to express grievances. This issue assumed a new degree of salience when the Maoists, in 2006, embraced democracy. Did Nepal have to go through the cycle of violence for the ultra-Left to return to what they had left behind—the Parliament?

As we walked down, I put the question to Baburam Bhattarai. He vigorously shook his head. 'No, it was just not possible then. Our People's War created the conditions for political transformation, for a republic, and set the stage for development.'

In 1998, two years after the first attacks, Baburam Bhattarai wrote a seminal tract justifying the revolution. Titled 'Economic-political Rationale of Nepal's People's War', it was first published in an inconspicuous party journal. Read alongside his PhD thesis, the two texts provide the ideological basis for Nepali Maoism. Bhattarai's diagnosis is contested and challenged by many; its assumptions are questionable; its economics sounds stale in the current climate where foreign capital is actively wooed; but understanding it is essential to get a sense of the minds of the men who decided that only a rebellion could decisively overturn Nepal's political order.

Baburam noted right at the outset that their aim was to end the existing 'socio-economic structure' and ruling arrangements, and establish Naulo Janabad, the New People's Democracy. Nepal, he said, was the second poorest country in the world. Seventy-one per cent of its citizens lived below the poverty line; 10 per cent controlled 46 per cent of the national income; 60 per cent were illiterate while 90 per cent of the population lived in rural areas.

Devoting a large section to the issue of Indian 'expansionism',

Baburam held the Delhi regime, and the operation of the multi-national companies—both Indian and foreign—based in India as being primarily responsible for Nepal's under-development. His argument was along the following lines.

Nepal's transport, trade and communication with the rest of the world were through India, and this made it a bandhua bazaar, a bonded market. The Sugauli Treaty of 1816—signed at the end of an Anglo-Nepal war which the British won despite stiff resistance—had put Nepal on the path of dependence. The balance of trade had been 5:1 in Nepal's favour until then. After the Treaty of Peace and Friendship was signed in 1950, Baburam argued, Nepal had become a safe market for Indian goods. The trade ratio dipped to 1:2 in India's favour, which was to increase to 1:7 by the early 1990s. Nepal exported raw material to India, while India exported value-added finished goods back to Nepal, which is a trademark of a colonial relationship. The treaty of 1950 gave Indian businessmen 'national treatment' in Nepal, with the result that a dozen Marwaris (an Indian-origin caste group of enterprising businessmen and traders) controlled the local economy, according to Baburam.

Nepal operated under the Indian financial and currency system. Nepalis served as mercenaries in the Indian Army. Foreign MNCs used India as a base to expand operations in Nepal; as a result of which, domestic industries like tea, as well as manufacturing units producing shoes, biscuits and paper were shutting down. Unequal water-sharing treaties, like those which governed the Kosi and the Gandak Rivers, allowed India to construct embankments within Nepal, while the downstream irrigation benefits went to India. Indians, through holding patterns, also controlled major revenue-earning sectors like tourism in Nepal.

If the external element formed one part of the crisis, Baburam dwelled at length on the internal agricultural crisis. The factors of production remained traditional in Nepal, with machines, fertilizers, seeds used on less than 1 per cent of the land. The fact that 81 per cent of the population was involved in agriculture was a sign of disguised unemployment. Only 13 per cent of the land was under irrigation, even though the Asian Development Bank—it was ironic to see the Maoists, in the middle of the war, quote a financial institution at the heart of the Washington Consensus—had claimed that 60 per cent land could be irrigated.

The root crisis, he said, was in the 'relations of production' and land-ownership patterns, with the concentration of ownership in limited hands. Labour relations were 'backward, feudal and oppressive'; tenancy rights were insecure; wages were low; sharecroppers were given minimal share of the product; absentee landlordism was rampant; exploitation was inherent in money-lending practices, with high interest rates; and practices of bonded labour, like the Kamaiya system in the western Tarai, remained entrenched. The need of the hour was 'revolutionary land reform'.

In due course, the Maoists would focus on Nepal's entrenched hierarchies as another element of the crisis. Though the party itself was led by men from Hindu castes from the hills, it argued that there was systematic discrimination and exclusion on the basis of caste, gender, region, nationality and ethnicity, besides class. Nepal was staggeringly diverse, but a tiny fragment of the Hindu upper castes from the hills—primarily Bahuns (Brahmins) and Chhetris—had monopolized power. The Madhesis, who lived in the plains and shared close ethnic and linguistic ties with people across the border

Battles of the New Republic

in India, were subject to an extractive relationship of internal colonialism. The Tarai's resources were gobbled up by the Centre, while its people were deprived of opportunities and access to power. Janjatis, the indigenous people of the hills and the plains, had to forsake their distinctive practices and accept the language and cultural mores of the Nepali Hindu castes. Dalits, both in the hills and the Tarai, continued to be subject to untouchability, while women suffered in an unequal patriarchal set-up.

All these groups, the Maoists argued, were victims of a centralized, patriarchal, elite-led, hill upper caste-dominated, Hindu, and India-backed state operating out of Kathmandu. There has been a raging debate on whether the Maoists were truly committed to the cause of these social groups, or whether it was a mere tactic to mobilize constituencies in their war. Irrespective of the motivation, the fact is that Nepal's militant communists were pioneers among Left groups in South Asia in fusing issues of class and identity.

For them, the source of both the external and internal crisis was Nepal's ruling arrangement. There was a symbiotic relationship between the Palace and the new ruling class at the top with the local landlords on the ground. The former depended on the latter to keep the social structure and polity 'stable'; the latter used the state's instruments to quell any challenge to their local hegemony. The big farmers and the emerging 'bourgeoisie' had pitched in its lot with the 'democratic' parties like the NC and the 'reformist Left' parties like the UML. In Marxist discourse, a major role is played by the 'comprador' elements—they are a part of the bourgeoisie, but do not add to national productivity. These 'middlemen' are brokers for foreign companies; 'agents' who sell goods produced by MNCs in the domestic market; traders who make a margin off the flow of goods, extracting the surplus value alongside the owners, even as the workers who actually produce the goods live in penury. Together and separately, in the ultra-Left's reading, these social groups formed the core of the system in the 1990s.

If the objective was to establish a 'People's Republic', the Maoists' objective was to overturn precisely this existing political and social order. This could not happen by playing according to the 'democratic rules' framed by the classes whom the Maoists sought to displace. The 'structural violence' in society could only be overcome by the 'violence of the oppressed'. The boy from Gorkha had decided that he would not rest until he defeated the ruling arrangement which underpinned the House of the Shahs of Gorkha.

~

If Baburam Bhattarai had provided the ideological direction to the Maoist movement, there is little doubt that Pushpa Kamal Dahal 'Prachanda' was the master tactician, the pragmatic politician, the charismatic but mysterious leader, the motivator-in-chief, the lead military planner—all rolled into one—of the Nepali revolution.

The two men, born into lower-middle-class families, around the same time, to upper-caste Bahun parents from the hills, would together form one of the most formidable political partnerships the country had ever seen. It was a relationship of cooperation and competition, a relationship in which both deeply resented each other's qualities but recognized that they were incomplete separately. To borrow from their Marxist dictionary, it was a dialectical relationship where both leaders presented the thesis and the antithesis for a new synthesis to emerge.

Prachanda was born in a village in Kaski in mid-west Nepal. Like many marginal farmers in the 1950s and the 1960s, encouraged by the state's policies, his father moved to Chitwan, on the edges of the Tarai, in the hope of securing a better livelihood. In his book about contemporary politics, *Prayogshala*, the Nepali journalist Sudheer Sharma mentions that Prachanda had toyed with the idea of joining the Royal Nepalese Army (RNA). But he did not follow through on the idea to serve the regime, a decision that may have altered the course of Nepali history.

Instead, Prachanda studied agriculture in a local campus, became influenced by Marxism and, after a brief working stint with a development project funded by the US government, joined in as a full-time communist worker at the district level in the 1970s. Prachanda has often said in his interviews that he was always interested in understanding the practical and ideological aspects of the armed struggle. Later, he joined other senior comrades to form the Communist Party of Nepal (Mashal). After a revolutionary bid led by him failed, Mohan Vaidya 'Kiran' resigned as the general secretary and nominated Prachanda as his successor. At his house in Gongabu, on Kathmandu's Ring Road, Kiran was to tell me in 2012, unable to conceal a tinge of pride, 'He was a young revolutionary talent. I recognized it.'

Prachanda remained underground for most of his communist career. Though he did engage with the various strands of the Left and, occasionally, with district-level NC leaders in his hometown of Chitwan, Prachanda's worldview was largely shaped by the writings of Marx, Stalin and Mao. Khagendra Sangroula, one of Nepal's leading Left literary figures, had translated Mao's texts as well as other writings from the Chinese revolution into Nepali. Prachanda would often tell Sangroula in later years, 'Dai, we grew up reading your work.' He was clear that unlike seniors like Mohan Bikram Singh, who spoke of revolution but waited perennially for objective conditions to ripen, or Manmohan Adhikari who had 'compromised' with the bourgeouisie democracy, he would neither surrender nor hold on forever. He saw himself as a man of action.

Unlike Baburam, he did not have the intellectual sophistication that comes from disciplined academic training. But Prachanda more than made up for it with his energy, an ability to reconcile conflicting strands, his oratory, organizational building efforts, and revolutionary rhetoric—all of which catapulted him to the top of the party in his early thirties. This was a remarkable achievement in a society and political culture which awards age and sees it as being synonymous with wisdom.

Backed by his early mentor, Kiran; the new entrant, Baburam; his old friend from Chitwan, Ram Bahadur Thapa 'Badal'; his colleague, Dev Gurung; and Chandra Prakash Gajurel 'Gaurav', a contemporary and competitor from his Mashal days, Prachanda decided in the early 1990s that it was time to commence the armed rebellion.

To establish Janabad, Prachanda planned to exploit the

contradictions in local power relations and cultivate the vast segments which remained excluded and angry—the landless labourer and tenant farmer who had little to lose and harboured resentment against their owners over low wages; a disenchanted brother who felt that he had no recourse to justice when other family members had taken over his rightful share of the property; the young semi-educated man who did not want to work the fields like his parents had done but had no access to a formal, organized economy, however meagre it may be; a first-generation student who had come to Kathmandu from the village, but felt alienated by the glitter and conspicuous consumption of the city; an energetic, feisty girl who was angry when her brother was sent to school while she had to walk miles to fetch water; a Magar in the mid-west hills or a Yadav in the Tarai who was often insulted and humiliated by an influential, upper-caste local.

The party's priority was to build a vast organizational apparatus; create trained district- and village-level leaders who understood the ideological framework and could convince the rest of the target groups; and build a coercive apparatus—their own militias and subsequently an army—which could stand up to state repression. The state, after all, rested on force. And only through force could it be defeated.

The multiple strategies would exacerbate the crisis of the state. It would expose the hollowness and limited support enjoyed by the regime. It would embolden newer constituencies, led by the Maoists, to first take over the villages, surround the capital, and then, in the phase of strategic offence, following Mao's dictum, capture the state. The naya satta, the new regime, would then—on the basis of the revolutionary upheaval—correct historical wrongs and establish Nepal as an egalitarian, autonomous, communist republic.

To operationalize the plan, the party had to begin with at least a rudimentary arsenal. Along with Badal and Dev Gurung, Prachanda went all the way up to Manang in the upper reaches of the Himalayas to pick up the first two guns for the revolution. These were the same rifles which had been air-dropped by the US in 1961 to help Tibetan rebels and incite a rebellion against China. The irony could

not have been starker. Many Nepali Maoist leaders received their initial armed training from retired soldiers who had worked in the Gorkha regiments in the Indian Army. Armed training also came from another source—Indian Maoists, waging a war against the Indian state. Nepal's Maoist commanders were to visit camps in Bihar and Andhra Pradesh to learn from their comrades across the border.

On 13 February 1996, as Prime Minister Sher Bahadur Deuba was sipping champagne with the then Indian ambassador to Nepal, K. V. Rajan, on a flight from Delhi to Hyderabad during an official state visit, news came in that Maoists had attacked a police post in Holeri in the Rolpa district in mid-west Nepal. The war had begun. The same rifles Prachanda and Dev Gurung had acquired from Manang were used by two young Janjati leaders—Nand Kishore Pun 'Pasang' and Barshaman Pun 'Ananta'—in the attack. The two were to become well-known military and political leaders over the years.

Rolpa was a traditional communist stronghold, where the Maoists had won a parliamentary seat in their over-ground incarnation as Janmorcha in 1991. The region had witnessed enormous police brutalities. It was to emerge as a 'base area' in the People's War, where the rebel forces displaced the state and other political parties early on, and was home to a large section of the Maoists' political and military leadership. It was a region with a high concentration of an ethnic minority group, the Magars, who were a natural constituency of support for the rebels because of their class and ethnic background. It was a district where the Maoists would consolidate power, set up communes, dispense justice, build roads, and provide a glimpse of the world they sought to create.

Far away from Rolpa, over a decade-and-a-half later, Prachanda recalled those heady early days of the war as we sipped coffee at the plush Oberoi Hotel in Delhi, where he was on a semi-official visit. I had got to know the Maoist chairman in my capacity as a reporter, and back in Kathmandu, our conversations and interviews usually revolved around the immediate layers of contemporary politics. The distance allowed the Maoist supremo to look back, perhaps.

When Pasang and Ananta launched the first attack, Prachanda was in Kathmandu, living in the homes of supporters in Harisiddhi in the Patan district. He was to stay there for twenty-two days. 'Once, the police came to the house where I lived two minutes after I had left. I often think what would have happened if I was caught then. The entire historical course would have been different.'

But the close shave warned him of the dangers of living in the capital. He pointed to his wife Sita, who was sitting with him when we spoke, and said, 'The two of us then moved to a place near Pokhara, the Lumle Agricultural Research Centre. It had been built by the British. The head of the office, a bureaucrat, was a friend of mine from Chitwan. We lived there for a while, and I prepared a document for the politburo meeting about the war.' We had met right after breakfast, and Sita Dahal interrupted to ask her husband if he had taken his medicines. He nodded. From Lumle, Prachanda moved to a village in Syangja, which was home to L. B. Thapa, a lecturer in the Pokhara campus and a sympathizer of the party. That is where the Maoist party held its first key, top-level conclave after embarking on the armed rebellion to decide the future course of action.

From Syangja in western Nepal, Prachanda travelled, inconspicuously, to Siliguri in West Bengal. It was becoming difficult to live in Nepal without being noticed and arrested. Thus began his long India years—by his own admission, he spent eight out of the ten years of the insurgency in various cities and towns in India—and the establishment of the Maoists' 'headquarters' south of the border, even as Nepal was engulfed in a radical political-social-economic overhaul through violent and non-violent means.

The quirks of history could not have been more startling.

A man who had once thought of joining the RNA decided to launch a war against the Nepali state. Three-and-a-half decades after the Central Intelligence Agency (CIA) dropped guns to foment rebellion against an enemy communist regime in the heyday of the Cold War, Nepali Maoists picked up the same rifles to launch their battles against 'royal feudalism, Indian expansionism and American imperialism' after the obituary of communism had been written. They were aided and trained by former soliders of the Indian Army—now living in Nepal on pension from the Indian state—as well as Indian Left militants. When the first attacks took place, Prachanda stayed in the heart of the state, where its coercive apparatus was strongest, even as the prime minister of the day was travelling with the Indian envoy across the border. The Maoist supremo, in the nascent stage of the rebellion, was supported by two mid-level functionaries of His Majesty's Government of Nepal—a bureaucrat and a teacher—indicating the blurred lines between those inside the system and those who wanted to destroy it. And through most of the war, the revolutionary leader lived in the country against which, he had warned his cadres, they may well have to fight their ultimate battle.

2

'The supreme commander of the People's Liberation Army [PLA] marched victoriously to Kathmandu and established the party's agenda as the national agenda. The supreme commander of the Royal Nepalese Army had to leave the Palace and surrender power,' said Prachanda, sitting on the first floor of his Naya Bazaar residence in central Kathmandu in 2009. He smiled, and then told me, 'It may have been a military stalemate, but this is our political victory.'

Exactly ten years after Prachanda had fled from the Kathmandu Valley, he returned, escorted by Home Minister Krishna Prasad Sitaula in a state helicopter on 16 June 2006. Sita, his wife, had been at his side in the early days of the war in Kaski district when he barely escaped police arrest; they had now been flown back from the same district. Sita was sitting next to him in the SUV—which flew a government flag—as they drove from the airport to the prime minister's residence in Baluwatar.

Mobbed by the media on the lawns, Prachanda spent the day locked inside, negotiating with Prime Minister G. P. Koirala. He then addressed a press conference late at night, accompanied by leaders of other parties and civil society leaders who had played an active role in the People's Movement. The Maoists were now in open politics, representing one pillar of the polity, as the Seven Party Alliance (SPA), led by the NC, led the other.

How did an outfit declared 'terrorist' by the governments of Nepal, India and the US; not recognized as 'Maoists' by China, a country which one would instinctively imagine to have been a source of support (China saw the label as a slur on its legendary leader); attacked by the internationally backed, 95,000-strong RNA and the specially created Armed Police Force and, before that, the Nepal Police; get here?

How did two men—one who had been underground for all of his political life, and had risen up the ranks from a district unit with no family connections or social capital; the other an obscure Marxist academic whose political socialization owed a lot to the country Nepali communists often declare an 'enemy', whose academic training was urban planning; and who had little mass base—wage an almost successful revolution in the twenty-first century?

Theorizing the problems with Nepal's socio-economic structure, as Baburam had done; or framing a strategy to implement the theory and conceive alliances, as Prachanda had attempted, was one thing. Implementing strategies and theories was a different ball game.

~

It used to be remote and inaccessible, and could be reached only after an ardous trek, but Holeri village is now a four-hour drive from Ghorahi in the Dang Deukhuri district over a rocky, steep and narrow road in the hills. From Holeri, one takes a bus up to Tila village over what is now the Shahid Smriti Marg, built by the Maoists. For those from the region, Murel village in the Rolpa district is a one-day walk from Tila. For those not used to the climb, it could take up to two days.

Mal Bahadur Budhamagar was born here in Rolpa in a family of small famers in 1979, the year when, far away in the capital, student protests had forced the royal regime to announce a referendum on the nature of the political system. The Panchayat regime would then defeat the idea of multiparty democracy.

Budhamagar was the only child of his family. For his Class 8 examinations, he attended a medium-secondary school in Chunbang village, and completed his School Leaving Certificate (SLC) examinations from Rukumkot town. It was in Chunbang, at the age of fifteen in 1994, that Budhamagar joined the Janmorcha's student front. It was also in Chunbang—over ten years later—that Maoists would take a historic decision to move from war to peace.

'All our elders, family members and teachers were in Janmorcha. Krishna Bahadur Mahara was a respected schoolteacher of the area, and he had become an MP in the 1991 elections. It was natural we would all join their student front,' Budhamagar recollected several years later. Their work was to 'go to the administration as a part of a delegation, do dharna, put forward demands of students'.

We were sitting in a PLA cantonment in Hattikhor in the Nawalparasi district in the central Tarai in February 2009. The cantonments were home to Maoist soldiers after they had joined the peace process. As prime minister, Prachanda had just made his first visit to the camp the previous day and had hailed the Maoist army's achievements, but had also told them that they were strictly under the state now. I had bumped into Budhamagar as he was setting up a stall, selling books and other material published by the party. He was a short, slightly stout man who looked older than his years. A popular song from the Nepali movie of the 1960s, *Maitighar*, was playing in the background.

Soon after Budhamagar passed out of school, the Janmorcha split on the question of whether they should wage a rebellion or not. His elders moved to the new Maoist party, and he followed suit. He was soon inducted into the Swayamsevak Dal, the Volunteer's Bureau, 'the predecessor of the People's Liberation Army', he told me proudly.

The NC-led government in Kathmandu had stepped up a security offensive in the hills of the Rolpa and Rukum districts. This was one of the few regions in the country where the ultra-Left had fared well in the 1991 elections, but the bureaucrats were NC nominees. NC loyalists, backed by the state, often engaged in clashes with the increasingly radical Janmorcha supporters. The actions of the police had played a key role in antagonizing several Maoist activists, predominantly of Magar background. The Nepal Police had launched Operation Romeo to suppress the political activities of the ultra-Left group. Activists from the ground then encouraged their own party leaders to launch the People's War as soon as possible.

I asked Budhamagar whether he had been aware of the long haul ahead when he had joined the new party. 'No, we didn't know that. All we knew was that we were fighting for the poor and the oppressed. Kacho dimaag thiyo hamro. [We were immature, then.] We had read Gorky's *Mother* and *Bright Red Star*, and were influenced.' What elements of the books—one about a Russian woman worker affected by her son's turn to socialism and the other a tale of young Chinese PLA warrior—had affected him? 'Many. I read many other books too, but have forgotten now,' he said, a bit sheepishly. It struck me that many other Maoists I had spoken to, across generations, had spoken of *Mother* as being their favourite novel.

Did he feel that there was no way to pursue political goals within the multiparty system? Budhamagar said that they were very 'happy' when the multiparty system was introduced in 1991. 'Those were the Janmorcha days. We knew we had to vote and we voted for the party.' But did he know, when he was joining the Maoists, that he was going to fight against the multiparty system? 'Not the multiparty system, but for the poor and oppressed.' He paused for a moment. 'It was against the feudal king, who had to be overthrown. Look, there are two classes in the country; the well-to-do and the poor. We had to pick up arms to defeat the rich.'

With that relatively simplistic outlook, Budhamagar became a part of the Sisne Sanskritik Parivar, the party's cultural arm, as a 'whole-timer'. They had four roles to perform—production, fighting, organization and publicity. 'As per necessity, we either went and fought or picked up tools and farmed. We also did publicity since there was no radio or TV.'

Budhamagar was asked to write people's songs, jansangit, which he enjoyed doing. He had also assumed a new party name, Mahesh Arohi, and asked me to use that instead of his birth name.

By 1997, Maoists had established local posts in forty-nine out of the fifty-one village development committees in Rolpa. During the day, his cultural group used to live inside the homes of party supporters. At night, they got out, 'collected all the people in the village', and then sang and danced for about thirty minutes.

I was curious about the kind of songs they deployed as tools of political mobilization. Arohi tried to string together a few words and hum, and then said, laughing, 'I have forgotten … but here was one. "Ko ho bhani na sodha kaile, ghar chadi hine ka yoddha lai." ["Don't ever ask a warrior who has left home who he is."] Our main message was there is oppression which needed to be fought and motivate them. A five-minute song is more effective than an hour-long political speech.'

The party was also projected as the only hope, which called for sacrifices. 'Mare shahid, bache mukti. [If you die, you are a martyr, and if you live, you are liberated.]' Arohi himself was married by then; his wife was a Maoist worker, too, but stayed mostly in their village. I asked him if he was scared. 'There was some fear. But my wife used to tell me to fight well. We knew that if something happened to me, the party would take care of the family.'

The party line at that time, relayed through the district committee to the area secretary and through him to cadres like Arohi, was 'to fight'. 'Banduk le tikeko rajyasatta banduk le dhalnu parcha. [A state which rests on the power of the gun must be defeated by the might of arms.] Our songs conveyed the message that a few people, a few rich, have everything even if they did not work, and the vast number are poor despite working.' What helped them, Arohi said, was police oppression. 'They did everything. They raped a woman in the presence of her husband and mutilated her private parts. They used to take innocent Rolpali Magars to the jungles and shoot them and claim it was an encounter. This made the state naked, this exposed them—otherwise the government would have won.'

In 1998, Arohi was sent to Kalikot, a neighbouring district in far-west Nepal, as a part of a fighting squad. The PLA had not yet been formed then. 'Imagine,' he said, looking around as hundreds of PLA combatants went about their daily lives in the cantonment around us, 'we had a small squad then and today, this is our army.' But he did not relish the moment of glory for too long and went back to his story. 'We used to attack the jamindars. They were rogues. We used to collect information from the local people and then attack. I remember Harsh Bahadur Shahi, who was known to rape poor women and take away land. We attacked his home, and damaged his foot.'

How did he feel about inflicting violence? Arohi paused, and said matter-of-factly, 'The party line was not to kill but to hack off their arms.' He did not elaborate on his own emotions through the process but said, reflectively, 'But some mistakes happened. Workers used to kill even when the instruction was to attack. Sometimes, nakli Maobaadis took our name and engaged in violence.'

But he returned to Rolpa soon after and joined the Jaljala Sanskritik Parivar of the party. This was when his interaction with the party's second-rung leaders grew, even though he did not see Prachanda till a much later stage in the war. 'We knew they had to stay safe. But in direct battles, you need direct leadership on the field too.' Krishna Bahadur Mahara, the popular schoolteacher of the 1980s who had gone on to become Janmorcha's Member of Parliament in 1991 when the Maoists had an over-ground avatar, spent a lot of time in the district. His pupils from school included Pasang and Ananta, who had become key military leaders of the party.

Mahara often visited the villages of Rolpa, sharing the party's future plans, and stayed with local sympathizers. Pasang never lived away from heartland of the war. 'He was also a schoolmaster once. I was quite close to him. He used to play, train with us, and share our joys and sorrows.' Arohi fondly recollected how Pasang had once made a rifle, basing it on a model of a rifle brought from Mustang. 'It was not automatic. You had to pull it back after shooting each time. But he took us to the jungle to show it worked. This was in 1998. We were very proud.'

The distinction between tactics and strategy, which Maoist texts place extraordinary emphasis on, percolated down to the foot soldiers. I asked Arohi about the ways in which they chose their target for karabahi, action, which could range from a relatively mild act of beating up someone to outright elimination.

'There is a main enemy and an assistant enemy. Earlier, the main enemy was the dalaal punjipati [the comprador bourgeoisie], represented by NC and UML. So for the first five years, we targeted their supporters. NC and UML leaders were chased out of villages. They were supported by police. So we fought the police. The king was inactive and so we did not touch his supporters and the old Panchas. The idea is to fight the person and the force which rears its head and is powerful at that moment.' Later, Arohi said, the focus shifted to the king and the army when they became increasingly significant in Kathmandu politics. 'We have always been alert that our aim is communism, but there is flexibility in working policy.'

The boundaries between being a member of the cultural group, of the army, and of a district committee often blurred. The cadre's primary duty was to the party and he could be shuffled around according to need. And so it was that Arohi was to work in all major fronts of the party's organization. He had participated in demonstrations as a part of the student front; he wrote songs and performed and motivated villagers through the cultural group. He was a member of the earlier avatar of the armed apparatus and attacked 'enemies'. He was transferred to other districts. And he was to participate in key, historic battles of the war—the first assault on Khara, and the march to Beni. And as much as I grilled him about why he gave up his youth, his life, and endured such hardship, Arohi's answer remained constant, 'For the liberation of the poor and oppressed and to defeat the king.'

The partial success of the Maoist project in Nepal had largely to do with its ability to motivate young men like Arohi. He did not join the party out of a deep understanding of communist ideology, neither was he clear and specific about the political system they were fighting for. But a mix of circumstances—being born in a belt which was among the most deprived in Nepal; belonging to a community of Kham Magars, an ethnic group which had never related to the Hindu caste-dominated political structure; early socialization where people around him were members of the Janmorcha; becoming a part of a larger political collective which must have given him a thrill during his student days; witnessing police high-handedness against neighbours, relatives and others of his community; the exposure to one view of the world and the absence of any avenue to access other viewpoints and opportunities— saw him remain a Maoist warrior through the war.

~

If Mahesh Arohi was the epitome of the committed Maoist warrior from their 'base area', the shifting of Krishna KC—a Maoist student leader who rose to prominence after being illegally detained and tortured by the state during the royal autocracy—towards the rebel insurgency indicated their growing appeal to newer constituencies and their ability to tap into the disenchantment with the parliamentary Left and the existing system.

Krishna was reluctant to meet when I called him up. We had bumped into each other at several Maoist party events in Kathmandu, but he did not remember me. He agreed only when I named several people who were common acquaintances and asked him to check with them. Krishna called me to Baneshwor Chowk, a busy city intersection, and we walked to his room in a back lane of the area. It was a sunny afternoon, the International Convention Centre which was to house the CA was in the background, and we sat on the terrace with a cup of tea each.

Born in Baglung district's Bhimpakda village in western Nepal, Krishna's father was first a farmer and had then worked in Shillong 'in the health sector'. Krishna completed his SLC examinations in Baglung, where he came under the spell of the 'Jhapalis'. 'The old Masal [Mohan Bikram Singh's party, which Baburam Bhattarai was a part of in the 1980s] was strong in our area. But I had heard many tales of the Jhapa kranti and that inspired me to fight injustice.'

An armed rebellion had erupted in Jhapa in the eastern Tarai in the late 1960s and early 1970s, inspired by India's Naxalite movement. A group of radical communist fighters had engaged in the 'annihilation' of class enemies, but the state cracked down rapidly, the activists were arrested and the movement fizzled out. The leaders of the Jhapali movement would moderate their instincts. Jhalanath Khanal, Khadga Prasad Oli, Chandra Prakash Mainali, Radha Krishna Mainali and Madhav Kumar Nepal had come from this political tradition and had led the Communist Party of Nepal (Marxist-Leninist). They remained underground during the Panchayat years. Their student wing was popularly called Akhil. CPN-ML merged with CPN (Marxist) led by Manmohan Adhikari to form the Communist Party of Nepal (Unified Marxist Leninist), the major moderate Left party of the 1990s.

Krishna started participating early in processions against the Panchayat. He was arrested when he was in Class 7, but was let off since he was considered too young to be jailed. Thirty-five of the forty-five students who passed their SLC examinations from Krishna's batch joined Akhil. Krishna himself came to the capital and attended the fairly well-known Siddhartha Vanasthali School. That he attended this school meant that Krishna had had a relatively better-off childhood than Mahesh Arohi of Rolpa. In Kathmandu, he had an opportunity to participate in more movements, senior party leaders got to know him and his work, and he rose to become a central committee member and even the central secretary of UML's students' front in the 1990s.

However, the mainstream Left was becoming increasingly wracked by internal divisions. The parent figure of the party, Manmohan Adhikari, was aging and had retreated to an honorary role. The bright young star of the party, Madan Bhandari, had pioneered the political line of Janata ko Bahudaliya Janabad, People's Multiparty Democracy, providing the ideological justification for a communist party to engage in competitive democratic politics. This had helped transform an erstwhile underground outfit into a political party which accepted the rules of the game. Bhandari had defeated the interim prime minister from the NC, Krishna Prasad Bhattarai, from Kathmandu in 1991 in a shock victory.

But the charismatic and popular Bhandari died in a car accident. The party had always hinted at a larger conspiracy behind his death, and I have hazy memories of days of strikes following his death. Madhav Kumar Nepal had become the new general secretary, and slowly expanded his control over the party organization. His key rival was Bamdev Gautam, a more radical-sounding leader.

An ideological tenet of the UML had been 'nationalism', which often translates into resisting the 'special relationship' with India in order to make Nepal a more autonomous state. UML, in its previous avatars, had often castigated the NC for being India's brokers. In G. P. Koirala's first term as prime minister, the party had opposed a hydropower arrangement with India. A moment of reckoning had, however, arrived for the party in 1994, when it came to power. It now had to engage with India on similar issues of bilateral cooperation. It agreed to a larger understanding whereby India would develop hydropower resources on the Mahakali, the major river in Nepal's far west, and construct storages; Nepal would, in turn, get additional electricity and water benefits. This was the famous Mahakali Treaty, which would eventually be signed when Sher Bahadur Deuba visited India in 1996—it was during this trip that the Maoists had begun their rebellion.

Krishna KC was not happy with the UML's decision to support the Mahakali Treaty in Parliament. His unease was a reflection of the unhappiness among a large section of Nepal's Left-wing politicians, who had grown up viewing India as a predator which exploited Nepal's resources and milked it dry. Past experiences with the Gandak and Kosi Treaties in central and eastern Nepal had not been encouraging either. In the dominant Nepali narrative, India had received all the benefits—of irrigation and control of the management of the barrage—while Nepal had to pay the price—the loss of land, citizens being displaced with no compensation being provided, and inequitable gains.

Krishna told me that day in Baneshwor, 'People in Rolpa and Rukum were fighting for a republic. These were poor people. Why were they fighting? Not to send their children abroad. No, it was for nationalism, for national respect. Nepalis had to own Nepal. And then I looked at my leaders in UML selling the country on Mahakali. I was furious.'

I asked Krishna about his concerns regarding the project, and how he felt it would amount to a sell-out. 'All experts said it. They would take our land, our water. Saala India would get the electricity and water for their fields.' Like Mahesh Arohi had not elaborated on the specifics of the feudal system he was fighting, Krishna offered little by way of specific criticism. It only reaffirmed that political rhetoric and slogans mattered more in motivating workers than minute policy details.

'I was also active in the movement against border encroachment. India wants to surround and take over Nepal. Nepal stretched from Teesta in the east to Kangra in the west but our land was taken away in the Second World War. But we don't want to lose Mechhi, Mahakali, Kalapani and Susta.' Krishna clearly had his politics, history and geography all mixed up. But what was revealing was the depth of passion directed at India and, by extension, his own party, the UML, for compromising with who he saw as the 'enemy'.

Krishna joined Bamdev Gautam and C. P. Mainali who had walked away from the UML to set up the Communist Party of Nepal (Marxist-Leninist) [ML]. 'They told us UML has betrayed the nation, that we will give a new direction to the party.' The ML adopted a staunchly ultra-nationalist platform; it was suspected to have a tactical understanding with the Maoists. But in the 1999 elections, it failed to win a single seat (despite winning a respectable vote-share). The ML's presence had led to the UML's defeat because it split Left votes, and ensured that the NC emerged victorious. The defeat was a sobering moment and, in due course, Gautam was to return to the parent party. But the radical young men did not return. Krishna was among them. He decided, instead, to travel even further to the Left and joined the Maoists.

'The present student union leader of the Maoists is from ML background. Many trade union leaders were from ML. Nineteen central committee members of the student front together shifted to the Maoists. The top guys stayed safe but, on the ground, the mood shifted because we realized there was no hope in the so-called mainstream Left of Nepali politics.'

Krishna was in charge of the students' union of Kathmandu, and convinced many students to switch allegiances. He was invited to meet the Maoist leadership in India, but did not go. But Krishna KC recalled travelling to Biratnagar and Chitwan with Krishna Mahara, and visiting a militia camp in Dang. Given his familiarity with Kathmandu, and the student politics of the capital, he began assisting the party's operations there. The army would eventually arrest and torture Krishna KC in the later stages of the war.

In Rolpa, the Maoists had taken advantage of the topography, their political history in the region, the deprivation of the Magars, their coercive apparatus, and the limited presence of the state. But it had also been able to adroitly benefit from the political churning in Kathmandu. As the mainstream parties fractured, as the parliamentary Left became increasingly enmeshed in the existing political-economic system, and gaps in the 1990s-style democracy became apparent, Nepal's new generation remained attached to ultra-nationalism— which saw India as the 'other'— and men like Krishna KC continued to be drawn to the Maoists.

~

Five years into the war, 1,700 people had been killed. Through this period, the state's reaction was marked by a paradoxical mix of arrogance and ignorance. Even before the war had begun, the NC-led government had deployed a security offensive, Operation Romeo, in the mid-western hills. As Arohi's account showed, it only boomeranged, breeding further alienation without substantially eroding the Maoists' capacities.

In an essay, 'Day of the Maoist', published in *Himal Southasian* magazine in the middle of 2001, the writer and analyst Deepak Thapa wrote about the first five years of the war, and how the insurgency was faring.

The Nepal Police was at the forefront of the battle with the Maoists, but it was thoroughly ill prepared for the job. It did not have intelligence on the Maoists and was confronted by surprise attacks. The Nepali state's penetration into the deepest parts of the mid-western hills was historically limited. As the Maoists slowly got rid of other political leaders from the villages, a political vacuum grew.

The police had become 'politicized' in recent years. Every step— from recruitment to promotions to the appointment of senior officers—happened on the basis of the personnel's ability to pay off their political masters. This led to widespread corruption across the force, destroying morale and leaving the foot soldiers with little incentive to stake their lives in the face of committed Maoists fighters. The police was also poorly equipped, saddled with .303 British rifles of Second World War vintage. Through the period, the RNA kept its distance even as the state faced the growing onslaught of the insurgents.

The security forces were operating in the backdrop of burgeoning political chaos in Kathmandu. Governments changed every six to nine months, but none of them could come up with a coherent and intelligent response. Parties espoused different approaches when in government and in the opposition.

The king and the democratic forces viewed each other with distrust, suspecting that the other was in bed with the Maoists. The Maoist leadership was to later disclose that they had a 'working unity' with the Palace, since they shared the objective of weakening the democratic Centre. Given that the RNA was under the joint control of the king and the elected government in theory, but under the Palace's control in practice, the prime minister of the day could not unilaterally decide on army deployment. For his part, Birendra had let it be known he did not want the army to be used to kill Nepali citizens.

Lip service was paid to the need for a 'political solution', even as the government deployed the police with the single-point agenda of crushing the Maoists. Like Operation Romeo in 1995, Operation Kilo Sierra 2 was launched in 1998 in Maoist-affected districts. Given the dismal state of the police force, the lack of intelligence inputs, the insensitivity towards issues of human rights, and the ability of the Maoists to become enmeshed in local society, it was inevitable that the pattern of violations would repeat itself. Human rights organizations which were sympathetic to parliamentary parties, too, condemned the government. 'Police high-handedness' became the single-most important factor for people to drift towards the Maoists.

As Deepak Thapa wrote, the 'haplessness' of the state, rather than extraordinary tactical brilliance on the part of the Maoists, had enabled them to come so far. 'After all, they confront a democratic state run by a government that is saddled with 1) an unmotivated bureaucracy, 2) a police force that is not trained to handle an insurgency, coupled with poor intelligence gathering, 3) infighting within the ruling party, 4) a belligerent opposition, 5) an uncooperative army, and 6) a king who, perhaps, holds his cards close to his chest.'

By 2000, five districts of mid-west Nepal were practically under the Maoists' control. Thapa wrote, 'The rebels had even set up their own "people's government" in these districts, complete with minor development works, "people's courts", and not a little bit of social policing against alcoholism, usury and so on.' They had set off explosions in at least two Indian MNCs in the Tarai; charged levy from households; and forcibly collected donations from businessmen and establishments across the country. The Maoist student wing, too, was active, shutting down schools and colleges to demand that the national anthem glorifying the king be revoked and that private education be stopped.

The Maoists had begun attacking the police even in district

headquarters, assumed to be safe, and were succeeding in inflicting ever greater casualties. Militias were getting bigger, more organized, better armed and structured in the run-up to the formation of the PLA in 2002. They had, Thapa noted, also expanded their arsenal and confiscated 600 'three-nought-three' rifles from the police, another couple of hundred weapons, and regularly used 'booby-traps, pipe-bombs and home-made grenades'. This trend was to continue as Maoists armed themselves with weaponry from the government's stock after successful battles. The party had also looted 250 million Nepali rupees from banks and other institutions.

~

The political class in Kathmandu could no longer afford to ignore and remain complacent about the rebellion. Neither would a half-hearted, badly thought out approach work.

Within democratic parties, some leaders had begun speaking of a rapprochement with the Maoists. It had not been a clean and easy run for the Maoists, too. They may have achieved more than anyone could have imagined, but the success had come at a cost. Cadres were getting frustrated about the end goal, which did not seem within grasp yet; the fundamental political structures of Kathmandu remained firmly in place.

Baburam Bhattarai told me that he had begun writing letters to the leadership in Kathmandu since 1996, emphasizing the need for a political solution. 'We knew we would have to talk finally.' What was remarkable about the conflict in Nepal was that at no point did dialogue cease between any of the key stakeholders—the Maoists and political parties, the Maoists and the king, and the king and the parties—as the legitimate constitutional forces had constantly been in touch.

But hopes that the conversations would translate into something tangible had to wait for some time.

In 1999, a new NC government led by Krishna Prasad Bhattarai took office. He set up a committee led by former prime minister Sher Bahadur Deuba to suggest ways to deal with the Maoists.

Deuba recognized it as a political problem and established contact with the Maoist leadership in 2000. Durga Subedi—a veteran NC leader who had been involved in a sensational plane hijacking as a mark of protest against the Panchayat regime way back in the 1970s—knew Baburam Bhattarai well. But the NC's other faction, led by G. P. Koirala, was against talks with the Maoists and pushed a military-based approach.

Before talks could materialize, Koirala orchestrated an internal party coup and forced Prime Minister Bhattarai to resign. Six years earlier, the latter had organized a dissident group against Koirala. Politics in the NC had come full circle but, in the process, the peace agenda went on to the back-burner. For the next year, confrontation between Koirala's government and the Maoists escalated. On India's prodding, and with logistical, financial and technical support from Delhi, the government also created the Armed Police Force (APF), a paramilitary force whose core objective was to tackle and defeat the Maoist insurgency.

The palace massacre of 1 June 2001 drastically altered the political situation. The traditional legitimacy of the monarchy was now under threat. For the first time, members of the royal family were being questioned. There was a widespread perception—false, in my opinion—that Gyanendra and Paras were behind the shootings. The Maoists alleged a grand conspiracy, and admitted being in touch with Birendra through his brother, Dhirendra. With the arrival of the international media in Kathmandu, the world got to know not only of the events in the palace, but also about the rising Maoist insurgency.

Meanwhile, the political bickering among parliamentary forces continued. The UML had accused Koirala of being involved in an aircraft scam, disrupting an entire parliamentary session at the end of 2000. The massacre dented the prime minster's reputation further. The final straw was an incident in Holeri in the Rolpa district—the same location from where the Maoists had launched their first attack, and the hub from where a bus and a walk would take us to Mahesh Arohi's home. The Maoists had attacked and kidnapped police personnel, and the prime minister wished to deploy the

RNA—which had a base in the vicinity—to conduct punitive and rescue operations. In the absence of clear directives from the new king, Gyanendra, this did not happen. This was a direct snub to the democratic notion of civilian control over the armed forces. Prime Minister Koirala resigned from office.

Deuba now took over and, within days, called for a ceasefire and for talks with the Maoists. The rebels reciprocated and the two sides—for the first time since the war had begun—formally launched a dialogue. The popular Rolpa leader and one-time MP, Krishna Bahadur Mahara, came over ground on behalf of the Maoists and led the team which would conduct the talks. But the Maoists had categorical demands—an interim government, a CA and a republic. The government was in no position to overhaul the constitutional structure of the state.

In retrospect, analysts concluded that the Maoists—if not the government—knew that there was no meeting point, and had only used the period to regroup and consolidate while propagating their point of view through legitimate channels and reaching out to new constituencies in the capital.

On 23 November 2001, the talks collapsed with the Maoists launching a multi-pronged attack, most prominently on RNA barracks in the Dang district of western Nepal. This was a deliberate invitation to escalate the conflict, as both sides had carefully avoided antagonizing each other till then. The Maoists were fully aware that this would bring the entire might of the state's military power against them, but it was a calculated decision to move on to the next stage of the offensive. In the process, the rebels also gained a large and relatively modern arsenal of weapons and ammunition which helped transform their military capacity. If there was any doubt about their intentions, the Maoists dispelled it by launching another fierce attack—their boldest one in eastern Nepal—a few days later. They attacked local government offices and destroyed the airport tower in Salleri town of the Solukhumbu district.

Back in the capital, this left Prime Minister Sher Bahadur Deuba—who had projected himself as the peacemaker as opposed to Koirala—stunned and betrayed. The RNA had made it clear that a declaration of a state of emergency was a precondition to its mobilization. The government agreed. Nepal was now in an emergency; fundamental rights were suspended and press censorship imposed; stringent anti-terrorism legislation, which allowed security forces to arrest without warrants being issued—and provided for long-term preventive detention—was passed.

The country was at war with itself.

3

If the first five years marked a conflict of low-to-medium intensity, confined to pockets, the next five years would numb and shake up Nepali society like never before.

Maoists had now concluded that they needed to move from the phase of 'strategic defence' to attaining 'strategic balance'. This required the conflict to be escalated, so that the state's capacity could be eroded and the party's presence expanded. It carried the risk of over-reach, but the rebels took the plunge.

From the Ladaku Dal and the Swayamsevak Dal that Mahesh Arohi had occasionally been a part of, the party had moved to creating militias in the late 1990s. Now, it set up the PLA. Mao's dictum—'without an army, the people have nothing'—is sacred for ultra-Left insurgencies and the formation of the PLA marked a major accomplishment.

The PLA was eventually structured like any professional armed force, with a general staff command, divisions, brigades, battalions, company, platoons and squads; the party also retained its militias. Recruitment was both voluntary and forced; with the party asking for one member per household in base areas to join their ranks.

The PLA suffered setbacks in many battles, but it also managed to inflict losses in its attacks on army and police posts, government installations, telecommunication towers, industrial plants and public utilities. It imposed blockades on highways, crippling supplies to major towns, including the capital. But as a report published by the research and advocacy organization, International Crisis Group (ICG), was to note in 2005, 'The Maoists are at heart a political party. They have developed military capacity but it is subordinate to political control ... they are neither Khmer Rouge clones nor is their campaign part of any global terrorism.'

The party also expanded its fraternal organizations. The students' union continued to make inroads into colleges and schools, raising the issue of exorbitant fees in private educational institutions. The trade union often brought industry to a standstill with struggles for higher wages and against foreign capital. The ethnic fronts were potent political platforms. They fit into the Maoists' projection of Nepal as a centralized Hindu state from which marginalized ethnic groups—the Magars and Gurungs of west Nepal, the Newars of Kathmandu Valley, the Tamangs of central Nepal, and the Rais and Limbus of eastern Nepal—needed liberation. And that was possible only through 'autonomous republics' with the 'right to self-determination'. The Maoist party, through its intellectual front, reached out to Kathmandu's professional organizations, and while its success, in this case, was relatively limited, it did manage to convey its message to the mainstream Left opinion-makers, 'progressive' lawyers, journalists and teachers.

Maintaining the PLA, as well as the larger organizational apparatus with whole-timers, was expensive. Many conspiracy theories did the

rounds in Kathmandu about their sources of funding, with some alluding to external backers, others to networks with an international terrorist network. But these appear to be without basis.

The party adopted an astute, though illegitimate, mix of strategies. Maoists relied largely on extortions, donations and loot from banks and financial institutions. Local units were tasked with raising their own resources through illegal trade and by imposing levies in their areas of operation. In India, the migrant community was tapped, as were Nepalis in the rest of the world—workers in the Gulf and sympathizers in Europe, particularly Belgium and United Kingdom.

The degree of coercion in the Maoist project cannot be underestimated. Their threats as well as the frequent use of violence played a big role in their eventual success. The seminal Nepal Conflict Report of the UN Office of the High Commissioner for Human Rights (UN-OHCHR) confirmed what multiple reported accounts had revealed about atrocities perpetrated by the Maoists. They engaged in the targeted killings of civilians, summary executions were ordered by the 'People's Court', and abductions were rampant. One emblematic case of violation took place in 2005. The Maoists destroyed a passenger bus in Maadi village of Chitwan district, killing thirty-nine people and injuring another seventy-two, using a bucket-bomb.

While the Maoists brushed aside the incident as a 'mistake', the party itself is not apologetic about the use of violence, though party sympathizers tend to discount the importance of this element. That would be a mistake. For it was only through this method that the Maoists succeeded in shutting out political rivals and diluting the authority and the presence of the state. Those who were not committed to the ideology, but lived in a village in an area controlled largely by the Maoists, had little choice but to follow the party's diktats. Families which received money from sons, husbands and fathers working in India, the Gulf and Malaysia had to part with it for the 'revolution' or face consequences. Many fled villages for the relative comfort of Kathmandu, causing massive internal displacement. Others who resisted the Maoists' hegemony in stronghold areas were killed for being 'class enemies', 'police informers' or 'feudals'.

The Maoists' violence did alienate many citizens. But unlike the state, the violence of the rebels was more targeted. It was also backed by the rhetoric of justice, by slogans of bringing about revolutionary change, and fighting an evil regime. State violence had been far more indiscriminate, resting on little more than the illegality of the insurgency. This led to a somewhat paradoxical situation. Arbitrary police and military brutalities indirectly helped the Maoists shore up their strength, but their own violence, too, helped in projecting power and enhancing political control. This throws up deeper questions about the use of violence, when it is effective and when counter-productive, and how, despite having legitimate monopoly over force, states often fail to exercise it wisely.

~

After 2001, the Nepali state had decided that enough was enough. The post-9/11 global discourse on the 'war on terror'; India's declaration of the Maoists as 'terrorists' even before the Nepal government categorized them as such; and a consensus in the international community in Kathmandu that the Maoists were to blame for breaking the ceasefire had created a favourable geopolitical context for the government to launch an offensive.

The RNA and the APF did inflict damage on the rebels. A fortnight after the war started, the Maoists attacked RNA camps, equipped with telecommunication towers, in Rolpa and Salyan in west Nepal. The army foiled the attacks. In January 2002, the Maoists attacked a police post in Panchthar in eastern Nepal; on their way back, the RNA killed several Maoist fighters in the neighbouring Terathum district.

The battles continued through the year. A cursory glance at the incidents reveals the breadth and scale of the violence. In February, the Maoists launched an assault on Mangalsen, the district headquarters of Achham in western Nepal. One hundred and thirty-eight people were killed.

A few days later, Maoists shot at an army helicopter which was trying to land on an airstrip in Kalikot district. On 24 February, security forces retaliated by killing construction labourers working on the airport project, suspecting that the Maoists were hiding amongst them. It later transpired that all of them were innocent. Many belonged to Jogimara village in the Dhading district of central Nepal, and had come to Kalikot—lured by the prospect of earning Rs 100 a day—a few months earlier. Six months later, Mohan Mainali, a journalist, reported from Jogimara that the killings had left behind ten widows, eighteen orphans and fourteen bereaved parents, 'trapped between the need to come to terms with the death of their loved ones, a future of destitution and despair, and a government that calls them relatives of terrorists'.

But it was clear, early on in this phase of war, that the army's bluster about 'finishing off the terrorists in six months'—as several generals, drunk with newly acquired power, used to put it—was precisely that, bluster. The Maoists' war machine and the popular support they enjoyed were more formidable than they had anticipated. For all its professional reputation, the RNA was more accustomed to ceremonial functions than fighting a guerrilla force. It seemed to cover its incompetence and inability to defeat the Maoists by engaging in the most egregious violations of the rules of war and the Nepali Constitution. This only alienated the local population even more, driving them towards the Maoists.

According to the UN-OHCHR report on the conflict, the army engaged in unlawful killings during search operations and patrols, and in collective retaliation like in Kalikot. There were deaths in detention facilities and barracks. In Bardiya's army barracks, hundreds of men and women of the Tharu community—which is among Nepal's most disadvantaged and excluded communities—were illegally detained. Many were killed; others were said to have 'disappeared'; and women were raped. A well-known case is that of Maina Sunwar. A young Dalit girl, Sunwar was picked up by the army in 2004 from Kavre district and taken to the Birendra Peace Operations Training Centre in the district. She was subjected to torture in the presence of seven army officers, including two captains. She died soon after. The army personnel then took her body outside and shot it in the back.

~

Even as the war intensified and innocents suffered, power politics was rapidly changing in Kathmandu.

In 2001, despite belonging to the same party, G. P. Koirala was in favour of a security-based approach even as Sher Bahadur Deuba advocated talks. But after the end of the ceasefire and the peace talks, the tables turned, with Deuba pushing for an all-out military offensive. Koirala, however, was wary of the increasing power of the royal–military establishment and adopted a more conciliatory approach towards the Maoists. Koirala opened up channels of communication with the rebels. Along with Chakra Prasad Bastola, a former foreign minister and Nepal's ambassador to India, he met the Maoist leaders in Delhi in early 2002.

Shekhar Koirala, Koirala's nephew, was then the head of the B. P. Koirala Institute of Health Sciences in Dharan in eastern Nepal. He told me several years later, 'Girijababu had spoken to Prachanda. In that conversation, Prachanda had told him to accept a republic while he would accept democracy. But Girijababu told him, let us make improvements in the political system, while keeping the preamble of the Constitution of 1990 intact.' Keeping the preamble would mean retaining the monarchy. This was not acceptable to the Maoists, but both leaders decided to continue their engagement.

According to Shekhar, Koirala told Gyanendra about the conversation. The monarch asked him to find out what the bottom-line would be, asking a revealing question, 'What will be my role?'

Koirala then sent senior leader Govind Raj Joshi and Shekhar Koirala to meet the Maoists in Delhi. Shekhar believes he was chosen, even though he was not an active politician, because official work often took him to India and his visit would not arouse suspicions. His old association with Baburam Bhattarai, from their days as students in Delhi, as well as the fact that he was a part of the Koirala family and could be trusted entirely, must have also played a role in his selection.

Bamdev Chhetri, a Maoist activist, took the NC's envoys in an autorickshaw to meet the Maoist leaders. 'I told him I would recognize Delhi blindfolded,' Shekhar Koirala recalled, laughing. 'It was a nice farmhouse in Mehrauli, with a beautiful garden.

Govind Raj Joshi also kept a secret recording of our talks. We reiterated to the Maoists what Girijababu said about retaining the 1990 Constitution preamble. But even as we were talking to them, we got the news that Prime Minister Deuba had dissolved the Parliament.'

By then, Deuba had sided almost entirely with the RNA, which insisted on an extension of the state of emergency as a precondition to continuing operations. Koirala had opposed the emergency, and was exploring the possibility of negotiations to stem the increasing role of the military in politics. But on the prodding of the Palace–military combine, Deuba unilaterally extended the emergency, dissolved the Parliament, and called for fresh elections. This infuriated Koirala, who threw him out of the party. Deuba went on to form the Nepali Congress (Democratic), but the split caused irreparable damage to the party.

Once again, internal tensions within the NC had blocked the possibility of negotiations with the Maoists. In 1999-2000, G. P. Koirala had played the spoiler, blocking the then prime minister Krishna Prasad Bhattarai's peace overtures. This time, Prime Minister Deuba played into the hands of the Right-wing establishment, blocking Koirala's efforts. Almost six years later, Shekhar Koirala said, piercingly, 'Deubaji is back in Congress with us now. But his role in this episode will remain a question mark.'

The more worrying trend was the gradual increase in Gyanendra's power. Unlike his elder brother, the new king publicly proclaimed that he would not be a mute spectator and had ambitions to go beyond his constitutional role. The RNA's loyalty was clearly towards its supreme commander, the monarch, rather than towards the democratic dispensation of the day. They took Sher Bahadur Deuba's orders because the prime minister had submitted himself to red-lines issued by the Palace and the RNA, unlike G. P. Koirala who had sought to maintain a degree of autonomy.

In August 2002, the term of the elected local bodies ended and, instead of extending it, Deuba let it lapse. This created a huge political vacuum on the ground. The political process, which was anyway under attack from the Maoists, was left with no legitimate and democratic mechanism. There was no check on the administration's excesses. Popular aspirations and dissatisfaction could not be channelled through peaceful means. The army colonel, deputed to fight the Maoists, was far more powerful in the district than the local administrator or the politician. It was a telling sign of creeping militarization. All of this led to further centralization of power in Kathmandu and, within the capital, in the hands of the Palace and the army headquarters in Bhadrakali.

On 4 October 2002, Gyanendra dismissed Prime Minister Deuba for failing to hold elections. This had been the Palace's strategy all along—of using Deuba to get rid of legitimate democratic institutions and then displacing him to take control. The gains of the 1990 movement, which had circumscribed the monarchy's role within strictly constitutional limits, were now in danger.

However the capital's elites, and the middle classes, disenchanted with the antics of the political class and blind to the dangers of authoritarianism, decided to give the king the benefit of the doubt. They also felt that only Gyanendra could tackle the Maoists once and for all. The king brought back a relic from the Panchayat era, Lokendra Bahadur Chand, whose party had won zero seats in the last elections held in 1999, and appointed him prime minister. Technocrats took over key ministries even as the king appointed a significant number of discredited figures—criminals and corrupt, incompetent individuals—displaying his shoddy political judgement.

The NC, led by G. P. Koirala, understood instinctively that this was a regressive move and began an agitation. Koirala realized that in a situation where elections were not immediately possible due to violence perpetrated by the Maoists in the countryside, and where the king had encroached on the turf of the elected executive, the only way to restore constitutionalism was by reinstating the House of Representatives, which Deuba had dissolved in May.

Meanwhile, the violence continued unabated. In one of their most high-profile attacks, the Maoists killed the APF chief, Krishna Mohan Shrestha, and his wife who were out on a morning walk in January. His daughter, Namita, was a year senior to me in school and we had got along well. I remember being numbed by the news and by the thought of what she and her two other sisters must have endured—like thousands of others who were either targeted, or became 'collateral damage', or suffered the loss of loved ones in the war. But a day after the Shresthas' killing, the government and the Maoists announced a ceasefire and called for talks. They had been in back-channel communication through Narayan Singh Pun, a retired army officer, an aviation entrepreneur and now a minister. This time, in perhaps a signal of the importance it attached to the talks, the Maoists sent a delegation led by Baburam Bhattarai.

The political logic of the Maoists holding talks with what was essentially the king's government was puzzling. After all, wasn't their aim a republic? Democrats fighting the monarch saw this as proof that the Maoists had no ideological commitment and were in the game for power, and both the extreme Right and the extreme Left had a common interest in squeezing out the democratic space. Indeed, the Nepali Left had been traditionally divided on the question of monarchy. But the Maoists offered the rationale that it was better to talk to the 'master' directly, as they felt that only the king had the authority to take decisions regarding the state structure—the parties would only toe his line.

Either way, the divide between the two sides was too fundamental for talks to succeed. The Maoists reiterated their demand for a round-table conference, an interim government and elections to a CA. Interestingly, they were willing to let the CA determine the fate of the monarchy and did not insist on a republic as a precondition. The king's government, however, ruled out any constitutional overhaul and, at best, offered an all-party national government, with participation by the Maoists, and reforms in the existing Constitution. The two sides could not resolve even seemingly tactical issues around the ceasefire, including limits on the army's movement, which the RNA refused to accept. The king had replaced Chand with another veteran leader from the Panchayat era, Surya Bahadur Thapa, as opposition had grown. But the stalemate persisted.

On 17 August 2003, even as the ceasefire was in place, the RNA summarily executed seventeen unarmed Maoists and two civilians in Doramba village in Ramechhap district. Nepal's second attempt at a political solution to the Maoist insurgency had collapsed. Besides the substantive differences on issues, the manner in which the talks concluded reflected a core problem confronting the polity—the impunity with which the army acted, the absence of any respect for the rules of war, and the design of an extremist section in Kathmandu's establishment to sabotage any peace effort.

The talks of 2003 would turn out to be the last chance for the king to preserve his position. Its collapse would also sharpen the emerging triangular conflict in the Nepali polity, one which had been simmering for a long time—between the Palace, the parties and the Maoists. The 1990 Constitution saw the monarch and the political parties as the pillars of the political order, working in unison. With the king carving out a direct political role for himself and excluding mainstream parties from the power structure, the two power centres were already at loggerheads. The Maoists, who saw a political opportunity in this division, constituted the third pillar of the conflict.

Even as the war resumed, politics in Kathmandu continued to become messier. The democratic opposition to Gyanendra continued, and he thought he was making partial amends when he re-appointed Sher Bahadur Deuba as prime minister in the middle of 2004. This was a clever political move, for it divided the alliance that was forming on the streets. UML, the moderate Left party which had become increasingly compromised, called it a 'partial correction of the regression' and joined the Deuba-led government.

G. P. Koirala, the old warhorse, once again stood firm as a pillar of democracy. He realized that the fight was not about an individual; it was about whether the king should have the prerogative and the power to appoint and sack prime ministers in the first place. It was about whether Nepal would be a democracy or operate according to the whims and fancies of an individual who was ruling on the basis of birthright and little else.

4

During the Dasain festival in 2004, King Gyanendra went on a retreat to his palace in Pokhara, the lakeside valley 200 kilometres from Kathmandu. The 2002 move had expanded his power, but a political solution was nowhere in sight. The state wasn't close to defeating the Maoist insurgency and the violence had only increased in the preceding two years. The NC was on the streets, protesting his proxy rule. There was increasing international pressure to show results.

The status quo had become untenable and the king had to make a choice. He could end the farce of controlling the state through token political leaders, take the next logical step and assume absolute control to fight the Maoists. Or he could hand over power to the parties on the streets, reinstate the dissolved Parliament, accept the leadership of the democratic forces and entrust them with resolving the conflict. Or he could try once again to re-engineer talks with the Maoist rebels and strike a direct deal. Royal advisors had been, till then, pursuing all three strategies partly, but simultaneously. They were in touch with Prachanda through intermediaries. They were exercising power through a weak government. And by replacing prime ministers, they hoped to find a meeting point with the democratic opposition or weaken it irreversibly. But it was not working, and something had to give.

Gyanendra needed advice and turned to an unlikely character.

Tulsi Giri had begun as an activist with the NC after completing his medical studies from Darbhanga in Bihar in the early 1950s. He even became a minister in the short-lived B. P. Koirala-led government of 1959-60. But he quit the NC a few months before the king, Mahendra, ousted Koirala in a coup and took control. The shift destroyed Giri's democratic credentials. But it was a smart political move, for Mahendra then appointed him as the Panchayat system's first prime minister. He became prime minister two more times. Giri went on to marry a Christian lady (his third wife), converted to his wife's faith and became a Jehovah's Witness, and left the country, first for Sri Lanka and then for Bangalore, in the middle of the 1980s.

Twenty years after Tulsi Giri had quit active politics, Gyanendra Shah—the son of the king who had first appointed him prime minister—called him to Pokhara. Giri was to later share the contents of the conversation with his old friend, and the man who served as home minister under him in the government in the early 1960s,

Bishwobandhu Thapa. Over coffee at his son's house in Gairidhara, Thapa recounted the conversation to me. Clear-headed as usual, Giri, who harboured not even a rhetorical commitment to democracy, had told the king, 'Sarkar, monarchy and democracy cannot go together. Sovereignty can either be with the people, or with you, the Palace. The choice is yours.'

Prodded on by a loyal coterie keen to expand its own power; driven by overweening ambition, self-righteousness and a staggering degree of self-belief; and heeding the advice of trusted interlocutors like Giri, Gyanendra took the plunge. Instead of diagnosing his earlier move of dismissing an elected government as a mistake, he felt that he had not gone far enough. On 1 February, with the aid of the RNA, Gyanendra took over executive power as the chairman of the Council of Ministers. He asked for three years to end the conflict, bring democracy back on track, and hold elections.

The Palace had made a choice. It had decided that sovereignty lay with the monarch, the country was his, and he would govern it in the manner he chose fit. It was now up to the other two forces, the political parties and the Maoists, to make their choices.

~

Eight years after the war started, the resilience of the Maoists had lessons for commentators in Kathmandu who had often written the movement's obituary. But it also had lessons for the Maoist leadership and cadre who were steeped in Marxist deterministic history of how events would unfold. Politics is non-linear, where circumstances beyond one's control, events, individual traits, leadership and luck play as much role as do the forces of history, economy and society.

The Maoists had made enormous strides in this period. They had become a national force, setting the agenda in Kathmandu. In large parts of the country, they exercised hegemonic control and determined the extent of political, developmental, administrative and donor activities. Prachanda and Baburam Bhattarai loomed large in the national consciousness. Through a clever tactic of sharpening the polarization and inviting a greater role for the monarch, they had exposed the weaknesses of the constitutional order of 1990. More and more people—in the mainstream polity—

were coming around to the view that the Palace-military combine was as much, if not a greater danger than the ultra-Left insurgency. The Maoists had also developed a coercive apparatus which could strike terror, almost at will.

But they were confronting major challenges, primarily due to a tough geopolitical context and military stalemate, which revealed the limits of what they could achieve.

Since 2001, some in the party leadership, particularly Baburam Bhattarai, had realized that outright 'state capture' was not possible. The Maoists simply did not have the firepower in terms of weapons and ammunition to do so. After the escalation of the war, and with India declaring the Maoists as terrorists, living in relative anonymity in pockets in India had become relatively difficult. Maoist leaders—Mohan Vaidya 'Kiran', C. P. Gajurel 'Gaurav', Suresh Ale Magar and Matrika Yadav—were arrested and either detained or deported to Kathmandu. Cases were filed against many others. Getting treatment in Indian hospitals across the border became tougher for injured Maoists.

Back home, the party had expanded in size quite dramatically, and in a short time-span, but this meant that ensuring the indoctrination and committment of recruits was no longer possible. The party was finding it difficult to exercise control in the manner that it once did. This had resulted in many 'mistakes' which, in party-speak, meant the unauthorized killing of innocents and the harassment of civilians; many district- and regional-level leaders were now seen to be using the party's clout to accumulate personal wealth and property. Across the country, there was a deep yearning for peace. From the cadres to the combatants in the line of fire, to their families, and civilians living in the conflict areas, fatigue had set in and revolutionary fervour was slowly dissipating.

The military dimension was as critical.

General Sam Cowan, a retired officer of the British Army and a veteran Nepal-watcher, has attempted what is, so far, the most authoritative analysis of the military dynamics between the two sides. After carefully studying battle videos, testimonies, and speaking to actors who were in decision-making positions, Cowan wrote in an essay in the *European Bulletin of Himalayan Research*, 'The RNA

fought a conventional war of attrition in which the emphasis was on the control of key territory, such as urban centres and district headquarters and on inflicting casualties through military engagements with the aim of weakening the Maoist will to fight through a gradual exhaustion of physical and moral resistance.'

The PLA, on the other hand, Cowan suggests, fought the war 'guided by a fundamentally different concept of conflict, as set down in the writings of Mao Tse Tung which in turn reflect many of the ideas of Sun Tsu', who had put forward a theory of war 2,500 years ago. The Maoists picked Sun Tsu's emphasis on the need to 'manipulate the enemy to create the opportunities for easy victories and lulling the enemy into untenable positions with prospects of gain, then attacking when they are exhausted'. Sun Tsu had also suggested that avoiding a strong force is not cowardice but wisdom, which found its way into one of Mao's most famous teachings, and into the practice of Nepali Maoists. 'The enemy advances, we retreat; the enemy camps, we harass; the enemy tires, we attack; the enemy retreats, we pursue.' The PLA, according to Cowan, also internalized another of Mao's maxims, that a 'revolutionary army must stay unified with the people it fights', who can then provide the 'recruits, supplies, information that the army needs, and can be politicized at the same time'. 'Revolution then comes about not after and as a result of victory, but through the process of war itself.' A failed attack on the district headquarters of Jumla in 2002 had made key Maoist commanders realize the limits of the military approach. Quoting Barshaman Pun 'Ananta', the young and dynamic fighter who had led the first attack on Holeri in 1996, Cowan writes, 'This was a setback the Maoists subsequently acknowledged to have been a turning point in the war, and one that required a serious downscaling in their aspirations for overall military victory.' PLA forces had also marched hundreds of kilometres and attacked Beni in 2004. This was a stunning battle, for it revealed the organizational abilities of the Maoists, the surprise with which they took on the state forces and its shoddy intelligence, and their capacity to wreck a town overnight. But the next morning, the PLA withdrew, indicating that they did not have the capacity to overrun, control and retain a district headquarters when faced with resistance.

Sam Cowan studied three battles. In Ganeshpur in the western Tarai, the Maoists suffered a setback when elite PLA fighters were killed in an ambush that went wrong. Khara in 2005 was a game changer in the war. This was, in a way, Prachanda's last gamble to test whether a military offensive would succeed in defeating the regime. In what appears to be a fit of rage and imprudence, and a desire to prove himself, the Maoist chairman personally instructed his army commanders to attack, for the second time in three years, a well-protected army base in Khara. Besides the weaknesses in the military plan, the PLA offensive was marked by a split and an ego tussle between two commanders leading the charge, Pasang and Prabhakar. The Maoists had moved away from guerilla warfare to a conventional war practice, morchabadda yuddha, but a crushing defeat at the hands of the RNA showed that they were not in a position to wage and win a conventional battle.

In the third battle Cowan analyses, the Maoists achieved a major victory when they overran a temporary army base in Pili, in Kalikot district, where the state forces had set up a camp to aid the construction of a road.

The PLA, Cowan argues, ranked high on the 'moral component', with combatants mentally prepared for fighting, possessing a high degree of motivation and purpose, and a willingness to put their lives on the line. Senior commanders were skilled, had experience at the company level, 'but lacked the training and experience to command and manoeuvre brigades in large contact battles'. And while they were not short of manpower, they 'woefully lacked firepower'. 'Large number of combatants did not have rifles, and machine guns and mortars were in short supply.'

The Maoists' success in drawing an internationally backed state army to a military stalemate is undeniable. But Cowan gets to heart of why the Maoists had to rethink their options, despite proclaiming that they would never give into 'reformism'. 'As a guerilla army using the tactics and strategy of that form of warfare set down by Mao, the PLA performed highly effectively. It lacked the capacity to successfully move to the level of conventional warfare.'

The Maoist leadership could read the signals, and felt that if they did not find a way out, they would suffer the same fate as many other failed insurgencies. Over a cup of tea at his Kathmandu residence several years later, Prachanda told me, 'I learnt from the negative experiences of other communist struggles. If we had continued blindly, we would have been like Myanmar's Karen rebels who are still fighting after sixty years, or communists in Malaya who were crushed by a ruthless operation or, more recently, like those in Peru.'

Like Gyanendra, they, too, had to make a choice. And it was here that an age-old debate within the communist movement of Nepal played out. One school in Nepal's ultra-Left viewed 'nationalism' as the core objective of the revolution; this tradition saw India as the principal enemy of the Nepali people and preferred a feudal despotic monarch to any understanding with democratic political parties, which were termed India's 'brokers'. After the royal coup of 1960, the Keshar Jung Raymajhi faction of the then Communist Party of Nepal used this principle to support the royal dictatorship. The other tradition saw 'feudalism' as the core enemy of the Nepali revolution, and argued for collaboration with the democratic parties, and India if necessary, to restore democracy as the first step to socialism and communism. Pushpa Lal was the most vocal proponent of this line.

Among the Nepali Maoists, Baburam Bhattarai followed in Pushpa Lal's footsteps. His exposure to India, to democratic political parties, and a civil society which operated beyond traditional Left categories had made him more liberal in outlook. He was also an ardent republican and could not countenance any tie-up with the king. He had been speaking about developing communism in the twenty-first century, and learning from the mistakes of past communist regimes, to slowly prepare the cadre for an eventual compromise with the multiparty system. Prachanda, the pragmatist, was more willing to consider working with the monarch. He rationalized this to me in a conversation, 'I had grown up with orthodox Left training. We were also indoctrinated to view India as the enemy.'

This debate in the party became so acrimonious that, by the end of 2004, Bhattarai had been suspended and put in PLA's custody. It was only with the royal coup that Prachanda realized the inherent contradiction with feudalism, and concluded that democracy was a more natural, and feasible, political goal.

~

The only unarmed player in Nepal's triangular conflict was the discredited, but resolutely democratic, NC. It led a loose coalition of parties against the extreme Right and the extreme Left. The UML had flirted with the Palace, and so had the NC splinter led by Deuba. But, with the royal coup, it was time to take a stand. Would they accept the Palace's supremacy and, by implication, a subordinate status in the political order? Or would G. P. Koirala give up his visceral anti-communism and engage with the more-than-willing Maoists? Or would it continue to chart a path of its own, which had clearly yielded limited dividends since 2002, with parties unable to energize the population to come to the streets against the regime and resist the Maoist onslaught?

In fact, the choice was a no-choice. Despite political parties reiterating their support for the institution of monarchy, the king had repeatedly kicked them out of the mainstream. Old democrats were tired, and a repeated refrain in the party offices in 2005 was, 'We fought Mahendra. We fought Birendra. And now we have to fight Gyanendra. Does each generation of Nepalis need to struggle for democracy? Isn't it time to resolve this quarrel once and for all?'

The pressure from the street was as intense.

~

Gagan Thapa's family was originally from the Solukhumbu district. But he had been a Kathmandu boy throughout his life. His father was a mid-ranking government official, and Gagan attended one of the capital's best-known schools. Young, charismatic and good-looking, Gagan joined the Tri Chandra College where he became involved with Nevisangh—the NC's students' union—politics. Gagan's oratory and inter-personal skills had made him a popular leader in the capital's campuses.

In 2003, during the movement against pratigaman, regression, Gagan went beyond the party's traditional line and became one of the first to raise a slogan that was, then, blasphemous in NC circles—the demand for a republic.

I first met him at a demonstration in Patan Durbar Square, and we soon became friends. Gagan told me several years later that he, in fact, had G. P. Koirala's sanction when he raised the flag for a republic, even though Koirala, publicly, still remained supportive of the constitutional monarchy. This was perhaps a way for the party patriarch to test the waters, and gauge the mood of the youth of Kathmandu. The message hit home, and Gagan's popularity shot up. But G. P. Koirala then sent him a message to retreat from the republican slogan and, while remaining critical of the monarch's moves, refrain from attacking the institution.

But once let loose, no leader can control outcomes. Gagan refused to pay heed. Despite belonging to a relatively conservative Chhetri family—where all his brothers followed conventional career paths and did what middle-class children are meant to do—Gagan had become a convert to the politics of radical change. Like Baburam had felt in Amrit Science College in the early 1970s, Gagan, too, could not see why Nepal needed to tolerate a birth-based political order and remain deprived of a modern, democratic political system.

Younger leaders from across parties had begun contemplating Nepal's political future without the king, and with the Maoists as a part of the broader democratic political system. They overturned the conventional political wisdom that the parties and the Palace needed to work together and, instead, argued that the Maoists and the other political parties needed to come together against the king.

This was the message the party leadership was getting from across districts in Nepal. The Maoists had introduced radical consciousness and awareness among the disenfranchised, among the excluded groups, and redefined the discourse. Parivartan, change, had become the defining cry. And to compete, parliamentary parties could not be seen as siding with an oppressive regime, incapable of providing peace, democracy, rights, good governance or prosperity.

But like there were Maoists sceptical of engaging with democrats, there were extremists in the democratic parties whose hatred for the Maoists exceeded their dislike for the monarchy. There was a backdrop to this—after all, the rebels had killed many NC and UML workers, displaced them from their districts and villages, and destroyed their politics. To work with the same force which had

castigated them as feudals and brokers was not easy. But Koirala, whose political stock had increased for being the only democrat to stand up to the king since 2002, made a choice. It was ironic that Nepal's oldest leader had the sharpest political impulse in both recognizing the dangers of the monarchy, and sensing the mood for an alliance with the Maoists, even as the second rung in his party remained stuck to the categories of the past.

~

India was a major direct, and indirect, factor in shaping the choices of all three domestic factors. Delhi's role will be dealt with extensively in Book 2, for the People's War waged by the Maoists, their accommodation in the new political structure, and the years when Nepal struggled to institutionalize peace cannot be understood without viewing India as an integral component of the political structure.

With the king deciding to go it alone, the Maoists recognizing the limits of their war, and the parties shedding their unwillingness to deal with the ultra-Left and move away from their support to the monarchy, new political possibilities opened up. NC and Maoist leaders began to meet in Delhi regularly in 2005, with G. P. Koirala himself seeing Prachanda and Baburam in June of that year. The agendas were clear—the Maoists would give up violence and accept democratic and peaceful change; the NC-led alliance would accept a republic. In November, a 12-point Understanding was signed between the two sides, and the 'end of autocratic monarchy' was declared the common aim.

This paved the way for a massive People's Movement, the Janandolan of April 2006. A multi-class, multi-ethnic alliance of individuals, communities and social groups came together across cities, districts and villages demanding an end to the monarchy, and full democracy. Nineteen days later, and after one address was rejected by the Nepali parties and the Maoists, Gyanendra made a second declaration on 24 April 2006. If, in line with Tulsi Giri's advice, he had decided that sovereignty vested with the Palace on 1 February 2005, he now conceded that sovereignty lay with the

Nepali people. Conceding to the consistent demand of the NC, he also restored the Parliament which had been dissolved in 2002 as a result of a conspiracy between the king and the army, in which Sher Bahadur Deuba had played the role of a conduit.

The Maoists had reservations, for they wished for a more radical solution decided by the streets or a round-table of all parties, rather than restoring a mechanism under the old 1990 Constitution. This had remained an outstanding difference even at the time of signing the 12-point Understanding. The Maoists were resentful that the NC-led Seven Party Alliance accepted the king's second declaration against their wishes, even though Maoist workers had played a key role in popular mobilization. But giving in to the popular mood, they responded to the newly appointed prime minister, G. P. Koirala's call for a ceasefire.

It was against this backdrop—riding on the ten-year-long People's War which had overturned Nepal's social order, the 12-point Understanding, the nineteen-day-long People's Movement, the political defeat of the monarchy—that Prachanda returned to Nepal's capital with his wife in tow in June 2006.

His arrival eventually led to the signing of a complex peace agreement—the key element of which was that PLA combatants would remain in cantonments across the country, to be eventually 'integrated and rehabilitated', while the Nepal Army (NA) would be 'democratized'. Nepal would also hold elections to a CA, a promise first made in 1951, which regimes had since consistently betrayed.

In April 2008, elections were held, throwing up the Maoists as surprise victors, reflecting the popular desire for peace and political change. It was this resounding verdict for full democracy, and for a republic, which forced the king to read the message on the wall. The world's youngest republic bid adieu to the 240-year-old monarchy as Gyanendra drove out of the palace after his final press conference.

Nepal's gradual revolution—through a mix of war, popular political mobilization, alliances, peace pacts and the democratic method of the ballot—had managed to defeat a 240-years-old institution. The nation remained. Its most feudal symbol was relegated to history.

BOOK 2

POLITICS OF PARTIAL SOVEREIGNTY

Sitting on the top floor of one of Delhi's premium hotels,
a former senior official of India's external intelligence agency,
Research and Analysis Wing (RAW), admitted, 'My organization's
engagement with the Nepali Maoists began in 2003.'

Later in the conversation, he added, 'We had heard a lot of good things
about Baburam Bhattarai and had even spoken to his schoolteacher from
Gorkha, who was a Malayali. We knew him a bit. But the real surprise
was Prachanda. We didn't know him earlier. He was a mysterious type of
figure. But we found him to be very balanced; he seemed to be a man of
vision. And that was the tilting factor for us.'

—Interview, February 2009

~

The crisis over the Maoists' attempt to dismiss the chief of the Nepal
Army, General Rukmangad Katawal, peaked in April 2009. Over coffee
at Illy café, close to the Indian embassy in Lazimpat, a senior
Kathmandu-based RAW official said, 'We are doing this for the
institution, not for General Katawal. We cannot let the Nepal Army fall.
It is time for the Maoists to engineer a course correction. They have
made a blunder.'

When I put to him the Maoists' argument that this was the only way for
them to push the peace process forward, he dismissed it. 'They should
have told us if General Katawal was being an obstacle on the peace
process. They should have conveyed their concerns. We would have
worked something out. The truth is they were not serious about the
integration of their combatants at all. This is about consolidating power,
about state capture. Prachanda has failed as a leader.'

—Interview, April 2009

From Rolpa to Kathmandu, via Delhi

After eight-and-a-half months at the helm, Pushpa Kamal Dahal 'Prachanda' resigned his prime ministership on 4 May 2009.

The previous morning, he had dismissed the chief of the Nepal Army (NA), General Rukmangad Katawal, and appointed General Kul Bahadur Khadka in his place as acting head. The decision had been preceded by a three-week stand-off, ever since the Maoist government asked General Katawal for a 'clarification' about his repeated defiance of civilian orders.

The timing was crucial for, in the normal course of events, General Katawal would have retired in three months. Senior Lt General Khadka would have retired before him, and the officer third in hierarchy, Lt General Chattraman Singh Gurung, would have become the new chief. By removing Katawal before Khadka's retirement, the Maoists had introduced a new dynamic in the army's chain of command. The move would elevate Khadka for the next three years, and kill the prospects of Gurung to emerge as the first chief from an indigenous background in the NA's long history.

The decision was not sudden, for all had not been well between the government and its army.

~

The Maoists had done exceedingly well, beating their own expectations, in the April 2008 elections. Four months later, they formed a majority-government with the support of the Communist Party of Nepal (Unified Marxist Leninist) [UML] and the new Madhesi forces of the plains. The politics of consensus, however, had broken down. The Nepali Congress (NC) wished to retain the defence portfolio in the new government, but the Maoists refused to give up their claim on the position. The NC decided to sit in the opposition.

At the end of 2008, the new defence minister, Ram Bahadur Thapa 'Badal'—a senior Maoist leader, one of Prachanda's oldest friends, and an inscrutable man who rarely spoke to the press or outside party platforms—had ordered the NA not to hire new recruits as it violated the Comprehensive Peace Agreement, which had stipulated that neither side would draft 'additional military forces'. A defiant chief, Katawal said that he would go ahead as the peace pact allowed the army to 'fill existing positions'.

A month later, the NA recommended the extension of tenure of eight brigadier generals, including the influential Pawan Pande. Pande belonged to one of Kathmandu's wealthiest and most powerful families. He was a well-regarded officer who headed the Department of Military Intelligence. Pande had extensive links across the political spectrum as well as within the international community. This time, Minister Badal had his revenge by refusing to give all eight officers an extension. In a sign of the distrust that marked the polity, critics of the Maoists interpreted this as a ploy to subvert the chain of command, create a vacuum at senior levels, and eventually fill the positions with soldiers drawn from the People's Liberation Army (PLA).

Both cases went to the Supreme Court.

In March, Prime Minister Prachanda allowed the PLA, which had been in cantonments under the supervision of the United Nations Mission in Nepal (UNMIN), to participate in the national games at the last moment. The NA immediately withdrew from the events in which the PLA was taking part, in a sign that it did not recognize the existence of a parallel army.

The incidents were merely a reflection of what many termed the 'war hangover'. The then Royal Nepalese Army (RNA) and the PLA had engaged in a bitter and dirty military conflict for more than five years. The war had ended in a stalemate. But, as the Maoists were fond of emphasizing, the RNA's supreme commander—King Gyanendra—had to demit his throne, even as the PLA's supreme commander—Chairman Prachanda—became the new prime minister. Past memories embittered the present relationship and threatened future stability.

There was also a core divergence in interests and outlook.

The Maoists were used to viewing the army as a 'private army of the king, and a feudal force'. In his first appearance over ground in June 2006, at a crowded press conference in the prime minister's residence, Prachanda had even called the army rapists, in a dark reference to its brutalities during the war. The former insurgents had mobilized ethnic groups who blamed the monarchy and the army for having taken away their territorial autonomy two centuries ago when the Shah-dynasty patriarch, Prithvi Narayan Shah, had conquered semi-independent principalities and forged a unified Nepal.

Only a few months earlier, the army chief had presented a long political paper to the Constituent Assembly (CA), suggesting that Nepal should go back to being a Hindu state, even though the country had been declared secular by the reinstated Parliament in 2006—a declaration which had also been legitimized by the CA in its first sitting. The Maoists felt that the army's position went fundamentally against the mandate of the Janandolan of 2006.

The army chief, Katawal, in particular, was seen as a hardliner. Indoctrinated in the royalist worldview, Katawal was a staunch champion of the state's offensive against the rebels during the war. He, it appeared, had not reconciled himself to the rise of the Maoists and the new ethnic forces in Nepali politics. Katawal also resisted the attempts to restructure the army, allow integration and make the armed forces more inclusive. The Maoists insisted that for the peace process to reach a logical conclusion, Katawal had to be pushed out.

And there was an over-riding realpolitik calculation. The Maoists knew that the only challenge to their ambition of establishing hegemonic rule was the army. They wanted a total overhaul of the military, and felt that the integration of their own soldiers into the NA on favourable terms would be an effective tool to change its political orientation.

Crucially, the prime minister was also under pressure from hardliners within the Maoist camp, who pushed him to take a drastic decision which would signal the party's commitment to change. Even relatively moderate voices like Finance Minister Baburam Bhattarai prodded Prachanda to step up the confrontation with the army. Bhattarai's motives in doing so have never been clear. Did he want to box Prachanda into a corner? Or was he motivated, like other senior leaders, with a desire to assert control and teach the army a lesson? Either way, the man who could have moderated the political temperature chose not to do so.

In mid-February, I was covering the thirteenth anniversary celebrations of the Maoist party, held in a PLA cantonment in the western Tarai district of Nawalparasi, where I had met Mahesh Arohi, one of the early recruits of the rebellion. The camp was about ten kilometres from the highway. After the ceremony, where the former rebel army put up an impressive show of strength, I was looking for a ride to the main road.

A PLA divisional commander, in his blue Hyundai Santro, asked me to hop in. As we made our way over the rocky road, I asked him what he felt about the rising tensions between the Maoists and the army. The commander, holding the steering wheel with one hand and smoking a cigarette with the other, responded, 'We gave the army a chance to cooperate, they did not take it. Now they will have to face the wrath of the people. There will be another confrontation. And they will lose whatever little they managed to preserve.'

The other side was bitter, too.

In the army's worldview, the Maoists were 'terrorists' and 'chor, daaka, phata [thieves, dacoits and rogues]'. The top brass saw the Maoists as enemies who made it good because of the failure of a 'stupid' king, 'useless' democratic parties, and an 'overly generous' international community. They urged interlocutors not to be fooled by the Maoists' rhetorical commitment to democracy.

A certain level of insecurity, and belligerence, was understandable. The army had been forced into accepting a political compromise it did not particularly like. The Maoists threatened not only their institutional structure, but also their vision of a unitary, monarchical,

Hindu elite-led Nepali state. Army generals disliked the idea of being equated with the PLA, and were deeply unhappy by the operational restrictions imposed on them under the peace accord.

The army also felt orphaned with the king gone, and with parties only reluctantly speaking up for them. Top officers claimed that they were being made the fall guys for the conflict, even though the war they had waged against Maoists had started under civilian orders in 2001. Many had lost friends, and relatives, and bitter personal memories often overwhelmed them. For instance, Pawan Pande, one of the brigadier generals who was denied an extension by the Maoist government, had seen his own brother and sister-in-law killed by the Maoists during the war.

However, it did not stop at that. There was a tinge of regret and guilt at not having been able to finish the job that they had been assigned. But instead of introspection, this resulted in wild rationalization. Generals insisted that if only they had another six months, they would have wiped out the Maoists—a claim that drew suppressed smiles and polite nods when they were around, and was ridiculed when they weren't. That is what the army chief had said in November 2001. Five-and-a-half years later, a guerilla force, 7,000 to 10,000 strong, had brought them to heel and entangled them in a military stalemate.

General Katawal was himself telling foreign diplomats how this was a battle between two ideologies, one which promised freedom and democracy, and was universally accepted, and the other which had been tried for over seventy years, but had failed and was now rejected by the world. Two Western diplomats confirmed such a conversation to me. Over two years later, I was to hear Katawal make exactly the same pitch at a conference in the Vivekananda International Foundation in Delhi. For good effect, he told interlocutors back in 2009 that Prachanda was a dictator. As an independent opinion, this would not have mattered. But for an army chief to voice such views about his own prime minister was absurd, and defied all norms of propriety.

Early 2009 was the period when the war against the Liberation Tigers of Tamil Eelam had reached its final stages in Sri Lanka. The army chief often drew an analogy, pointing out how the Sri Lankan model should have been emulated against Maoists in Nepal, and expressed open admiration for President Mahinda Rajapaksa.

Another army general, after a few beers during an afternoon lunch, clenched his fist and told me at that time, 'You know, when I see a Maoist on television or in person, any Maoist, I want to punch his face.'

Well, it turned out that the Maoists threw the first punch when they sought to dismiss General Katawal. But the stakes were too high for the game to be confined only to the two warring sides. From fighters out in the cold after the electoral hemorrhage to the presidential referee who assumed the mantle of a player; from behind-the-scenes managers to commentators who wore the veneer of neutrality—all threw their hats into the ring. Counterpunches and kicks flew. The rules of the game no longer mattered. The Maoists had to be punished for their pre-emptive strike.

~

The army chief lobbied intensively with political forces to protect his position, claiming that this was an attempt by the Maoists to take over the army and capture the state. His case was strengthened by reports which suggested that the man supposed to replace him, Kul Bahadur Khadka, had struck a secret deal with the Maoists, pledging that he would ensure the full-scale integration of the PLA into the Nepal Army. Rivals saw in the Maoists' action the intention to subvert the institution from within and create a pliable chain of command.

The other parties, the NC and the UML—unable to mount a political challenge to the Maoists on the ground—felt that the army was the only check against the Maoists' power. They opposed the government's move.

Ironies abounded—it was the same army, and the same generals, who had launched a brutal crackdown on the same parties less than four years ago in the coup engineered by the Palace with help from the military. The parties had then allied with the Maoists to counter the challenge from the Right. Today, they stood with the army, united in their fear of the Maoists. As the political polarization deepened, the line between conservatives and liberals in civil society and media blurred. Those who had earlier written against the army's royalist antecedents now felt that the greater threat was from the Maoists.

The Maoists' actions over the past nine months—their attempt to appoint their loyalists in state institutions, the use of their paramilitary structure to coerce rivals, their effort to obliterate the line between the party and the state—strengthened these apprehensions. The fact that they had their own private army and retained a politico-military organizational structure made their case for civilian supremacy sound hollow to many.

But the local dissent against the Maoists formed only a part of the picture. There was another power centre—sometimes visible, sometimes invisible—that was exercising real influence and shaping events, including encouraging all the anti-Maoist forces to band together. Like at other key moments in Nepal's political history, its stand would determine the course of domestic events.

The Indian state had put its foot down.

~

The Indian ambassador to Nepal, Rakesh Sood, met Prime Minister Prachanda close to half a dozen times over a span of two weeks, advising and warning him not to dismiss General Katawal. These meetings were widely reported in the national media, triggering speculation about the nature of the conversations and the message that India wanted to send out.

A bearded man in his mid-fifties, Sood was earlier the Indian envoy to Kabul—when Delhi was expanding its activities there. He was best known for his pioneering role in setting up the disarmament division of the Ministry of External Affairs (MEA) back in Delhi. Sood had been a part of the nuclear establishment in the late 1990s during the debates over the Comprehensive Test Ban Treaty and the nuclear tests of 1998.

Sood was a key negotiator during the Strobe Talbott-Jaswant Singh talks of the late 1990s, which broke the Indo-US impasse on nuclear issues. In his book, *Engaging India*, Talbott has written of Sood with respect, as a man with mastery over technical aspects of the deal. He also mentions, in a lighter vein, Sood's penchant for astrology and his belief that planetary movements would affect the outcome of the negotiations.

Unlike his predecessor in Kathmandu, the amiable Shiv Shanker Mukherjee, Sood's inter-personal skills were weak for a diplomat operating in an intensely political setting. He was a straightforward man, not one to mince words, and was businesslike in all his interactions. But this made him come across as brash, and disrespectful of local sensitivities and hierarchies. He often told interlocutors that he was in Kathmandu 'to protect national interest, not to win a popularity contest'. Sood's social circle was confined to those whom he saw as 'the true friends of India'. In practice, this meant that he was often most comfortable with the old aristocratic elite of Kathmandu and the business community.

The Punjabi diplomat had been appointed envoy in early 2008 but took charge only after the April elections. He recognized that the Maoists had a legitimate claim over government after the elections, and prodded the then prime minister, G. P. Koirala, to make way for Prachanda. But Sood also had deep reservations about the way the peace process had been envisaged—in particular, the way in which the NA and the PLA had been equated in the peace and arms-monitoring agreements. This, he seemed to feel, was the original sin which had allowed the Maoists to get more than their fair share in negotiations for peace. His assessment, however, missed the crucial fact that at the time when the peace pact was being negotiated, the NA was a force seen to be loyal to the Palace, while the PLA had been an essential element in the success of the democratic struggles of 2005-06. The two armies had also been equated for the simple reason that the military conflict had ended in a stalemate, with neither scoring a decisive victory over the other.

Sood's reservations about the Maoists' intent had deepened when, at the end of 2008, Prachanda veered towards the party's dogmatic wing at a party conclave and declared that the next stage of the revolt would be against 'expansionists and its brokers'—in the ultra-Left's dictionary, this translated into India and the democratic parties.

At an India-Nepal conference in Patna two years later, over lunch during a leisurely boat ride on the Ganga, Rakesh Sood told me that he had repeatedly pushed Prachanda to deliver on the peace process and to resolve the PLA issue when he was at the peak of his political power and could take tough decisions. The Maoist supremo had cited internal difficulties and, as India saw it, refused to take the plunge and transform his party into an entirely civilian outfit. Instead, by taking on the NA, egged on by dogmatists, Prachanda— in the Indian view—had returned to his revolutionary roots.

~

On the issue of sacking General Katawal, India publicly urged the government to take a decision only on the basis of consensus. It was an interesting postulation, since Delhi privately urged the other parties not to back Katawal's sacking—thus reducing the chances of any domestic consensus.

But to be fair, Delhi was not playing a double game in this. The Indians had consistently warned Prachanda that if he went ahead, the fine balance of power on which the peace process rested would collapse. Indian embassy officials told me that they had advised the Maoists to let Katawal off with a warning and defuse the issue. Two months earlier, on a visit to Kathmandu, the foreign secretary Shiv Shankar Menon had pushed a message along similar lines to the Maoists, and had urged them to focus on completing the peace process instead. Wikileaks (Cable: 09 KATHMANDU 137_a) has now shown that Sood met his US interlocutors in Kathmandu and told them what Menon had conveyed to Prachanda, particularly on the need to respect the army.

During his remarkably successful visit to Delhi soon after becoming prime minister in September 2008, Prachanda had promised that he would not take any action regarding the army without a political consensus. Shyam Saran, who was then Prime Minister Manmohan Singh's special envoy and knew Nepal extraordinarily well, later told me, 'The Maoists shifted goalposts. We did not say do not touch the army. All we told them was that if you take any step on a sensitive issue, it must be based on the broadest political consensus among all of Nepal's main forces.'

Soon after the elections, but before the Maoists were sworn into office, I had made the rounds of South Block, which houses the Prime Minister's Office (PMO) and the MEA, to understand India's policy approach.

A top Indian official, who had been involved in the Nepali peace process since its inception, had said then, 'If the Maoists play by multiparty democratic rules, we will not have a problem. But they must not disturb the Nepal Army's chain of command and hurt its institutional interests. That will invite a backlash.' Another official said that the fact that the Maoists still retained the PLA could not be forgotten while judging their moves on the NA. 'They already have their own army, and because of elections, have also got charge of the state army. This is a very unusual situation, an uneven playing field and their actions must be carefully scrutinized.'

Over coffee at the Illy café, close to the Indian embassy in Lazimpat, an officer of the Research and Analysis Wing (RAW), India's external intelligence agency, told me as the crisis over the Maoists' attempt to dismiss the army chief peaked in April 2009, 'We are doing this for the institution, not for General Katawal. We cannot let the Nepal Army fall. It is time for the Maoists to engineer a course correction. They have made a blunder.'

When I put to him the Maoists' argument that this was the only way for them to push the peace process forward, he dismissed it. 'They should have told us if General Katawal was being an obstacle on integration. They should have conveyed their concerns. We would have worked something out. The truth is they were not serious about the integration of their combatants at all. This is about consolidating power. Prachanda has failed as a leader.'

Earlier in the year, when reports had first surfaced about the Maoists seeking to increase their control over the state apparatus, the same official had defended the Maoists, arguing that each party sought to do so when in power. 'Didn't Girijababu do it? Didn't Nepali Congress put its own people in the bureaucracy and police?' But his, and by extension, RAW's position had shifted when it came to the question of the army.

So what made the Indians bat for the NA?

Delhi's logic was simple—they saw the army as a 'silent partner' in the peace process. Indian officials often recalled that the RNA, at India's insistence, had urged Gyanendra to surrender power when popular protests swelled on the streets of Kathmandu in April 2006. They pointed out that the army had cooperated in the transition; it had even cut off its ties with the Palace and had not obstructed the declaration of the republic. The army had played along because India had assured that its chain of command, structure, privileges and interests would be protected.

India also viewed the NA as the final bulwark which would resist any attempt by the Maoists to grab power. A joint secretary heading the northern desk of South Block—which tracks Nepal and Bhutan—had remarked in December 2007, 'This is the only state institution that remains intact; everything else has been dismantled. We will never allow the Maoists to mess with the army.'

India was also deeply uncomfortable with the idea of former Maoist fighters being integrated into the national army. Soon after the peace pact was signed, Foreign Minister Pranab Mukherjee had told visiting NC leaders that they had made a major mistake by agreeing to the integration. He, like many others in the Indian establishment, cited the example of how the Indian National Army was never accommodated within the Indian Army after Independence, despite the proven patriotism and nationalism of the Subhas Chandra Bose-led troops. The idea, Indian officials argued, was to maintain the 'sanctity, the professionalism, and the apolitical character of any state army'.

For Delhi, the NA was an extension of its own security architecture. The NA and the Indian Army share deep fraternal ties. In fact, in the final days of the People's Movement, when the end of the monarchy became imminent, senior officers of the NA had told India that they did not want their relationship with the Indian Army affected in any way because of the political change. India was quick to put those apprehensions to rest, and assured the officers that the ties were equally important for them.

The Indian Army chief's first bilateral visit, after taking office, is to Nepal where, in a formal investiture ceremony, the head of state awards him the rank of honorary general of the Nepal Army. The NA chief makes his first visit to Delhi, and India reciprocates the gesture. Nepali citizens serve in the Gorkha regiments in the Indian Army, and over 100,000 retired personnel are paid pension by the government of India in Nepal. Nepali cadets and officers are trained in India in all key military institutions—the National Defence Academy at Khadakvasla, the Indian Military Academy in Dehradun, and the Defence Services Staff College for mid-ranking officers. Indian officers training at the Staff College visit Nepal on an academic programme every year. India remains, by treaty, Nepal's primary supplier of weapons and is known to have been concerned when the NA diversified acquisitions during the war. While unstated, the close ties with the Nepali state's strongest institution is also important for Delhi to ensure that they have a position of strategic advantage vis-à-vis China south of the Himalayas.

All of this meant that India took a close interest in Nepal's military. It sought predictability and prior information in its operations and acquisitions. It was keen to maintain excellent relations with those in NA's higher echelons. And it was wary of an uncertain shuffling of personnel that could adversely impact its comfort level with the institution.

The institutional ties often find reflection in the close personal bonds between officers of the two countries. In 2009, this assumed political significance as General Katawal had a firm supporter in the chief of the Indian Army, Deepak Kapoor—the two had attended the IMA in Dehradun together. General Kapoor is reported to have put his foot down when reports of the Maoists' attempt to dismiss Katawal emerged.

So here was a rare moment of policy convergence in Delhi. In April and May of 2009, all agencies handing Nepal policy in India—the MEA, the Ministry of Defence and the Indian Army, RAW, and the political leadership—decided that they had to 'save the institution, the Nepal Army'. And when a firm, unanimous decision is taken on Nepal in Delhi's otherwise heterogeneous bureaucracy with conflicting agendas, India usually has its way. The government, led by the Maoists, would pay a high price for refusing to heed India's advice on how to deal with its own army.

~

By the evening of 3 May, the day Prime Minister Prachanda dismissed General Katawal, his key coalition partners had withdrawn support. At night, the first President of the republic, Ram Baran Yadav, took the unprecedented step of writing directly to the army chief, asking him to stick on to his position and defy the prime minister's orders. The President had clearly overstepped his constitutional brief and legal mandate in bypassing the elected executive. But so had the prime minister when he directly dismissed the army chief instead of recommending to the President that he do so.

India had played a major behind-the-scenes role in persuading supporting parties to pull out and reduce the Maoists to a minority. A senior Indian minister, and an old Nepal hand, called up the President assuring him of India's 'support' and asked him to block the implementation of Prachanda's decision. Top Indian embassy officials had met President Ram Baran Yadav earlier in the week, and had discussed the emerging crisis with him. The Indians had told Yadav that they would look up to him to ward off any crisis if Prachanda engaged in 'adventurism' with the army chief. Embassy officials had also maintained close contact with the President's advisors as the episode unfolded.

The next afternoon, after a meeting of the Maoist secretariat, Prachanda resigned on national television. The prime minister blamed the President's unconstitutional action, the repeated defiance of civilian orders by Katawal, and foreign interventionist forces as the triggers for the crisis. 'The days when Nepali governments bowed to foreign lords to stay in power are over,' he announced. 'This is a fight for our national sovereignty.'

For those who missed the signal, the Maoists organized a huge protest rally immediately afterwards. The defining slogan was, 'End Indian interference'. The defining image was stark—a charred effigy of Ambassador Sood.

~

Six days later, as Prachanda was presiding over a caretaker government, he gave an interview to Siddharth Varadarajan, then the strategic affairs editor of *The Hindu*.

The Maoist supremo had got along well with the erudite journalist, since giving him what Prachanda often referred to as a 'breakthrough' interview after the 12-point Understanding was signed. Siddharth possesses that rare blend of an academic's distant perspective and a journalist's intimate knowledge. He had kept in touch with matters relating to Nepal and was one of the few to have sensed that the Maoists were winning the elections after travelling across the country a fortnight before the polls in 2008.

In the interview, Prachanda said that he had repeatedly tried to reach out to the Indian establishment. Two days before sacking the army chief, he claimed to have requested Ambassador Sood to ask Delhi to send Foreign Secretary Shiv Shankar Menon or some other senior official for talks.

'We knew there was some confusion between the Maoist-led government and India on the question [of the army chief]. I wanted to settle this issue through interactions and discussions with high-level officials from Delhi. But unfortunately, the ambassador informed me that this cannot happen now because the election campaign is going on, that nobody is there, that it is very difficult.'

The interview was published on Monday morning in Delhi. By the afternoon, the lead story across FM stations, TV channels and afternoon papers in Kathmandu was that Prachanda had asked for India's help in the incident with the army chief. Opposition leaders jumped on to the issue and portrayed it as an instance of hypocrisy on the part of the Maoists. A radio-show host could not hide his glee. He asked, 'What intervention is Prachanda talking of when he invited India to help himself? Isn't his nationalism rhetoric hollow?'

Siddharth himself had flown back to Delhi. I sent him an SMS about how his conversation with the prime minister was playing out in the local media. Taken aback, Siddharth replied instantly, saying, 'That's absurd. Don't they realize Prachanda needed the Indian special envoy because the "patriotic" opposition would not listen to anyone else?!'

He was correct.

The parties opposing the Maoists' move had shown themselves to be totally amenable to India's instructions. They had escalated their nascent opposition to Katawal's dismissal when they knew which side India was on. Prachanda had, in fact, secured the approval of Jhalanath Khanal, chairman of the UML, and Upendra Yadav, chairman of the Madhesi Janadhikar Forum, the government's two key partners, before taking the decision. The Maoist chairman knew that talking to the parties without convincing India was an exercise in futility; they would toe the line dictated by their neighbour. This fact became even clearer as the efforts to form an alternative government gathered pace.

The Maoists were also trying to communicate a deeper political point. There was a contradiction in India's position. On the one hand, it urged the Maoists to complete the peace process, synonymous with the integration of former combatants. On the other, it supported the NA's conservative position, which was opposed to any integration—a sentiment many in Delhi shared under the excuse of retaining the 'professional and apolitical' character of the NA. The Maoists interpreted this as India wanting them to 'surrender' the PLA and disarm, and not integrate it on respectful terms as envisaged by the peace accord.

If the Indian establishment saw the former rebels as shifting goalposts and retaining ambitions of 'state capture', the Maoists saw India as backtracking from its role as an honest, non-partisan guarantor of the peace accord—by resisting integration and supporting elements like Katawal who were publicly against the 12-point Understanding and the accommodation of the Maoists in the mainstream. This was at the core of the gulf between the India and the Maoists.

Delhi, in consultation with G. P. Koirala, had narrowed down on UML leader Madhav Kumar Nepal—who had lost elections from two constituencies—as an acceptable face. Instead of propping up a far-Right regime, the Indian calculation was that a 'moderate Left' party, which still carried the label of being communist, would be best positioned to take on the 'far Left' Maoists.

Madhav Kumar Nepal's image as a reconciler helped his cause. But it was bureaucrats from Delhi who helped him to get to the magic figure of 301 in the legislature. The embassy persuaded the Madhesi parties whom they had generously funded during elections to back the hill-centric UML. When there was resistance by the Madhesi leader Upendra Yadav, who thought he could become the prime minister with backing from the Maoists, Indian diplomats and intelligence officials encouraged his MPs to move away and form a splinter outfit.

As one Indian official put it to me, 'We opposed the Maoist move on sacking the army chief. It was our stand that gave the other parties the guts to stand up to the Maoists. This led to Prachanda's resignation. Now, obviously, we will extend whatever support is needed—political, financial, and moral—to the other parties to form a new government. There cannot be a vacuum.'

~

But all this did not take away from the Maoists' doublespeak.

The former rebels had raised the rhetoric about Indian interference only when they realized that Delhi had taken a stern position that went against the Maoists' stand on Katawal. At key moments—during the insurgency when the top leaders stayed in the Indian capital, while entering the pact with the other political parties in Delhi, during the peace-process negotiations, in the run-up to elections, and while forming the government after polls when the old fox G. P. Koirala was refusing to step down—Maoists had been happy to engage with India, and seek favours from it.

But this was not unique to them. The former rebels were only following an age-old political tradition.

Gyanendra had lobbied hard during the endgame with the monarchy—sending private envoys to Delhi, making assurances to Indian diplomats that he would deliver on economic interests, reaching out to his natural allies like rulers of erstwhile princely states and the Hindu Right—to win South Block over. But when support was not forthcoming, he adopted the nationalism rhetoric and entirely blamed Delhi for patronizing and funding the People's Movement.

During the turbulent 1990s, which saw ten governments in as many years, all parties—from the Right to the Left—lobbied for support from India to come to power, and accused it of 'intervention' as soon as they were out in the opposition.

Or go back half a century. The oligarchic Rana regime survived because it played along with the British India government. But the same clan began ranting against India when the independent Indian government led by Jawaharlal Nehru provided refuge to the monarch in Delhi and allowed the NC to use Indian soil to fight the Rana regime. The rulers accused Delhi of 'intervention'. The Panchayat regime crafted an entire ideology based on 'anti-Indianism' because Delhi had given refuge to anti-feudal and democratic leaders like B. P. Koirala.

The fundamental fact of India's leverage over Nepal, and its ability and inclination to shape local politics, had not changed. Only the actors had.

The Maoists had a problem not with Indian intervention, but with the fact that Indian intervention went against their interests this time around. Where the Maoists differed from the other actors, though, was in the fact that they had a huge domestic support base, which gave them the confidence to stick to their stand instead of toeing Delhi's line. But Prachanda could not have forgotten that only a few years earlier, he had reached out to Delhi—and, were it not for India's mediation, accommodating the Maoists in mainstream politics would not have been possible.

1

On 23 November 2001, the Maoists attacked an army barrack in Dang district in the western Tarai, shattering a fragile, five-month-old ceasefire. The attack on the RNA signified an escalation in the conflict—till then, only the Nepal Police had been battling the Maoists on behalf of the state. The government declared an emergency, and battles between the two sides picked up in frequency, intensity and severity unprecedented in Nepal's modern political history.

The Maoists' 'headquarters' was then based in India. Both Prachanda and Baburam Bhattarai lived in small north Indian towns, travelled in crowded buses and trains to avoid being caught, and were careful not to leave any trace behind—to the extent that

Bhattarai once travelled from Allahabad to Varanasi just to make a phone call, as he recounted to me years later.

They lived with Nepali migrant workers loyal to the party, they lived in small rented rooms under pseudonyms, and they made it a point to shift locations regularly. Lucknow, Patna and Siliguri were regular destinations. Major party conclaves were held in Punjab. Top leaders occasionally went across the border to base areas in Nepal to assess operations, motivate cadres and build up the organization. The mid-level fighters on the ground came over to India to meet their leaders and plan strategy in secret locations.

This worked rather successfully.

The Nepali state was unable to develop a coherent and unified response to the rebellion. Busy with internal political wrangles, mainstream parties swung from advocating a policy of outright suppression or engagement, depending on whether they were in government or the opposition. Brutal police operations only alienated innocent civilians and created precisely the kind of polarization that Maoists sought—of pitting the state against the people.

It was against this domestic backdrop that the Maoist political leadership stayed in India incognito. The Indian government did not take the insurgency seriously when it began, and saw it as merely a domestic law-and-order issue. The lack of clarity and urgency within the Nepal government, and the dismal intelligence at their disposal, meant that Kathmandu never raised the issue of the Maoist leaders living clandestinely in India on a priority basis.

India, as a result, did not invest administrative resources in nabbing Nepal's rebels in a land where it would have anyway been difficult to locate them, given how easy it was to blend in with the gigantic Nepali diaspora or cross, and recross, the open border. India saw the Maoists as an irritant, but one that the Nepali government had to deal with. The Maoists saw India as an 'expansionist' power, an obstacle in their quest to complete the revolution, and projected Delhi as an enemy in their rhetoric. Their literature was built up on the traditional Nepali communist themes of how Indian capital extracted raw materials from Nepal and used cheap Nepali labour to fuel its growth; and on the relationship of political dependence. But they were prudent enough to know that they needed to use Indian territory, and did not take steps which would make the Indian political and intelligence apparatus take action against them.

By 2001, things changed.

The Maoists were now a significant force in the Nepali polity, and a rising threat to the existing political order. The royal massacre of 2001 had shaken the foundations of the polity. Baburam Bhattarai wrote an article in *Kantipur*, Nepal's largest daily, on 6 June 2001, blaming, among others, Indian intelligence agencies for engineering the massacre. With the September 11 attacks, the global discourse on violence changed, and rebel groups in any one country were seen as a possible threat to stability across the region.

The government of India, under the Bharatiya Janata Party (BJP), now changed track. In a visit to Kathmandu, the then foreign minister Jaswant Singh called the Maoists 'terrorists' even before the Nepal government had made any such categorization and while talks between the government and rebels were underway. India now also stepped up security assistance. In a sign of their increased confidence, as well as their calculated risk-taking abilities, the Maoists launched a counter-offensive when they broke the ceasefire and attacked the RNA. Delhi and the Maoists could no longer afford to ignore each other.

~

Sitting in his Sanepa residence in early 2011, Baburam Bhattarai recalled the tense months after the war resumed. Aditya Adhikari and I were speaking to him. He told us that they realized that with the domestic conflict intensifying, and the government projecting them as 'terrorists', the Maoists needed to reach out to international actors, particularly India. There had been a tradition of 'anti-feudal struggles' in Nepal seeking solidarity from India's democratic classes, and the Maoists hoped to explain their point of view and evoke some degree of sympathy and support in Delhi.

But they had a problem: even though they stayed in India, they had no contact with, and no access at all to, the Delhi establishment.

Bhattarai reached out to former colleagues from his time at Jawaharlal Nehru University (JNU), and comrades in the various Left parties in India. Yet, no leader was willing to meet him, worried about the implications of associating with a 'terrorist'. The most radical of Indian politicians did not want to upset the government of India, which had taken a tough public position against the Nepali Maoists.

Over breakfast at the India International Centre, the hub of Delhi's policy wonks, an Indian diplomat who shaped Nepali policy for a major part of that period explained his government's approach to me. 'In 2001-02, the aim was to neutralize the Maoists. The idea was to strengthen security forces and try to get the two constitutional forces, the monarchy and parties, together to isolate the Maoists. The combined might of military pressure and political consensus would then force the Maoists to come to the table on terms favourable to the constitutional forces.'

The diplomat focused on the importance of the RNA in their scheme of things, and defended what is seen by many in Nepal as India's lapse in not nabbing the Maoist leaders during the early years of the war. RNA, he said, had never fought an insurgency. 'We were ready to help with everything—weapons, intelligence-sharing and training. But when you have a 1,700-kilometres open border, it is impossible to control all movement. But there were successful instances of the Intelligence Bureau passing on inputs and acting on their information.' But, he said, they realized the key would be in getting the Palace and the democratic parties to work together against the 'common challenge'.

Bhattarai was looking to explain his position to Delhi at such a time, when India was firmly backing the Nepali state in its war against the Maoists.

That is where S. D. Muni, a widely respected professor in JNU, whom Bhattarai knew from his student days in the 1970s and 1980s, came in. Muni Sir, as he was known to generations of students, was a Nepal veteran who knew the country well since the 1960s. He was close to the Koiralas, as well as to Pushpa Lal, the communist leader who had argued in favour of allying with the democrats against the monarchy. Muni had also been a consistent republican and had supported the movement for democracy in 1990. Though he had briefly served as the Indian ambassador to Laos, Muni had broadly maintained a voice independent of the Indian government on issues related to Nepal. Neither was he affiliated to any of Nepal's parties, even though his sympathies clearly were with the NC for its long struggle for democracy.

Bhattarai reached out to Muni. The message was simple—we are not terrorists but are fighting for genuine political goals against the backdrop of a feudal and exploitative history; we are not anti-India, but seek to redefine bilateral relations.

In June 2002, Muni communicated the Maoists' message to Brajesh Mishra, then the National Security Advisor (NSA), the man who, by all accounts, actually ran India's PMO. In a seminal chapter in the book, *Nepal in Transition: From People's War to Fragile Peace*, Muni writes how the PMO initially reacted hesitantly to overtures from the Maoists, and then insisted that they communicate in writing. The Maoists then communicated through a letter that they sought the best of ties with India. Despite reservations, Brajesh Mishra did not shut the doors on the Maoists. Muni writes that the response came a few months later, when 'intelligence surveillance and restrictions on the Maoists' movements in India were relaxed and an IB team held discussions with Maoist representatives'. Subsequently, it was RAW which developed contacts with the Maoists.

I asked a former RAW official, who was well acquainted with Nepal's affairs and even served as the organization's head at one point, about India's initial engagement with the Maoists. Sitting on the top floor of one of Delhi's premium hotels, he said, 'My organization's engagement with the Maoists began in 2003. It was also the time when they were in talks with the king's nominated government back in Nepal.'

But didn't declaring the rebel group as terrorists and supporting Nepal's security forces, yet keeping channels of communication open with the Maoists and allowing the top leaders to stay in India, reflect conflicting objectives at best and devious intent at worst? The Palace, generals of the army, and a dominant section of the NC saw

Indian 'doublespeak' as the primary reason for the Maoists' success, and blamed Delhi for covertly supporting the rebels.

The former intelligence official responded, 'This is not true at all. We had links, we had communication. But that is the nature of intelligence organizations. We keep in touch with the enemy and we establish channels so that if at any point, our policy-makers shift tracks, there is a pathway to implement it.'

He may have been right, about agencies developing ties and relationships with actors across the ideological and political spectrum. But there was surely more to it if the engagement was happening with a group that was supposedly hostile to India's interests. Analysts have long pondered the connection between India and the Maoists.

An important factor that shaped India's willingness to engage with the rebels was its unease with the existing mainstream political players in Nepal. In a footnote in his chapter on bringing the Maoists down from the hills, Muni writes of a discussion in the Indian PMO about how the monarchy had never really been sensitive to India's security and development interests in Nepal—which saw them softening their stance and agreeing to listen to what the Maoists had to say. The Delhi establishment had always been distrustful of Gyanendra Shah, who had been a palace hardliner in the late 1980s when his brother was more reconciled to accepting multiparty democracy. The former RAW official confirmed this to me, saying, 'Birendra was willing to work within the constitutional framework but Gyanendra was negative right from the outset.'

India's comfort levels with the NC, the party which, in public perception, was Delhi's 'natural ally', had also dipped. The late 1990s, in the assessment of Indian security agencies, had witnessed a steady increase in activity by the Inter-Services Intelligence (ISI) on Nepali territory which was inimical to India's interests. In 1999, Flight IC-814 was hijacked from the Tribhuvan International Airport in Kathmandu, at a time when an NC government was in power. Even though the episode reflected the weakness and the inability of Nepali state, rather than a desire to harm India, Delhi was furious.

A top Indian official serving in Kathmandu at that time remarked how the incident was a turning point. 'Something snapped in Delhi. Before that, when I spoke to the prime minister, Atal Bihari Vajpayee, about Nepal, there was genuine warmth, support, affection. But something changed after the hijacking. The mood was that if something like this could happen under a Krishna Prasad Bhattarai-led Congress government, our friends, what meaning did the special relationship have?' A chill in relations set in, and it took diligent political and diplomatic work on Nepal's part to normalize ties.

Just before a visit by Brajesh Mishra to Kathmandu in 2000, sections of the Indian government leaked a major intelligence report—titled 'Nepal Gameplan'—to *India Today* which was published in June 2000. The report named politicians across the spectrum, including some of the then prime minister Girija Prasad Koirala's relatives and close aides, as working at the behest of Pakistan's military-intelligence complex, the ISI. The Indian agencies alleged that there had been an increase in the number of madrasas in the Tarai near the border and insinuated that this was being used as a breeding ground for extremism. They also accused Nepal of turning a blind eye to the infiltration of Pakistani 'terrorists' and counterfeit Indian currency notes through the open border into Indian territory.

Hari Sharma, who was then working as Koirala's principal secretary, received Mishra at the Kathmandu airport, and asked pointedly what message India was trying to send by leaking such a story. Sharma narrated to me years later that he had, at another time, posed a question to Mishra when Nepal's commitment to India's security interests was being questioned, 'How many bodies came to your village after the Kargil war?' Mishra kept silent, and Sharma added, 'Four came to my village. Six came to Foreign Minister Chakra Bastola's village. Nepalis have paid with their blood for India's security. Please don't question us.'

If the gulf between India and Nepal's mainstream actors was one factor, the growing involvement of the rest of the international community, particularly the US, in Nepal was an important consideration too.

While India had been RNA's primary supplier of weapons, Nepal's military was now diversifying its supplies. Wikileaks (Cable: 03

KATHMANDU280_a) now reveals how India had subtly conveyed the message that Delhi could meet all of RNA's requirements, that they need not look elsewhere and other internationals did not need to step in. While India's relations with the US were improving, the days of the strategic partnership between the two were still some time away. India had traditionally been averse to allowing any 'third country' involvement in the region; this was particularly true of Nepal, which it saw as its own backyard. The Palace, the then prime minister, Sher Bahadur Deuba, and the RNA were all perceived as being close to the 'US lobby', in the words of one former bureaucrat. They had sought to bypass Delhi in their military engagement with the US.

It was also a time when everyone was talking to everyone else in Nepal. The RAW official I spoke to emphasized this point and argued that India could not be behind the curve. 'We knew the Palace and Maoists had been in touch in the early years of the war and still retained contact through intermediaries. We knew that both factions in the NC—Sher Bahadur Deuba and Koirala—kept channels open with the Maoists. We knew that various Left leaders had met Maoists in India. We had consistently asked all parties and the Palace to work together against the Maoists, but they just did not understand the gravity of the situation. It was clear to us that, eventually, a political solution would need to be found. In statecraft, you build up leverage when you can.'

~

Those who were then serving in the Indian establishment take great pains to emphasize that being in touch could not be construed as support. And as proof, they point to how several Maoist leaders were arrested in India during that period.

C. P. Gajurel 'Gaurav' was picked up in Chennai when he was travelling on a fake passport to England. The party's ideologue, and Prachanda's political guru, Mohan Vaidya 'Kiran', was arrested in Siliguri. The Maoist leader from the Madhes, Matrika Yadav, was arrested and handed over to Nepal. (Yadav's arrest seems to have been a result of a difference in outlook between the IB and RAW. The RNA had passed on information about Yadav to an IB official who was visiting Nepal with an Indian minister's entourage; and a RAW functionary once mentioned to me how IB had 'messed up' by arresting a key source.) Upendra Yadav, who was known to be close to the Maoists, though his exact relationship with the party remained ambiguous, was picked up, but then mysteriously let off. Suresh Ale Magar, the ethnic theorist for the Maoist party, was arrested and so were Ram Karki, who had served as an important link of the party with India's radical movements, and Bamdev Chhetri. Cases were filed against many Maoist cadres. It became a lot more difficult for the top leadership to travel in India as compared to the late 1990s.

There have been hints of a conspiracy regarding the arrests, since both Mohan Vaidya 'Kiran' and Gaurav happened to be the more dogmatic leaders, and were perceived to be leading the 'anti-India' faction in the party. Their loyalists have often darkly suggested that the leadership of the party itself got the more doctrinaire members arrested. But this seems more imagination than fact, for Prachanda and Bhattarai loyalists were also picked up by Indian security forces. What could be possible is that Indian agencies focused on the people they perceived as being more troublesome, and impediments to a future political settlement.

The arrests caused a ripple within the Maoist organization. Despite the sporadic communication his party representatives had with Delhi, Prachanda was now convinced that the principal contradiction of the people was with the 'expansionists', meaning India. Worried about their safety, both he and Bhattarai returned to Rolpa in 2004 and began living in their base areas. Prachanda even announced that they would eventually have to fight a war with India, and called for trenches to be dug for that purpose.

Bhattarai was uncomfortable with the rhetoric, for he continued to view the Palace and the monarchy as the key problem, the enemy which needed to be vanquished, not India. As recounted in Book 1, the tension had historical roots, with different schools of the Nepali Left prioritizing either 'nationalism' or 'democracy'.

These debates within the Maoists' camp became sharper in 2004, as India's support to the RNA increased and its crackdown on rebel leaders on Indian soil picked up in scale and intensity. Prachanda was now in favour of speaking directly with the king to initiate peace talks and work together, bypassing the mainstream democratic forces altogether. As a committed republican, Bhattarai was aghast and strongly challenged this line in party conclaves at the end of 2004, which led to him and his close comrades being suspended from the party. The Maoist army, which Bhattarai had done so much to build, was now tasked with keeping him under arrest even as Prachanda stepped up his engagement with the Palace and the rhetoric against India.

India's support for an offensive against the Maoists increased. And the thaw in relations that had been initiated by Bhattarai, through Muni, was a closed chapter for now. From India ignoring the Maoists and the Maoists avoiding antagonizing Delhi in the early years, to a brief phase of communication, the new phase was marked by both sides, institutionally, treating each other as adversaries. The relationship, however, was to go through another cycle. And the trigger was Gyanendra Shah.

2

The coup of 1 February 2005 shocked Prachanda. He had been expecting a gesture of reconciliation from the king. Instead, what he got was a royal proclamation which declared that the monarch had assumed executive power to defeat the 'terrorists'.

The move vindicated Bhattarai's political line, but it took a while for Prachanda to realize his folly and make corrections.

Aides of both leaders recall how their respective camps were bitter. Prachanda's advisors continued to urge him to not reach out to Bhattarai, whom they castigated as being an Indian 'agent'. Bhattarai's colleagues saw Prachanda as an 'opportunist', with no ideological spine, and urged him to split away. But despite differences, both leaders knew the value of working with each other. One of Bhattarai's aides told me that Prachanda's wife, Sita Dahal, who had been at his side when he initiated the war and then returned to Kathmandu with him, has always been a key political advisor of the Maoist chairman—she repeatedly urged Prachanda to make up with Bhattarai.

The two leaders began talking about the new political situation. But what turned the scales in Bhattarai's favour was when Prachanda realized the impossibility of a military victory after a major setback in Khara where the RNA repelled a PLA offensive in the spring of 2005. The leadership then took an official decision to send Bhattarai and another senior leader, Krishna Bahadur Mahara, to Delhi to reach out to the government of India as well as to leaders of the political parties of Nepal.

Meanwhile, Delhi was furious with the king for his coup. India had repeatedly warned the monarch not to embark on an adventurist path, and seek ways to work with political parties. Yet, his actions had only further alienated the democratic forces. The NC had been on the streets since the king dismissed the elected Deuba government in 2002; now, the other forces joined the NC-led agitation. The royal coup was followed by a declaration of an emergency, the suspension of civil liberties, a crackdown on the press, the deployment of the army to arrest political and civil society leaders in Kathmandu and the districts, a freeze in all communication networks, censorship, and the stifling of the democratic space. In one stroke, Gyanendra had killed the prospects of the two pillars of the 1990 Constitution—the monarchy and the parties—working together against the third force operating outside the legitimate framework, the Maoists. The triangular conflict had now become sharper.

India had issued a strong statement soon after the coup, stating that the move would only 'strengthen forces that not only wish to undermine democracy but also the institution of monarchy itself'. It was categorical in laying the blame on the king for 'violating' the 'twin-pillar' policy of multiparty democracy and constitutional monarchy. Supporting its uncharacteristically strong statement with action, India pulled out of a SAARC summit to be held in Dhaka that month to avoid giving Gyanendra any kind of international legitimacy. Arms supplies to Nepal were halted. Bilateral meetings were called off, and the army chief cancelled a pre-scheduled visit to Kathmandu.

In subsequent weeks, the king's emissaries visited Delhi to lobby for support and, according to Indian officials, even offered economic subjugation in return for political support for the regime. Delhi's consistent message was that he must correct his actions first. Prime Minister Manmohan Singh met the king on the sidelines of a multilateral summit in Jakarta and urged him to release political leaders, lift the emergency, restore democratic freedoms and work to create a broad political consensus. The king assured him that he would do so, but took only half-hearted measures, which only made Delhi more distrustful of the monarch. It encouraged the democratic parties to work together and form a Seven Party Alliance (SPA).

The distance between Delhi and Narayanhiti was a boon for the Maoists, and exactly the opening they were looking for to sell their case in India. Baburam Bhattarai was now able to meet the political leaders who had avoided him in 2002. He saw Prakash Karat, general secretary of the Communist Party of India (Marxist) [CPI (M)], which was then a key ally of the government and provided it support from outside. Devi Prasad Tripathi, general secretary of the Sharad Pawar-led Nationalist Congress Party, which was in government, played an active role in encouraging the anti-monarchy forces. Tripathi had moved from being a communist student leader in the 1970s in JNU to mainstream parties, first the Congress and then the NCP. He had friends across the political spectrum and in officialdom. His engagement helped the Maoists earn political capital. Bhattarai discreetly met other members of the Nepal Democracy Solidarity Committee, a group led by Indian politicians supporting the anti-monarchy struggle. On behalf of the party, he also deepened contacts with the Indian agencies, which had turned a blind eye to the activities of the 'terrorists' on Indian soil.

The Maoists' message, this time, marked a great leap forward in their political imagination. They promised to join democratic politics, accept norms of the multiparty system, and ally with the older parliamentary forces. In return, they urged the parties to launch a joint struggle against the monarchy and accept a republican platform. The Maoists sought India's good offices to facilitate such an agreement and assured Delhi that they were committed to excellent bilateral ties.

The fact that policymakers in Delhi knew Nepal well helped in enabling a 'triangular conversation' between India, the Maoists and the parties.

Foreign Secretary Shyam Saran had served as ambassador in Kathmandu when the conflict was intensifying. He had broken new ground in Indian diplomacy in Nepal by reaching out to constituencies outside Kathmandu and engaging with stakeholders in the rest of the country, particularly the Tarai. The RAW chief, P. K. Hormis Tharakan, had been the station chief in Nepal during a crucial period between 1998 and 2001, including the time of the royal massacre. He had taken over as chief on 31 January 2005, a day before the royal coup, and Nepal was the first file on his table. Tharakan was from the Kerala cadre and had witnessed the rise of Naxalism in the late 1960s. But unlike many of his colleagues in the Indian Police Service, that exposure had made him sensitive to the root causes of such rebellions, even if he disagreed with the violence. His stint in Kathmandu had also shown him the degenerate nature of the democracy that the mainstream politicians of Nepal were practising. The Indian ambassador to Nepal, Shiv Shanker Mukherjee, was an excellent diplomat with sharp political understanding and a willingness to invest his political capital and make recommendations without worrying about how they would be seen in Delhi. Well aware that there were multiple constituencies of support for the king in Delhi, he did not spare the monarch's actions in his messages back to the government. After his retirement, Mukherjee often recounted to me, and to his other Nepali friends, how he had to fight internal battles in Delhi to gradually convert the establishment towards a republican line. All three played a crucial role in 2005, assisted by the joint secretary in the MEA handling Nepal, Ranjit Rae, and his counterpart on the Delhi desk in RAW, Amitabh 'Tony' Mathur.

One official involved in policymaking at the time explained the evolving Indian stance. 'February 1 was a turning point in Indian perceptions; we realized convincing the king was not going to work. Instead of the Maoists being the main problem, we realized the king was the main problem. He had dug himself in a deeper hole.' India, he said, kept urging the king on to the constitutional route, but the 'man just did not act on his promises'. Another official said the coup 'was an insult'. It 'reversed the process that had started in the 90s, and hardened the mood on our front'.

Both the RAW and the MEA were slowly arriving at a common understanding about the Maoists, no mean feat given the regular policy battles that occur between diplomats and spooks. One MEA official said, 'The best thing was that the Maoists came around on their own. They reviewed the failures of communism in the twentieth century and realized that the dictatorial approach to government was not working.' An intelligence official added that they were impressed with Prachanda. 'We had heard a lot of good things about Bhattarai and had even spoken to his school teacher from Gorkha, who was a Malayali. We knew him a bit. But the real surprise was Prachanda. We didn't know him earlier. He was a mysterious type of figure. But we found him to be very balanced; he seemed to be a man of vision. And that was the tilting factor for us.'

~

Delhi's nod enabled a series of meetings between Nepal's mainstream leaders and Maoists in the suburbs of New Delhi. G. P. Koirala met Prachanda and Baburam Bhattarai in the early summer of 2005. In that historic meeting, Prachanda is understood to have assured Koirala that they would accept democracy and work within the multiparty system, and urged him to shift to a republican platform. Koirala was not completely convinced, but asked his aides in Delhi—

particularly Krishna Prasad Sitaula, Shekhar Koirala and Amresh Kumar Singh—to continue the conversation with the Maoists. Discreet meetings continued through the summer and monsoon in various locales in the National Capital Region of India—in Noida, Badarpur, Faridabad, hostel rooms in JNU, Yusuf Sarai—as mainstream politicians and rebels tested and challenged each other's position, and sought to bridge the trust deficit when faced with a 'common enemy'.

Even as parties were talking to each other, they were also engaged in internal reassessments. The Maoists held a major party conclave in Chunbang village in the Rolpa district in October 2005, where they revised the party line and declared that their political objective was to achieve a Democratic Republic. This was a major shift from the earlier position of calling for a People's Republic. The shift in their demand indicated that the party was now willing to embrace the idea of 'multiparty competition', unlike the orthodox Maoists who dismissed the idea of political pluralism. The Chunbang meeting declared that the Nepali revolution's principal contradiction was with 'feudalism', as symbolized by the monarchy, and which needed to be destroyed. It marked the formal rapprochement between Prachanda and Baburam Bhattarai—the former adopted the latter's political line, while Bhattarai accepted Prachanda's leadership.

There was also increased pressure on the parliamentary parties from their radicalized rank and file to break ranks with the monarchy. Student wings, civil society and the media took a stridently anti-Gyanendra position, leaving the relatively conservative leadership to either support republicanism or get left behind. If the Maoists needed the parties for legitimacy, the parties needed the Maoists for organizational muscle, street power, and to sell the promise of a new, peaceful and just political order.

Devendra Raj Panday, who had been active in the 1990 movement, was now a leader of the Citizen's Movement for Democracy and Peace (CMDP). Along with others, senior activists, academics and writers of different political persuasions like Krishna Pahadi, Daman Nath Dhungana, Padma Ratna Tuladhar, Krishna Khanal, Khagendra Sangroula, Shyam Shrestha and others, Panday played a key role in pushing the political parties and the Maoists closer.

Panday had first met Prachanda in the early 2000s. He told me, 'I had kept telling the Maoist leadership that the entire social democratic space in the Nepali polity was vacant. They just needed to accept democracy, and occupy that space.' Simultaneously, the king's actions had radicalized former bureaucrats like Panday into moving away from a position of supporting constitutional monarchy to supporting a republic. 'Our message to the parties was simple. It was time to learn from their mistakes of the past, to understand that the monarchy posed a threat to democracy, and move forward.'

The policy battles were intense in Delhi, too. The king had deployed all possible resources to cultivate support. The Hindu Right, which fortunately wielded little influence in the United Progressive Alliance (UPA) government; the erstwhile rulers of the princely states, many of whom happened to be the king's relatives; and the Indian Army leadership, which felt duty bound to support the RNA and had conjured up an unlikely theory of how Gorkha troops in their own army would feel alienated if India did not back the king, were his key constituencies of support.

But the RAW and the MEA, led respectively by Tharakan and Saran, stood firm in favour of encouraging a rapprochement between the Maoists and the other parties. It helped this school of thought that the ruling government's key supporter, the CPI (M), invested political capital in pushing a similar line. The CPI (M) had fraternal ties with the UML back in Nepal, but it had also deepened its engagement with the Maoists, with Sitaram Yechury and Maoist leaders cultivating each other.

There is a perception that the CPI (M)'s presence pushed the UPA government to reach out to the Maoists. But this seems to be a mistaken interpretation. The establishment had clearly reached its own conclusions about the emerging political reality in Nepal but, as the government could not be seen as engaging directly with a rebel group, they gave Yechury the green signal to build a political relationship with the Maoists. Having said that, the CPI (M)'s opposition to resuming arms supplies to the Nepali regime did put pressure on the government to not reverse course and neutralized the more conservative elements like the IB and former princely rulers.

But through the process, Indian policymakers were very clear that the engagement between the SPA and the Maoists must happen on terms that would favour the parliamentary parties. As a policymaker put it to me, 'We were not going to hand things over on a platter to the Maoists. There was no blank cheque. It was a very carefully thought out, calibrated process of conditional engagement which depended on whether they met their commitments.'

The king did not stop trying. He sent more emissaries, and I asked interlocutors in Delhi what his message was. 'The regular bullshit. I am your closest friend. These parties are useless. If they take charge, they will ruin the country. I can do things for you—that was the essence of his position.' Another official who had met some of Gyanendra's envoys concurred. 'They were totally detached from reality, and told us all was under control and they just needed a little help. It was a disastrous administration; the conflict was getting worse; and they thought they could fool us.'

If that was not enough, the king shot himself in the foot in Dhaka in November at a crucial SAARC Summit. Not only did he propose China's entry as an observer—a red-line as far as India was concerned then—but he also sought to block Afghanistan's entry into the regional grouping, even as Delhi had invested political capital in getting Kabul into SAARC. A bureaucrat told me, 'That really irritated us. Here was someone who had trampled on democracy, deepened the conflict in his own country. And now, he was playing strategic games that directly impinged our interests.'

The precise Indian role during the period is shrouded in mystery and, depending on their respective political position, various domestic actors in Nepal have either denied Delhi had any role at all or have alleged that the entire endeavour to 'mainstream the Maoists' was plotted by India. I asked concerned officials about what they actually did, and the extent to which they pushed the democratic parties to work together and ally with the Maoists.

A senior source, then in the MEA, said carefully, 'There wasn't as much Indian role as it is sometimes made out to be. Our role was to nudge the parties into an understanding with the Maoists and vice versa. Much before we became active, the parties had been speaking to the Maoists; they had a relationship. We just helped them communicate and encouraged the interaction. This gave them a sense of assurance. Parties would have otherwise felt vulnerable to the Maoists and our involvement gave them the confidence.' A former intelligence official looked back similarly. 'We just helped put them in touch with the main political actors. The GOI was a facilitator and not a mediator; that is a very important difference. They did it on their own. One thing I have learnt is that everyone has their self-respect. We were a facilitator and then left it to them.'

The political leadership was more candid, with Pranab Mukherjee taking credit in an Al-Jazeera interview on 27 January 2009 for India's role in convincing the Maoists to give up arms and join the political process.

So a range of factors had now come together—the Maoists' internal decision to work with democratic parties; the churning within the democratic political class and the realization that they needed the Maoists against the king; Nepali civil society's pressure on the Maoists and the parties to reconcile; and the willingness in Delhi to work with new stakeholders, including the rebels who were still officially categorized as terrorists. This led to the historic 12-point Understanding being signed between the SPA and the Maoists, a draft of which was seen by Indian officials before it was formally ratified.

There was a difference in the exact letter and the spirit of that pact. In spirit, it was a one-point deal—the Maoists were to accept the discipline of democracy and give up violence; the parties would accept a republic and commit to socio-economic transformation. But the text was more careful. It spoke of the aim to end 'autocratic monarchy' and establish 'full democracy', but avoided the term republic completely. It was announced separately by the SPA and the Maoists; the fact that it was just an understanding and not an agreement was also important, for the parties did not want to award the Maoists full political legitimacy just yet. There was also a clear difference in how the two sides viewed the future political roadmap. The SPA wanted the reinstatement of the old Parliament while the Maoists sought a national political conference which would lead to elections for a new CA.

The 12-point Understanding was to become the basis of a revolutionary change in Nepal, the accommodation of the Maoists in open politics, and the restructuring of the Nepali state. And it had been made possible by the shift in Delhi's approach towards the Maoists.

~

Six months later, the Janandolan rocked Nepal. And, as at previous key moments in Nepali history, India was to play a decisive role in it.

Delhi supported the popular mobilization against the king. In fact, its facilitation of the pact between the Maoists and the parties was based on the assumption that, jointly, the two forces would be able to mount a popular challenge to Gyanendra Shah. But the script went beyond anyone's imagination. Millions took to the streets. The Maoists played a key role in organizing the movement across the country and, crucially, organizing citizens from Kathmandu's neighbouring districts to join the protests in the capital. Key points on the Ring Road were occupied by Maoist cadres, peacefully, where they were joined by NC and UML workers. The state resorted to brutality, shooting down over a dozen protestors, and imposed curfews which were defied every day. It continued its crackdown on the political class and civil society by putting them behind bars and sought to project the movement as being anarchic and supported by 'terrorists'.

India kept a close watch on the developments. But it was grappling with a major policy dilemma. Its instinct was to support the protests and teach the king a lesson. At the same time, Delhi did not want the movement to go out of control, and turn completely violent and anarchic. It also did not want the protests to culminate in a manner which would allow the Maoists to claim victory and achieve a decisive edge in future negotiations. What the policy mandarins forgot was that when people come out on to the streets, outcomes cannot be as easily controlled as they can when negotiations are happening, behind closed doors, with men who depend upon you for political patronage.

A fortnight after the movement, on 19 April, India sent Karan Singh—the former ruler of Jammu and Kashmir, Congress leader,

and a relative of the Nepali king—to Kathmandu with a mandate to find ways to break the political deadlock. But his appointment as the envoy generated suspicions that India was trying to save the monarchy, even though the public mood was stridently republican.

These suspicions were confirmed when, on 21 April, the king issued a royal proclamation. He asked the political parties to nominate a common prime ministerial candidate, and offered to appoint such a person as the head of government. Royalists saw this as a concession, but people on the streets resoundingly rejected the offer. When the demand was for the transformation of a regime, a token change which would not address the fundamental issue of whether sovereignty vests with the people or with the Palace, was a joke. While some conservatives within the NC, who were keen on an alliance with the monarch and unhappy about the 12-point

Understanding, welcomed the king's announcement, the protestors shot it down. The Maoists saw no reason to play along with the king—victory was within grasp and, if they could storm the palace, the end of monarchy was nigh.

India, however, jumped the gun and welcomed the king's statement. Foreign Minister Pranab Mukherjee is understood to have even made calls to Nepali leaders and asked them to accept the offer. This only confirmed the view that Karan Singh had encouraged the monarch, and it was an India-mediated effort. All of Delhi's work over the past year of building the Broad Democratic Alliance, and earning the goodwill of a majority of Nepali citizens, was about to go waste.

But, the establishment, led by Shyam Saran, quickly changed course once they understood the mood on the ground and received critical feedback from the embassy in Kathmandu. On 22 April, Saran held a press conference, claimed that India supported the struggle for democracy, and emphasized that whatever was acceptable to the Nepali people was acceptable to Delhi. For the first time in over fifteen years, India did not stick to its 'twin-pillar theory' about Nepal needing both a constitutional monarchy and multiparty democracy. The silence on the monarchy, accompanied with the emphasis on democracy, signified that Delhi had crossed the Rubicon and would have no objections to a republican Nepal.

I asked key officials who were then serving in Nepal why Karan Singh had been chosen. A former RAW official said, 'Do you think the king would have listened to anyone else? And do not forget that was the breakthrough in a way, he did come down one step. Parties welcomed it and then so did we. When the mood of the parties changed, we changed our positions. There was a perception that the king would listen to a Karan Singh type of person. It was a necessary complication that happened to get to the ultimate outcome.'

A former MEA official concurred, adding, 'Our basic concern was who can speak to him and tell him that he was endangering his own life and position. That is why Karan Singh.' But a diplomat then serving in the Indian embassy in Kathmandu put it more bluntly, 'Delhi's political leadership wanted to save the king. We were very angry when they selected Karan Singh. He almost ruined all our work.'

A far more significant meeting that occurred during the brief visit by the Karan Singh–Shyam Saran duo was between Saran and the chief of the RNA, Pyare Jung Thapa. The monarch had depended almost entirely on the army to quell dissent, crack down on protestors, arrest political leaders, defeat the insurgency and secure his political and personal survival. But India's deep institutional ties with the RNA were to prove more important than the army's traditional loyalty to the monarch.

Saran told me that he had conveyed to the chief that it would be a 'good idea to convey to His Majesty that the situation was more serious than he thought'. Saran warned the chief that the demonstrations were massive and told him, 'If there were orders to shoot, and there was a big incident, it would be impossible to control and you should think about the effort required to tackle 250,000 people.' Saran also emphasized that there was no military solution to either the Janandolan or the Maoist insurgency. A similar message was passed on to the RNA from the chief of the Indian Army. The Indian assessment was that the RNA chief had 'understood the gravity of the situation', and then played a 'positive role' in communicating to the monarch that the status quo was not tenable. 'That is why Thapa is not too popular with the royalists anymore. But he took the correct decision, which saved the army,' Saran was to recount to me years later.

This factor—of the army having listened to India in the past as a mark of the special relationship—would play a crucial role through the transition. Delhi would feel duty bound to support the army when the latter saw a threat to its institutional integrity, whether real or perceived.

The continuing protests, the firm Indian position in favour of full democracy, and the shift in the army's position now left the monarch with no option but to give up. For the most part, G. P. Koirala and the UML general secretary, Madhav Kumar Nepal, framed the text of the king's second proclamation. The king wanted to issue it as a 'press statement', but Madhav Nepal insisted—rightly—that he must appear on national television once again. Maoist leaders were still in Delhi, and were kept in the loop. Royalists have often claimed that Koirala and India had privately agreed that the Palace's interests and Gyanendra's position would be made secure. But other actors have rubbished the claim. Publicly, this time, the king declared categorically that sovereignty rested with the people of Nepal, ending a long battle between the Palace and democrats; he reinstated the House of Representatives, dissolved in 2002—a key demand of the SPA—and he accepted the SPA's roadmap to peace and democracy. The announcement was greeted with jubilation.

And while the Maoists had reservations—they would have preferred an outright confrontation, or a round-table conference, instead of a settlement on terms laid out by the NC and the UML—they realized that the balance of power did not allow for a complete victory. They, however, had reason to be satisfied.

What many had dismissed as a fringe demand—republicanism—had become a national goal. What started out as a little revolt in the remote north-western district of Rolpa with two rifles had driven a People's Movement. The one-time fringe ultra-Left group, riding on the back of its decade-long insurgency, was about to become a decisive political player in Kathmandu—with a little help from their new friends in the citadel of the 'expansionists', Delhi. But precisely because they had sought India's support in this transformation, they would have to pay the price of crossing 'red-lines' set by the Indian establishment, as they learnt during the crisis over the attempted dismissal of General Rukmangad Katawal.

Notes from the Extremes

As I stepped out of the Gorakhpur Junction, a line of hotels, and big billboards with Bollywood stars selling the latest consumer products, stared me in the face. A group of men surrounded me instantly.

One of them carried a pamphlet that read, in uppercase: 'KATHMANDU TRAVAL IN 8 HOURS'. A second person nudged me towards a taxi and said, 'Aage ka seat denge sahib, seema tak bas sau. [You can have the front seat, sahib. Only 100 rupees till the border.]' The competitive bidding was in full swing as yet another man pointed towards a rickety bus plying for the Uttar Pradesh State Road Transport Corporation, and said out loud, '35 main bus hai. [The bus fare is 35 rupees.]'

Most of my co-passengers from the train who had, like me, boarded the train in Delhi to reach this bustling town in eastern UP headed further north up to the border at Sunauli. A quick walk from there—through an ugly gate, over ten yards of no-man's land, past paan-chewing Sashastra Seema Bal (SSB) soldiers on the Indian side and blue-uniformed cops on the Nepali side, both united in their yearning to extract cash, goodies, or even a tip for chai-paani from tired travellers—would get us to the southern Nepali town of Bhairhawa.

A one-way flight ticket between the Indian and Nepali capitals costs anywhere between 6,000 to 9,000 Indian rupees; a mix of train and road travel could get you from Delhi to Kathmandu for 1,000 Indian rupees. The air route takes an hour and a half; the latter may take up to twenty-four hours. But for migrant workers, students, tourists on a budget, soldiers in the Gorkha regiments in India, people visiting for medical treatment, and many others, the logic of hard cash saved always wins over the long hours spent looking out of train and bus windows.

Gorakhpur in UP, Raxaul in Bihar and Siliguri in West Bengal have built up a hospitality- and travel-based economy dependant entirely on serving those in transit. For Nepalis spread far and wide across India, the smell of these towns meant home was just next door. I had often taken this route while I was a student in Delhi University. But, in August 2007, I stayed on to explore the town's political dynamics and its impact on Nepali politics.

1

It was after the Janandolan. Gyanendra, then still a king living in the palace but stripped of all powers, was lobbying intensively to preserve the institution. Rumours of his grandson—a four-year-old born to the notorious crown prince Paras—becoming the 'baby king' as a part of a compromise had picked up. News reports suggested that the monarchy's Hindutva allies in Nepal and India had begun a campaign, a final effort, to protect the Shah dynasty. Earlier in the year, when the Madhes movement had sprung up, there had been dark references to how it was a 'regressive' movement backed by 'reactionaries' from across the border.

Common to these plots to destabilize the peace process was the figure of Yogi Adityanath, the acting head of the Gorakhnath Math, and a leader of the Bharatiya Janata Party (BJP).

The math had a historical relationship with the Shah dynasty. The presiding deity of the House of Shahs was Guru Gorakhnath. Legend had it that when Prithvi Narayan Shah, then only a ruler of the Gorkha principality in the central Nepali hills, embarked on his mission to conquer other states in the middle of the eighteenth century, he was blessed by the head of the temple. There was another legend, too: of a sadhu's curse on Shah that his dynasty would end with the tenth king; a tale that attained retrospective anecdotal relevance after the royal massacre of June 2001.

The temple owned property, ran schools and hospitals, and exerted influence across eastern UP and the Nepali Tarai and the hills. A mahant of the math in the 1940s, Digvijaynath, became active in Hindutva politics. His successor, Mahant Avaidyanath, took the legacy forward by initially leading the Hindu Mahasabha, and then becoming a BJP MP. Avaidyanath was among those who brought the Nepali monarchy closer to the Rashtriya Swayamsevak Sangh (RSS) and its fraternal organizations.

But it was the younger mahant, Adityanath, who had infused energy and dynamism into the conservative politics of this part of the Hindi heartland. Besides managing the temple's affairs, he wore many badges—MP in the Lok Sabha; national president of the Indian chapter of Vishwa Hindu Mahasangh (VHM), which maintained its headquarters in Nepal; founder of the extremist Hindu Yuva Vahini, which considered the BJP and even the Hindu militant organization, the Vishwa Hindu Parishad (VHP), moderate.

Manoj Kumar Singh, a Gorakhpur journalist, was to tell me later, 'We may not like him, but he has many things going for him. He is clean, young and aggressive; he inherited the temple's influence and is a Hindutva mascot.'

During the 2006 UP assembly elections, one of his key campaign planks was to oppose the link between the Nepali Maoists and all the Indian Left parties. In the Lok Sabha, he had often raised the issue of ISI-sponsored madrasas in the Nepali Tarai and UP. And right before the Madhesi movement for rights had broken out in Nepal's southern plains in January 2007—which will be discussed at length in the next section—he had hosted a meeting of Madhesi leaders, including Upendra Yadav, to encourage them to start an anti-Maoist agitation. He was also at the forefront to oppose any moves to abolish the Hindu character of the Nepali kingdom.

The larger Hindutva movement in India had consistently supported the Nepali monarchy. The Indian ambassador to Nepal in the 1960s, Shriman Narayan, writes in *India and Nepal: An Exercise in Open Democracy*, an account of his tenure, how King Mahendra was invited by the RSS to speak to a large gathering in India. Their interests converged—the king wanted to cultivate constituencies in Delhi at a time when his relationship with the Congress government was not strong. The RSS found a Hindu mascot; saw its vision of a Hindu kingdom, a 'Ram Rajya' unpolluted by Muslim invasion, fulfilled in Nepal; and imagined this to be one more step towards fulfilling its vision of an Akhanda Bharat, an undivided India.

As Birendra faced democratic protests against the Panchayat system, the VHP organized a huge congregation in Kathmandu to crown him the 'Vishwa Hindu Samrat', the emperor of all the Hindus of the world. The legacy continued when Gyanendra was bestowed a similar honour after the royal massacre. When he attempted a partial takeover in October 2002 by sacking an elected government, he won the support of the Atal Bihari Vajpayee government in Delhi. Diplomats serving at the time suggest that the MEA was not enthused, but the pressure exerted on the government by the RSS and the VHP was one of the factors that led to India's support for the move.

Two days before the royal coup in 2005, I had interviewed Acharya Giriraj Kishore of the VHP in Delhi for *Tehelka* magazine, who said, 'We want the king to act and take over; we will support the move.' In hindsight, it was clear that they were better informed about the king's impending move than the establishment in Delhi was. Through 2005, even as the Indian government veered away from its twin-pillar theory of supporting monarchy and democracy, the Indian Hindu Right, along with the old princely states, remained the primary backers of the Nepali monarchy.

There were multiple examples of the symbiotic relationship. Nepali monarchy acquired traditional legitimacy and political support from the Hindu Right. The Hindutva organizations received royal patronage and support to expand their activities in Nepal. Religion provided the cover; at the core, it was a realpolitik quid pro quo deal.

~

After checking into Hotel Ganga Deluxe I headed straight for the main temple.

Right next to the grand temple, giving it architectural competition, stood Yogi Adityanath's palatial house-cum-office. Taking off my sandals, I walked into the massive hall. A dozen people, men and women in dhotis and saris, sat cross-legged on the floor. In front of them was a long wooden table piled with stacks of paper. A vacant chair awaited its master. On their right, three men were sitting on mats, working behind knee-high tables. With spectacles slipping down their noses, they bore an eerie resemblance to the munshijis [accountants of landed estates] of the Hindi movies of the 1950s. The walls were covered with huge portraits of earlier Mahants.

I did not have an appointment, but upon hearing that I was from Nepal, one of the munshis asked me to wait at the other end of the room.

As Adityanath walked in, everyone stood up. He waved his hand and sat down on the vacant chair behind the table. There was a sudden scramble and I could see people crawling under the table. The dhotis and saris carpeted the floor. An old man slithered under the table, touched the thirty-five-year-old master's feet, slithered out, and bowed in reverence again after standing up. The cycle was repeated—with old women, young babies and middle-aged men all paying obeisance. The saffron-clad, clean-shaven Adityanath, busy signing papers and giving instructions to his three assistants, barely looked up to acknowledge the devotees and the supplicants.

I waited. After ten minutes, Adityanath pointed to me and said, 'Speak.'

I introduced myself and asked him what he thought of the situation in Nepal.

He said, 'All of you have spoilt a paradise. There is anarchy. The Maoists haven't given up arms and want to grab power through goonda raj. They want to extend their influence from Pashupati to Tirupati. Nepal might disintegrate. The unifying force in Nepal, like the soul that unites the body, is the Hindu king and Hindu culture. Yeh secularism kyon laad diya waha pe? [Why was secularism imposed there?]'

He was referring to the decision made by the restored Nepali Parliament in May 2006 to effect a fundamental change in the Nepali state structure. The House had ended Nepal's status as a Hindu kingdom by declaring it secular; the same democratic declaration had also curtailed the monarch's privileges and brought the army under civilian control.

Adityanath's support for the king was not unexpected. But the moves made by the monarchy in 2005 had led to fissures within the broader Sangh Parivar in India on Nepal. Some 'moderates' in the BJP and the RSS felt that the king had made a mistake and should have worked with the political parties against the Maoists. After the People's Movement of 2006, some of them even propagated the concept of the 'Hindu republic', pushing the line that their core interest in Nepal was preserving the Hindu state, not necessarily the monarchy.

But Adityanath clearly disagreed.

He went on. 'The problem was that the raja was not aggressive enough. His mistake was he was too soft. I have not met him since 2004 but my assessment is he gave up too easily. He should have gone after everyone who opposed him. The king should not be silent and must take matters in his hand. He has our support. Hindu monarchy and Hindu state cannot be divorced from each other.'

And why did he think the king was so central to the Nepali nation?

'India's unification, out of 550-plus princely states, was possible because there was one umbrella party and the states were too small to rebel. In Nepal today, you have too many parties with limited base and growing regionalism. This never happened during monarchy. There was no discrimination. The king does not loot people like politicians. For 250 years, there was no discrimination in Nepal under royalty, now everyone is divided. What is going to keep your country as one? Who is the king is not important. What is essential is that he should be a Hindu. It is the soul that unites that body ...'

We were back to that old argument that many in Nepal had made for decades; the only thing that unites this diverse country is the monarchy.

But there seemed to be a contradiction in the young yogi's assessment of the king—as the unifying figure—and his support for the Madhesi movement of the plains—whose leaders blamed the nationalism imposed by the monarchy for having reduced them to second-class citizens. He did not see it that way. 'See, Madhesis must have social and economic equality in Nepal. But we don't support their demand for a separate country. What we want is a unified Nepal as a Hindu state.'

I had heard from informed sources in Kathmandu and Delhi that the Gorakhnath temple's interest in Nepal was not merely spiritual or religious. It was said to own property in the country, which had been confiscated by the Maoists. Adityanath's fellow BJP MPs from the region also possessed landed estates across the border. They had even sent some of their hired goons to support the military-sponsored anti-Maoist vigilante groups in the Tarai during the war.

I asked Adityanath if they had commercial interests in Nepal. 'Tum pagal ho kya? [Are you mad?] The temple cannot have economic interests. Ever. Whatever we have is for religious purposes. I do not own any land. But the math has some property in Dang in western Tarai, Gorkha and Kathmandu.'

The question had rubbed him the wrong way. He continued, 'Who has fed you all this? Are you a Maoist? Ab yahan se jao.'

The last thing I wanted was to antagonize the powerful politician on his home turf. I requested him to answer one last question— what did he think of the government of India's Nepal policy?

'They are fools. Only Nehru understood India.'

That was strange, a Hindutva mascot agreeing with the Nehruvian vision of the region.

'Nehru knew monarchy was necessary in Nepal and restored the king after the Rana rule. Anything that happens in Nepal will affect us. We have a 1,751-kilometre border, and people like us who live next to it suffer the most. There has to be a stable and peaceful Nepal and only monarchy can provide that. India is destroying that institution. From the 12-point Agreement, Maoist agenda has expanded. The Maoists and our Naxalites work together. In India, too, Naxalite influence has grown because of this government's leniency. If BJP was in power, this would never have happened. The country has been handed over to the Maoists. It is terrible.'

'Nepal developments are terrible.'

Two months after meeting Yogi Adityanath, I heard the same refrain from a diametrically opposite perspective.

I was sitting on a sofa in the drawing room of a middle-class apartment, next to a flyover in Hyderabad. It seemed like an unlikely residence for a revolutionary. But Varavara Rao is not your usual gun-wielding Naxalite activist.

Rao was an ideologue who, along with balladeer Gadar, had helped the movement win popular legitimacy through their writings and songs. He set up the Revolutionary Writers' Organization (Virasam in Telugu), soon after the first Naxalite upsurge in the late 1960s, bringing together artists and littérateurs sympathetic to the radical Left. He had been hounded by different regimes and had spent close to seven years in prison, including during the Emergency in the mid-1970s.

In 2004, Rao was an emissary between the government and the then Communist Party of India (Marxist-Leninist). When the 'peace process' collapsed soon after, Virasam was banned and he was kept in detention for seven months.

Local journalists told me not to entertain hopes of meeting the party leadership directly. It was a time when they were on the run because of the Greyhound—a special police force—offensive in Andhra Pradesh, and the Salwa Judum campaign in the jungles of Chhattisgarh. To understand the Naxalite view of the Nepali Maoists, my best bet was an over-ground sympathizer, aware of their inner workings.

One of Rao's many sons-in-law, Kurmananth—a journalist at *The Hindu Business Line*—had helped fix up the meeting. It was Dussehra and the whole family had just returned after visiting the caves of Ajanta and Ellora. A Maoist who found so much wrong with Indian history and the country's cultural past had just come back after adoring the architectural splendour of the caves and carvings.

What Rao definitely did not adore was the trajectory adopted by the Nepali Maoists.

He told me passionately, 'The aim of any Maoist movement is not just to abolish the symbol of feudalism. It is to radically overhaul the socio-economic relations. Your Maoists have given up on all the real issues, livelihood issues, land issues, caste issues. They have become a part of the system. How can a party that works with reactionaries like Girija Koirala's Nepali Congress, social fascists like Madhav Nepal's UML, and cozies up to the Indian state, be revolutionary?'

~

The Communist Party of Nepal (Maoist) and the Communist Party of India (Maoist)—also known as Naxalites, or, in their earlier avatar, the People's War Group (PWG) of Andhra Pradesh and the Maoist Communist Centre (MCC) of Bihar and Jharkhand—had close ideological and operational links. Some reports suggested that Prachanda had played a part in convincing the MCC and the PWG to unite and form the CPI (Maoist) in 2004. After emerging over ground, PLA commanders revealed that they had been trained in Naxal camps in Andhra Pradesh. During the war, they had often made joint appeals against American imperialism and Indian expansionism. When they were on the run from the Nepali security forces, and crossed the border, the Naxals often provided hospitality and medical care to their Nepali comrades.

Reminiscing about the past, the CPI (M) wrote to the Nepali Maoists on 20 May 2009, 'High-level delegations of our two CCs [central committees] had exchanged our respective experiences of struggle against revisionism, discussed the universal significance and contemporary relevance of Maoism, historic GPCR of China, glorious Naxalbari uprising and the experiences of people's war in India. We were enthused when finally your Party made a firm decision to initiate people's war in Nepal, made great strides and achieved highly significant achievements with considerable speed within a span of a few years. Throughout this period—from the preparatory period for launching the people's war through the initiation and development of people's war—our Party in India supported your Party, condemned the intervention by the Indian expansionists and tried to build solidarity for the revolution in Nepal. And as part of this, both our CCs took the initiative in 2001 to set up the CCOMPOSA [Co-ordination Committee of Maoist Parties and Organizations in South Asia] to wage a united struggle against Indian expansionism and imperialist intervention in South Asia. And also as part of our proletarian internationalist duty we rendered assistance in all possible ways to the people's war in Nepal.'

One of the primary motivations of the Indian government in engaging with the Nepali Maoists was to break the nexus between the Naxals and the Maoists. They facilitated a deal between the Nepali parties and the Maoists in Delhi to present, in the words of a senior official, a 'role model' to the Naxalites. The message was simple: if you give up violence, the doors of electoral politics will open up and you can win domestic and international legitimacy.

For moderate Left leaders like Sitaram Yechury, this was a key motivation in taking interest in the Nepali process. It allowed him to score brownie points against his radical Left rivals back home.

Prachanda was politically astute enough to know that if he wanted to win support among the Indian policymakers, including security hawks, he should relay the same message to the Indian Naxals. In the 'breakthrough' interview with Siddharth Varadarajan in *The Hindu* in February 2006, when asked whether his line of multiparty democracy applied to Indian Maoist movements, Prachanda replied, 'We believe it applies to them too. They have to understand this and go down this route. Both on the questions of leadership and on multiparty democracy, or rather multiparty competition, those who call themselves revolutionaries in India need to think about these issues. And there is a need to go in the direction of that practice. We wish to debate with them on this. If revolutionaries are not going to look at the need for ideological development, then they will not go anywhere.'

Delhi succeeded, but only partially. The gulf between the two radical Left forces increased—to the extent that the Indian home ministry repeatedly told the Indian Parliament in 2007 and 2008 that there were no operational links between the Naxalites and the Maoists.

The Naxalites had also learnt a lesson from the Nepali experience, but it was not the one that the RAW and the MEA had hoped for.

~

The Nepali Maoists and the Indian Naxalites had a falling out after the 12-point Understanding was signed. Initially, it was friendly criticism which then descended into bitterness and accusations, with the Maoists accusing the Naxals of not understanding 'objective conditions' and falling into a 'dogmatic trap', and the Naxals brushing the Maoists aside for becoming 'revisionists'.

To cut through the jargon, I asked Varavara Rao how sticking to armed revolt would have helped the party and the Nepali masses.

'Whoever said that there is a shortcut to liberation? We in India have also been in this long struggle. The Maoists have sold out. After all those years of struggle, all those years of success, look at what they have come to. Working with imperialist and expansionist forces; giving up all their arms and army to the United Nations which is merely a tool of the United States of America; returning property to the landlords. We had high hopes from the movement but it is all dashed. And to top it off, they tell us to learn a lesson.'

But if the Naxals wanted to wish continued violence on another society, those who had to live and suffer through violence perpetrated by the Naxals were looking to Nepal with renewed hope. In Warangal district and Bhadrachalam town of Andhra Pradesh, which had witnessed civil strife in bursts since the late 1960s; in Chhattisgarh's Konta tehsil, where the government had encouraged strategic hamlets and vigilante groups to stand up to brutalities perpetrated by Naxalites; in Jharkhand's Ranchi and Hazaribagh districts, where people were sick of the exploitative state and the degeneration of the Maoists into criminals; or Bihar's Gaya district, where Naxalites often killed innocents, I was struck by the level of interest and awareness about developments in Nepal.

Lawyers, journalists, political activists and businessmen asked, 'Kya Maobaadi rajniti main aa gaye hain? [Have the Maoists fully entered politics?] We hope they succeed. Our government and Maoists may also follow suit then.'

In Dantewada district of the Bastar division—the base of the Naxalites and the site of a brutal government-sponsored vigilante campaign, Salwa Judum—I met a Left leader and a critic of both the warring sides, Manish Kunjam, a little away from the main town on the road towards Jagdalpur. Kunjam said, 'The Maoists fought a just war, but they have realized smartly that they must participate in the democratic process. Nepal holds the promise of communism and change. Our Naxals must learn.'

Hundreds of miles away, in his small office in Patna, Ram Jatan Sharma of the Communist Party of India (Marxist-Leninist) Liberation—which stood further left from Kunjam's Communist Party of India in India's sectarian and seemingly incomprehensible maze of Left politics—echoed the sentiment. Sharma had once been a part of the armed underground movement. He traced his origin to the Naxalbari movement of the 1960s, and still called himself a Naxalite, but participated in the democratic processes.

'Our Maoists do not understand that mass mobilization comes before you can give a call for "revolution". Your Maoists understood that. Our Maoists do not understand that the primary task is to utilize the existing institutions of the bourgeoisie system and break the illusions of the people. Nepali Maoists are on that track now. Most importantly, our Maoists contribute little by anarcho-militarism and mindless violence, apart from giving the state a pretext for repression. Your Maoists understood the limits of that approach.'

The Naxalites scoffed at these criticisms and told me during that trip in 2007, 'Don't listen to these revisionists who have sold out to feudalism and the comprador bourgeoisie. The Nepali revolution is over.'

In the Power Corridors

The Right and the Left may have their own grand preferences and visions for Nepal but, it is the Centre, in Delhi, which determines the trajectory of the bilateral relationship.

India had opened up to the Maoists, not because there was any revolutionary transformation in South Block, but because they were left with little choice but to work with the polity's biggest force to ensure a degree of systemic stability which was broadly in line with India's interests.

India saw that the Maoists represented the aspirations of a large section of the population. They needed to be involved in the power structure if there was to be peace, and peace was in India's interest, for instability was spilling over the border. The Maoists, while at war, had developed close links with Naxalites and India hoped that getting the former involved in the din of mainstream politics might detach it from the latter. Obstinacy on the part of the monarchy had created the domestic context in which the Maoists could become a part of a broader democratic alliance.

The Maoists' ideological texts still viewed Nepal as sharing a semi-colonial relationship with India. But this also gave Delhi leverage in Nepal, with the other political parties, with the 'national bourgeouisie', and with the military. Confrontation with India was not an option. And so engagement was indispensable if the Maoists were to carve out space in the mainstream political structure.

So both sides came to each other with very cautious instincts and a lot of baggage. India would engage with the Maoists and help them gain legitimacy with the international community. But it would do so with the intention of detaching the rebels from their revolutionary antecedents, their coercive apparatus and their extremist ideology; it would force them to work within the confines of democracy with its diffuse power arrangements and compromises; it would also get them to shed their resistance to India's influence.

The Maoists would reach out India, remain broadly sensitive to its security interests vis-à-vis any third country (read Pakistan or China). But they hoped to use Delhi's openness to expand their strength within the Nepali political sphere, establish a degree of hegemony by overwhelming domestic rivals, and push the agenda for which they had fought a decade-long war.

These fundamentally different interests of both the sides, and the divergent objectives they had continued to pursue even as their engagement with each other deepened, created a tense dynamic. And once the Maoists and the political parties signed a ceasefire accord in May 2006, and the rebel leadership emerged over ground, this was to play out in many ways.

1

The Maoists wanted to invite the United Nations (UN) to monitor the peace process in general, and the arms and armies of both sides in particular. While the more dogmatic elements in the party saw the UN as a 'tool of US imperialism', the Maoist leadership felt that the international organization could serve as a guarantor of the political process.

The Maoists were also worried about their own physical safety. They had given up their wartime structures, but there was a bloody history and many 'enemies' were still out there. The UN could be a credible witness in case of any ceasefire violation or the breakdown of the process. Ian Martin, the widely respected diplomat, human rights activist and humanitarian worker, had led the UN's Office of the High Commissioner for Human Rights (UN-OHCHR) in Nepal during the endgame of the royal autocracy. His firm stand in favour of democratic freedoms had given him credibility with the mainstream parties as well as with the Maoists.

But India had been reluctant to allow the UN a role in its neighbourhood. The presence of a UN observer group in Kashmir was an irritant in Delhi's relations with New York, since India was opposed to any 'third-party' intervention or the 'internationalization' of the Kashmir issue. South Block felt that the UN's entry into Nepal would only embolden the organization's bureaucracy, backed by major powers, to expand its role in the region. Foreign Secretary Shyam Saran initially also had reservations that a UN-type of body would give a sense of equivalence to both the Maoists and the parties. India did not want any such equivalence as Saran believed that the pressure ought to be exerted solely on the Maoists to move away from their revolutionary past.

What helped the Maoists, though, was the fact that the new prime minister, G. P. Koirala, backed the UN's role in Nepal. His aides told me later that this stemmed from his genuine commitment to the peace process, but also because he felt that the international community would check any excesses and efforts by the Maoists to shift goalposts. In his visit to Delhi in June 2006, soon after the movement ended, Koirala—whose stock with the Indian establishment was high, and who commanded great political capital for having led the People's Movement—lobbied for India to green-signal the UN's role.

There was now a rethink in Delhi. Though unhappy about the idea, diplomats were coming around to the view that the UN's involvement was perhaps necessary to kickstart the peace process and manage the Maoists' military apparatus. But wary of what they saw as the possibility of 'mission creep', coupled with a general distrust of the UN, India set strict conditions on the UN's involvement in Nepal. It was to have a very 'light footprint', and there would be no 'boots on the ground', ruling out a traditional peacekeeping operation. The UN would have 'no political role', in an effort to stall the chances of the UN bosses using their offices to mediate discussions between Nepali forces. The insistence on non-military presence, combined with a limited mandate, meant that the UN had no enforcement authority. So if there was a ceasefire violation, it could report it but not act on it.

In an instance of the kind of balancing act each side had to perform, India withdrew its objections to a UN presence, shedding its geopolitical inhibitions, given the larger objective of accommodating the Maoists and providing them with a sense of security. But it circumscribed the UN's role to such an extent that the organization had little power to influence developments and outcomes.

Delhi's calibrated engagement was on display as negotiations over arms management, the interim Constitution, and the Maoists' participation in the interim government sharpened. India's approach was in contrast to that of the Americans who, under the loud, brash and arrogant James Moriarty as ambassador, used a black-and-white prism to judge the Maoists. The US, under the influence of the Nepali Right wing, wanted the Maoists to surrender all their weapons and complete the rehabilitation of all their former combatants before they could be allowed to participate in mainstream politics. The Maoists, for their part, preferred an arrangement where they could come to power while retaining their coercive apparatus in full strength or after getting it integrated into security forces in a manner which would give the former rebels greater control over the state.

India was with Nepali democrats in pushing hard for disarmament, but when they realized that the Maoists—at that early stage of the peace process when the political path was not certain—would not give in, they were willing to live with a compromise formula. Maoist combatants would be registered and verified by the UN; they would live in cantonments; their weapons would be stored under a single-lock system, the key to which would remain with the Maoists, monitored via a device by the UN; and the NA, too, would place the same number of weapons as the Maoists in the barracks. All NA and PLA personnel were to remain in barracks or cantonments, subject to a maximum percentage of leave and permitted NA activities. And once that happened, Maoists would receive space in the interim legislature and participate in the government. This was a long process and was subject to endless negotiations. But India's twin objectives—of accommodating the Maoists yet 'defanging' them to the maximum possible extent—went together.

Compromises made by the Maoists helped them gain access to

legitimate political structures and share power with the mainstream parties. India enabled this process, pushing the Maoists away from their wartime structures and prodding the parties to open up to the former rebels and give them important ministries.

But political processes cannot be pre-designed. For, at some point, negotiations move out of closed doors and involve the janata, the people, for whom politics is conducted and the state is run. There is no one people, but when they speak and are allowed to speak—either through mass movements or elections—citizens articulate their preferences in ways which no punditry can predict, no political party can pre-determine, no intelligence operation can manipulate, and no external power can dictate.

On 10 April 2008, the Nepali people voted in the Maoists as the single-largest political force in the new CA. The former rebels, two years after entering open politics, had won the popular mandate to govern the country and lead the Constitution-writing process. They could not do it unilaterally, and needed allies; but neither could the other parties move an inch without the Maoists, who now had legitimate veto power. The Maoists needed no one's certificate of good conduct anymore. Or so they thought.

2

'Why is he making life difficult? The domestic consensus in Nepal has broken. The old sceptical voices in Delhi are back, and we don't know what to say when they give us that smug "I told you so" look about Maoist misdemeanours. And Prachanda keeps giving them more and more ammunition,' said an exasperated official of the Indian embassy as we sat down for a drink at the bar in Hotel Himalaya in Kathmandu.

We were in early 2009. After months of power-sharing negotiations, the Maoist chairman had finally taken over as prime minister the previous year in August. India was not happy with the election results. They had got it terribly wrong, predicting that the Maoists would fare a distant third. It also upset their careful plans of keeping the Maoists as a junior partner in the power structure. But

Delhi put up a brave front. At a conference in Patna two weeks after the results, Shyam Saran was emphatic that India had no favourites and only wished for democracy in Nepal. This was clearly not true, for the national security advisor, M. K. Narayanan, had even stated that Delhi would prefer the NC to succeed. But India now sought to make amends—when G. P. Koirala showed reluctance to leave office, the newly appointed ambassador, Rakesh Sood, nudged him to hand over power.

Prachanda's first act after taking office was to declare that he would be travelling to Beijing to attend the concluding ceremony of the Olympics. It broke a long-standing political tradition: a newly elected Nepali prime minister made his first official trip to Delhi. Coming as it did from a Left party, and that too an ultra-Left outfit that had made equidistance between India and China Nepali foreign policy's stated objective, the security establishment in India was quick to note the development.

But it went beyond the bureaucrats. Sharad Yadav, the Indian opposition leader and a former socialist who was sympathetic to the Maoists, had attended Prachanda's swearing-in ceremony. He heard about the planned China visit as soon as he arrived in Delhi from Kathmandu and called up Anand Swarup Verma, a radical Left journalist-cum-activist who was close to the Maoist supremo. Yadav told Verma that Prachanda's plans would create a 'misunderstanding', and ruin their efforts to improve ties between the two countries. Verma narrated the conversation to me a few months later.

The Maoist leadership said that they did not understand what the fuss was about. Here was a sovereign prime minister visiting a neighbouring country which had successfully hosted the world's biggest event. The new prime minister stuck to his stand and went ahead with his visit. He projected it as a 'break in continuity', or kram bhang, in Nepali history. But the Maoists also did not want to antagonize Delhi and, on his return to Kathmandu, Prachanda said that his first 'political visit' would be to Delhi.

Diplomacy is made up of grand gestures, of summit meetings, of statesmanship and wars, but it is the often seemingly mundane incidents that feed into wider policymaking. Officially, the government of India brushed the incident under the carpet, but it remained suspicious about the Maoists' intent regarding the geopolitical balance south of the Himalayas.

India welcomed Prachanda in Delhi the next month. I was a part of the prime minister's delegation, covering the visit for the Nepali magazine *Himal*. There was little doubt that Delhi had laid out the red carpet for the prime minister.

He was put up at Hotel Taj Man Singh; he received access to the most powerful people in the land, including Sonia Gandhi; the joint statement addressed many of Nepal's concerns, including a commitment to review the 1950 treaty; in private briefings, Indian foreign ministry officials told journalists that Prachanda was a 'statesman' worthy of respect and recognition. But privately, they had also conveyed to the Maoist leader that he should complete the peace process and not take steps regarding the NA without a broad consensus. Disregarding this vital message, couched in diplomatic terms, was to later haunt Prachanda.

Sharad Yadav, Prachanda's friend, hosted a mega-lunch for him at his residence on Tughlak Road, with leaders from across India's political spectrum in attendance, warmly congratulating the Maoists. It was here that the Maoist leader, speaking in Hindi, admitted for the first time that he had spent eight years during the insurgency in India.

But the romance was to be short lived. Soon after his return, Prachanda became entangled in intra-party ideological battles. The dogmatic faction, led by Mohan Vaidya 'Kiran', had never reconciled itself to the peace process on terms agreed to by India, other parties and the Maoist leadership in 2005-06. For him, achieving a Democratic Republic was just a tactic to reach the larger goal of a People's Republic.

At a party plenum on the outskirts of Kathmandu, Kiran made a push. Now that the monarchy was abolished, it was time to move on to the next stage and declare India and its perceived 'brokers' in Nepal, particularly the NC, as the principal enemies. Despite strong opposition from Bhattarai, Prachanda adopted Kiran's line. With this ideological shifting of goalposts, actions which may have been innocuous and emanating from specific situations began to be read as the Maoists' intent to destabilize existing structures and establish a 'communist dictatorship'.

So when the Prachanda-led government sought to end the age-old tradition of appointing Indian priests at Pashupatinath temple and replace them with Nepali priests, religious conservatives in Kathmandu saw it as an attack on Hinduism. Many in Delhi perceived it as an affront to the 'special relationship', with the BJP upping the ante and calling it an instance of the failure of UPA's foreign policy. BJP leader L. K. Advani called up Prachanda to register his protest. When a management-labour dispute in a media house over the issue of forming a party-affiliated trade union resulted in Maoist activists physically assaulting the publisher, it was construed as an assault on the freedom of the press and how the former rebels were still attached to violence. When Finance Minister Baburam Bhattarai pushed for a strict tax mobilization drive to increase state revenues, sceptics perceived it as an attack on the private sector.

So here were powerful sections—businessmen, owners of media houses, Hindu conservatives and mainstream political rivals—coalescing around a single-point agenda, to oust the Maoist-led government. Like the Maoists had reached out to Delhi when the domestic conflict had sharpened, these interest groups, too, reached out to lobby with the Indian establishment. Surya Bahadur Thapa, a former PM who was perceived as being close to powers in Delhi, visited the Indian capital to sell the idea of a Broad Democratic Alliance of non-Maoist forces which would prevent the communists from engineering a 'state capture'. The NC president G. P. Koirala visited Delhi, too, and while he did not get the reception and access he was expecting, the supreme leader of the 2006 movement did not spare the opportunity to criticize the Maoists. Nepal Army generals, too, had reached out to their counterparts in the Indian Army and briefed them about what they saw as the Maoists' efforts to 'capture' the army, but what the Maoist political leadership argued were genuine moves to institute 'civilian control'.

The domestic tensions were coupled with an external element. Since March 2008, when 'Free Tibet' protests had erupted in Kathmandu, China had stepped up its engagement with the Nepali government. They had a one-point agenda: crack down on Tibetan unrest. They were unhappy with what they saw as the then NC-led government's lenient treatment of the protests. Beijing had now taken a conscious decision to step up its interactions with Nepal's political class across the spectrum, as well as to directly reach out to security forces and the bureaucracy. Several high-level delegations now visited Kathmandu. The Maoists were happy with this, for Prachanda saw it as an opportunity—like many rulers before him did—to counter India. Unconfirmed reports started trickling in of how China had even offered to train a Maoist PLA commander in one of their academies. This was never verified, but it fed into the perception that China was siding with the Maoists on the debate over integration—where India had clear views and concerns. At a time when the Maoists had spoken of revising the 1950 treaty with India, China proposed a new treaty of friendship with Nepal which would ease visa restrictions.

This was the backdrop to my conversation with my source at the Indian embassy that evening in early 2009. He continued, 'Prachanda had a chance to be a reconciler. He could have been Mandela, taken everyone along. But he has tried to be a ruthless maximizer, opening multiple fronts and slowly burning bridges with us. Take it from me; like 1990, the 2006 change will be squandered away.'

The Maoists saw the entire situation differently. Leaders told me that if India wanted them to be as pliant as the past regimes, it was mistaken. A top leader said, 'We have a mass base. We are now legitimately elected. And we are still committed to our agenda of change. It is none of India's business how we govern the country.' On China, the Maoists repeatedly reiterated that there was a 'unique' relationship with India which was more wide-ranging than that with any other country. But this was not enough to assure the sceptics in Delhi.

Three months later, the Katawal episode caused the most serious schism between the key stakeholders of the Nepali peace process and disturbed the major relationships that formed its core—between the Maoists and the parliamentary parties; between the Maoists and the NA; and between the Maoists and India.

3

By the middle of 2009, Prachanda was out of power. An anti-Maoist coalition—on the lines of the Broad Democratic Alliance suggested by the former prime minister, Surya Bahadur Thapa, on his visit to Delhi—was in place.

The Maoists were now on the streets with a range of slogans. They demanded 'civilian supremacy', raising the legitimate question of who controlled Nepal's armed forces and whether a prime minister had the right to dismiss the army chief. They opposed the President's 'unconstitutional move' to write directly to General Katawal and demanded a parliamentary discussion on the issue—which was rejected. They protested 'foreign interference', making public the issue of India's role in the Katawal episode.

The Indian Maoists now felt vindicated. Echoing the voice of the party's dogmatists, they wrote to the Nepali Maoists patronizingly: 'Now that the government headed by comrade Prachanda has collapsed after the withdrawal of support by the UML and others at the behest of the Indian ruling classes, American imperialists and the local reactionaries, the Party leadership should be better placed to understand how the reactionaries can manage the show from the sidelines or outside and obstruct even moves such as sacking of the army chief by a prime minister. This is a clear warning to the Maoists in Nepal that they cannot do whatever they like through their elected government against the wishes of the imperialists and Indian expansionists.'

The Indian Maoists prescribed a clear roadmap stating what the Nepali far-Left should now do, 'At least now they should realize the futility of going into the electoral game and, instead, should concentrate on building class struggle and advancing the people's war in the countryside. They should pull out the PLA from the UN-supervised barracks which are virtually like prisons for the fighters, reconstruct the organs of people's revolutionary power at various levels, retake and consolidate the base areas, and expand the guerrilla war, and class and mass struggles throughout the country. There is no short cut to achieve real power to the people. If the Party leadership hesitates to continue the people's war at this critical juncture of history and persists in the present Right opportunist line then history will hold the present leadership responsible for the abortion of revolution in Nepal.'

If such extremist advice was gaining traction with the Maoists on the one hand, on the other, the nuanced approach adopted by the government of India—of using engagement as a policy to wean the Maoists off their radical politics—was now dead. Instead, Delhi had decided that only isolating the Maoists would work.

After speaking to key Indian officials in both the RAW and the MEA, I broke a story in the middle of June 2009 for the *Nepali Times*, a weekly published from Kathmandu. India wanted the Maoists to make a 'course correction', and laid out specific parameters on which it would judge the Maoists. At the heart of it was the condition that the Maoists give up the PLA and its armed apparatus, which had created an 'uneven' playing field in India's assessment.

India said that the Maoists needed to demonstrate a 'clear and credible commitment to multiparty democracy', which was missing during their nine-month tenure. 'The Maoists have to give up dreams of state capture. They have to change course to a moderate left-of-centre party from their dogmatic line,' said an intelligence official who had earlier been sympathetic to the Maoists' position. India wanted Prachanda to stop offering 'excuses' of how he was under pressure from hardliners. 'If it is a tactic, we are not falling for it. If it is real, it is time for the leader to assert himself and either bring the hardliners in or marginalize them.' The peace process must end but a 'large-scale integration' of former Maoist combatants into the NA was not acceptable; Maoists must also return 'seized properties'. An MEA official said that along with the domestic element, the Maoists must stop 'playing games to jeopardize the geopolitical balance' of the region, and stop their 'anti-India slogans'.

Until the Maoists convinced India of their commitment to democracy, marginalized those who India saw as the more troublesome elements in their party, reoriented their rhetoric and stopped flirting with China, and gave up their military wing, India would continue to support the Broad Democratic Alliance. An official in Delhi explained the logic to me, 'The only way the

Maoists would reform is if they know they cannot get back to power without reforming. Otherwise, they will have no incentive to become a democratic force. The proof of reform is in giving up PLA and sidelining Kiran.'

There were tremendous political implications of such a policy line.

The Maoists, despite being the biggest party in the house, sat in the opposition. Twenty-two of the twenty-four parties in the house had come together to form a government with the explicit objective of excluding them. While the Maoists had only themselves to blame for their utter political failure in antagonizing so many forces at the same time, they felt victimized and betrayed. Their exclusion from the power structure gave ammunition to the hardliners within the party, who now turned around to claim that the entire project of participating in open politics had been flawed. It was time to return to their radical roots. This was a clever postulation for these hardliners, led by Kiran, had been responsible for the Maoists' isolation in the first place because they had pushed policies and actions that the balance of power did not permit.

If India insisted on the PLA's settlement as a precondition to any change in government, the Maoists insisted that a change in government would have to precede any deal which would be struck vis-à-vis the PLA.

The Maoists' political effort was now geared towards breaking up the anti-Maoist ruling alliance and discrediting it; obstructing Parliament and governance; and gaining political capital by pitching the battle as one between principles, between maintaining the status quo and revolution, between those who wanted to reverse the gains of 2006 and those who wished to institutionalize it, between those who were Indian 'puppets'—as they called the Madhav Nepal dispensation—and those who sought greater national autonomy and sovereignty, between those who resorted to unconstitutional means and those who stuck to the letter of the interim Constitution, and between those who sought military supremacy and those who fought for civilian rule. They intensified street protests.

This may have been a fight for principle and power from the

perspective of the former rebels. And to be fair to them, they could not but have put up an opposition to the manner in which they had been pushed out of power. But the politics of obstruction would not win them popular sympathy and support.

It also did not help that Prachanda's short stint in power had failed to impress those swing voters who had cast their ballot for the party. The Maoists had appeared to emulate the worst of Nepal's political culture. Party leaders had fought endlessly amongst themselves for portfolios. Once they had secured lucrative ministries, the focus was on abusing the perks of office and displaying power rather than improving the government's functioning and services for the people. Ordinary Nepali people were coming around to the view that it did not quite matter who was in power. There would be little improvement on issues that mattered—the long hours of power cuts, the lack of employment prospects, inflation, dysfunctional government schools and an exorbitant private educational system, bad roads, the difficulties in obtaining official licenses and permits in a transparent manner, the corruption. If the Maoists would not focus on such issues either, why invest energy in bringing the party back to power—even if it was their rightful claim? The confrontational posture of the Maoists, which delayed the budget, paralysed governance and disrupted livelihoods, was alienating citizens.

But the former rebels, deeply immersed in the big ideological and power battles of the day, were not listening to the voices on the ground. Their focus was on high politics.

~

Despite the public tension with India, Prachanda did not spare any effort in trying to woo Delhi back. In August 2009, the Maoist chairman went to London to meet RAW officials. He sought to assure them that the Maoists were committed to democracy; that the fiasco with the army chief was a result of internal pressure, and they cherished the special relationship with India. The senior officials reiterated India's official line to Prachanda: until words were translated into action, they could not do anything. Prachanda told them that he would soon act on his commitments, but he could not cooperate with the current government. Both sides have confirmed the meeting to me. Two months later, in November, Prachanda went to Singapore and met Indian officials once again in an effort to bridge the gap.

But Delhi did not budge.

In December 2009, at a reception hosted by the Nepal embassy in Delhi for the new chief of the NA, Chhatraman Gurung, then on his first visit, a group of us accosted the chief of the Indian Army Deepak Kapoor, and asked him about his views on the NA.

'We want a democratic, professional and apolitical army.' This was the stated Indian position; the subtext of which was that the integration of the Maoist combatants could dilute the army's professional standards and introduce partisan loyalties. When asked specifically about integration, General Kapoor went a step ahead. He said that the Maoists were 'untrustworthy', that the NA was the only 'stable institution' of Nepal and that the Maoists wished to 'politicize' the NA and compromise its 'institutional integrity'. He also added that the Maoists were free to join the NA as ordinary citizens once they met the requirements of the army. When it was pointed out that the Maoists saw the NA as 'feudal' and integration as the way to democratize the army, the Indian chief shot back, pointing to General Gurung who was standing some distance away, 'Is your present army chief a feudal? Don't fall for Maoist rhetoric.'

Since the conversation happened at a cocktail reception, and its terms were not clear, I played safe and couched it as background from a top defence official for my weekly column back home. But *Kantipur* and *The Kathmandu Post*, whose reporter was present, ran it as a front-page story and attributed it directly to General Kapoor. The story created a sensation and confirmed suspicions that India was not in favour of integration at all. It appeared that Delhi wanted to keep the Maoists in the doghouse and force it to surrender on what would only be humiliating terms for the former rebels.

A week later, at a mass meeting in Kathmandu's New Baneshwor crossing, next to the building which houses the CA, Prachanda responded. If the President and the NC-UML alliance had been the primary targets till now, the Maoists now shed all inhibitions in attacking India. The Maoists had concluded that the policy of engagement had not quite worked, and it was time to up the ante. This would polarize Nepali polity and society on the question of sovereignty, and send the message back to Delhi that the Maoists represented nationalist forces which could not be ignored. Prachanda also saw it as an effective measure to keep the radical faction within his party happy.

The Maoist chairman announced that the party would now launch a 'national independence awareness campaign'. He pointed to the 'unequal' Treaty of Peace and Friendship of 1950, the soaring trade deficit, and Indian 'border encroachment' into Nepali territory as instances of the unequal ties between the two countries. 'The Maoists are not Surya Bahadur Thapa or Nepali Congress or UML. In the new context, in the twenty-first century, in republican Nepal, India-Nepal ties must be redefined in a new manner.' He declared that Nepali political forces were mere puppets, and his talks with domestic forces had failed since they were being guided from outside. Now, Prachanda said, he would only talk to the 'master', Delhi.

I spoke to a diplomat soon after the speech to get India's reaction. He was dismissive. 'They are getting desperate and digging themselves in a hole. This is immature politics. Prachanda's new strategy will not work.'

The confrontation between India and the Maoists was now only getting worse. Maoist leaders followed up on Prachanda's speech by visiting disputed border areas and giving speeches accusing Delhi of 'encroaching on Nepali territory', in tune with its 'expansionist designs'. This only strengthened the consensus in Delhi that the Maoists could not be trusted at all. The governing anti-Maoist alliance benefited from this gulf, as it could count on India's continued support, particularly during the six-day-long strike called by the Maoists that spring.

Meanwhile, in March 2010, the one man who had the stature to re-engineer the broken domestic consensus, as well as to re-create the right external climate for the peace process, died. Girija Prasad

Koirala—the man whose mistakes in the 1990s had discredited democracy but who salvaged his credibility by standing up to the monarch during the years of royal authoritarianism; the veteran who had the wisdom to shed his aversion to communists and partner with the Maoists for the sake of peace and democracy; and the last of the founding leaders of Nepal's democracy movement— had passed away. He was disappointed with the Maoists for not having delivered on their commitments on the peace process while in power, but family insiders told me that he was not happy with India either because of its belligerence. His death left a huge void in Nepali politics.

In May 2010, the Maoists brought hundreds of thousands on to the streets across the country, demanding the government's resignation, and claiming that this was a struggle to protect national sovereignty. This was the most widespread popular mobilization on the streets of Kathmandu after the Janandolan of 2006. Despite the increasing disillusionment with the Maoists, the show of strength indicated that they remained Nepal's biggest, best organized and most powerful political force. The party had brought cadres from several surrounding districts to the capital and put them up in universities, colleges, hotels, in make-shift camps and in the homes

of sympathizers. The andolan began with a massive rally in Kathmandu's Khula Manch on 1 May. On each subsequent day, meetings were held across the country; demonstrations were organized, transport was crippled, schools and offices were shut, and economic activity crashed.

The Maoists' argument was along the following lines—this government was illegitimate; the protests showed that the poorest and the most marginalized citizens of Nepal widely supported the party; it was time for Madhav Nepal to make way for a Maoist-led government, respecting the mandate of the 2008 elections. Like the decision to adopt a more radical ideological orientation at the end of 2008 and to sack General Katawal in 2009, it was the Maoist dogmatists, led by Mohan Vaidya 'Kiran', who had pushed for an indefinite strike.

But Prime Minister Nepal—firmly backed by India—stayed put. The ruling parties strongly rebutted the Maoists, and argued that in a constitutional democracy, the only way to oust a government was through an established process in Parliament or through elections. If the government caved in, it would pave the way for anarchy and establish a bad precedent. They projected the Maoists' campaign as a way to incite an urban insurrection to capture state power, which was to be resisted at all costs.

But it was not the political opposition, as much as the public defiance of the strike, that would force the Maoists to reconsider their stance. Six days into the agitation, the former rebels realized that they were on the verge of alienating Kathmandu's population almost irreversibly. Not only were the capital's middle classes thoroughly disgusted with the Maoists' tactics, even the working class and labourers, who depended on daily wages, were impatient and angry at losing the opportunity to generate income. Elite professionals, backed by business chambers and media houses, organized a counter demonstration and a 'peace rally' against the Maoists, which was widely attended. On the evening of 7 May, Prachanda announced the withdrawal of the strike.

This failure would moderate Maoists' instincts considerably and reveal to them the limits of their power and the impossibility of an urban revolt. It would also bring to light the increasing power of the 'counter-revolutionary forces', or anti-Maoist segments of the polity, to resist the pressure of the former insurgents. At the same time, those seven days in May showed India, the NC and the UML that the Maoists were down but not out, and could not be completely marginalized. They did retain the organizational ability, and the popularity, to mobilize crowds—particularly from outside Kathmandu.

~

28 May 2010 would mark the formal end of the term of the CA as stipulated in the interim Constitution. The only way to extend its two-year term would be for two-thirds of the house to support an amendment in the interim Constitution.

Royalists believed that if the CA failed, its declaration of the republic would stand invalid and the monarchy stood a chance of a comeback. Nepali conservatives, schooled in the ideas of controlled democracy, perceived popular aspirations as a threat to the existing order and were uncomfortable with the idea of an elected CA writing the Constitution in the first place. This sentiment had only become more entrenched with the election results. The victories achieved by the newer forces which had fought for state restructuring worried the older parliamentary parties who were still comfortable with the unitary state structure. They calculated that if a Federal Democratic Republic Constitution was drafted, the Maoists would have an enormous political advantage as it would be seen as the success of their agenda. Top leaders of the older parties, from NC's acting president Sushil Koirala to UML's senior leader K. P. Sharma Oli, had lost their seats and had little commitment to the CA.

For Delhi, the CA was a source of strength for the Maoists. It provided them legitimacy, it allowed them to claim that they were the biggest elected force in the house, and the CA's existence meant that the Maoists could return to power any time the parliamentary arithmetic changed slightly.

There was a widespread perception in Kathmandu that India was pushing for an end to the CA. Delhi's stated reason, conveyed to its allies in private, was that the parties had failed to draft a Constitution within the stipulated period, the CA's term was ending, and it was time to return to the people for a fresh mandate. But the unstated calculation was that the end of the CA's term of operation would deprive the Maoists of any opportunity to return to power, end their legitimate political strength, sharpen the internal divisions between moderates like Baburam Bhattarai who were committed to ensuring peace and writing the Constitution—the peace-and-Constitution line—and dogmatists like Kiran who were pushing for another revolt in order to achieve a communist republic—known as the People's Revolt line—and force Prachanda to finally make a choice between pragmatism and extremism. The onus, according to this school of thought, should be placed entirely on the Maoists. If they wished to save the CA, they ought to 'reform' first, learn to be a 'constructive opposition', make a 'clear-cut choice' in favour of democracy, and 'complete the peace process'.

As the deadline approached, India's message to its friends in the UML-NC combine, which was ruling at the time, was simple—do not blink. The Maoists too played hardball and said that unless Madhav Nepal resigned, they would not support an extension to the CA.

Subel Bhandari, a fellow journalist and friend, and I walked around inside the CA complex as negotiations carried on late in the evening. A makeshift canteen was set up to prepare dinner for the MPs. Some of them walked down to a nearby restaurant, the Beijing Duck, for a drink, even as their leaders were holed up inside the CA's private chambers.

Leaders explained the state of play to us. NC and UML negotiators had told the Maoists, as Delhi suggested, that the ball was entirely in their court. If they wanted an extension, they had better live with the current government. The status quo did not suit the Maoists at all. They had spent the past year seeking to oust Madhav Nepal, and realized that their bargaining power was at its peak that night. They may have needed the CA, but the other parties did not have much of a choice, either. While Prime Minister Nepal had argued that he would remain in office even after the CA reached the end of its term, the Maoists had said that neither the government nor the

President would have any legitimacy in the absence of the house which had elected them in the first place. What was certain was that a dangerous political-constitutional vacuum would ensue. MPs across party lines were keen to save their jobs and generated pressure on the leadership to compromise.

That is when the internal tensions within the UML surfaced. Chairman Jhalanath Khanal had not been comfortable with Prime Minister Nepal's government right from the start of his tenure, for the party head thought that he was more deserving of the prime ministership. Khanal's aides had consistently criticized Nepal in public, and had argued for engagement with the Maoists. But even MPs who were loyal to the Madhav Nepal and K. P. Oli factions within the party were now getting jittery. As Oli walked into the house at night, his aides, Pradeep Gyawali, for instance, immediately raised questions about why the CA was being sacrificed to save a government—history would never forgive the UML if the CA failed. Women MPs had begun raising slogans in the CA complex to extend the tenure. NC, too, was a divided house, with parliamentary party leader Ram Chandra Poudel and popular young MPs like Gagan Thapa, who had been an advocate of political change, emphasizing the need to save the CA.

This worked perfectly for the Maoists, who were depending on the other side to blink first. An agreement was reached late at night. Madhav Nepal would make way for a new government. Sources said an informal, verbal agreement had been reached that he would do so in five days, but this was not specified in the text. Parties also committed to complete the peace process. Each side, barring Madhav Nepal, could now claim that this was a win-win deal. The Maoists had got the prime minister to commit to resign. The ruling alliance had got the Maoists to agree to complete the peace process. The sequencing was not mentioned, which left both sides to interpret it as they wished. Most crucially, this had preserved Nepal's Constituent Assembly.

Nepal's political leaders had defeated India's design to kill the country's only elected institution—the outcome of a six-decade-long democratic struggle—which could determine the fate of its citizens.

~

India may have lost the war to kill the CA, but its battle to keep the Maoists out of power structure, and isolate any political or non-political force which supported them, continued with Madhav Nepal's resignation in June 2010.

Prachanda filed his nomination for the prime ministership in the Legislature-Parliament; his rival was the parliamentary party leader of the NC, Ram Chandra Poudel. While a section of the UML, led by K. P. Oli and Madhav Nepal, were in favour of supporting the NC in return for its support of the past year, Chairman Jhalanath Khanal was a strong advocate of engaging with the Maoists. Through the parliamentary party, he ensured a decision whereby the UML would stay neutral during the vote and support only a national unity government. With the UML out of the picture, Poudel would not have reached the magic figure of 301 in the house of 601 to become prime minister even if the Madhesi parties had supported him. Victory for the NC was a distant proposition. But Prachanda would have gone through if the Madhesi parties had supported him.

India invested enormous political and financial capital in preventing the Madhesi parties from supporting the Maoists in the contest. RAW was understood to have offered much money to the Madhesi parties to lure them away from the incentives Prachanda was offering. Two Madhesi leaders who received the cash confirmed the exchange. The stick came along with the carrot and, when cash didn't work, they threatened MPs who were planning to cross the floor. One Madhesi leader of the Maoist party, Ram Kumar Sharma, alleged that a RAW official had warned him that if he continued lobbying for Prachanda, his daughter's admission to a school patronized by the Indian embassy would be in jeopardy.

In August 2009, Delhi also sent Shyam Saran as a special envoy to put pressure on the Madhesi leaders, who knew and respected him, to stay in line, and also to speak to the Maoists. A few months later, Saran gave some of us an account of his trip to Kathmandu and his dialogue with the Maoists at a closed-door meeting at the Centre for Policy Research in Delhi, which Saran had joined after retirement.

Accompanied by Ambassador Sood, Saran went to Prachanda's residence the morning after his arrival. The meeting began on a formal and stiff tone, which surprised Saran given their past familiarity. But that was not the only change. Earlier, Saran had only met Prachanda and Bhattarai from the Maoist party. But this time, all the office bearers of the party, including leaders of the dogmatic faction, were present.

Prachanda complained in the meeting that they felt India was targeting the Maoists. The thrust of Saran's message was that Delhi had no hidden agenda. But the Maoists 'needed to make a choice'. Saran cautioned the Maoists. 'Do you wish to be a revolutionary force or a civilian democratic political party? You cannot be both.' To drive the point home, especially in front of his more radical colleagues, Saran reminded Prachanda of the commitments he had made in 2005 when the 12-point Understanding was being drawn up. Prachanda reiterated the party's commitment to 'multiparty competition'—avoiding the term democracy which only raised suspicions among Indians; he also emphasized that there was a need to redefine ties with India in the new context.

While the meeting was tense, the formal tone gave way soon when Prachanda switched to Hindi—the language in which the Maoists and Saran had earlier communicated. That relaxed the mood, and Saran returned with the feeling that all was not lost.

That trip, however, made Saran more sceptical of the Maoists than he had ever been in the past. He had stuck his neck out to push for engagement between the Maoists and the parties. He had genuinely felt that the Maoists represented the aspirations of a large section of Nepali people. Saran often remarked how two changes had occurred in Nepali society—a generational transformation, and the assertion of the marginalized. The former rebels were more in tune with those changes than any other party. But this time, as he drove in front of Kathmandu's foreign office housed in the old Narayanhiti Palace and saw long queues of citizens waiting for their passports to leave the country, Saran could not help feeling that even the Maoists had lost the plot.

Prachanda, after seven rounds of futile contests in Parliament, realized that India would not let him become prime minister. The turning point was Saran's fairly blunt advice to the Madhesi parties that it may not be in their best interest to side with the Maoists as long as their political line did not change. Prachanda withdrew his nomination.

The Maoists then held an intra-party conclave at the end of 2010, where the latent ultra-nationalism was to emerge visibly—not least because of the hardline position taken by India. While admitting that ties with India needed to be redefined, Bhattarai, the original proponent of the peace-and-Constitution line and the original advocate of engagement with India, termed the 'remnants of feudalism' as the principal enemy of the Nepali revolution. His line was, however, challenged by both Kiran and Prachanda, who categorized the battle with India as the principal contradiction for the movement.

The almost public knowledge of Delhi's actions of the past year, coupled with the sense that India was stoking Bhattarai's ambitions to counter Prachanda, strengthened the Prachanda-Kiran camp in the party. The belligerent line that the Maoists took was underscored by actions its radical leaders encouraged in sensitive districts. In Solukhumbu, an influential leader, Gopal Kiranti, led protests against Ambassador Sood when he arrived on a visit and Maoist cadres threw shoes and stones at him.

India had succeeded in keeping the Maoists from power, but it could not create a sustainable political alternative. The stalemate continued and Madhav Nepal stayed on as caretaker prime minister through 2010.

India had the capacity to destroy and obstruct, but its ability to nourish—as it had done in 2005—had clearly diminished.

~

Like many other Nepalis, I was angered by India's policy, actions and behaviour in that period. Having covered the political process day in and out, I had seen the depths to which the Indian establishment had plunged to isolate the Maoists, with little regard for the notions of sovereignty, democratic norms and processes, or political ethics.

India's actions appeared to confirm long-held apprehensions in Nepal that Delhi was not comfortable with any domestic force with a sizeable mass base, and one which refused to take dictation from the babus of South Block. Delhi's desire to be in control of events and actors in Kathmandu has often preceded any other objective. In 1960, the Nehru-B. P. Koirala relationship had become uneasy when Koirala had struck out and asserted his strong and independent personality. In the 1990s, minor incidents disrupted India's ties with the NC which eventually benefited the Palace. And now, India had a problem with the two forces who had been most successful in the 2008 elections—the Maoists nationally, and the Madhesi Janadhikar Forum (MJF) in the plains. It seemed India really wanted pliant agents, and was just not mature enough to deal with autonomous political agents in a neighbouring country.

I have often wondered where this penchant for control comes from. There are several popular explanations in Kathmandu. The Nepali Left, as Baburam Bhattarai's initial tract justifying the war suggested, sees India as being motivated by a desire to keep the country economically subservient to serve its capitalist classes. While Nepal's economic dependence gives Delhi enormous leverage, I am not sure if policymakers are really concerned with the economic dimensions of the relationship. The most influential of India's business elites, who shape policy in Delhi, have barely any economic stakes in Nepal as they have diversified on the global stage with a range of other interests. India would be happy to use Nepal's hydropower potential but, given the history of failure in operationalizing the big deals, few in Delhi are losing sleep over this.

Others argue the core issue is that South Block is the true inheritor of the British imperial legacy and, in the tradition of Lord Curzon, sees the neighbourhood as its sphere of influence. They focus on the strategic calculations, citing, primarily, Jawaharlal Nehru's speech which projected the Himalayas as India's security frontier. If this is the case, Delhi needs a friendly regime in Kathmandu to prevent China from gaining space at its expense. There is merit in the argument that India's core interest in Nepal is security, especially given the fact that the two countries share an open border.

I asked a thoughtful RAW official why they could not let go and allow domestic processes in Nepal to play out, irrespective of outcomes, without meddling. 'If you have an open border, there has to be a special security relationship. We could have lived with a Maoist dictatorship if it was 5,000 miles away but, across an open border, we cannot risk it.'

What India was attempting with the Maoists was not a simplistic strategy of isolation, though. It was emulating a highly sophisticated tradition of statecraft it had practiced, with mixed results, in Kashmir with the Hurriyat Conference and, in the Northeast, with the National Socialist Council of Nagaland (Isak-Muivah).

Engage, coerce, divide, frustrate, exhaust, corrupt, lure, repeat the cycle, and give nothing. It had never stopped talking to the Maoists even when the war of words was at its worst. It had isolated them to show them the high costs of not listening to advice. It had encouraged Baburam Bhattarai as a counter to Prachanda in order to sharpen the divisions within the party. It had created a situation where the leadership could deliver nothing to the cadre, frustrating them and increasing the gulf between the top and the bottom. It offered inducements and showed the benefits of cooperating and playing along with the existing political-economic networks. And it kept up the strategies until the incentives for the other side changed, and caused a transformation in its behaviour which suited the establishment.

I knew that the traditional nationalist argument—that no external power has the right to intervene in another sovereign country's internal affairs—did not quite work, particularly in the context of India and Nepal.

The idea of absolute sovereignty is becoming increasingly irrelevant in an inter-connected and inter-dependent world. Smaller countries like Nepal have to take into account the security concerns of bigger neighbours like China and India even as regional powers like India cannot afford to ignore the concerns of global powers like the US. With each state wooing international capital, foreign investors often have the power and the leverage to influence laws and policies. Global civil society networks have made it difficult for regimes to get away with blatant human rights violations. It is still an anarchic world, and nation-states are the fundamental units of the international order, but their autonomy has become squeezed.

In our case, all actors in Kathmandu were well aware of the 'special relationship' with India, and had even accepted Delhi's role in Kathmandu's internal politics. As someone who had cheered on the Indian role during the 12-point Understanding, and lauded South Block's willingness to shed its anti-Maoist baggage to engage with Nepal's progressive forces, how could I suddenly turn around and say that India had no business getting involved in Nepali politics? What moral ground did we have to welcome India's role during one specific episode, and decry it at another time when it went against our preferences?

But, there was also a difference.

In 2005, there had been a genuine attack on democracy by the king. Nepali citizens wanted democracy and peace. Delhi had read the mood correctly, and had helped facilitate a deal between the two representative forces. It was an enlightened approach, and failing to engage would have left India behind the curve. Nepal would have, sooner or later, succeeded in defeating the king and Delhi would have been on the wrong side of history. It was a transformative moment in the history of a close neighbour, and universal values like freedom and democracy were genuinely at stake. There was a request for assistance by Nepal's representative political forces, and

Delhi's actions were not necessarily an imposition—as much as the royalists would have liked to portray it as such.

But this time, India was intervening not in favour of universal values but to influence outcomes in a fragmented but democratic political landscape. There was no reason for Delhi to play favourites among Nepali politicians, for no one—including the Maoists—had harmed India's security interests. They could have let domestic political processes take their own course instead of preventing a natural equilibrium from emerging. For a neighbour to actively intervene in order to try and kill another country's elected institution, and target one political force, went beyond any acceptable norm of inter-state relations.

But besides the objections on the basis of principle, which do not count for much in realpolitik, my problem with the Indian approach was on pragmatic grounds.

I was never convinced by the Indian reading, as the RAW official had starkly put it, that Maoists represented a threat to democracy and would establish a dictatorship. The former rebels did indeed have an ideological attachment to the one-party system; they had disdain for the compromises required in parliamentary politics; and they were openly contemptuous of what they called bourgeoisie freedoms and we saw as fundamental rights.

But the Nepali Maoists, despite this baggage, had come around to the new political reality. They had participated in the elections and won legitimately. Despite sporadic incidents, they had allowed a free and extremely critical press to flourish. They had given up their base areas and opened it up to political competition so that other political parties could operate there. They had dissolved their parallel courts and had agreed to have their former army put into cantonments. Prachanda had resigned when faced with an uncomfortable political situation, and was making a bid to return to power by gaining a majority on the floor of the house.

The Maoists did indeed harbour hopes of establishing a degree of political hegemony where they would out-compete all other rivals. Like with other communists, the line between the state and the party was blurred for them. And during Prachanda's short nine-month tenure, this featured prominently as government decisions were pushed through by party mechanisms. But even if they had the intention to push through political hegemony, they did not have the capacity to do so anymore since they had to compete in a crowded, fragmented political landscape and operate in a society replete with contradictions and discontent. They could not even win a simple majority on their own; they could not dismiss an army chief when they wished to; they could not return to power despite being the largest party in the house; and we were being told that they would establish a dictatorship. This seemed like fiction to me.

If it was felt by the powers-that-be that the Maoists' ambitions needed to be tamed, and the only way was for them to let the political process evolve. The onus was on the other parties to go back to the people, carve out alternative and more attractive political platforms, and expose the weaknesses of the Maoists. It required hard work, it required organization-building, it required spending days and nights with communities to build a relationship of trust, it required the deepening of patronage networks and the enabling of constituents to extract benefits from the state, and it required political innovation—the stuff democratic politics is made of. Propping up an artificial alliance, and keeping the biggest political force of the country out of the power structure, was not the way forward.

My other problem with the Indian approach was that it did not take into account the insecurities of the Maoists at all. Delhi had a point when it said that the Maoists could not indefinitely retain the advantage of having an armed apparatus. In fact, this point was made more vocally by large sections of Nepal's political class and civil society as well.

But here was a rebel force which had given up its wartime structures for the most part. It had moved away from its radical past. In return, Delhi (and others) had assured the Maoists that its agenda of writing a Constitution through the CA would be accepted and it would be a part of the power-sharing arrangement. Instead, Delhi had pushed the Maoists to the wall, squeezed it out of the mainstream, and then told the former rebels to give up—on terms set by the non-Maoist political class and the NA—the PLA. In such adverse circumstances, the PLA was the only insurance policy the

Maoists possessed. To expect them to surrender—when they had achieved a military stalemate, brought in the political change of 2006, and won elections—was naïve.

India was not only attacking the Maoists, but also all those who were seen to be sympathetic to the rebels or those who believed that keeping them out was no solution. The Kantipur Media Group, Nepal's biggest media house, was openly critical of the Madhav Nepal government. It had also exposed India's shenanigans in influencing parties not to vote for the Maoists. This had vexed the Indian embassy in Kathmandu. What did it for them was when Kantipur insinuated that India's covert agencies may have had a role in the killing of some controversial individuals, linked to the ISI, and who were known to be 'anti-India' elements.

Then, one day, the Kantipur group mysteriously declared that it was short on newsprint. Over lunch at Nanglo café in Kathmandu, Akhilesh Upadhyaya, editor of *The Kathmandu Post*, published by the Kantipur group confided to me his suspicion that it was probably the Indian embassy which had blocked the newsprint meant for the media house at the Kolkata port. Indian companies running joint ventures with Nepali corporates also stopped advertising with the group. A top Indian CEO in-charge of a joint venture in Nepal told me how he was called in to the embassy and was shown clippings of 'anti-India' reportage published by the Kantipur group. They were requested to stop advertising in the 'national interest'. The corporates complied.

And if that was not enough, India's plans to stop the extension of the CA would have killed the dreams of all those who had struggled, and given up their lives, for a restructured, inclusive and federal Nepali state. How would it have helped them achieve their long-term objective of democratizing the Maoists? The former rebels would have been in the opposition, along with all the other marginalized groups. The hardliners among the Maoists would be vindicated about the limits of the constitutional approach and argue for a fresh revolt. The government's legitimacy would have been in tatters. And Nepal would have been locked into yet another cycle of conflict.

Indian policy carried the risk of derailing the Nepali transition; it damaged the national psyche; it wasted precious time which could have been used otherwise in ensuring peace and writing the Constitution. Those of us who shared close ties with India at several levels—personal, family, kinship, linguistic and cultural—and believed that Nepal's future lay in greater cooperation with India, could see that the cumulative impact of such flawed policies would give rise to more resentment against India. And we hoped, fervently, that Delhi would change course before it was too late. Fortunately, that was to happen, enabled by a set of circumstances which showed that domestic actors could still set the agenda.

4

For India, propping up the Broad Democratic Alliance was the pillar of their anti-Maoist strategy. For the Maoists, breaking precisely this alliance was the only way to end their political isolation and return to power which, in turn, would give them the political security to maintain peace, push the Constitution-writing process forward and institutionalize the Federal Democratic Republic, which was their political baby.

The former rebels had failed to wean the Madhesis away. But there was a chink in the armour of the Broad Democratic Alliance— the UML's Left-leaning faction led by Chairman Jhalanath Khanal. This group had consistently maintained that the Maoists must be brought back in government; Khanal had done his best to undermine his own party's prime minister, Madhav Nepal, as the consistent criticism levelled by his aides against Nepal revealed; he had stood in favour of granting the CA an extension; and he withstood the challenge posed by the conservatives in his party to support the NC candidate. More than ideological convictions, personal ambition was driving Khanal.

He felt that he was one of the few leaders in the party who had won his seat in the CA even as Madhav Nepal and K. P. Oli had lost theirs; he had been elected chairman of the party through a democratic convention; and he deserved the prime ministership. Yet Nepal had walked away with the trophy in 2009, with support from G. P. Koirala and India.

With a stalemate persisting through 2010, a fresh round of voting to elect the prime minister on the floor of the house was called for in early 2011. Parliamentary rules had now changed, and no party could remain neutral, thus preventing a result. Prachanda filed his nomination. But the ground had not shifted, with India maintaining pressure on Madhesi parties to not switch sides. A senior RAW official was sent from Delhi to prevent Prachanda's elevation. But they were fighting a losing battle this time, for the Maoist supremo realized even before the first round of voting that he would not make it. And, in a sudden move, he called a meeting of the party's standing committee and decided that the Maoists would support Jhalanath Khanal for prime minister.

Baburam Bhattarai opposed the move, arguing that only a national unity government could resolve the current crisis, but he was overruled. Prachanda's loyalists in the party, including Barshaman Pun 'Ananta' and Haribol Gajurel, had then told me that Bhattarai's opposition was motivated by his desire to become prime minister rather than a principled stand. That morning, the Maoists and the UML had signed a secret 7-point deal, the key element of which was protecting national independence and sovereignty—a clear indication that the alliance was born to resist Indian influence.

The new prime minister sent a tough message to Delhi. In an interview with me for *The Hindu* soon after taking charge, Khanal said that he would be sensitive to India's security interests. But he also added, 'It is up to the Indian policymakers to review their Nepal policy, how it is conducted, and how much India has benefited from it... We should respect each other's independence, sovereignty and interests. We may be small or big, but we are equal. That has to be the guiding principle and sentiment in building the relationship. If we move forward like that, then the anti-India sentiment that is sometimes seen in Nepal will disappear on its own.'

There has been speculation in Kathmandu that the alliance was backed by the Chinese. Beijing's engagement had grown in Nepal since the 'Free Tibet' protests of March 2008, as recounted earlier. While it had engaged with all political actors, China's most regular interlocutors were from the UML's Khanal faction and the Maoist leaders, particularly Prachanda and Kiran, who backed Khanal even as Baburam Bhattarai opposed the alliance. The Chinese ambassador congratulated Khanal in unusually quick time after his election, and some political sources suggested that the ambassador, in fact, had encouraged the Maoist chairman to back Khanal.

Despite talking to multiple sources, I could not get an authoritative account of whether there was indeed a Chinese role in the episode. I doubt that Beijing engineered the Maoist-UML alliance. There were sufficient domestic factors to enable the new government to come up, and Beijing did not really have the political leverage yet to decisively influence government formation. But China, no doubt, saw it as an alignment that would be friendly to its interests and sought to deepen its relationship with the new dispensation.

India did not trust Khanal. It saw him as a man of the 'Chinese lobby', as one intelligence official put it to me. Khanal had given the green signal to Prachanda to dismiss Katawal, and had been on a visit to Beijing when the crisis erupted. When an Indian minister spoke to him during that time, he was quick to revise his position, but that was not enough to win him support in Delhi. When Khanal tried to reach out to Delhi and visited the Indian capital in 2009, he was kept waiting for a meeting with Prime Minister Manmohan Singh for days and was called back from the airport for a short interaction just as he was about to depart.

Several incidents confirmed prevailing suspicions in Delhi that the Khanal government was 'made in China'. Prachanda's ambitious project to get 3 billion US dollars from a Chinese NGO (an oxymoron if one existed, given that little happens in China on this scale, involving a strategic neighbour, that is 'non-government') to develop the Lumbini region picked up during Khanal's tenure—though the prime minister was careful not to give it official sanction. There was an even firmer crackdown on Tibetan refugees and their movement by the government of the day. The home ministry was headed by Krishna Bahadur Mahara, who had been caught on tape the previous year asking for 50 million Nepali rupees from a Chinese businessman. (The tape was leaked by RAW to the Nepali media, which had dented the credibility of the allegations against Mahara.)

Lila Mani Poudel, who had served as Consul General in Lhasa, and was perceived by India to be a China loyalist, was appointed home secretary.

Indian officials also viewed the government as one of 'anti-India forces', given that it shared a relationship of deep distrust with all three key protagonists of the alliance—Khanal, Prachanda and Upendra Yadav, the only Madhesi leader in the bloc and the one Madhesi leader India was not fond of. The embassy in Kathmandu went through the motions in dealing with the government, but offered the UML-Maoist alliance no political support. And Khanal became the first prime minister in post-2006 Nepal who was not invited to India for an official visit. When I asked an official in Delhi whether he saw any chance that the policy would be revised, he responded, 'Not till this poisonous phase is over.'

The lack of movement on the peace process weakened Khanal's government, for his entire political line was based on the principle that giving the Maoists a share in the power structure would lead to the integration and the rehabilitation of its former combatants. The Maoists were now embroiled in their own internal battles, with Baburam Bhattarai undermining the Khanal government and allying with his ideological rival, Kiran, to undercut Prachanda's authority in the party. The NC and the Madhesi parties were on the streets, baying for Khanal's blood, and warning the nation that this was a Left dictatorship in the making. India supported the opposition's movement politically and financially.

Another constitutional deadline, that of 27 May 2011, approached. The CA's term was ending and, this time, the bargaining power was with the NC. Just as the Maoists had demanded Madhav Nepal's resignation as a precondition for extending the CA's term in the previous year, this time, the NC asked for Khanal's resignation and firm actionable commitments by the Maoists on the peace process before supporting the CA extension. In the run-up to the deadline, India had once again played a role by encouraging a split within Upendra Yadav's party in order to ensure that the UML-led government did not have the two-thirds majority it needed to extend the CA on its own.

Negotiations went on, like in 2010, till late at night and ended with an agreement that Khanal would make way for a national unity government and the CA's term would be extended, but only for three more months. Jhalanath Khanal's government was now on its way out, but it had served a useful function. By enabling the Maoists to return to the power structure, it had given Prachanda much needed space to take on the hardliners in his party and correct the Maoists' official line. It had also forced India to realize that keeping the Maoists out of power for all time to come was not feasible.

5

I met the Maoist chairman for an extended interview for *The Hindu* even as a crucial central committee meeting of his party was underway in April 2011. We sat in his drawing room on the first floor of his residence in Naya Bajar. It was late evening. His nephew and aide, Sameer Dahal, brought in his own recorder. This was new, for I hadn't seen it the many times that I had spoken to Prachanda in the past. I asked Sameer, half in jest, whether it was meant to ensure that I did not misquote the chairman. He laughed and responded, 'No. It is to help in case your recorder does not work!'

Prachanda walked in and sat comfortably on his favourite sofa. Before we started, he remarked, 'You are really interviewing me at a historical time. The CC decision is path-breaking.' I asked him to elaborate, and he candidly admitted that there were divergent views within the party—on whether to create conditions for a People's Revolt, as Mohan Vaidya 'Kiran' had been arguing, or to stick to the peace-and-Constitution line which Baburam Bhattarai had consistently recommended. He said he led the third school. 'We should focus on peace and Constitution, but if there are conspiracies, there may be a need to get people on the streets to revolt.' He denied that this was a 'dual line', and insisted that his party's proposed model was not contradictory to liberal democratic precepts.

But it was when I asked Prachanda about his relations with India that he came up with what I thought was the most coherent explanation of the background of their ties and the current state of play.

'The first thing is we are not anti-India. Relations between India and Nepal are unique on the basis of history, culture, geography and economy. No one can think of weakening this. Our party also believes in strengthening these links.' He said that India had played a 'supporting role' during the signing of the 12-point Understanding and the peace accord, and the elections to the CA. In a major admission, he said, 'The 12-point Understanding was signed in Delhi and without India's direct or indirect support, it would not have been possible.' But Prachanda said he felt that when the Maoists became the largest party and led the government, and tried to 'address the people's aspiration for change', 'I did not get the support from India. Instead I began to feel there was non-cooperation and in the Katawal case, this became clear. Our relations chilled.'

I tried to interrupt and ask a question about the supposed 'anti-India activities' of the Maoists, but the Maoist chairman cut me short and said, 'Give me two minutes. I know what you want to ask and will answer everything.'

Resuming his chain of thought, Prachanda said that in a meeting with Foreign Minister S. M. Krishna, who had visited Nepal the previous week, they had had a 'frank conversation'. 'I asked him who is responsible. Being a bigger country, with a rising economy, and an international power player, now that there is a chill in relations, whose responsibility is it to improve these ties?' The foreign minister asked Prachanda why the Maoists were 'stoking anti-Indianism, defacing the Indian flag, and attacking the Indian ambassador'. Prachanda said he had told Krishna that they respected the Indian flag, and 'could not even think of insulting the emotions of the Indian people'. Obstructing the ambassador was not policy either. 'But India must also introspect whether they have created difficulties for the Maoists, who are the biggest party of the country and an agent for change. We are all very sensitive to India's security and economic interests. India should also creatively think about how to generate trust in a country passing through a historical transition.'

As the interview concluded, I informally asked Prachanda if he thought that ties would improve. He was optimistic that India would understand the significance of the shift in the party's line, but added that in his opinion, the problem was that Delhi was getting the wrong inputs from Kathmandu. He hoped that this would soon change.

The Maoists had known all along that the political process would not move forward in the face of strident Indian opposition. They had, in 2009 and 2010, sought to redefine the terms of engagement in their favour. But Delhi had stuck to its policy line. By electing Khanal, the Maoists showed to India the limits of how far they could dictate domestic politics. But the fact that Prachanda himself, or the Maoists institutionally, could not lead the government also revealed to the former rebels the limits of their power and the extent of India's power. Prachanda made a course correction to allay the apprehensions of the Indian security establishment—by recommitting to democracy and giving up on the anti-India rhetoric. The Maoists also sought to convince Delhi that they would settle the future of the PLA as soon as they returned to power. But this was not possible by being in the opposition, for it would spark an unmanageable backlash by the hardliners. Internal tensions among the Maoists—where Prachanda faced a strong challenge from Bhattarai and Kiran—also forced him to recalibrate his position.

~

But the period also forced Delhi to introspect.

The polity had become more unstable—contradicting India's stated objective of ensuring a stable neighbourhood. It was clear that keeping the Maoists out of power would not lead to progress in the peace process; defeating the Indian objective of detaching the Maoists from their coercive arm and ending the existence of the PLA.

India's hardline position had only given birth to an alliance of forces which Delhi disliked and over which it had limited leverage. Beijing now had greater space to manoeuvre in Nepal—conflicting with the unstated Indian objective of keeping Nepal firmly within

Delhi's sphere of influence. The refusal to deal with Nepal's biggest political force meant that none of India's core economic projects in Nepal could become operationalized—stalling the objective of creating dense networks of interdependence in South Asia. And implementing the flawed policy line had forced India to intervene blatantly and publicly in Nepali affairs, sparking widespread resentment—adding to the list of countries in the neighbourhood where India's stock was getting lower.

There was also a change of personnel in the Indian establishment. And as we had seen in 2005-06, individuals played a major role in shaping policy. Sanjeev Tripathi had taken over RAW in January 2011, and he was understood to be in favour of re-engaging with the Maoists. Alok Joshi had taken over as special secretary who looked after key neighbouring countries. Joshi had served as the station chief in Nepal between 2008 and 2010. A product of JNU, and an Indian Police Service officer from the Haryana cadre, he had sharp political sense and knew the lay of the land in Nepal.

RAW did not believe in giving the Maoists a blank cheque and recognized the importance of challenging them in order to get them to deliver on commitments. But it could also see that the experiment of keeping the Maoists out of power had perhaps outlived its utility, and the Indian position needed revision. It argued to the national security advisor, Shiv Shanker Menon, that the Maoists should be given 'one final chance'.

Rakesh Sood had left Kathmandu for Paris, and the new ambassador, Jayant Prasad, had not yet arrived in Kathmandu. A soft-spoken, brilliant diplomat, with uncanny political sense and a commitment to basic democratic ethos, Prasad had an old Nepal connection. His father, Bimal Prasad, a former professor in JNU, had been India's envoy to Kathmandu in the early 1990s and had a reputation of being close to the NC. But Jayant Prasad had visited Nepal only once during his father's tenure and carried little baggage. A 'free-thinker' in his student days in JNU, where he distinguished himself academically, Prasad could empathize with broad socialist and Left political thinking, but carried no dogma. While Prasad did not take charge till August-end, Sood's departure had already helped to partially detoxify the India-Maoist relationship.

Prachanda had met senior Indian intelligence officials during his trips to various Southeast Asian cities through the summer of 2011. In early August, they met in Kuala Lumpur where Prachanda once again committed to completing the peace process as soon as the Maoists led the government. He briefed them on internal tensions within the party, and said that after Khanal resigned, the Maoists would put forward Baburam Bhattarai as the party's prime ministerial candidate. Indian officials are learnt to have told him that they would not object if the Maoists observed all democratic processes and mustered a majority on the floor of the house. This was a significant meeting in rebuilding the relationship between the two sides. While the mistrust was deep, both sides were slowly inching back to the more nuanced approach they had with each other between 2005 and 2008. To borrow Prachanda's metaphor, the warmth may not have returned, but there was a thaw. A rapprochement was on the horizon.

Would it finally enable the successful accommodation of the Maoists into the formal power structure? Would it help integrate the Maoist combatants into the NA—an issue which was at the heart of the tensions over the UN's role in Nepal, over General Katawal's dismissal, over the Maoists' re-entry into government, and the yardstick for whether the rebels had indeed transformed into a democratic force? Would it finally push forward the Constitution-writing project, which had been in limbo as power games overwhelmed Kathmandu politics? Would the renewed engagement between India and the Maoists bring back the focus on the core political goal of restructuring the Nepali state and Nepali nationalism?

BOOK 3

POLITICS OF INCLUSIVE NATIONALISM

All I had to suffer for my surname, for speaking in Hindi and Maithili,
for being a 'dhoti', for having relatives across the border in India, were a
few taunts. But for precisely the same reasons, millions of people in
Nepal have had no access to power, have been subjects of systemic
discrimination, have remained deprived of services, and have lived
everyday with the burden of having to prove that they are, indeed, Nepali.

We are the Madhesis of Nepal.

~

The spirit of the movement, in Tula Sah's imagination,
Jwala Singh's karabahi, Rajeev Jha's anger, Upendra Yadav's political
programme and, eventually, the election results, envisaged a shift in the
power structure. This unnerved those who belonged to groups which had
traditionally exercised power. It made the disenfranchised politically
assertive, determined to stake their claim and not miss the bus again.
And it tested the intent and imagination of the Madhes's political
leadership, of whether they were seeking to create an accommodative
and plural society or replicate one form of hegemony with another.

Being Nepali

It took me a while to realize that there was something different about us.

I used to study at the Modern Indian School in Kathmandu, and remember clinging to my mother, who taught English there, in the bus on my way to school.

In class and outside, we usually spoke in Hindi. India was the reference point in most of our subjects and conversations. Mahatma Gandhi and the *Panchatantra* were as much a part of our consciousnesses as *The Jungle Book* and *Mahabharata* serials on Doordarshan; Independence Day was 15 August and Children's Day was 14 November. The prayers we chanted during school assemblies were old Indian bhajans. Many of my classmates were Marwaris and Sikhs—making me infinitely more familiar with Indian-origin ethnicities than the multiple surnames which punctuate the Nepali social landscape.

Life was comfortable, for there was a seamless linguistic and cultural homogeneity between school and home.

My parents spoke to each other, and to me, in English and in Hindi. I spoke to my brother in Maithili. My grandfather, Tatta as we called him, used to listen to both Nepali and Hindi news on the radio as we played with him in the evenings. Games meant cricket and Saturday afternoons were reserved for watching Hindi films on television. Aunts from Patna visited us during their summer holidays; in December, it was our turn to go to Delhi and spend the long winter holidays with our mausis. We occasionally made the eight-hour drive down to meet relatives in Rajbiraj which, we were told, was our hometown in southern Nepal.

I remember being conscious that Nepal and India were different countries; that they had different prime ministers; that Indian and Nepali news were broadcast in different languages; and that I was a Nepali, which meant that I was not an Indian like many of my cousins.

But the lines were too blurred, and I was too young, for these national distinctions to mean anything. It was as normal and happy a childhood as one could have.

There were some unnatural moments, however. When we used to go out to New Road to shop or Papa used to take us out for a meal, anyone speaking in Hindi was immediately hushed up. It is a memory that has stayed with me; there was something wrong about being ourselves, and speaking in the language that we felt most comfortable in, when others were around.

And then, in Class 5, when I was eight years old, my parents shifted me to a new school—Loyola.

The first day was a blur.

We were having lunch in the common mess. Two classmates who I had seen but not spoken to in the morning were sitting opposite me with their plates.

One of them asked where I was from.

Kathmandu.

He asked, 'Jha pani Kathmandu ko huncha? [Can a Jha hail from Kathmandu?] He is Indian.'

The other immediately chimed in, 'Euta aru dhoti aayo. [One more dhoti has arrived.] The maade will get a friend now. Ha ha!'

I smiled weakly, not knowing what either dhoti or maade meant, and continued eating.

But there appeared to be a connection between being made fun of because of my surname, and being told that I was Indian. And I realized that there was a reason why my father asked us not to speak in Hindi. It was important to run away from who you were, when confronted by outsiders, by normal people, by the 'true' Nepalis.

In hindsight, there were possibly two reactions a child could have had to what was a bit of a scarring conversation—go into a shell, or try to be more 'normal'. And for some reason, perhaps due to the typical schoolkid instinct of recognizing where power resides in a classroom, I decided to do the latter.

So I hung out with the cool Kathmandu kids. I could not hide my poor Nepali, but fortunately the school had a speak-only-in-English rule which was quite strictly enforced. I joined the others in calling those with Indian-sounding surnames—Bararias, Agarwals, Mishras, Chowdhurys—dhotis, which I learnt was a generic, derogatory term to dismiss anyone 'Indian', or maades, which was short for Marwaris. Cultural religious practices within my family were at odds with the other 'Nepalis'. On Dussehra, we turned vegetarian; they feasted on meat. At the end of the festival, the elders of the family blessed others with tika, which was a big event in the calendar; we did nothing of the sort. But I did not tell my new friends that and pretended that we did the same at home.

In a few years, I left to study in Delhi. And I felt far more at home than I did in school in Kathmandu, where I had not only constructed a divide between school friends and home, but also created a web of lies to sustain the fiction that I was as 'Nepali' as any other student in the classroom.

But the problem did not disappear, and the first thing classmates in Delhi's Sardar Patel Vidyalaya asked was how I could be a Nepali—'You don't look like a Nepali at all.' Or 'Are you a Bahadur too? We have one who guards our apartment.' A bit older by now, I had developed a somewhat more coherent response—you could be a Nepali without being a 'Bahadur' or 'looking' Nepali. In the common perception, Nepalis always have Mongoloid features.

It was only much later that I realized that I was not unique. I was privileged, for I came from an upper-middle-class, upper-caste family which sent me to Delhi to acquire a better education. My class allowed me to escape the handicaps that came with my identity, and access the best opportunities available.

All I had to suffer for my surname, for speaking in Hindi and Maithili, for being a 'dhoti', for having relatives across in India, were a few taunts.

But for precisely the same reasons, millions of people in Nepal have had no access to power, have been subjects of systemic discrimination, have remained deprived of services, and have lived everyday with the burden of having to prove that they are, indeed, Nepali.

We are the Madhesis of Nepal.

The Madhesi Mutinies

Lahan can pass off as just another small decrepit town on the East-West Highway in Nepal's southern plains. But unlike the other anonymous bazaars that punctuate Nepal's arterial road, Lahan is central in the consciousnesses of the travellers who cross the Tarai. Long-distance buses travelling from Kakarbitta—a town on Nepal's eastern border with Siliguri in West Bengal—to Kathmandu stop here so that passengers can refresh themselves; truck drivers halt here for the night; and ramshackle private buses from Janakpur to Biratnagar wait here the longest, with conductors screeching to attract the most passengers. A hospitality industry—from small dhabas serving daal-bhaat to 'premium' hotels like Godhuli—has sprung up to cater to a diverse clientele.

But despite its small size—Lahan is all of one long road with a few small lanes branching off it—the town is more than just a passenger stopover.

Major government offices are located in Siraha bazaar, the district headquarters fifteen miles off the main highway to the south, right at the border with Bihar's Jainagar district. One of Nepal's best, the Sagarmatha Chowdhury Eye Hospital is on the main road. Most local journalists, and NGO representatives, use Lahan as a base to cover neighbouring districts like Saptari and Dhanusha. The landed classes of the nearby rural areas, professionals of Siraha origin, and workers from the region in Malaysia, India and the Gulf, who send money back home, all want to buy land or a house in Lahan.

Perhaps it is the constant movement of vehicles, and the mixed demography, with both people of hill and plains origin, which lends the town an unexpected energy, discernible in district politics if not in the stagnant economy. Influential locals meet every evening over paan and chai to exchange gossip—be it about the new government official who has just taken office, the big construction contracts in the pipeline, property disputes wrecking prominent local families, the newest caste-based power alliance, or the political machinations in the distant capital.

It was here, right in the middle of the highway town, that Ramesh Mahato was killed on 19 January 2007.

1

Three days earlier, 240 legislators—including eighty-three Maoists who had been nominated to an interim Parliament—had adopted a new interim Constitution.

For seven months, ever since the end of the second Janandolan, major parties, especially the Nepali Congress (NC) and the Maoists, had engaged in tough peace negotiations. At the end of November, an intricate Comprehensive Peace Agreement had been signed, formally marking the end of the war. In mid-December, the interim Constitution was negotiated, which declared that Nepal's 'unitary structure would end'.

Nepali politicians, mostly of hill origin, had spent all their time fighting each other, then fighting the king, and finally arriving at a multiparty alliance. Immersed in the divides between the monarchy, the parliamentary parties and the Maoists, and blind to the fact that it was six hill Brahmin—and a couple of Chhetri—men who were making all the decisions, they could not sense the simmering discontent on the ground—showing how disconnected all of them, including the Maoists, had become in the capital.

There was a backlash of unexpected ferocity from an unexpected quarter, challenging long-held notions of nationalism and putting Nepal firmly, and perhaps irreversibly, on the path to federalism.

~

Upendra Yadav—a schoolteacher turned mainstream Left politician turned Maoist sympathizer turned semi-underground regional leader—burnt a copy of the interim Constitution at Maitighar Mandala, an open green space in the middle of Kathmandu's power zone. In its vicinity lies the army road, home to the Nepal Army (NA) headquarters and its adjunct offices—the road was closed to the public after the military was deployed in the war against the Maoists. The Supreme Court and the Nepal Bar Association are a minute's walk away. And half a kilometre away is the Singha Durbar, the secretariat complex which is home to key ministries as well as the Parliament where the interim Constitution had been promulgated the night before.

Despite its proximity to state power, or because of it, the Mandala had emerged as the favourite site for protestors, from those organizing peace rallies to groups challenging the authorities. The democratic government post April 2006 usually deployed additional police, but treated protestors indulgently, perhaps because those running the government had themselves been on the streets till very recently.

But not this time.

Yadav, along with his supporters of the Madhesi Janadhikar Forum (MJF), then a cross-party forum, were immediately arrested, shoved into a van, and taken to Hanuman Dhoka—the capital's police hub familiar to most political activists, all of whom had spent a few nights locked up there at some point or the other in their careers.

Few people in Kathmandu knew either Yadav, or the MJF's, background.

The MJF's protests were not sudden. The Forum, as it came to be popularly known, had repeatedly warned of protests if the interim Constitution did not make a firm commitment to federalism. Madhesis—people who live largely, but not exclusively, in Nepal's southern plains; speak languages like Maithili, Urdu, Bhojpuri, Awadhi and Hindi; and maintain close linguistic, cultural, ethnic ties with people across the border in Bihar and Uttar Pradesh—felt a deep sense of resentment against the Nepali state, and the hill-centric political elite's discriminatory practices. They had historically seen regional autonomy in their own territory, the Tarai, as the only way of political empowerment.

The ambiguous phraseology in the interim Constitution about 'ending the unitary structure', while remaining non-committal about the future state structure, was perceived as another way to concentrate all power in Kathmandu. Ironically, it was the Maoists who first pushed this demand, but they did not make it their central plank after coming over ground. The MJF also asked for greater political representation from the Tarai in Parliament and the future Constituent Assembly (CA) through an increase in electoral seats.

A month earlier, the only established party claiming to speak for Madhesi interests, the Sadbhavana Party, had made similar demands. A Sadbhavana minister was in government. Their strike in the western Tarai town of Nepalgunj opposing the interim Constitution had led to a riot-like situation between people of hill origin, backed by the local police, and Madhesi activists of plains origin in December 2006. This was perceived by Madhesis across the Tarai as yet another instance of the discrimination, the insensitivity and the racism of the state—compact discs containing videos of the 'Nepalgunj riots' were being circulated across Tarai towns.

But the government did not pay heed, smug that these groups were too small to affect macro politics. The Maoists felt that disillusionment with the state would translate into support for them, little realizing that there was also widespread resentment against the former rebels for not having pushed the federal agenda enough. Powerful social groups in the Tarai, who had suffered during the insurgency, and other political rivals were instrumental in painting the Maoists as 'betrayers' along with the 'pahadi' state which was projected as an 'oppressor for the past 240 years'. In what was to be a costly political error, the Sadbhavana did not resign from the government or launch a mass movement.

No established political force was able to read the signal from the Tarai, no one could read the agitational mood that was building up. And this allowed the relatively anonymous Upendra Yadav to occupy the political vacuum and emerge as the face of Tarai politics, whose seeds had been planted more than five decades earlier.

2

In 1951, soon after the first democratic revolution against the clan-based Rana oligarchy, a Tarai leader, Vedanand Jha, disillusioned with the Nepali Congress (NC), had formed the Nepal Tarai Congress. Its main demands included the use of Hindi as an official language, and autonomy for the Tarai. In the mid-1950s, when the then government decided to introduce Nepali as the sole official language of the country, there was resistance in the plains, even leading to clashes in Biratnagar in the eastern Tarai between groups supporting Nepali and Hindi. Those supporting Nepali were largely people of hill origin, pahadis, who were recent migrants to the Tarai; those demanding Hindi were people of plains origin, Madhesis, and Marwaris. The medium of instruction in educational institutions in the Tarai till then had been Hindi, with teachers from neighbouring areas of Bihar running schools. Locals feared that the imposition of Nepali would not only block the growth of their languages, but also disrupt livelihoods and reduce opportunities for growth.

But the ground was not yet ripe for ethnic identity- or language-driven politics. The big battle of the decade was for prajatantra, democracy, and the symbol of the democratic struggle was the B. P. Koirala-led NC. Structurally modelled on the Indian National Congress, the NC drew inspiration from the democratic and socialist guard of the Indian politics and gave space to leaders from diverse regions and ethnicities, including those of plains origin. Along with Kathmandu, it was the Taraibasis, the Tarai-dwellers, who were most active in the politics. The Koirala family itself was a pahadi family from Biratnagar, and the major battles against the Rana regime were fought in the Tarai towns.

Unlike royalist or communist parties, the NC was also the most inclusive in its symbols. Its leaders had spent a long time in exile in Banaras, Patna and Calcutta and were comfortable with the culture, lifestyle and habits of the Gangetic plain and North India. This helped the people in the Nepali plains relate to NC leaders at various levels—when they saw them wear dhotis, eat paan, speak in Hindi, or use familiar idioms, the pahadi-Taraibaasi divide became

2

secondary. That many of these leaders had been associated with the Indian freedom struggle, and with political stalwarts across the border, gave them an additional aura.

All this meant that in the first elections of 1959, the Nepal Tarai Congress suffered a rout, and even Vedanand Jha lost his election deposit. The NC swept the polls nationwide, winning a two-thirds majority. In the Tarai, its image of a national, democratic and inclusive party, the co-option of the relatively influential upper-caste leaders of plains origin, and its appeal to the intermediate castes and the landless with a radical land-reform agenda helped. Identity and regional politics had lost out for now, both due to limited political mobilization around these issues but also because the NC had remained sensitive, at least symbolically, to the concerns of the people in the plains, it had treated them like citizens, and had won their confidence.

But the NC's efforts to build Nepali nationalism and the state in an inclusive, non-violent, liberal, gradual and democratic manner— which may or may not have succeeded—received a jolt almost immediately. The royalist project of aggressive nation-building, with faith in coercion, homogenization, integration and the construction of the 'other', began in full earnest. Nationalism as propagated by Mahendra kept the land united, but it divided the people, apparent in the mutinies which were to rock Nepal four decades later.

~

King Mahendra took over in a royal coup in December 1960, sacking the elected government, dissolving the Parliament, and arresting all the top party leaders.

Mahendra's apologists built a case for autocracy. Their argument went along familiar lines—the monarch was concerned about keeping the 'territorial unity' of the country intact. Nepal was among the 'least developed' countries in the world. Literacy was in the single digits; geography had been unkind, with rough terrain and inaccessible mountains; the state had little money; and the country was just not ready for the populist aspirations a Westminster parliamentary democracy would have unleashed. A democracy 'suited to the soil', akin to Ayub Khan- or Sukarno-style guided democracies in Pakistan and Indonesia, was more appropriate. An elaborate Panchayat system was designed, with layers of notionally representative bodies, culminating into a national Panchayat. But the bottom line was clear—the Palace was the source of all authority.

For the king, the biggest challenge in sustaining a relatively autonomous, autocratic regime was India.

The day after Mahendra's takeover, Jawaharlal Nehru called the move a 'setback to democracy' in the Lok Sabha of the Indian Parliament. Recent accounts have suggested that Nehru knew of the coup in advance but did little to prevent it, for he shared an uneasy relationship with Bishweshwor Prasad Koirala and was happy to see him go. Senior Nepali lawyer Ganesh Raj Sharma, who was a close confidante of B. P. Koirala, believes that Nehru knew that the king would dismiss the government but not that he would dissolve Parliament. This goes against the image of Nehru as a committed democrat, but the idea is plausible, for India's approach, in dealings with Nepal at the time, was imperial in nature. This is reflected quite clearly in the letters of 'advice' Nehru wrote to Matrika Koirala, a Nepali prime minister during the 1950s and BP's elder half-brother—which have been made public now—and the actions of some of the earlier Indian ambassadors who behaved, in BP's words, as though they had been sent to run a district, not represent a foreign country.

But soon after the takeover, the government of India did provide a degree of support to NC dissidents who had escaped arrest and were based in India. Mahendra, his aides recall, felt that India would constantly try to weaken and topple him by using arashtra tatva, anti-national elements, which became synonymous with NC in the decades of Panchayat rule.

Mahendra got lucky, for China and India went to war.

As relations between Nepal's neighbours to the north and south deteriorated, he played what has come to be known as the 'China card', subtly threatening the Indian establishment with the prospect of Nepal developing closer ties with Beijing, both politically and in terms of greater infrastructural connectivity. This would have left

India vulnerable on another front. The policy of using the Himalayas as India's security frontier—as articulated by Nehru—would be in tatters, and Nepal would no longer remain a buffer state under the Indian arc of influence. Delhi quickly realized that it had to develop a more cordial working relationship with the Palace. Even if the king did not go all the way with China, the risks of antagonizing him entirely were too high. India snapped the support it was offering to Nepali democratic activists in exile; an armed movement launched by a section of the NC, using India as its base, fizzled out; and Mahendra found enough space and time to consolidate his regime.

But to do so, he had to deal with his biggest internal challenge, the Tarai, for two reasons. The plains were an NC stronghold, and had been the site of the struggle for democracy in the past. 'Royalist nationalists' were insecure that activists for democracy, either on their own or prodded by India, could use the open border to destabilize the regime through actions in the plains. The short-lived armed movement after the coup, led by NC exiles, was concentrated in towns in the Tarai which reinforced the fear and led to the feeling that the plains must be controlled.

The other reason was the fact that the ruling elite just did not trust the Madhesis. They were seen as 'migrants', 'people of Indian origin' or 'Indians', who had continued to maintain cultural practices and spoke languages which were distinct from the hill Nepalis. Their national loyalties were suspect, and the Palace felt that this was India's natural constituency which it could use to weaken the regime, or even to 'break the country'.

Besides being lucky, Mahendra was shrewd—perhaps the shrewdest leader Nepal has seen in modern times.

He constructed a narrative in which the monarchy was the symbol of the unity of the nation. And faith in the 'glorious' history of the Shah dynasty, a common language (Nepali), a common religion (Hinduism), and a common dress (daura-saluwar) tied the country together. This definition of a 'true Nepali' immediately privileged a certain group of people—the hill Bahuns and Chhetris— who fulfilled the above criteria. His suspicion of India as the biggest threat to 'national unity' and 'Indian-origin people' as swamping

Nepali territory was visible in internal formulations as well, since Nepali citizenship required one to possess attributes which would distinctly set one apart from 'Indians'.

Like nationalisms of all hues, Mahendra's nationalism was fundamentally exclusionary. Muslims were second-class citizens since the state was officially Hindu. There was little chance that Dalits would be able to rise up and challenge the caste hierarchy given the manner in which the Hindu religion, with its entrenched hierarchies, had been given formal state sanction. The bulk of the indigenous people—Tharus, Magars, Tamangs, Gurungs, Newars, Limbus, Rais and others—were left outside the mainstream since many were neither Hindus, nor did they speak the Nepali language, and continued to maintain distinct cultural practices.

The Madhesis, too, were not true Nepalis since they could not speak the Nepali language, continued to wear dhotis which were reflective of a distinct culture and lifestyle, could not be trusted to support monarchy, and had 'Indian attributes' given cross-border links and a shared culture.

Their exclusion happened not merely in theory, but in practice.

An education policy, with the primary objective of perpetuating the royal regime and its version of nationalism, was introduced. Nepali was the sole medium of instruction. Textbooks told children that Nepal was the creation of the Shah kings, conveniently glossing over the fact that the unification was seen as a conquest by most indigenous people who cherished their own tales of resistance, and that much of the Tarai's inclusion in Nepal was a result of arbitrary border demarcation after the Anglo-Nepal War of 1816.

The rulers were lauded for keeping the country independent even when India next door was colonized. Students were, of course, not told that Nepal had been humiliated in the 1816 war; the Rana rulers had accepted a subservient status to British India; Nepali Gorkhas, largely from ethnic communities, served as mercenary soldiers for the colonial army; and Nepali rulers had a slavish attitude to the British masters, reflected starkly in the way they rushed to their aid during the Sepoy Revolt of 1857. Nepali exceptionalism was based on Mount Everest and Lumbini, privileging spaces which merely happened to be in Nepal. And, along with pride, a sense of vulnerability was planted—Nepal was a landlocked country, external powers posed constant threats but the great king had successfully protected 'national unity'.

From a historical and political perspective, the Tarai found no mention at all in school curricula, except as a breadbasket. There was little a Madhesi could relate to when he was taught in classrooms—the language of instruction, the historical figures which were being mythologized, and the hill-centric cultural practices were all alien to him. But that was the aim, to make him more Nepali through pedagogy and force him to be ashamed of his own roots.

Discriminatory citizenship laws with impossible requirements to prove 'descent' and to speak Nepali were framed, making it difficult for those of plains origin to acquire citizenship papers. This virtually disenfranchised them, since they could not buy land, access state services, or participate in politics. They had little choice but to be meek and pliant for survival. At the same time, people of 'Nepali descent'—which could include Nepali speakers from Darjeeling and Sikkim in India, or Bhutan—were granted citizenship and encouraged to move to the Nepali hills and plains.

Mahendra also systematically built up on the trend that had first begun in the 1950s. With the clearing of forests and the eradication of malaria, people from the hills had slowly started moving down to the Tarai in large numbers. This was, to some extent, a natural process since the hills remained remote and the plains were seen as the path to progress and prosperity. But he made it state policy to encourage this migration, changing the demographic balance of the region and ensuring that it was not the Madhesis but hill-origin people who controlled local politics and economy. The Rana regime had distributed enormous tracts of land through the nineteenth and twentieth centuries in the Tarai to their loyalists, relatives and bureaucrats—all of hill origin. Through a flawed and selectively implemented Land Reforms Act, Mahendra did the same, giving land to recent settlers of hill origin while using the Act to make those influential landowners of the Tarai, who were potential dissenters, fall in line.

His suspicion of India and Madhesis was clear from the way in which the East-West Highway was constructed. An old postal road, Hulaki, connected the various Tarai towns, and was a mile off the Nepal-India border. Instead of upgrading that, the Palace made a conscious decision to construct the national highway several kilometres away from the border, even if that meant destroying extensive forest areas. The underlying fear was that building it next to the border, in Madhesi-populated areas, would give India enormous leverage. Instead, poor pahadi families from the hills were settled to the north and south of the new highway where small towns and economies sprung up. Lahan in the Siraha district, Dhalkebar in the Dhanusha district, Bardibas in the Mahottari district, Navalpur in the Sarlahi district, and Chandranighapur in the Rautahat district—all with a sizeable pahadi population—grew in importance at the time and became alternate political centres.

The country was also divided into zones where the Tarai, the hills, and the upper Himalayas were clubbed together vertically. So, for instance, the Sagarmatha zone had both the Everest Base Camp in the extreme north and Rajbiraj town—which shares a border with Bihar—in the same zonal unit, which made little administrative sense. Advocates of the model at the time used two arguments to justify the division—the optimum utilization of resources, especially river systems, and 'national unity' which would result from the cohabiting of people of different regions. Madhesi activists have since claimed that this was a deliberate ploy to keep Madhesi-populated areas from developing a coherent regional identity. Either way, what is indisputable is that all the zones, and even the Tarai districts, were run by pahadi officials who viewed the Madhesis as outsiders.

Mahendra made room for the elites of all communities, including Madhesi castes, to be included in the Panchayat polity. If they were willing to accept the monarchy's legitimacy and hegemony, and become more 'Nepali', a Jha, a Mishra or a Chaudhary could be accommodated in local power structures; be allowed to impose his writ and continue with his zamindari in localized areas; be given membership of the national Panchayat or bureaucracy and receive opportunities in the state-dependent economy.

My grandfather, Jogendra Jha, or Tatta, as we called him, was among those Madhesis who actively supported the monarchy. He was a trained doctor, but set up Nepal's first private construction firm. He indirectly dabbled in politics, financing leaders like Tulsi Giri, who was the first prime minister under the Panchayat system. Giri and Tatta had studied medicine together in Darbhanga, and Giri had encouraged my grandfather to migrate to Nepal after they completed their degrees. Bishwobandhu Thapa, who would serve as Giri's home minister, was a close family friend. Giri's and Thapa's children, and my father and aunts, grew up together.

Tatta had close links with political actors in Delhi, and often served as an intermediary between the royal regime and the Indian establishment as well as the Rashtriya Swayamsevak Sangh (RSS), which he had joined as a student at the Banaras Hindu University in the early 1940s. Before his death in 2001, he had often told me that he served as an intermediary between Mahendra and Pandit Nehru in the run-up to the royal coup in 1960. Nehru, he claimed, was in the loop about B. P. Koirala's dismissal.

On King Mahendra's request, Tatta co-produced Nepal's first private feature film, *Maitighar*. In the 1970s, he partnered with Mahendra's younger brother, Prince Basundhara, to set up Nepal's first private shipping company—a wildly ambitious project that fell flat, leaving him financially vulnerable. My grandmother would always remain furious at his overreach, but Tatta was a first-generation entrepreneur, a risk taker, and a survivor who knew how to navigate the power corridors of his times.

The point here is to highlight the fact that despite being a Madhesi, he was close to the establishment of the day. This indicated the slight opening that the system had for people of varied ethnic backgrounds. In return for loyalty, he got unprecedented access and opportunities—and we have benefited from those privileges. But he, and people like him, operating in the Tarai districts on a much smaller scale, were exceptions.

The larger pattern of how the Madhesis were to be dealt with was clear. Deprive them of citizenship and the rights that come with it; inculcate a deep suspicion about their 'nationalism' among other population segments through organized propaganda; destroy their self-esteem by making them feel like outsiders in a land they consider their own; ensure that they have little political power; give control of areas where they are in the majority to state officials and people of hill origin; use their resources without granting representation; co-opt, bribe and coerce local upper-caste elites so that they maintain peace and order in a feudal, patronage-based economy; and locate the entire strategy in a broader context of a 'foreign hand' which is out to attack 'national integrity'.

What you then get is an image that was common across the Tarai. A poor Madhesi villager visits a distant government office in the district headquarters, his hands folded, speaking subserviently to a pahadi official, struggling to stitch together a line in Nepali for the sahib who does not know the language of the area which he has been sent to administer, and pleads for citizenship, to become Nepali. And the only response he would receive: 'Oye saale dhoti, go back to where you belong.'

This was Mahendra's abiding gift to the Nepali nation.

3

The major political struggle for thirty years between 1960 and 1990, when Mahendra and his son Birendra ran Nepal like a fiefdom, was to restore democracy.

NC leaders tried all possible modes of protest—courting arrest; waging non-violent campaigns; fighting from exile in India; resorting to violence, including hijacking an aircraft; and adopting a policy of reconciliation in the hope that this would pressure the king to become more accommodative. The Communist Party of Nepal splintered into different factions—some supported the monarchy for the sake of 'nationalism' (read resistance to India); others argued for an alliance with the NC for 'democracy'. A radical fringe, inspired by the Naxalite revolt in West Bengal, experimented with a 'revolutionary approach', including class annihilation. Most of these battles were fought in the Tarai. The NC hijacked a plane from Biratnagar, and the ultra-Left started its revolution from the eastern Tarai district, Jhapa.

Madhesi leaders and activists were a part of this larger national battle. Many continued to support the NC, both because of their implicit belief in democracy and the faith that a free political system would empower the people of the plains. At a time when there was little hope that the monarchy could be defeated, they led lives of extraordinary struggle. The regime treated all dissenters harshly, but Madhesi democratic activists were particularly vulnerable. Many were imprisoned, some were killed, and many disappeared in mysterious circumstances.

Politics around Madhesi identity was limited, with scattered groups demanding federalism and autonomy. Raghunath Thakur was one such revolutionary Madhesi figure who identified key issues of discrimination against the Tarai and sought to mobilize opinion around it in the plains as well as in Delhi. His tract on the Tarai, *Paratantra Madhes aur Uski Sanskriti*, is still considered a bible by Madhesi activists. But his politics never gained momentum, and Thakur died in mysterious circumstances. Regional politics received a boost in the early 1980s when a former NC leader, Gajendra Narayan Singh, formed the Nepal Sadbhavana Parishad. The immediate trigger was a government commission report which recommended the sealing of the Indo-Nepal border, and suggested that the Madhesis were people of Indian origin, which outraged the Tarai leaders who insisted that while there may have been migration, many people had always lived on the same land for generations. The Sadbhavana demanded recognition of the Hindi language, citizenship for Tarai dwellers, federalism, and inclusion in state organs.

An alliance between the NC and various factions of the Left, and Indian support to the movement for democracy, finally led to the end of the Panchayat system in 1990.

The Sadbhavana turned into a political party, even though most Madhesi leaders continued in the bigger national parties like the NC and the newly formed Communist Party of Nepal (Unified Marxist Leninist) [UML]. But it struck a note of dissent on all major political events of the time. As a Constitution Drafting Committee comprising representatives of a few political parties and the king set out to write a democratic Constitution, Sadbhavana demanded elections to a CA. It reiterated the original Tarai claim for a federal province, arguing that power must move out from Kathmandu. It asked for affirmative action policies for Madhesis and other oppressed communities. These would be conventional wisdom a decade later, but were almost blasphemous then—the deeply entrenched hill-centric mindset saw these demands as 'anti-national'.

But Sadbhavana's fate was similar to the Nepal Tarai Congress in electoral politics. It won a few seats in the parliamentary polls of the 1990s, but could never build an organization and expand beyond a narrow upper-caste base of a few select districts.

It framed the Madhesi issue in terms of rights and justice, but could never link it to livelihoods and mobilize people. Madhesi voting patterns revealed that broader party affiliations (NC-UML) and narrow caste loyalties (forward-Yadav-backward-Dalit) trumped any broader allegiance to a 'Madhes' region, which remained a cultural rather than a political identity. The Sadbhavana itself got sucked into the power politics of Kathmandu, and Gajendra Narayan Singh became content with a ministership in the Cabinet.

But away from the capital's politics, tremendous changes were happening in the Tarai. It was a time when politics around ethnic and regional identities had become sharper, both globally and regionally. In Nepal, indigenous people, the Janjatis—with international support—were slowly consolidating themselves and openly challenging the hegemony of a few castes over the Nepali state.

Young people from the plains now visited Kathmandu, interacted with the state, and recognized that they were treated differently and derisively. Missed opportunities were linked to systemic discrimination—'How can I get a job, these pahadis will take it?' was a common refrain among Madhesis who had applied for positions in government. Language movements, aimed at protecting Maithili, Bhojpuri, Awadhi, Urdu and Hindi, had picked up. Madhesi students in Kathmandu slowly began asserting their distinct cultural practices by organizing events like the Saraswati Puja. The 'democracy' of the 1990s had led to greater awareness, but also to disillusionment and anger about the absence of greater access to opportunities, resources and representation. The Maoists, too, were slowly entering the Tarai and shaking up its political, social and economic structures.

~

Born in a rural family in the Saptari district, Upendra Yadav had gravitated towards Left politics during his student days in Biratnagar. He was a foot soldier in the battle for democracy in the 1980s, and became a part of the UML after the restoration of democracy. He contested and lost elections in the 1990s from the neighbouring Sunsari district, while continuing to teach mathematics in a high school in Biratnagar. Old timers remember seeing Yadav on a cycle, carrying a bag full of books around the Jatua village on Biratanagar's outskirts, a few miles from the border with Bihar's Jogbani town.

Yadav was slowly beginning to see the limits of the orthodox Left approach which focused on class—which was the orientation of his party bosses in UML in the capital. It was clear that people living in the plains—in Saptari where Yadav was born, in Sunsari from where he had contested elections, or Morang where he was working—suffered from an identity crisis and were not equal citizens. But he had problems with the sanitized, parliamentary approach adopted by the Sadbhavana, too. Yadav read up on the politics of recognition and began presenting papers about systemic discrimination against the Madhes in seminars around the mid-1990s. He set up the Madhesi Janadhikar Forum as a cross-party platform to discuss the 'Madhesi agenda' and build political awareness around it.

By the late 1990s, the Maoists had begun recognizing the potency of the ethnic issue as a tool for political mobilization. They hoped to convince the marginalized ethnicities that the source of their problems was the centralized, discriminatory state structure, controlled by a tiny ruling hill elite. The solution was federalism with autonomous homelands, and the Maoists would deliver it.

Ideologue Baburam Bhattarai was among the first to frame the issue of the Tarai in terms of 'internal colonialism', where the central state had extracted resources from the plains, and treated the people as second-class citizens without giving them adequate political power and rights. The Maoists had set up many ethnic fronts, including the Madhesi Liberation Front, which was initially headed by Jai Krishna Goit and Matrika Yadav—two leaders who would, for various reasons, go on to become fairly well known when the Madhes movement finally erupted.

Upendra Yadav felt that the problem of the Tarai fit into this framework, and ideologically veered towards the radical Left rebels. Yadav himself had always been ambiguous about his relationship with the Maoists. But there is little doubt—based on the accounts provided by Yadav's aides as well as the Maoists—that he had close links with the rebels. The state had begun its crackdown on the Maoists, and Yadav's Biratnagar home was raided a few times in the late 1990s.

The MJF got a boost when a NC leader, Jay Prakash Gupta, joined the platform. Originally from Yadav's home district of Saptari, Gupta started off as an NC student activist, worked as a journalist during the Panchayat days in papers sympathetic to democracy, and then became a close aide of G. P. Koirala—first serving as his press advisor when Koirala was prime minister and then, in a later Cabinet, as information minister. But they had a falling out. Gupta was subsequently implicated in a corruption scandal and imprisoned, where he wrote a memoir and began to think seriously about the question of the Tarai and about issues of identity. After his release, he became a full-time activist on Madhesi issues.

Yadav was arrested in 2003 in Delhi on charges of being a Maoist. He was mysteriously released though the other Maoist leaders, including Matrika Yadav, who had been picked up along with him were deported to Nepal. This was a turning point, for it marked Yadav's break from the Maoists on a bitter note and the beginning of his multi-layered relations with various state and non-state actors in India.

Yadav himself continued to live in India, and wrote and worked from there. Walking on Chennai's Marina beach, peanuts in hand, or sitting in a small apartment in central Patna, his central focus was on how to build the MJF. Gupta, too, spent time in Chennai to study the Sri Lankan Tamil question and draw parallels with the Madhes situation—the discrimination of a sizeable minority concentrated in a geographical area by a centralized state structure; exclusionary language policies; under-representation in state organs; existence of kinship networks across the border; the yearning for federalism and autonomy; and the possibility of a regional, or even a separatist struggle.

As Yadav was semi-underground in India, his close aides often took groups of young Madhesis to Forbesganj in the Araria district of Bihar or to Patna to meet the MJF chairman. Here, he would indoctrinate them on issues related to the Madhes and convince them to join the MJF. Yadav's old association with the Gopal Samiti, a Yadav organization, helped recruit caste members. Gupta, for his part, travelled within Nepal, expanding the organization and speaking at public forums on the Madhes.

Critics, especially other Tarai leaders, dismissed the MJF as an attempt of two failed mainstream politicians to remain relevant, one (Yadav) who could not even win an election and the other (Gupta) who had lost his patron in the NC. But both leaders wrote books together, outlining the history of the Tarai, claiming that the Madhesis had been discriminated against, documenting the implications of Mahendra's policies, and making a political case for federalism, autonomy and political representation. A MJF delegation visited Delhi and lobbied for political support for the Madhes soon after the 12-point Understanding was signed in November 2005. And while they participated in the Janandolan, their primary objective remained the achievement of rights for the Madhesis. Their political moment arrived in January 2007, with the interim Constitution, when Madhesi protestors finally took to the streets.

4

Ramesh Mahato was born into a poor peasant family in the Majhaura village of the Siraha district. The youngest of four brothers, Mahato was a student in Class 9, and had no political affiliation.

Upendra Yadav's arrest in Kathmandu, while protesting the Constitution's silence on federalism, had triggered a bidyarthi andolan, student unrest, in MJF-stronghold districts like Siraha. Mahato had joined his friends and elders to chant slogans, burn tyres, and block all vehicular movement on the East-West Highway.

The agitation had the usual ingredients of anger, energy and excitement, laced with the fear that the police would crack down on them. Their immediate demand was Upendra Yadav's release, but the movement would continue till the interim Constitution guaranteed federalism, increased electoral representation from the Tarai, and promised proportionate representation to Madhesis in all state organs.

For two days, reports of the Tarai bandh trickled into Kathmandu, but with little impact. The capital's residents were known to be indifferent to events outside the Ring Road, as long as their lives were not interrupted. Through the decade-long People's War, the only occasion when the citizens of Kathmandu became agitated was when the Maoists imposed a blockade and fuel supplies were halted, or when the conflict-displaced people from other parts of Nepal settled down in Kathmandu, crowding the city and causing traffic snarls and congestion. This time, things would be different—and Mahato was to be the unlikely catalyst of that change.

~

On 19 January, a Maoist team was travelling from eastern Nepal to Birgunj, a town in the central Tarai. Senior Maoist leaders were in a jeep while other Maoist activists had crowded into a couple of mini-buses. In Lahan, the team came across Ramesh Mahato and other protestors from the MJF who refused to allow them to proceed. They stopped their vehicles next to the town's petrol pump. A skirmish followed, with young men of both sides jostling each other. Suddenly, eyewitness accounts say, Siyaram Thakur, a Maoist, pulled out a gun and fired. The bullet struck Mahato on his chest.

Rajlal Yadav, who went on to become an elected Member of the Constituent Assembly from the area, and heads the Ramesh Mahato Academy, told me several years later that they took one look and knew that the young boy was dead. The Madhesi protestors were furious and beat up Thakur, before dragging him to the police station. They also burnt down the buses in which the Maoists were travelling, along with other vehicles parked on the Lahan road. They then carried his body in a procession and kept it at the town's main crossing.

Mahato's body remained at the Lahan crossing, with discussions raging among other protestors about how to do justice to Mahato's sacrifice and advance the andolan. The protestors eventually demanded that the town's crossing, Loktantrik Chowk, be renamed the Martyr Ramesh Chowk; the family be given 2.5 million Nepali rupees as compensation and that a relative be provided government employment; the home minister, Krishna Prasad Sitaula, resign with immediate effect; and the prime minister publicly apologize. Till then, Mahato's body would not be cremated. The students affiliated with MJF then took the body in a procession around town.

Word of Mahato's killing spread across Tarai districts. Informal Madhesi kinship and political networks sprang into action, with fury growing at the unfolding events. If the compact discs containing footage of the Nepalgunj riots of the previous month, the interim Constitution's discriminatory provisions, and Upendra Yadav's arrest had stoked Madhesi public opinion against the state and refreshed the memories of historic injustices, Mahato's killing gave the mood a distinct anti-Maoist flavour.

As the Maoists sensed the growing anger against them, instead of retreating and apologizing, they went on the offensive. A day after Mahato's killing, at 9 p.m. on 21 January, even as his friends, family and protestors waited with his body at the Lahan crossing, a mob of Maoists arrived on a dozen motorcycles, a jeep and two mini-trucks; they had sticks and began beating up the grieving protestors. Matrika Yadav himself led the crowd. The Maoists then grabbed Mahato's body and asked one of his brothers to come along. In a jeep, they took Mahato to a river bank some distance away and cremated his body. His brother lit the funeral pyre, and the Maoists then sent him off with 15,000 Nepali rupees.

The communists had made a fatal error of judgement. In a religious and conservative society that still abided by the norms of the Hindu caste system, even one's worst enemy was treated with respect in death.

~

The relationship between the Maoists and the Madhesi social groups had been complex. The rebels had entered the eastern plains late in the war, only after consolidating their base areas in the middle and far-western hills. The party had attracted some ideologues like Upendra Yadav, who agreed with the thesis of 'internal colonialism' of the Tarai. But the foot soldiers in the plains consisted of what the Marxists call the 'lumpen proletariat', who did not hesitate to loot, bully and kill in the name of revolution, thus alienating citizens.

The genuine revolutionary attempts by the Maoists—of seizing land and distributing it to the landless, of mobilizing Dalits to speak out against the upper castes—had won it supporters but also alienated several powerful sections. The upper castes and the middle classes of Madhes had always been 'democratic' (read supporters of the NC), and their contempt and opposition for communist politics had persisted despite its pro-Madhes rhetoric.

Maoist leaders of plains origin had gradually begun leaving the party for different reasons. Some accused it of being a 'pahadi' outfit, which was only using the Madhes for its selfish ends, and went on to form their own armed groups; Jai Krishna Goit and Nagendra Paswan, a.k.a. Jwala Singh, were the most prominent among them. Upendra Yadav himself had fallen out with the Maoists after his arrest and mysterious release in India. Some others quit because of the leadership style of the key Maoist Madhesi leader, Matrika Yadav. Yadav was lauded for his radicalism; he had painted Kathmandu red with the slogan—'Say with pride I am a Madhesi, not a traitor but a son of the soil.' But his arrogance alienated many of his colleagues. And even sympathizers who had given the Maoists the benefit of the doubt on the issue of federalism felt disappointed after their silence during the framing of the interim Constitution.

The turning point was Mahato's killing and the way the Maoist leadership projected the Madhes movement. Calling it a royalist, Hindu Right-wing conspiracy, the chairman of the Maoist party, Prachanda, floated the idea of sending the NA (the force the Maoists had fought a bitter war against till only six months before, and had treated as an enemy) and the party's PLA, jointly, to crack down on the protestors. Nothing could better illustrate how supposed liberators turn into oppressors. Within six months of becoming a part of mainstream politics, the Maoists had well and truly become a part of the establishment. By stripping the first martyr of the Madhes andolan of his right to a dignified death, the Maoists had unleashed the latent resentment which had been festering among residents of the Tarai for decades.

~

The Tarai began burning.

The Maoists' rivals on the ground—including NC activists—felt that this was the moment to 'finish off' the former rebels in the Tarai. They could not hide their glee when the Madhesi Street turned against the Maoists, with many even joining in the subsequent protests, chanting anti-Maoist slogans. But they misread the popular mood. The Maoists' actions may have been the trigger but, in the popular narrative, the battle was with the 'pahadi satta' and 'sarkar', the hill regime and government.

The NC-led political dispensation in Kathmandu reacted in the same manner that the royal regime had treated democratic protests only eight months earlier. They shot protestors in an attempt to scare the crowds away. Home Minister Sitaula was also the key negotiator in the peace process talks with the Maoists, and did not want to antagonize them by reaching out to their rivals in the Tarai. The state's attitude—Upendra Yadav was not released, local authorities did nothing when Ramesh Mahato was killed and his body taken away for cremation, political demands were ignored, and the policy of suppression was adopted—sparked further unrest.

As different chapters in *Madhes Bidrohko Nalibeli*, a compilation on those heady days of the movement edited by the researcher Bhaskar Gautam, documented, the movement picked up intensity from 21 January as the news of the martyrdom of Ramesh Mahato spread. In Lahan, in a coordinated attack on state institutions, protestors burnt down the buildings of the Nepal Food Corporation, the Agricultural Development Bank, the town municipality, the Internal Revenue, Area Postal and District Forest offices and the Road and Water Departments. In Siraha bazaar and Rajbiraj, the headquarters of the neighbouring Saptari district, effigies of Prachanda were torched. In the next few days, the villages of the Madhes woke up and thousands of people marched into key district towns.

The pattern repeated itself across the Tarai. People congregated at strategic locations, be it a highway crossing or district headquarters. They chanted slogans, attacked police personnel and government offices, replaced the words 'Nepal government' with 'Madhes government' on official signage boards, vandalized the statues of national figures of hill origin, including former monarchs and prime ministers. In places, when people of hill origin sought to defy the bandh or organized counter-protests, inter-community tensions grew and led to clashes. In Rautahat, Madhesi homes were set afire in pahadi-dominated areas near the highway; Madhesi protestors retaliated by torching pahadi homes in Madhesi-dominated villages. In Biratnagar, when transport workers of pahadi origin defied the bandh, clashes erupted between the groups. In a few areas, Maoists and Madhesi protestors clashed.

The police sought to impose order by imposing curfews, but they were defied. They fired bullets and several rounds of tear gas, but this resulted in casualties, including deaths. This provided more ammunition to the protestors, whose number swelled as more and more villages joined the movement. The cremation of each 'martyr' was attended by thousands. These killings also took on a communal colour since protestors blamed the 'pahadi police', in a reference to its unrepresentative character, for suppressing protests. The fact that those killed came from all communities in the Tarai—Hindu upper castes, Yadavs, Tharus, Muslims, people belonging to the Other Backward Classes, and Dalits—gave a sense of unprecedented unity to the people of the plains. Public pressure was such that Madhesi leaders belonging to ruling parties, including the NC, the UML, and even the Maoists, participated in the protests. It was no longer a political protest by MJF sympathizers, but a popular agitation spread across the Tarai.

The highway was blocked through this period, and so were supplies from the Tarai or India to Kathmandu. The capital was finally feeling the heat, as fuel and food shortages and spiralling prices began to hit residents. There was now increasing pressure on the government to reach out to the protestors, who had made it clear that they would not pull back till their minimal demands—an unequivocal commitment to federalism in the interim Constitution and an increase in electoral representation from the Tarai—were met. The UN Office of the High Commissioner for Human Rights (UN-OHCHR), which had been in Nepal since the royal autocracy in 2005, expressed concern about the police reaction. India—which did not engineer the Madhes movement, but was pleased when it started since it saw it as a way to weaken the Maoists—began quiet diplomacy to push Prime Minister Koirala to recognize the reality on the ground and give in to the demands of the Madhesis.

The pressure appeared to work and, on 31 January, Prime Minister Koirala addressed the nation. However, he neither recognized the struggle of the Madhesi people, nor did he utter a word about the loss of life in the Tarai or about police brutality. He was also silent on federalism and ended with a generic appeal for peace and calm.

The address boomeranged. Madhesis felt that the state had not only glossed over their demands, but also disrespected their martyrs. The MJF said that it would continue protests; NGOs, professional associations, government employee unions, and even business chambers of several Tarai districts expressed their solidarity. The anger had only increased. Women in Siraha took out 'broomstick' processions. A large rally was organized in Inaruwa, the headquarters of the Sunsari district. Clashes continued between police and protestors, and killings triggered ever-larger demonstrations. Madhesi journalists wore black arm bands to oppose the government. District units of the national parties pressed their leadership to make a categorical commitment, and concede to demands. The Maoists, too, engaged in that classic communist practice of 'self-criticism', and extended moral support to the Madhes movement. In Kathmandu, MPs from the Tarai, across party lines, pressed the prime minister to address the nation again.

A week later, on 7 February, Prime Minister G. P. Koirala appeared on television screens and could be heard on radio stations across the nation. This time, he seemed to have learnt a lesson. He began by expressing the government's 'commitment' to meet the 'legitimate demands' of the Madhes movement. He added that electoral constituencies would increase proportionately to the Madhes's population, and there would be a corresponding increase in seats under the proportional representation system. He also categorically mentioned that a federal system of governance would be created.

Koirala committed to amending the interim Constitution to include both these changes regarding the electoral system and federalism. Madhesis, Dalits, ethnic and indigenous groups, women, peasants and workers, and those from the backward classes and regions would be included in all state organs in proportion to their population. Citizenship certificates would be distributed—this was a long-standing demand of the Madhesis, who had been deliberately left stateless. In a departure from the previous address, attempting to strike an emotional chord with the protestors, he appreciated the contribution of the Madhes to the struggles for democracy and also paid tribute to those who had lost lives in the course of the movement.

~

The announcement was greeted with jubilation across the plains of Nepal. For the first time, population groups of the Tarai—Madhesis, Tharus, Muslims and others—had managed to exercise their democratic right of protest and win fundamental group and individual rights.

It was indeed a historic address, for the Nepali state was now locked into certain irreversible commitments—to reform the electoral system and enhance the political representation of groups who had so far been excluded, to guarantee their inclusion in state organs to which they barely had any access, to convert the unitary Kathmandu-centered state structure into a federal system, and to give a sense of ownership of the Nepali nation to marginalized groups.

Forty-five years after Mahendra Bir Bikram Shah Dev institutionalized an assimilative Nepali nationalism and a centralized state which sought to suppress diversity, the anonymous Ramesh Mahato participated in an agitation for multi-cultural nationalism and federalism. In his death, the sixteen-year-old boy defeated the political and ideological basis of the 240-year-old monarchy and the Nepali state.

A Year in the Plains

Janakpur was hot, congested, messy—and angry.

The poorly maintained road from Dhalkebar on the East-West Highway gave no inkling that one was approaching Nepal's iconic temple town, the cradle of Mithila civilization where, according to mythology, the Hindu god Ram wed Sita, daughter of king Janak. The ramshackle passenger bus shook every few seconds, and the driver often had to veer off the main road to avoid pot-holes.

After getting off at the bus stand, I took a rickshaw to Hotel Welcome through narrow alleys, avoiding honking vehicles, piles of garbage and pedestrians. The hotel was near Shiv Chowk. From the window of my room, I could see one road leading down to the Janakpur station, where Nepal's only railway line to Jainagar across the border in Bihar started, while another went up to Janaki Mandir.

I called up Rajeev Jha. An acquaintance had passed on his number, and had said that he was well connected. Rajeev had been alerted, and was expecting my call. He offered to come over to my hotel.

Later that afternoon, Rajeev said that he was a samajik karyakarta, a social activist, who had set up the Tarai Samrakshan Samiti during the movement. 'Goondas had started collecting funds in the name of the Madhes mudda, and used the money to drink. I thought it was important to systematize it and worked with the Janakpur chamber of commerce. We opened a bank account, I raised donations, and we used it for the treatment of the injured.' He also ran an NGO, Grassroots Nepal.

It was a few months after the movement. We were speaking in Maithili, and I asked him about the events in January. 'First, you should understand that MJF got a lottery. They neither planned the andolan nor expected it. Once it happened, they became the face.

But Upendra Yadav is too arrogant and will not be able to take advantage of it.' But the MJF, he grudgingly admitted, had given Madhesis the dignity that Sadbhavana had failed to in the past.

His fury was reserved for the national parties. The Maoists were full of 'anti-social' elements and only those who had nowhere else to go had joined. People had understood that the NC and the UML had taken them for a ride. In Dhanusha 2 constituency, which has only 12 per cent pahadis, Jha asked, why did NC's Lila Koirala always win? In the neighbouring Mahottarai constituency, with only 3 per cent pahadis, why did Sharad Singh Bhandari—a former royal minister turned NC leader—get elected? 'We have always got fooled, but now people are waking up and have left these parties,' he fumed, raising his voice for the first time in the conversation. The only hope for the Tarai was for the Madhesi leaders, across party lines, to join together and form a Madhesi front. 'We Madhesis need to be bold now. It is time to be bold.'

Rajeev's excitement quickened when speaking of the militants. 'Prashantji, Nepal sarkar would have suppressed the entire issue but for armed groups. They have deployed the Armed Police Force in eighteen Tarai districts. The armed militants played a key role and made many sacrifices during the andolan. Many of them were killed.'

The phenomenon of sashastra samuha, armed groups, had gained momentum after the movement, with regular reports of bombings, abductions, extortion, killings and threats to people of hill origin. Many former Maoist activists had shifted loyalties to such groups.

Like others, Rajeev mentioned the Janatantrik Tarai Mukti Morcha (JTMM) faction led by Jai Krishna Goit and Jwala Singh. 'Goitji is systematic, he thinks and plans. But Jwala is fast, he believes in karabahi.' I asked him about the perception that many in these groups were criminals. 'Arre, goonda sab ta rakhe ke pade che, Sir [They have to keep goons, Sir]. Who will pick up the gun and join otherwise? Will our shahari buddhijibis [urban intellectuals], fight for a single day for the cause?'

What did he think of their demands? 'Both Goit and Jwala say they are not Nepalis, that we are from Madhyadesh and had our own Tirhutiya Army. It was, let me think, almost 15,000 strong and we had even defeated Prithvi Narayan Shah.' Stumbling in his narration, Rajeev said that Goit would be better equipped to tell me the history. 'But I know we were cheated, Madhes is a colony of the pahadi rulers.'

A few days earlier, Jwala Singh had issued a circular warning all pahadi government officers in the Tarai to leave. Rajeev supported the move. 'Ninety per cent of the Nepal sarkar even in Madhes is full of pahadis. They are all rich feudals. Corrupt to the core. Even the pahadi driver of the pahadi district officer has bought a house in Janaki Chowk. When Madhesis go to a sarkari karyalaya [government office], Nepali-speaking officers can't understand our language.'

So was independence, as the armed groups had been demanding, the solution? He replied, 'If we don't ask for independence, we won't even get an autonomous state. Pahadis will divide Madhes into five states. And if that happens, then Madhesis will only rule in Mithila. There will be pahadi chief ministers everywhere else. They have migrated everywhere.' Rajeev then became quiet and looked thoughtful for a moment. Sipping tea, he said, 'So they will never give us one Madhes, we will never give it up. There is no option but to fight.'

The coherent defence of armed groups, and the open admiration for their actions, was striking. Rajeev seemed more than just a distant observer; he spoke like a passionate insider. I asked him, a bit hesitantly, whether he could get me in touch with either Goit or Jwala Singh. He nodded, 'Jwala Singh knows me well. I will call him. Wait.' He immediately fished out his cellphone and dialled a number. 'All these people are in Bihar you know.' After speaking to someone on the other end, he said that he would let me know by the evening if something could be worked out. And if it did, he would be happy to take me across the next day.

~

That evening, I went out to try out the town's famous fish delicacies at Navrang, a roadside restaurant next to the hotel I was staying in. Half a dozen motorcycles were parked outside, and all the tables were occupied. Navrang was loud and raucous, with customers screaming across to the waiters to quickly complete their orders. Tuborg beer and Royal Stag whisky, and the fried fish, seemed to be the favourites. A waiter said that the place was as crowded every day. 'Sir, Janakpur me paisa chhe. Qatar ke paisa. [Sir, Janakpur has money. Money from Qatar.]'

Like the rest of the country, remittances drove the consumption boom here. Workers from Dhanusha, Mahottari, Siraha and Saptari, four Tarai districts, made up almost one-fourth of Nepal's migrant workers. Some of these workers were small-sized landowners, landless labourers, construction contractors, taxi-drivers and rickshaw-pullers. They belonged to a wide spectrum of castes: Brahmins, Yadavs, Telis, Dalits. Some were illiterate, others had failed their School Leaving Certificate examinations, and still others were college graduates. A young brother who did not get along with his elders; a son for whom there was no land to be inherited; a father who tried, unsuccessfully, to get a job in the few factories that operated a few hours away near Birgunj; a middle-aged man who had failed to get a government job because an unwritten code had excluded Madhesis from the mainstream—everyone, across class, caste and education divides, left or was preparing to leave.

They took loans, sometimes at as high a rate of interest as 60 per cent a year from local moneylenders, to pay manpower agencies for a passport, a visa, a ticket and a job. And then they went to Qatar, where 400,000 Nepalis now outnumbered the Qataris themselves. They went to Saudi Arabia, where another 400,000 fellow citizens worked. They went to Malaysia. Many more crossed the open border. They went to Punjab during the harvest season, they went to Delhi and Mumbai and became the anonymous workers who construct these mega cities, they went to Assam, they became domestic help and guards in townships across North India. But unlike hill Nepalis, who were stereotyped as Bahadurs or Gurkhas, Nepali workers from the plains remained indistinguishable and were lumped with the Biharis.

They sent money home, and Western Union Money Transfer became the country's lifeline. More than 20 million rupees— 2 crore in Nepali currency—came to banks in Janakpur from these workers every day. And this wasn't unique to the town. A money-transfer agent in Mirchaiya bazaar, on the highway in neighbouring Siraha district, told me that they received 10 million Nepali rupees daily, and he catered only to ten to fifteen villages in the vicinity. In one generation, remittance had become an integral element of the Tarai's political economy, as central as agriculture had been for centuries. Families lived on it. Debts were slowly repaid. Kids went to private schools. In a sign of the psychological attachment to land and how it accorded dignity and status in everyday life, everyone's big plans hovered around how to buy more property. The landless Dalits, for the first time in their lives, thought of purchasing a gharedi, a small plot enough to build a hut, in their village. Those from the villages wanted to buy land in the nearest bazaar, those from the bazaar wanted to buy land and build a house in Janakpur. Other routes to upward mobility were also adopted. Muslim workers helped build madrasas and mosques; Hindus spent more on weddings and funerals.

It exposed many to the best and worst of the capitalist world and gave them confidence to speak up. Once on a Kathmandu-Dhaka-Kuala Lumpur flight, I found myself sitting next to Lakhandar Mukhiya. As the meal was served, he stared blankly. After seeing me peel the foil off the food tray and take a fork out, he cautiously did the same. He then blurted out, 'My first time. But can I use my hands?' He spoke only Maithili, he did not know which city he would land up in, or what work he was supposed to do. All he had was a jacket with the name of a manpower agency emblazoned on it. 'Someone from the company will be there... But I am scared.'

During my return flight a few days later, I was sitting next to Mohammad Sadiq, a worker from Saptari. When I asked whether international travel made him nervous, he laughed, 'Earlier, I was scared of roads, airports, planes, factories. I used to feel if I made a mistake, people would abuse me. But now I have done Doha twice, and Malaysia once, Sir. I walk with my head held high. If I have to fill a form, I write my name somehow and leave the rest of the form blank. Then you deal with the person at the counter.' He had picked up a few words of English. 'People are the same everywhere Sir. They will help.' And what did he think of Nepal after working abroad? 'Bekar jagah chhe, Sir. [It is a useless place, Sir.] Even Kathmandu is backward. Till there are factories, a place is useless. Nepal needs factories, more factories.'

Migration was not about negotiating airport terminals or travel etiquette. It was about gaining the confidence to express a view; to navigate in an unfamiliar setting; diagnose, whether correctly or not, the flaws of one's own society. Many Lakhandar Mukhiyas were turning into Mohammad Sadiqs.

But things weren't altogether harmonious. Hundreds of coffins returned home every year, with workers dying in foreign lands. Their destinations, particularly in the Gulf and Southeast Asia, were ruled by oppressive regimes, hospitable to capital but hostile to labour. The quid pro quo was simple—the mazdoors would receive their wages, but would have no rights. If they dared protest, they would be expelled from the country or framed in false cases. Waging a revolution had further pauperized the poor in Nepal and had left them with no choice but to surrender abroad and become a part of the new trans-national proletariat.

Back home, family disputes, especially between the wife and the father of the worker, often broke out over who had the first right over the money. Marriages were breaking down, a phenomenon which, so far, had been unheard of in the conservative and patriarchal Madhesi society. Many workers returned home in search of opportunities but when they could find nothing, fell into depression. Once the money ran out, they went through the same cycle of taking loans, paying manpower agents, and flying out. As Rajeev, whose brother was in Saudi, too, had put it to me that afternoon, 'You either pick up a passport here or pick up a gun. What else is there to do?'

It was predominantly men in-between jobs, and the brothers and sons of workers who had sent money from the Gulf who were at Navrang that evening. The Qatari emir's dreams of hosting a football World Cup, a Malaysian oligarch's plans to expand his factory, and the Punjabi farmer's bumper harvests helped pay the bills for the beer and fish at Navrang, and sustained the economy of Janakpur.

I had just finished my drink when Rajeev called. 'JS will meet us tomorrow. We should leave by ten in the morning. I will come to your hotel.' I returned to my room, read a bit, and dozed off.

1

Rajeev picked me up on his bike and said that we had to go to Darbhanga.

I was excited. My grandfather had become a doctor in Darbhanga in the late 1940s. It was here that he had become friends with Tulsi Giri, a quirk of fate which would make him migrate to Nepal and make us Nepali citizens. Rajeev said that he, too, like many Madhesis, had finished his higher education in the city. Families living in the Tarai usually took their ill to Darbhanga, north Bihar's biggest centre for medical care. Every other household in Nepal's Mithila belt had a relative or two in the greater Darbhanga-Madhubani region. Maithili language activists organized conferences to emphasize their shared heritage here, and it was home to a strong movement for a separate Mithila state in India.

We set off, but not before buying a pack of Surya cigarettes. A product of one of the royal family's multiple business ventures, this was Jwala Singh's favourite brand. Rajeev drove over rocky rural roads—the route was shorter, he said. We stopped over at his village right on the border and then drove across fields to enter Bihar. There was no boundary, no check, and crossing the international border was like taking a stroll in a park. Few things better defined the unique relationship between Nepal and India than this open border.

The only cross-border rail-link, the Janakpur-Jainagar train, crawled on a track parallel to the road, packed with passengers. On the way, we picked up an Indian SIM card. I asked Rajeev how members of these armed groups lived in India. Did they carry weapons? Did India support them? 'All of us have relatives here. We know people, we can pass off as Biharis. Society supports them here, there is support for Madhesis. People on the border know that Madhesis are exploited in Nepal. I don't know about the government,' he screamed above the noise of the bike engine. 'Some police officers and district administrators may know about them. But militants don't carry weapons openly here, they don't commit any crime this side of the border. As long as they are quiet, they are not disturbed.'

Jwala Singh had asked Rajeev to call after entering Darbhanga.

He did so, and was given the name of a hotel. We crossed the city and checked in. But Singh called once more and asked us to shift somewhere else. Rajeev turned to me and said, 'He thinks there could be informers here. What should we do?' We were both tired and a bit irritated by this game of hide-and-seek; the possibility of a direct threat to Singh in this crowded city seemed farfetched. But we played along. Singh told Rajeev the name of the new hotel; we bought half a bottle of whisky and waited there.

Nagendra Paswan had been a journalist in Siraha. He, in fact, had even served as an office bearer for the district unit of the Federation of Nepalese Journalists, an umbrella organization of media personnel. He joined the Maoists sometime during the civil war and adopted a new name, Jwala Singh. But when Jai Krishna Goit, the tallest Maoist Madhesi leader, walked out of the party, Singh followed. Goit had several complaints against the Maoist leadership. He wrote about how the revolutionary party, too, practised discrimination, and installed pahadi party secretaries in Madhes districts; Goit was opposed to the slicing off of a Tharu autonomous republic in the western plains from the Tarai province as proposed by the Maoists. But the actual trigger was more personal. The Maoists had replaced Goit with Matrika Yadav—the younger leader whose actions had sparked the Madhes andolan in Lahan in January—as the head of their Madhesi front. Goit walked out and sounded a call for independence. The JTMM was born.

Singh, the grapevine had it, had different motivations. Under him, the Maoists had captured a plot of land from an absentee landlord in Mirchaiya in the name of 'revolutionary land reform' to distribute to landless tillers. But he had begun treating it as personal property. When Maoists, and later Goit, asked him to surrender it, Paswan rebelled and set up the Janatantrik Tarai Mukti Morcha (Jwala Singh). What struck me, however, was that in a caste-conscious and hierarchical society like the Madhes, a Dalit had first become a journalist and was now leading a militant group which sought to liberate all of the Madhes. In less than a year, Jwala Singh's group was rumoured to have become stronger than the parent outfit, and, as Rajeev had put it the previous day, undertaken more karabahi, action, a euphemism for killings and abductions.

At around 9 p.m., as we wondered whether he would show up at all, Jwala Singh walked into the room with two aides. He was tall and wore spectacles. In a blue shirt and grey trousers, Singh could have passed off as any other middle-class professional. He sat on the bed, chatted with Rajeev for a bit, and said that he had to ask us to change the hotel since he had reliable information that Nepali spies and the Bihar police were now working together. He then looked at me and asked what I wanted.

I returned the question. 'What do *you* want?'

'An independent Madhes,' he replied curtly. And why could the Nepali state itself not be reformed? Singh recited what had become a staple text for all activists in the Tarai—of how they had suffered under a centralized, monarchical setup for 240 years, how Mahendra had treated them as Indians, how their land and resources had been taken away, how Kathmandu would never accept federalism, and how it was time to break the shackles.

I asked him whether this was indeed their bottom-line. 'Since you have come with Rajeev, and since you are a Madhesi, I will be honest. Our minimum demand is one Madhes prant, nothing less.' But, he continued, 'You must know that Tarai was also independent. We were cheated by the Shahs, then by the British, and then by the Indians. So asking for atma-nirnaya [self-determination] is correct.' Immediately, though, his movement was focused on creating a 'Madhes for Madhesis'. Throw out the pahadis, appoint Madhesi officers, he said.

But how would he achieve his goal of swatantrata? He was living in Bihar, his activists in the Tarai were scattered and were seen more as criminals than revolutionaries, and the armed groups were themselves divided.

Singh said sharply, 'What do you mean? I can't do anything, haan? Let me tell you. I told Upendra Yadav to burn the interim Constitution, and he did it. If he had continued the movement instead of giving up after Koirala's second address, Madhes would have become independent. But he failed. He only wants to become a minister. Prachanda called me up to reunify with the Maoists. I told him to support an independent Tarai first, to have 50 per cent

Madhesis in his own party. And you think I can't do anything.' He was visibly angry. 'Even the UN people are in touch with me. That shows they recognize me as a politician, not a criminal. All the money that is raised is for the Madhes kranti. I don't keep any of it.' He then softened, and said that he needed people like us to support him. 'Ham sab ta lathaith chhi, dimaag ta aahan sab jena Brahmin ke paas chhe. [We are just strongmen. Brahmins like you have the brains.] I need a legal face. Join the movement.' I laughed off the offer, but realized that by referring to my caste, he was highlighting his Dalit identity as well. Continuing the thread, he added, 'Look, the problem in Madhes is Yadav-vaad. Upendra's party, Goitji, all of them believe in jativaad. It is time for us to set up a non-Yadav force. That is why I left Goitji also.'

Pointing to one of the two young men who had come with him, he said, 'He is Toofan Singh. He is a Dalit. And both of you are Brahmins. We need to do what Mayawati did.' The firebrand Indian Dalit leader had just won the assembly elections in Uttar Pradesh, and her key strategy had been to carve out an alliance of the upper castes and Dalits, along with sections of the backward classes and Muslims, to undercut the Yadav base of her rival, Mulayam Singh Yadav. Singh wanted to replicate that. The direct contradiction in land relations in the Tarai was not between 'forwards' and Dalits, but between intermediate castes and Dalits. But it was not going to be easy, for that locked these caste groups into a patron-client relationship. The Brahmins, Rajputs, Kayasthas and Bhumihars were numerically insignificant and, as the democratic space opened up, their importance would only diminish.

His candour about caste gave me the opening I was looking for. There were persistent rumours that Ram Vilas Paswan, Bihar's Dalit leader and a former union minister, was supporting Jwala Singh. Was that true? 'No I have never met him.' Did he have support from anyone else in India? Singh retorted, 'If I had support, you think I would travel on a stolen bike, buses and trains. I don't have money on my mobile. I am always running, on the move to escape being caught. You saw that today also.'

Singh then went to the bathroom. Taking the opportunity,

Rajeev whispered that we should perhaps offer him a drink. When Singh came back, I asked, cautiously, whether he would like some whisky. 'No, no bhai. I don't drink. Drinking is the enemy of revolution.' But he agreed to join us for dinner at the dhaba below the hotel. The conversation was a lot more informal over the meal, but Singh's attention was on Rajeev. He asked, 'When will you join us?' Rajeev said, 'Arre Sir, I am with you only. I am supporting you from outside.' No, Singh insisted, this is not joining the sangathan. 'Become a part of the structure, nothing will be achieved with NGO work.'

Turning to me, he said, 'What do you think, shouldn't he join?' I kept quiet and waited for Rajeev to answer. 'Sir, give me time. I will think about it,' he said. There isn't time, Singh countered, we have to start the next phase of the offensive soon. 'There will be no elections for a Constituent Assembly. Madhes will be betrayed again. We have to prepare for both armed and street movement. It is time to sacrifice.' Singh's sidekicks joined in to encourage Rajeev. We soon wrapped up, I paid the bill and Jwala went off on a bike.

We returned to the room and, finally, cracked open the bottle of whisky. I asked Rajeev if he planned to join the armed movement. 'Ham dharma sankat ma chhiye. [I am in a dilemma.] I have two children, a wife, parents, many brothers. Who will take care of them? But I also know that till we raise the banner of revolt, without violence, the pahadi satta will give nothing, Madhes will gain nothing.' It was only a matter of time, I thought then, before he chose the gun over the passport.

The next morning, we drove back quietly, lost in our thoughts— on the rough border roads yet to be upgraded by Nitish Kumar's state government, crossing Benipatti, Jainagar, Unnau and Jathi, and, this time, through an official border checkpost marking the end of one nation state and the beginning of the other—into Nepal.

2

Upendra Yadav had disappeared.

In the summer of 2007, the man who had triggered the biggest mass mobilization on the issue of identity in Nepali history by setting fire to the interim Constitution, who had created the MJF, which was now synonymous with the Madhes issue, had gone semi-underground.

And the reason was to be found in the rice fields of Gaur, at the southernmost edge of Rautahat district touching the border with India.

On 21 March, the MJF had called for a mass meeting in Gaur. The Maoists, who remained bitter for having been projected as the villain in the Madhes andolan, even though they had first spoken of autonomy and self-determination for the Tarai, had called for a separate gathering at the same venue, on the same day. Clashes between the Maoists and the MJF had taken place in the weeks after the Madhes movement in several locations in the Tarai. Maoists had beaten up MJF activists on a few of these occasions, and had disrupted their rallies. The Gaur meeting was, to those who were aware of it, a potential flashpoint.

This time, as a report by the UN-OHCHR subsequently documented, MJF workers, almost all of whom were Madhesis from neighbouring villages and districts, had come prepared with sharp bamboo sticks. They numbered in the thousands. Hundreds of Maoists, the report added, were armed with 'slingshots, one fire arm, socket bombs, and detonation equipment'. Many of them were pahadis.

In the afternoon, ten to fifteen MJF supporters, disobeying the command of their leaders, vandalized the stage where the Maoists were holding their gathering. The Maoists reciprocated and attacked the MJF corner of the field. In the ensuing chaos, shots were fired— by the Maoists, by the MJF, and by the local police who were trying to restore order. MJF activists, who had retreated when the Maoists attacked, now returned. And, with their decisive numerical advantage, the MJF activists launched a ferocious attack on the former insurgents.

In the next two hours, twenty-seven individuals associated with the Maoist party, including four women and a seventeen-year-old girl, were killed. They died in the rice fields of Gaur, and in the narrow alleyways of the town. One person, according to the UN report, was killed just outside the town's police headquarters with over thirty cops watching. Fifteen Maoists were killed in neighbouring villages. And almost all of them died, according to the forensic reports, from blows to the head.

The Gaur massacre threatened to destroy the peace agreement barely four months after it had been signed. It had been less than a year since the Maoists had emerged over ground. Through the period, Maoist leaders had been concerned about the security of their workers. They had sought guarantees that they would not be physically attacked, that the state would protect them after they had deposited their weapons in UN-monitored containers in cantonments. The tensions between the Maoists and the Madhesi forces had grown during and after the Madhes andolan. But few episodes, even during the war, came close to the brutality and ruthlessness of what happened in Gaur.

The Maoists were to blame for organizing a rally in the same venue as the MJF. But their restraint after the incident marked political maturity, and revealed the tight command structure that still prevailed in the party. The leadership controlled the anger of the cadre; there were no retaliations and the Maoists recommitted themselves to the peace process. Instead, the Maoists used the incident to reinforce their claims that the Madhes movement was being engineered by Right-wing elements, by the 'Palace and the Hindu Right', which wanted to destroy the peace process.

The MJF's reaction was mixed. Officially, they took no responsibility for the incident. They accused the Maoists of provocation, and claimed that criminals from 'across the border' had engineered the incident. But privately, the mood in Madhesi political circles was triumphant. A few months after the incident, a Madhesi activist in Gaur took me across the field where the massacre happened, and then walked me all the way through the alleys, the municipality, and across a bridge to some of the neighbouring villages where the killings had taken place. He said proudly, 'These Maoists had caused aatank [terror]. We had to teach them a lesson.'

The incident made Upendra Yadav a hero among the anti-Maoist segments of Madhesi society, and helped expand his base. He was seen as the only one capable of standing up to the former rebels. But it eroded his credibility in Kathmandu politics, his commitment to non-violence, democracy and the larger peace process came under doubt, and his association with the Palace became a matter of speculation.

Yadav was reported to have crossed over to Bihar, and subsequently moved to Delhi. Sources in Delhi later told me that he had reached out to Indian officials through common political friends, reactivated the contacts he had built up in the intelligence establishment of India, and touched base with the BJP leaders who had helped get him off the hook when he had been arrested in 2002. He, according to leaders who had introduced him to officials in Delhi, sought Indian assistance for a legitimate 'safe-landing' in national politics.

~

But Yadav used to make quiet trips to the Tarai. I had been in touch with the MJF's unofficial legal advisor in Kathmandu, Awadesh Singh, and he had promised to arrange a meeting. After several failed attempts—which included spending nights waiting for him in Tarai towns only to be told he could not make it, or getting stuck in the Tarai's notoriously frequent highway bandhs and missing scheduled meetings—MJF leaders called me over to Birgunj.

At a dharamshala in the city, I met two of Yadav's close aides, Jitendra Sonar and B. P. Yadav. Like all other activists, they narrated to me the '240-year-old history of discrimination of Madhesis', and how the time had come for a revolt. I was more interested in knowing how the Madhesi leadership planned to capitalize on their successful movement. Yadav, it was generally felt, had displayed poor political judgement. He had revived the movement ten days after the demands had been met by Prime Minister Koirala's second address; predictably, it had failed. He had made the resignation of the home minister a non-negotiable demand, frittering away the chance to strike a deal with the government. And the MJF was still not a political party, and whether it would contest elections was unclear.

A little later, when I met Yadav in a house next to the Birgunj-Raxaul border checkpost, he seemed well aware of the challenges facing him. 'The key now is institutionalizing the achievements of the movement. Conflict management needs to happen through dialogue.' Reflecting on the current moment, he said, 'The old system has gone and the new system is not there anymore. The constitutional monarchy is about to go, but has still not given up. The federal republic is not yet established. That is why there is uncertainty, and politics has not crystallized.'

How did he view the country's situation? 'Dalits, Madhesis and Janjatis are two-thirds of this country. Madhes andolan was a historic necessity, a response to discrimination. The administrative system is anti-Madhesi, there is discrimination in resources, and there is no presence in decision-making processes. That is the problem.' And his prescriptions: federalism and autonomy— 'Without autonomy, it is like a skeleton'—and proportional representation in resource allocation, administration and politics— 'An inclusive PR electoral system is far better than direct elections'.

Yadav then spoke about the challenge of converting the MJF into a party, building an organization since 'no pahadi party could address the needs of Madhesi people'. He claimed that elections to a CA were desirable, but impossible unless the Madhesi agenda was addressed. He reiterated the point about the continued discriminatory nature of the state. Yadav was ambivalent about violence, and linked it to the 'structural violence' of the state. Circumspect about the Gaur incident, he blamed it on a conspiracy and tried to shift the blame on to others. And meaningfully, he reached out to the pahadis of the region, denying this was a 'communal agitation' at all. 'They have wrong information. We are also fighting in the national interest, to make Nepal stronger.'

In contrast to his image in the Kathmandu media, Yadav came across as a sharp political thinker. His strategic goal for the Madhes was clear. But he had either not been able to formulate clear tactics about how to achieve it, or was reluctant to share it with me at that point in time. Yadav's emphasis on the shared history of discrimination with other marginalized communities showed that like the Maoists, he realized the need for a broader alliance. Even as Jwala Singh was drawing up plans to impose the politics of identity chauvinism, the stocky schoolteacher-turned-Madhesi-messiah had realized the need to reach out to the pahadis, who comprised one-third of the population of the Tarai, and make them feel secure.

But if there was one element that stood out—despite his long and complicated political history, his widely criticized errors in political judgement, and the post-Gaur context where he was desperately short of political credibility—it was Yadav's confidence in the future. 'Young Madhesis have finally risen up. There is awareness everywhere. People in villages know the intricacies of politics. This generation will not give up the struggle for pahichan and pratinidhitva [identity and representation]. They came on to the streets in January and they will return again.'

3

Travelling on the East-West Highway, we started from Biratnagar; rushed through the rapidly mushrooming town of Itahari, home to migrants of all hues, returnees from foreign armies, and the point of diversion for the town of Dharan and the eastern hill districts; got caught in a traffic snarl in Inaruwa; drove past the Kosi River, the source of livelihood and sorrow for communities in both the Tarai and Bihar; across the Kosi barrage on the Indo-Nepal border, where a breach was to result in devastating floods in 2008, veered back to the highway overlooking fertile green fields; and approached Bharda in the Saptari district. A narrow road off the highway led to a cluster of villages.

My travelling companion, Tula Narayan Sah, was born in 1971 in one of these villages, Goithi.

Tula had written some sharp opinion pieces in the Nepali press after the Madhes movement, and I had met him briefly in the capital. Sometime later, we bumped into each other at a seminar in Biratnagar, and decided to take the bus together to Lahan for a meeting of Madhesi journalists. During the journey, as we went past places which marked his childhood, Tula began telling me about his life. It turned out to be a story which captured the multi-layered changes that had occurred in the Tarai in the last five decades, and chronicled the emergence of the generation on which Upendra Yadav had pinned his hopes.

Tula's grandfather was 'very poor', but hardworking. He practised the traditional family occupation of trade in mustard oil—sourcing oil from the hills and taking it across the border to India. The business flourished and the family managed to accumulate property. 'He had nothing at ten. But when he died at sixty-two, he had twenty-five bighas,' Tula said with a tinge of pride. Tula's father inherited six of those bighas of land. One bigha is roughly equivalent to 6,700 square metres.

To understand the 'geopolitics' of the districts that we had just crossed, and his own village, Tula said, it was important to realize the enormous significance of the Kosi barrage. 'The Indians built the barrage in the 1950s and 60s, and everyone's lives changed.' I was vaguely familiar with the Kosi story. My grandfather, who had set up Nepal's first private sector construction company, had worked on the construction of the embankment in eastern Kosi and, later, on the Western Kosi canal. Tula continued, 'There were big companies, and then there were many petty thekedars who emerged in Tarai. Among them was Nunu Jha. He used to get boulders from the pahad and supply it for barrage construction. There were others too, Krishna Deo Jha, Devendra Jha, Bachha Jha. They all rose together, and the entire Bharda belt was ruled by Brahmins.'

But inevitably, Tula added, there was a conflict among them and the 'big men' carved out their respective spheres of influence, 'like the big parties divide the pie now'. Goithi, which was then in Madhuapur Village Development Committee (VDC), fell under Nunu Jha. 'All the Musahars used to attend to him. He extorted at will, he and his people came and took away the field produce. Anyone with property had to be his chela. We used to do darshan of Nunu Jha, and bow to Jagdish Jha, who was anchaladish [zonal commissioner]. Both knew the king.' During the Panchayat system, the commissioners for Nepal's fourteen zones were all-powerful and, deriving authority straight from the royal durbar, ran their administrative units with fierce control.

Tula continued, 'My father had six bighas and so he had a

compulsion to do hajiri at Nunu's darbar. We didn't have to pay money. But Nunu's people used to come and harass. They said that maalik has asked for two kilos of this or that. That kind of exploitation happened. So my father joined Nunu's camp to get the harassment stopped. He later became a ward member.'

And like now, Tula said, politicians were unemployed even then. 'Their character has remained the same. Netas roamed around the villages, visited houses. We had to serve chai, nashta and beedi. Then they did panchayatis and resolved disputes, many of which they had created in the first place.' Reflecting for a moment, Tula said, 'See, the reasons for joining politics remain the same also. My father joined Nunu to protect his property. Many people are now joining armed groups for protection from other armed groups.'

Trikaul VDC was next to Goithi, and had become well known in recent years as the home of Jai Krishna Goit, the radical secessionist leader. 'If we were under Nunu, Trikaul was under Krishna Deo Jha. There were many Yadavs in the village, but Jha's men did not allow Yadavs to speak at all and harassed them a lot.'

According to Tula, Goit, a Yadav himself, had just graduated from a college in nearby Birpur, a town in Bihar. He was furious at the harassment. The Brahmin lords of the area had the direct support of the anchaladish and the Panchayat system, the NC was seen as 'soft-liner', and Goit was thus attracted to the radical communists. 'He joined Left politics, and participated in movements with the slogan, "Jamindaar ka moochh ukhado".' The phrase means, literally, 'Pluck out the landlord's moustache', which serves as a metaphor to strip the exploiter of his pride.

Tula grew up in this political milieu and walked to school a few miles away in the neighbouring Diman village. One day, when he was eight, there was a hartal in school. A large procession walked past him, with people chanting the slogan: 'Bahudal jindabad! [Long live the multiparty system!]'. Along with other students, he joined the rally before a relative spotted him and sent him home.

Zulfiqar Ali Bhutto's hanging in Pakistan had sparked student unrest in Kathmandu and, using the moment, the banned political parties, particularly the NC, had demanded the restoration of democracy. King Birendra agreed to hold a referendum to allow the people to choose between a reformed Panchayat system and multiparty democracy. In a vote widely suspected to have been rigged, the establishment won and democracy lost. But the political space had opened up, and Tula had, unknowingly, participated in a rally of political rebels even as his father's fate was now tied with that of Nunu Jha, who derived his power from the Panchayat system.

But things were changing. Goithi had become a separate VDC, and political expenses had begun to pinch Tula's father who had remained a ward member. 'People came and ate at our home,' Tula recalled. 'Nunu had many lathaits [strongmen] and, during elections, we were expected to feed them. There was no time to till the fields.' In the 1980s, other social groups, too, had begun asserting themselves and, in western Saptari, some Yadav families had now replicated what the Jhas had done in the Bharda belt. This created a new dynamic. 'The main job of the ward member was to sit in panchayats and resolve disputes. Earlier, no one questioned the judgement of Nunu Jha's people. But now, when you took a side, others became resentful. They sometimes destroyed your crops. Slowly, as the Yadavs became strong, Nunu Jha's protection diluted. My father felt he was unnecessarily getting into local conflicts, and got out of the Panchayat.'

~

Tula struggled in school.

'I am telling you Prashantji, for years and years, I went to class, sat there, and did not understand a single word.' But the impetus to continue came from two sources. Tula's maternal uncle had gone on to finish his postgraduate studies—'he had mugged up the entire advanced law dictionary'—and his mother was keen that he study. Tula's father was inspired by another man in the village who used to make his son study for six hours a day, and gifted dhoti-kurtas to his schoolteachers to take special care of his child. 'We are a business community, so the literacy rate is low. My father's persistence—he woke us up every morning at 4 to study—was rare,' Tula recollected.

The problem was that the medium of instruction in school was Nepali, while Tula, like others in his village, had only ever spoken in Maithili at home and had only a nodding familiarity with Hindi. 'Our teacher, a Thakur, was from Jhanjarpur in Bihar, and realized the standard of his students. So then he taught Maths also in Maithili. Out of thirty people in class, ten took the Class 10 School Leaving Certificate exam. Only four passed, and I got the lowest among them, 41 per cent. Third division, but I at least passed.'

After 'matriculation exams', Tarai students used to attend colleges in Darbhanga, Madhubani, Madhepura and Birpur in Bihar. 'It was easy to cheat there and get high marks or buy fake certificates. They finished intermediate there and returned with high marks to apply to the Indian embassy in Kathmandu to send them back to good Indian institutes with scholarships for graduate studies.'

Tula did not want to do that and decided to stick to the Nepali education system, which was, as he expressed it, 'tighter'. He applied to study science in the Janakpur campus, his first preference, and the Siraha campus as a back-up but, with a third division, failed to gain admission into either. Dejected and lost, his first time in a bazaar, he stood outside the Siraha campus between 10 in the morning till 4 in the evening, waiting. Tula then met the accountant who, luckily, belonged to the same caste as he did and who encouraged him to meet the campus chief, Ashok Singh, who turned out to be from Saptari, Tula's home district. 'The accountant's caste, and the chief's district, worked for me. They added my name to the list. I respected Ashok Singh a lot and he even came for my wedding later.'

For six months, Tula went to classes religiously but understood very little. 'I saw English books for the first time. They were so thick and I tried to mug up but failed. So one day, I decided to quit and, without informing anyone, I left for Janakpur. My plan was to attend tuition classes and apply again the following year when I was better equipped to deal with the classes.'

When he arrived in Janakpur, student elections were approaching. Tula then heard, for the first time, the name Nevisangh, the Nepal Students' Union (NSU), which was affiliated to the NC. Meanwhile,

Ashok Singh, his mentor in Siraha, had recommended Tula's name to be included on the NSU panel for the Siraha students' union elections. It was 1988-89, and royalists and NC students had joined hands in the campus to defeat the communists. 'In collaboration with government officials, the communist students were beaten up and NSU won. I was now an elected student union office bearer, and I didn't even know it.'

Tula's entry into politics may have been accidental, but when fellow students from Siraha conveyed the news to him, and word spread, he saw an opportunity. The NSU student leaders in Janakpur now wanted to recruit him into their own group, and quarrelled with the campus chief to get him admission there. He made it. 'My father got into local politics for property. And I ended up becoming active in politics to ensure my admission. My identity was now Nevisangh. My friends were those from Congress families. And I joined them on occasions like BP jayanti to plant trees. Campus leaders fought for me and I repaid my loyalty to the party.'

From an innocent bystander in the 1979 protests, Tula had turned into an active foot soldier of the democracy movement. In early 1990, a major political meeting was organized at the Kathmandu residence of NC's tallest leader, Ganesh Man Singh. Indian leaders, including Chandra Shekhar, had joined in to express their solidarity. Tula was in his lodgings in Janakpur when a cassette arrived through party circles. He and his friends heard the recordings of the meeting in the capital in their room. 'Chandra Shekharji's speech had a major impact. I still remember his powerful lines— duniya main tumhein koi shakti rok nahin sakti hai, apne man se dar ko nikalo. [No power on earth can stop you, banish fear from your minds.]' Janakpur became the second-most important centre of democratic protests after Kathmandu. Many courted arrest. Six people were killed in Jadhukhua village at the beginning of the movement. And young NC leaders, Bimalendra Nidhi and Brikesh Chandra Lal, went underground to conduct the movement. Tula and other NSU activists were responsible for organizing and sustaining street demonstrations every day.

It was in Janakpur that Tula came across people of other social backgrounds for the first time. He used to visit the home of his friend, Bishwaraj Gautam, whose family was originally from the hills. 'It was the first time I had entered someone's house in a bazaar. The bedsheet was so clean. There was no place to keep cows, or the paddy. I tried to speak like them, but I did not know Nepali. So when they asked, when did you arrive, Tula, I used to say bholi or parsi [tomorrow or day after], instead of hijo or asti [yesterday or day before]. But they were nice and tried to teach me. It made me realize that there was a difference in our culture, our language.'

~

After finishing his intermediate education, Tula came to Kathmandu. He had applied to an engineering college, but could not make it. And so he got admitted, with a little help from his Nevisangh friends, into a BSc course in the capital's premier Tri Chandra

College. He shared a room with a friend in Maitidevi. 'This is where I began to feel the pahadi-Madhesi thing strongly,' he recalled. 'The person in the next room used to drink a lot, every day. And we used to be scared. I felt fear, and that fear has stayed with me. Whenever I enter Kathmandu, even today, I feel this deep fear. When I am walking, when I am with my children, I am always extra careful. That man just came one day and told us to move out. We asked why. And he said, just move out. We did not have the courage to ask him who he was to tell us to leave. We just packed our bags and left. But that fear has remained.'

Tula then shifted to Shivram Yadav's rented room in Kupondole. Shivram was two batches senior to him in school in Diman, hailed from a communist family, and had become a student leader in Biratnagar. A third friend from school, Balram Yadav, also occasionally came over to live with them.

'The pahadi-Madhesi consciousness became stronger here. We used to speak in Maithili and laugh a lot, and this Newar neighbour always used to say Madhesis laugh too much. I felt a bit scared of him. There was another thing. The landlord did not get our septic tank repaired, and we had stopped paying rent to him for two months. His son came and said, "Madise haru, pay up or get out".' Another time, Shivram and Tula went to the tailor to get a blanket cover. Shivram then tried to negotiate and cut down the cost. The tailor reacted sharply, "Yo Madise haru, jaile kich kich garcha! [These Madises, they are always cribbing!]"'

That night, Shivram reacted furiously, 'These motherfuckers, they always call us Madises. Why can't they show us some respect, treat us with dignity? Why can't they at least call us Madhesi instead of Madise? We must do something.' Tula suggested that they should try organizing the vegetable vendors, who were predominantly dhoti-clad Madhesis. He felt that they were both exploited, and in large enough numbers to register their revolt. 'The idea was to collect one rupee from 1,000 vendors every day. That would make 1,000 rupees, and one of them could keep it. If we could do that for two years, we would build a corpus. And then, they could go on a strike for a week and that corpus could sustain them.'

The two friends thought that it was a good idea and, the next morning, pitched the idea to a Sadbhavana Party leader, Hridayesh Tripathi. Sadbhavana was the only political force that articulated the concerns of the Madhesis at that time. Tripathi sniggered at them and asked, 'You must be in Nevisangh.' Shivram responded, 'No, Akhil [the communist student organization].' Tripathi said, 'You must have been abused yesterday and so have come here. Come and join us first instead of giving free advice and teaching us.' Tula told me that in hindsight, he felt that the leader was right and that their commitment could not be trusted if they themselves remained with the bigger parties. The plan went nowhere and they soon became busy with other issues.

But the anger was simmering. One afternoon, Tula got off a bus to see a Madhesi banana-seller surrounded by pahadi customers. The vendor was complaining that they had picked up bananas without paying for them, while the customers were making fun of him. A traffic policeman nearby looked on quietly. Tula's father was visiting him in Kathmandu, where he was receiving medical treatment. One day, Tula's father urinated on a wall next to the house. The occupant of the house pelted the old man with a stone. This incident proved to be a turning point for Tula. 'That bastard could have said something instead. My father came and told me that a pahadi had thrown a stone. I swallowed the pain and walked on. The next day, when we went out, he was there again. And he tried to pull my father's dhoti off. I tried to protect him at first, and then we ran away. It was torture,' said Tula, his voice shaking with pain twenty years after the incident.

Tula continued his student activism in Kathmandu. He lobbied with old contacts to get a ticket to contest on the NSU panel and, for the first time in the history of Tri Chandra, the oldest college in Nepal, a Madhesi received the ticket. 'I did all the activism. Unlike the village, politics here was about shaking hands, saying Jai Nepal, going to NSU central office and listening to leaders.' He became embroiled in factional struggles in the student front, began giving tuition lessons to sustain himself, completed his BSc, and then secured admission to the Institute of Engineering in Pulchowk.

'I was a big leader and became the president of the NSU chapter. Our speeches were only about abusing Akhil. All Madhesis were in Nevisangh. During clashes in the university, Madhesis were usually targeted. My intention was to defend Madhesis under the Nevisangh banner. Seniors, too, abused us, calling us Madises.' During cricket matches, Madhesi students usually supported India while pahadis backed the team opposing India. In one such encounter, Tula told me, a pahadi student stomped on his roommate's palms and crushed them. Such incidents continued.

Tula and a few of his friends, once again, felt a strong urge to do something about the discrimination. They thought of setting up an underground outfit, the Tarai State Establishment Front Nepal, and, to mark their commitment to the cause, used a burning candle to brand themselves on their arms. 'A few of us were badly injured and asked a health assistant we knew to give us first aid.' The Front did not go far, but the sentiment that had motivated Vedanand Jha in the 1950s, Raghunath Thakur in the 1960s and 1970s, and Gajendra Narayan Singh in the 1980s, was only getting more radical.

What struck Tula was how most of their Madhesi seniors did not react to or resist the discrimination, taunts and humiliation inflicted on them by pahadi students. He asked a senior about it and was told, 'This happens in all countries. Gora sab kaala ke ena kare chhe. [All whites do this to blacks.] Let it be.' Thinking about the comment, Tula later said, 'The problem with Madhesis was because they were so insecure, they sought to ally with power. The generation before us tried some low-key activities, organized Saraswati Pujas in Kathmandu; they were angry but they were also greedy and lacked confidence. So they opted for mainstream parties and could not resist traditional Nepali symbols, the language, the dress, the culture of pahadis.'

But there were rebels. One night, Dipak Sah, a Madhesi student who had received a scholarship to study in Bangladesh, was beaten up by some pahadi students a few days before he was to leave. He decided to shelve his plans and joined a karate class in Patan instead. He then trained his way up to a black belt. Dipak distributed pamphlets, beat up pahadi students who were harassing Madhesis, coached Tarai students for college entrance exams, even trained them in karate, and went on to head the Tarai Madhesi Navjagaran Samaj which spread awareness about Madhesi rights.

In this period, Tula had also become close to a senior NC leader, Jay Prakash Gupta, who had served as Prime Minister Koirala's press advisor in 1991 and would go on to lead the MJF in the future. Jay Prakash was from Saptari as well, and had recruited Tula to help him during his election campaign in 1994. When Jay Prakash became a Cabinet minister for information and communication in 1998, he asked Tula to become his personal assistant, with the rank of a deputy secretary. But soon after, Jay Prakash diluted the position, appointed a pahadi officer as his personal assistant, and gave Tula a section officer-level position. This rankled, but Tula took the job. 'I used it to give my friends phone connections,' he recalled, laughing about it.

But the minister and he soon fell out due to a misunderstanding. Tula was taking Jay Prakash's election pamphlets to Saptari when a UML leader complained that this was a violation of the election code. A policeman in Thankot, on the outskirts of the capital, confiscated the pamphlets. But Jay Prakash felt that Tula had got it captured on purpose and told him, 'You will get me caught.' For the next seven years, the two would not speak to each other. Jay Prakash also got Tula's name struck off as a proposed NSU central committee member. Tula then took an exam to secure a job with the Nepal Electricity Authority, but did not make it. 'NC's Bijay Gachhedar was the concerned minister then. But I did not get a job despite NC being in government, while activists junior to me were recruited. I decided then that I would take revenge and quit NC.' Tula filed his nomination as a presidential candidate in the Nepal Engineering Association presidential polls, which were fought on party platforms. 'I managed to cut NC's votes and, for the first time, communists won. That was my badla [revenge], and I left the Congress after that.'

Tula became a journalist with a local Nepali daily, covering water resource issues. He also lobbied with the secretary of the ministry he covered for a government job, and landed a position in an office responsible for the maintenance of Singha Durbar, the government secretariat. The two jobs gave him a combined salary of over 15,000 Nepali rupees. After three-and-a-half years, as the newspaper he worked in started to crumble and he was left with little time for familial responsibilities, Tula shifted again, this time to a research think tank.

Tula then set up the Tarai Engineer Samaj, where he got senior professionals to present papers on subjects covering infrastructure, irrigation and agriculture in the Tarai. Shivram Yadav, Tula's schoolmate and then flat-mate in Kathmandu, had become a student leader in the Patan campus and had then gone on to join the Maoists. He was the Saptari commander for the party during the war, when rumours of his death surfaced. The news was false, and Shivram emerged over ground after the ceasefire. Balram, Tula's third school friend who used to visit them sometimes, had continued living in the Tarai and had developed ties with the MJF. Balram took Tula to some MJF meetings in Kathmandu but, Tula, mistakenly, did not feel that much would come out of it. This is when he met Jay Prakash Gupta, whom he had grown distant from, and they sorted out their misunderstandings.

After the Madhes movement, Tula finally gathered courage to write about the Madhes, something he had avoided doing even while working in the mainstream press. He also realized that a full-time job and Madhes activism was not possible and, in 2007, set up the Nepal Madhes Foundation, one of Nepal's first research institutes and think tanks devoted to the Tarai.

~

Tula's life story is a microcosm of the transformation of the Tarai. He was born when the Panchayat system was at its most oppressive, and his father had to make compromises with the Palace's local agents to survive. He grew up when political and social changes were underway, and the power of the old feudal lords was on the decline. Through a mix of circumstances and personal choice, he became a part of the umbrella Congress formation. But as his exposure to pahadis, to Kathmandu, and to the state, increased, his alienation increased as well. Once the consciousness that Nepal had different ethnic groups which were not equally treated seeped in, even normal everyday incidents, which may not have had anything to do with ethnicity, were seen through that lens. This deepened resentment. Many of the plans he and his friends hatched in college went nowhere, but they revealed the underlying anger that had been brewing on the Tarai Street.

Tula's story was representative, for it provided an insight into the insecurities and the life trajectory of a first-generation, literate, Madhesi young man who had migrated to the capital. It was also exceptional, for he showed entrepreneurial and risk-taking skills which could not be judged in any black-and-white framework.

His choices were not a result of abstract theoretical principles, but sprang from what life had thrown at him. Politics was a way for upward mobility, for security and for revenge but it was eventually pressed into the service of larger cause where the personal and the political were inextricably tied together. He felt vulnerable, yet represented the new generation which would not hesitate to use the available political space to resist what it perceived as acts of humiliation—sometimes overtly and often behind the scenes through quiet mobilization.

Tula said he had not made many hisaab-kitaab, calculations, before jumping into Madhesi activism. 'One generation will have to sacrifice. I know pahadis will get irritated with me. Financially also, I have not done well. My friend, who was secretary in my union, now has a house in Baluwatar. My brother-in-law lives abroad. My son sometimes asks me, why don't you have a car? I should have thought more about all this. But my inspiration is the writer C. K. Lal. He thought, wrote, spoke without any selfish interest. He has sacrificed so much. We should be like that.'

Tula went back to contemplating his village, where we had started the story, where both politics and the economy had changed. Earlier, land had been the only determinant of prosperity. Now, those with other skills, who worked with wood and iron, mattered. As urbanization increased, the value of carpenters, for instance, rose. Labour could extract more for their services due to opportunities offered by mobility. Those who went to Punjab for six months returned with 10,000 Indian rupees, while those who lived in Goithi through the year could barely save 2,000 Nepali rupees. 'Those who were poor definitely have more money now. But the traditionally privileged have focused on education, and advanced even more.'

All of this had an impact on politics. Earlier, western Saptari was controlled by the Yadavs and eastern Saptari by the Jhas, Nunu and Krishna Deo. But with the restoration of democracy in 1990, Saptari had five constituencies, which threw up five leaders, and each had several competitors. The NC and the UML became powerful. More parties emerged and choices increased. Tula added, 'When government budgets started entering the villages, more and more people became interested in politics. Criminalization and corruption increased.' The Maoists were then the gamechanger. They mobilized the Dalits, who began questioning the caste hierarchy. NGOs, too, played an active role in this regard and, in the neighbouring Siraha district, social activists supported Dalits who refused to dispose of the carcasses of cattle—their traditional occupation—and thus antagonized the upper castes.

Battles of the New Republic

'We lived under the terror of Nunu Jha, who was supported by the Palace. The Bharda road was his personal property. Today, a Dalit can beat up Nunu Jha's sons at Bharda chowk and no one can do anything. That is change. And we have to replicate the same change in Kathmandu. That is the spirit of the Madhes movement.'

4

The spirit of the movement—in Tula Sah's imagination, Jwala Singh's karabahi, Rajeev Jha's anger, Upendra Yadav's political programme and, eventually, the election results—demanded a shift in the power structure. This unnerved those who belonged to the groups which had traditionally exercised power. It made the disenfranchised politically assertive, determined to stake their claim and not miss the bus again. And it tested the intent and imagination of the Madhes's political leadership, of whether they were seeking to create an accommodative and plural society or replace one form of hegemony with another.

Birgunj's location in south-central Nepal—as the Tarai town closest to Kathmandu, touching Bihar's Raxaul border, with access to both eastern and western towns of the plains—defines its character.

Every morning, tankers line up on the 'No Man's Bridge' at the border, bringing fuel from Indian Oil's Barauni refinery to meet Nepal's ever-increasing energy needs. Trucks carry products to and from the Kolkata port, which continues to serve as the landlocked country's access to international seas and trading. Stones and boulders, extracted from Nepal's Chure hills and forests, are taken across to supply material for the relentless expansion of highways and roads in north India.

The scale of the informal, and illegal, trade across the forests and open fields that divide the two countries far exceeds the official trade across checkpoints. Small arms are smuggled in from Bihar, while counterfeit Indian currency notes—according to the Indian security establishment—are sent across to infiltrate India's economy. Sacks of paddy and fertilizer, subsidized in India, are diverted for use by Nepali farmers while Nepali women are trafficked all the way to brothels in Delhi, Mumbai, Kolkata and, increasingly, to other countries.

The stretch from Birgunj to the town of Simra in the neighbouring Bara district, through Jitpur bazaar, also happens to be home to Nepal's most prosperous industries, including joint venture companies. The Dabur factory produces different flavours of Real Fruit Juice, which is then exported for consumption to India. The factory which produces the Surya brand of cigarettes, co-owned by ITC Limited, is situated here. Many other units have shut down in recent years, though, largely due to conflict and trade union militancy.

The geography, economics and the politics all gave Birgunj a mixed demography. People from neighbouring districts of the Tarai, from Dhanusha to Bara, saw migration to the town as a way for upward mobility. Maithili and Bhojpuri speakers were in a majority, but many pahadi families, too, had settled here over the years. The increased migration from the hills had, among other reasons, led to a drastic increase in population density in the district. Birgunj represented what had become an increasing pattern across plains. One-third of the Tarai's population consisted of people of hill origin, Bahuns and Chhetris, as well as Janjatis from the hills.

I was staying at Hotel Heera Plaza, conveniently located between Ghantaghar, the town's most famous landmark, and the bus park, and had stepped down to have dinner at the restaurant. Four men were drinking in one corner, while I sat quietly and read, waiting for my meal. They were all speaking in Nepali, but interspersed with English. They were all well dressed, and car keys and the latest cellphones were strewn on the table. They appeared to be either visitors from Kathmandu or belonged to the town's upper crust. The familiarity with the waiters—who were being called by their first names—indicated that they were regulars.

A little while later, one of the men called out and said hello. We chatted. His name was Sanjay Giri, and he owned the hotel. He said that the place was named after his father, Heera Giri. The name rang a bell, and I asked Sanjay if they were from the Giri family of Bastipur VDC in the Siraha district. He nodded. The family had thrown up two political figures, the royalist prime minister Tulsi Giri and the NC leader Pradeep Giri, whom I had met in Delhi on the day Gyanendra Shah had pulled off a coup in February 2005. Sanjay's father had shifted to Birgunj and had gone into business. His mother was from Gujarat and the family owned some industrial plants.

He then introduced me to others around the table. Among them was a Newar businessman who ran a sweetmeats shop in town. As soon as I told them that I was a journalist covering Madhesi politics, the conversation took a turn.

'Ke ko Madhes, bhai? [What Madhes, brother?] Let me tell you this is all business. Every day, we get calls on our mobiles from unknown numbers. They ask for money, or threaten to vandalize the hotel. This is the real face of the so-called armed groups who go around talking about Madhes,' said Sanjay.

The Newar sweetmeats-shop owner chipped in. 'It was all peaceful. Nepalis lived together with the Madises. But now that feeling has gone.' Pahadis in the Tarai often use the two terms—either deliberately or without realizing its full implications—to distinguish themselves from the more dark-skinned, non-Nepali speakers. They are the Nepalis, the latter are the Madises. I had heard a taxi driver refer to the communities precisely in the same manner a few days earlier. 'Pahadi' and 'Nepali' are synonymous, and can be used interchangeably, while other Tarai-dwellers are Madises, considered a derogatory substitute for Madhesi. The lack of empathy in understanding the difference between the words Madhesi and Madise was precisely what the Madhesis were struggling against.

'That's true,' Sanjay said. 'My family has been in the Tarai for centuries. We have been in Birgunj for two generations. I speak Bhojpuri, Hindi and Maithili better than most. And now, they call us pahadis outsiders, they tell us to pay or leave.'

A third friend, who had been concentrating on his drink thus far, spoke up, 'Outsiders! *They* are the outsiders. All of them Indians who took fake citizenship and became Nepalis twenty years ago. And let me tell you, if it was not for us, Tarai would be far poorer than it is. Look at the towns which have money, Bhairhawa, Birgunj,

Biratanagar. What is common? So-called pahadi population. All this development is because of us.'

They disagreed with the complaint that Madhesis did not have space in the power structure. 'See, Birgunj's leaders are Surendra Chaudhary, Ajay Chaurasia, Ajay Dwivedi, Bimal Srivastava. Aren't they Madhesis?' What about the demand for respecting Madhesi identity? 'What Madhesi identity? This society is so divided in castes. Here Brahmins hate Bhumihars who hate Rajputs who hate Kayasthas. They all hate Yadavs. And everyone hates Dalits. What identity?'

Sanjay and his friends agreed with federalism, though. 'Yes, it will be good if there are provinces. After all, there will be more opportunities for us, too. Birgunj can be the capital. But it should not be called Madhes state.'

~

If Birgunj derives its cosmopolitanism from its location and trade, Biratnagar's legacy rests on its being home to the democracy warriors of Nepal, as the citadel of the NC.

Krishna Prasad Koirala 'Pitaji', the patriarch of the Koirala family, was a leading figure in the town in the early twentieth century before the Ranas expelled him from the country. Three of his sons—Matrika Prasad, Bishweshwor Prasad and Girija Prasad—went on to become the country's prime ministers. G. P. Koirala, along with communist activist and another future prime minister, Manmohan Adhikari, had cut his political teeth with the Biratnagar jute mill strike in the late 1940s, which marked the arrival of militant anti-Rana politics. The NC organization remained strong in the region even during the Panchayat years and Morang district, of which Biratnagar was the headquarters, produced the party's tallest leaders and future ministers. The Koirala Niwas was like a pilgrimage spot for old NC activists, and G. P. Koirala had continued to return to Biratnagar to sharpen his political strategies and make public announcements.

The strength, intensity and duration of the Madhes movement in a place that the NC considered its stronghold shocked the party's leaders, mostly of pahadi origin.

Pitamber Dahal was the NC's district secretary. We met at the city's Traffic Chowk, and walked down to a nearby restaurant for a cup of tea. I asked him what he thought of the Madhes andolan. 'Their demands are valid. But the process of movement, the manner in which it was conducted, we cannot agree with it at all. They claimed non-violence, but used violent tactics. Social harmony between communities who have lived in peace for centuries has broken down. The smell of communalism is everywhere.'

If their demands were valid, why had the NC not accepted it in the first place? But we have, Dahal insisted. The NC was committed to federalism. It could not accept a fully proportional representation-based electoral system because 'it broke the link between the citizens and their representative'. Neither could they even entertain the possibility of a separate Madhes, as demanded by armed extremists. 'Madhesis are Nepalis. Their rights must be assured. And there should be no discrimination. But this is going down the LTTE path. The current mood is backward looking.'

I asked whether NC's Madhesi workers were unhappy. Dahal had opened up by now. He said, 'Well, many supported the movement but have returned to the party. But it is our responsibility to give more Madhesis election tickets, involve them more, and give them leadership positions. Or they will rebel.'

Dahal returned to the theme of the social fabric in the Morang district, how they had always peacefully co-existed, and how there was no discrimination in everyday life, including in political affairs. 'Let me give you an example. In a ward in Pokharia VDC, there is only one pahadi family, the Adhikaris. But Adhikariji has won two ward elections in a row. His voters are Madhesis.' I reacted sharply and said that was exactly the point that Madhesi activists were making; that they did not have sufficient political representation even though they had the numbers. Dahal countered, 'But in ward number nine of Durbisa village, there are 3,500 pahadis. But a Dalit, a Paswan, has won the election. There are only 150 Paswans there. So see, if a candidate is popular, people vote for him. We should not look at caste, ethnicity. This is regressive.' There were pahadi families, he said, which had been in the Tarai for the last 150 years. 'How can we be called outsiders, and Madhesis who have come from India be called citizens? Let us stop communalism.'

Morang had an even demographic balance with almost 50 per cent pahadis and 50 per cent Madhesis. The balance lent the city a tenuous calm, since no side could impose its hegemony on the other. But reports had begun trickling in of pahadi families leaving towns like Rajbiraj, which had an outright Madhesi majority.

Shiv Hari Bhattarai was among Rajbiraj's most senior journalists. He was of pahadi origin, but widely respected by journalists across the spectrum for his independent and non-partisan outlook, no mean feat in those polarized times.

'Forty percent of the pahadi families in Rajbiraj have left in less than a year, since the Madhes movement. But the question is of state presence. People lost faith in the government. After the movement, armed groups proliferated, many of them using politics as a cover for crime. The cops usually took a cut from these groups, politicians offered them protection, kidnapping and extortion increased. And so those who had resources left. Pahadi families left, Marwaris left, and even well-to-do Madhesis are leaving. Tell me, who would want to stay in Rajbiraj?'

Frankly, no one.

Tatta had migrated from Bihar to Rajbiraj after completing his medical studies, and worked in the government hospital there in the late 1940s and early 1950s. But he soon realized that limited opportunities were available, and was among the earliest professionals from the Tarai to migrate to Kathmandu in the early 1950s. Neither my father nor his three siblings studied in the town. An uncle, who worked in construction, and an aunt, who taught in the local college, shifted to Patna in the 1990s when they could not find any good school for my cousins.

Central Rajbiraj was all of one long road, with a couple of cybercafés, the dilapidated Star Hotel with broken beds in mosquito-infested rooms, two shops selling newspapers, and a line of medical stores next to the zonal hospital where Tatta had begun his career. The town's campus administrators spent all their time in endless intrigues to suck up to political masters and become the principal or the rector of the campus while higher education irreversibly decayed. A specially created industrial estate, named after the Sadbhavana founder Gajendra Narayan Singh, lay barren. The town had the Tarai's first airport, which had been dysfunctional and out of use for years. The numerous national-level politicians who called Rajbiraj home had never returned to invest any energy in transforming the place. Like some other towns in the Tarai, notably Gaur in Rautahat district and Taulihawa in Kapilbastu district, if one word described Rajbiraj, it was stagnation.

Bhattarai interrupted my thoughts. 'No one wants to live here. That is the core point. Those who can leave are leaving. But yes, the pace at which pahadis are leaving has increased. The lack of opportunity is now compounded with insecurity.' I asked him whether he planned to leave, too. 'No, we discussed it in the family. I have old parents and a wife. My children are already studying outside, one in Kathmandu and one in India. Where will I go now? And what will I do? I know people here, people know me. I am too old to shift now, and I don't have the money to buy a house in Kathmandu either.'

Like Pitamber Dahal, Bhattarai longed for the past when 'social and political integration' of the different communities had been intact. 'Pahadis were leaders even in Madhesi-dominated villages. They sat on the charpoy in their dhotis, eating paan and speaking in Maithili. That is the symbol of harmony.' When I pointed out that political under-representation was precisely the complaint made by the Madhesis, he agreed. 'Yes, they should have more representatives. But you know, right now, it is pahadi-Madhesi. Tomorrow, it will be about forward-backward, Yadav-non Yadav, Madhesi-Tharu, Hindu-Muslim in the Tarai.'

~

If the insecurity and the resistance of the pahadi population of the Tarai constituted one element of the political crisis, the search for identity by the other communities who were of plains origin, but were unsure of the direction being taken by the Madhes movement, represented another challenge.

Abdul Sattar Ansari was a member of the Madhesi Intellectual Society in Biratnagar. The society, he told me, had sprung up soon after the Madhes andolan and was close to the MJF leadership. He organized a small 'focus group discussion' to give me a chance to meet the society's office bearers, all of whom were Madhesi Hindus. They narrated the story of discrimination against the Madhes and how it was time to fight for adhikar and pahichan, rights and identity.

But I was more interested in Sattar, as his friends called him. In the wider meeting, Sattar had passionately advocated the Madhesi cause. 'The government is not interested in a solution. They just want to use force, the army and the Armed Police Force to crush Madhes.' If Kathmandu uses force, he warned, there would be bloodshed. Madhes would not give up this time unless it got federalism.

We left the meeting together in a rickshaw. I asked Sattar whether he saw himself as a Madhesi or as a Muslim.

'Madhesi Muslim,' he said without batting an eyelid. 'How can I be anything else? I am from Mirzapur village in Sarlahi district, where there are almost no pahadis. I have grown up and studied in the Tarai. I speak Maithili like my Hindu friends. When I go to Kathmandu, people call me dhoti. Unless I tell them my name, no one knows I am a Muslim. But as soon as they see me, they know I am from Madhes.' At the same time, Sattar added, he was also a Muslim. His family was religious. He read his namaaz, albeit not as regularly as he was supposed to. He had read the *Quran* and spoke in Urdu, and occasionally helped out at a madrasa.

According to the 2001 census, Muslims constituted a little over 4 per cent of Nepal's population. But activists had always claimed that the figure was higher. They maintained that counting heads when the country remained a Hindu kingdom smacked of prejudice, and incentivized the under-representation of minorities. Over 95 percent of the country's Muslims lived in the Tarai.

Sattar said that there was a debate among Muslims about their relationship with the Madhesi parties. 'Pahadi Muslims are more advanced and vocal. They are at the forefront of projecting Madhesis and Muslims as antagonists. And in this, they are supported by

Muslim leaders of big parties like the UML.' But, he added that there were also genuine apprehensions among some Muslims in the Tarai. How would they benefit if pahadi rule was replaced by the hegemony of the Madhesi Hindus? What would they get in return for supporting the movement?

Sattar was strongly in favour of allying with the Madhesis for a simple reason. 'See, we have to live here. If we begin fighting Madhesis on issues that are genuine, issues that will benefit us, too, like inclusion and federalism, then Muslims will never be liberated. Demographically, too, Muslims can advance by cooperating with Madhesis. Our common enemy is the old state structure.'

Sattar took me to a madrasa next to the Salt Trading Chowk in town. It was in a dilapidated condition. The roof was crumbling and the classrooms were tiny. A young maulana sat in the courtyard and asked us to look around. 'We have no support. There are some government provisions for support to madrasa education but getting it out of the local administration office requires a lot of connections with the powerful. How can we educate Muslim children this way?' I asked him why they didn't send children to government schools instead. 'See, we are providing modern education here. But alongside, as Muslims, we are supposed to know certain things. Urdu and Arabic, *Quran*. Do our namaaz. Here, we can teach children to be true Muslims and true citizens.'

Later, while discussing Muslim politics over a drink—Sattar did not let religion come in the way of alcohol—he warned that they would lose the battle if the Madhesi leadership did not reform; if they did not give space to Muslims in their party and in the leadership structure; if they did not raise Muslim 'issues' like declaring Eid a national holiday, allowing Muslims to implement the Sharia law, recognizing Muslims as a marginalized group in the Constitution; or creating a National Muslim Commission—Muslims would start doubting the intent of the Madhesi Hindus. 'Madhesi leaders will need to take Muslims along,' Sattar asserted.

~

At the other end of the Tarai, Ekraj Chaudhary was not willing to be as kind as Abdul Sattar Ansari had been.

Nepalgunj, the headquarters of Banke district, is western Tarai's most important urban centre. It is next to the India border, touching Bahraich district of Uttar Pradesh. In the eastern plains, especially the belt between Biratnagar and Birgunj, Madhesis enjoyed an outright majority, but the demography in the west was more mixed. Madhesi Hindu castes, hill migrants—including landowners as well as poor pahadi migrants from the western hills, and Muslims lived alongside Tharus, the Tarai's biggest indigenous community, their numbers varying in the different districts. Tharus constituted almost 7 per cent of the national population.

Chaudhary identified himself as a social activist and a journalist associated with the Nepalgunj Media Centre. He told me that the Madhesi demands for representation and participation were valid. 'The government's intention is bad. They don't want to give us proportional representation in the state.' He criticized the Maoists, a party which had been in the forefront of raising the issue of 'Tharu liberation'. 'Look at their central committee and politburo. There is no Tharu. They just used us like they used the Madhesis.'

But he hastened to add that he did not mean that the intent of the Madhesi movement was right. 'Madhesi leaders keep saying Tharus are Madhesis. Let me tell you, I am a Tharu and I am not a Madhesi. I am an adivasi. We are the original inhabitants. See the Tharu samaj. We have a family assembly, joint-family decision-making mechanisms, a village assembly, distinct marriage rituals, our own language, and these have nothing in common with Madhesis.' Both pahadis and Madhesis, he said, had entered their land and exploited Tharus. 'Madhesis were cowherds, and the rulers had allowed them to settle here; the pahadis were given huge tracts of land by the Rana and Shah regimes. Jal, jangal, jamin [water, forest and land] were taken away from the Tharus who were then systematically enslaved. We have suffered the most.'

Chaudhary had a point about the continued pauperization of the community. The Kamaiya practice, in which pahadi landed families of the region selected Tharus to work as bonded labour for them, had been banned only in 2000 after a sustained campaign. Tharus were even more dismally represented in the state structures than Madhesi Hindu castes, and some of the lowest human development indices in the country applied to them. During the war, Tharus were subject to some of the military's worst brutality during the war, and Bardiya—a district where over half the population was Tharu—reported the highest number of disappearances.

A key grievance of the Tharu political and community leadership against the Madhesi movement was its quest for a single Madhes pradesh across the Tarai. Across party lines, Tharu leaders claimed that this was an effort by Madhesis to impose their 'hegemony' over the Tharus. Nepalgunj was abuzz with the activities of Laxman Tharu, a young leader who had quit the Maoists and accused the former rebels of merely using the community. He had also said there was 'no Madhes' in Nepal and, to counter the Madhesi demand, insisted that the entire plains be named Tharuhat Pradesh.

Chaudhary told me, 'All big Madhesi leaders are from the east. Many belong to one or two districts. If Madhesis are given the whole plains, entire Nepal should be renamed Madhes.' The compromise formula, he suggested, was for the eastern Tarai to be a Madhes province and for the western Tarai to be a Tharu province, Tharuhat, with minority rights for Tharus in the east and Madhesis in the west within the democratic setting.

Chaudhary was now sounding conciliatory and, like Sattar in Biratnagar, urged the Madhesi leaders to reform. 'Tharus want the same thing as Madhesis—our own state and completely PR system where 6 per cent Tharus means there should be 6 per cent Tharus in the Parliament. We tell Madhesi leaders to raise issues like liberating Kamaiyas, talk of our rights, and include Tharus in leadership positions. They need to win our trust and include our demands. Only then can the two communities work together.'

5

In the year following the mass movement in the Tarai, every one was fighting with each other—the Maoists and the Madhesis, the

Madhesis and the government, the Madhesis and their own party leaders, the pahadis and the Madhesis, the Madhesis and the Tharus. With the opening of the democratic space, and the assertion of marginalized groups, a new phase of political churning was underway. The pro-Madhes sentiment that had been so visible during my trips in the Tarai soon manifested in party-formation processes.

Upendra Yadav turned the MJF, which had been a cross-party platform, into a political party and registered it with the Election Commission. The MJF already had district-level units on the ground; Yadav could tap into his strong caste network; and the MJF had appropriated the mantle of having led the andolan. All of this gave him a political advantage but, when Yadav signed a 22-point agreement with the government in August 2007—which promised proportional representation to Madhesis in state organs, autonomous states, and declared those who died in the movement as martyrs—a section of his party split, accusing him of selling out. This was a precursor to the fragmentation that was to ravage Madhesi politics over the next five years.

Meanwhile, pressure had been building up on Madhesi leaders in mainstream parties, from their own constituencies in the Tarai, to speak up. And everyone was looking towards Mahant Thakur—an old NC stalwart and a trusted advisor to G. P. Koirala.

Mahantji, as he was known in political circles, had been a minister in several governments in the 1990s and, during the January movement, had led the government team negotiating with Madhesi protestors. Always clad in a kurta-pyjama, Mahantji's soft-spoken and gentle style lent sobriety to an overly aggressive political theatre; his impeccable integrity and simple lifestyle gave him unmatched credibility among Tarai leaders; and his national stature, his commitment to democracy and his advocacy of republicanism added to his cross-party appeal.

In the charged atmosphere of identity-driven politics, he was under tremendous pressure from his support base in the Tarai to rebel against the NC and return 'home', to his community. Established Madhesi leaders in mainstream parties saw Upendra Yadav as an upstart, and did not plan to join the MJF. They needed an alternative Madhesi platform if they wished to be politically successful in the region, and looked up to Mahantji as a leader. The impulse to set up a new party also emerged from the non-Yadav communities in the Tarai, when the MJF appeared to give the Yadavs more space in the party structure. The final push came from the Indian establishment, which was looking for a reliable partner in the maze of the Tarai's politics.

All of this led to the birth of the Tarai Madhes Loktantrik Party (TMLP) in December 2007, with many influential leaders of the NC, the UML, the Sadbhavana Party, and MJF dissidents coming together. This had huge political and symbolic significance, for it indicated the limits to which the Madhesi agenda could be pushed from within the national parties and shook up the structure of the older forces in the plains. Regional politics was seen as the future.

The third pillar of mainstream Madhesi party politics remained the Sadbhavana Party. While the party had slowly begun splintering into several small factions, the biggest of them was led by the Rajendra Mahato-Anil Kumar Jha duo. While its organization was weak, the party's advantage was its almost two-decades-old legacy.

The Sadbhavana leaders were bitter that while they had invested years in the struggle, others had run away with the credit of leading the movement. As party general secretary Jha, who eventually became a close friend, said over coffee at a Babar Mahal café, 'We raised the Madhesi issue when it was not fashionable to do so. Twenty years ago, I put up posters in Kathmandu which propagated a Constituent Assembly election and federalism when Madhesi leaders in big parties were busy sucking up to pahadi leaders to become ministers.' But this was the party's own fault, as Jha admitted in a moment of candour. They had decided to stick to the government during the promulgation of the interim Constitution instead of resigning and hitting the streets—considerably eroding their credibility.

~

At the end of 2007, almost a year after the Madhesi movement, the resentment in the Tarai was still festering. Activists narrated a litany of complaints to anyone who cared to listen—the home minister was still in office even though his police force had shot down Madhesi protestors; promises of inclusion had not been implemented; Madhesis still did not pass entrance exams for government jobs; the pahadi regime wanted to use force to suppress protests instead of empathizing and negotiating with the protestors; the state was quick to declare a pahadi killed by an armed group a martyr but victims of police firing during the movement were not compensated; Madhesis would not be fairly represented in the CA; Prime Minister Koirala's statement that the Madhes problem could be solved in merely a minute if India so wanted, showed that Kathmandu still saw all Madhesis as Indians or agents of India.

These political grievances were articulated when the three Madhesi parties allied and formed a broader front, a Madhesi Morcha, and announced a movement. Their key stated objective was to bring about further revisions in the electoral system, and extract a firm guarantee on a future federal state in the Tarai. But the unstated aim, as a leader of one of the parties had told me, was to 'create a hawa, unleash passion and energy, and carry the andolan spirit on to the next elections so that Madhesi parties do well'.

The Morcha shut the Tarai down in February 2008, and their message was clear—accommodate our demands or there will be no elections in the Tarai. Madhesi professional organizations supported the movement and held rallies in Tarai towns. The East-West Highway was blocked once again, travellers were stranded and, crucially, essential supplies could not be transported to Kathmandu which generated pressure on the government to resolve the impasse. Prices shot up in the capital and fuel scarcity crippled the transport sector. The government, like in the 2007 andolan, reacted belligerently and fired upon protestors—this, expectedly, inflamed passions. Protests and violence greeted candidates who tried to file their nomination papers for the CA elections, announced for April.

G. P. Koirala and his aides reached out to Madhesi parties, but negotiations repeatedly failed. The first issue was the substance of the agreement; the Madhesi parties pushed for firmer commitment to creating a single autonomous Madhes province—ek swyattata Madhes pradesh—while the government wanted to leave the issue for the CA to decide upon once it was elected. The implementation mechanism was another area of contention, since the government had a poor track record of meeting promises. Upendra Yadav demanded an amendment which would incorporate the deal in the interim Constitution and guarantee that it would be enforced, while Koirala's aides were not willing to go beyond a written agreement. Late one night, even as protests continued in the Tarai, the different sides were able to reconcile their stated positions, but the agreement fell through on the question of who would sign the pact. Madhesi parties demanded that the prime minister himself must represent the government, while the state wished to depute the home minister or the minister for peace and reconstruction, both of whom were discredited figures in the Tarai.

The Indian ambassador, Shiv Shanker Mukherjee, mediated the negotiations between representatives of the NC and the Madhesi leaders, many of which were held at the sprawling India House—the envoy's residence—inside the embassy. India was determined to push for elections in April, and had been disappointed when the polls had been postponed earlier. Yet, it realized that the concerns of the Madhesi parties needed to be accommodated for the polls to happen. Ambassador Mukherjee encouraged the government to be more responsive and flexible, while urging the Madhesi leaders to step back from their maximalist demands.

Several weeks later, I asked a key Indian official why the embassy had adopted such a visible role, contrary to their usual behind-the-scenes involvement. He replied, 'It was deliberate. Gyanendra saw disturbances in Madhes as his last opportunity to derail the CA elections, and stall the transformation to a republican order. If we had not intervened, he would have succeeded and the peace process would have been in danger. We had to intervene and send a clear message.'

Upendra Yadav, whose political links have always been murky, was suspected to be closely engaging with the royalists. In fact, when he was flown into Kathmandu from the Tarai for negotiations during the protests, he had gone straight from the talks to meet key royalist interlocutors who were making a desperate attempt to prevent an agreement, and thus stop elections. A close aide of one of the royalist politicians confirmed the meeting to me. But when the Indian establishment invested its political capital, the MJF leaders fell in line and went along with efforts to find an agreement.

On 28 February, Tula Narayan Sah, the Madhesi activist, and I went to the prime minister's residence in Baluwatar. We had heard that a deal was in the offing, and saw that a tent had been put up in the lawns. Refreshments were being prepared, and a large press contingent had slowly trooped in. We all waited expectantly for the leaders. Girijababu, followed closely by other party leaders, ministers and the dissenting Madhesi party chairmen, walked in.

The leaders announced that they had agreed to an 8-point understanding. Its key provisions included a commitment to creating an autonomous Madhes state, ensuring the 'group entry' of Madhesis into the NA, declaring all those who had died in the movement as martyrs, and amending the electoral laws in a way which would ensure that the Madhesi parties could exclusively represent Madhesi groups of the plains and were not forced to put hill candidates on their proportional representation list.

In a significant symbolic gesture, Prime Minister Koirala spoke in Hindi, and recalled his association with the Tarai. Reciprocating the spirit of the moment, Mahant Thakur chose to speak in Nepali and reaffirmed the Madhes's commitment to the territorial integrity of Nepal. The mood was euphoric, and Tula Sah, sitting next to me, whispered, 'I never thought I would see a day when Madhesis would take over Baluwatar and get their claims recognized. I never thought Nepal's PM would speak in Hindi in Kathmandu. We have won!' Over tea, Home Minister Krishna Sitaula declared to reporters, 'Now elections are certain. Nothing can stop it.'

The first Madhes andolan of 2007 was a result of the long-standing historic grievances, channelled cleverly by the MJF and supported by a wide cross-section of the Madhesi population. It brought their issues on to the national stage. It made federalism an irreversible reality that was enshrined in the Constitution. But the discontent, festering over decades, would not dissipate so easily. Through the year, the Madhes went through a period of political churning—anger and resentment grew, political entrepreneurs jumped on to the identity bandwagon, older forces weakened, and agitators sought even more solid guarantees on representation in the CA and the space the Madhes would occupy in a future federal structure.

These impulses led to the second Madhes andolan of 2008. It was more limited in participation and scale. Unlike the year before, when leaders had merely followed the spontaneous upsurge of the masses, this time around, the parties had mobilized protestors and were clearly in command. Its results were tangible, for the Nepali state now committed itself to a future Madhes pradesh, and promised representation to the Madhesis in that institution of the state in which they had the least stake—the NA. By proving that peaceful politics could win rights for the Madhes, the andolan weakened the Madhesi extremists who had called for a boycott of the polls. The royalists' hope of subverting the process were foiled. Nepal would finally hold elections to an inclusive and representative CA—promised way back in 1951—on 10 April 2008.

Dhotis in Singha Durbar

Bokraha village is off the East-West Highway in Sunsari, a little before the Kosi barrage. The traditional constituency of G. P. Koirala, his daughter, Sujata, was contesting polls from Bokraha as Girijababu had stayed out of the campaign. Her rival was the 'messiah of the Madhes', Upendra Yadav.

Sankarshan Thakur, a senior Indian journalist and a close friend, had come over to cover the polls. We travelled together to Biratnagar, hired a car, drove for an hour, and turned right at Laukaha, leaving the comfort of the highway for the rough gravel road towards Bokraha, to witness Koirala's campaigning.

As she drove by, crowds chanted, 'Sujata didi, jindabad.' At a primary school close by, she addressed a mass meeting and touched on themes that had become the NC's staple—of how the party had fought for democracy; of how her family had made extraordinary sacrifices in the struggle; of how they had fought the monarchy as well as restored peace by bringing the Maoists 'into the mainstream'; and how the Koiralas had been sensitive to Madhesis throughout their political lives.

We were standing at a distance and were soon accosted by a crowd. Maithili- and Urdu-speaking men in dhotis and kurtas, and young sari-draped women with heads covered, were not impressed by the slogans. 'Look at the road. Look at my torn clothes. Look at my children who have no school to go to, nowhere to work. We have always voted for the Koiralas and this is what we have got.'

The Madhesi leadership was hoping to combine precisely this disenchantment over livelihood concerns and link it to the identities of voters. We followed Upendra Yadav's convoy to a nearby school, and his pitch to the 1,000-strong meeting was, 'Let us stop this slavery to the Koiralas, Acharyas and Upadhyayas. They have only used us. Have they ever treated you as equal citizens? Let us take back what is ours. Let us ask for our adhikar, izzat, pahichan [rights, dignity, identity].' He, and his colleagues fighting elections across the Tarai, repeatedly emphasized how this was a one-time opportunity to draft their own Constitution, their own laws and, if the Madhesis failed to elect their own representatives, the opportunity would be lost forever.

The Koirala-Yadav battle was representative of the political struggle in the Tarai in the elections of 2008. On one side were the old 'democracy warriors' of the NC and the radicals-turned-establishment figures of the UML, returning to their traditional base after a successful struggle against the monarchy. These predominantly hill-origin leaders had been repeatedly elected, but there was always a gulf between the representative and the voter, with both eyeing the other with suspicion born out of their prejudice regarding the others' identity. On the other side were the new faces of the new parties. They did not have a six-decades-old democratic legacy, but they had, to their credit, the success of the Madhes andolan; they had the surnames and complexions which the voters could identify with; and they were contesting on the platform of inclusion and federalism, which sounded more meaningful than the mere rhetoric of democracy.

The old national parties received a severe drubbing and, symbolically for the NC, three of the four Koiralas who fought elections, including the discredited Sujata who had come to represent the worst of the nepotistic and corrupt democracy of the 1990s, lost. The Maoists managed a respectable performance in the plains, with the support of the Tharus and the pahadis in the western Tarai, and Dalits and other intermediate castes in pockets of the eastern Tarai. But the three Madhesi parties, given their short histories, were the big story—they won eighty-three seats in the CA. Across party lines, there were to be 200 Madhesis in the 601-strong CA, fulfilling the idea of proportional representation for the first time. Ramesh Mahato's sacrifice had not gone in vain. The manner in which the Madhes would become the swing force in Nepali politics became apparent very soon, with the election of the first President of the republic.

1

G. P. Koirala's daughter may have lost the elections. His party may have come a dismal second, winning thirty-seven out of the 240 directly elected seats and having only 110 representatives in the 601-strong house where the Maoists had two hundred and forty. He may have stayed out of the election campaign entirely. But, after having spent six decades in democratic politics, become prime minister five times, signed the 12-point Understanding which initiated the peace process, engineered NC's shift away from the monarchy and, in the words of his party colleague Pradeep Giri, 'being pathologically obsessed with political power', Girjababu felt it was his right to become Nepal's first elected head of state.

His expectation was not unnatural, for the Maoists, according to NC leaders, had reportedly assured him that they would support him for the position. Indeed, many of G. P. Koirala's aides later admitted that one of the factors that motivated the NC president to move away from the king was the promise of the presidency.

But the election results changed the incentive for all sides.

The Maoists' electoral success had scared the NC. Sceptics within the party, and professional Maoist baiters, were quick to conclude that the Maoists would use the electoral legitimacy to 'capture the state'. G. P. Koirala was himself reluctant to transfer power, and took over four months to make way for Prachanda.

The interim Constitution had imagined that the politics of consensus would define the political transition. In order to tackle the bane of governmental instability that had marked the 1990s, and ensure that the focus remained on Constitution-writing, the statute stipulated that a two-thirds majority would be needed to vote out the elected government. As long as the NC expected to return to power, they had no problem with this provision—in fact, they saw it as a way to ensure that the parliamentary arithmetic remained in their favour. But they now feared that the Maoists would use precisely the same provision to consolidate power. The NC and the UML shifted goalposts, and came up with a new demand—the Constitution must be amended to allow governments to be voted out on the floor of the house with a simple majority.

The Maoists resisted the move, and warned that this would mark the end of consensual politics. But G. P. Koirala remained firm and the older parties made this specific constitutional amendment the prerequisite for declaring the country a republic on 28 May 2008. The Maoists eventually gave in.

But all of this was to add to the mistrust, and harden the Maoists' position on the presidency. The former rebels now felt strongly that the NC and the UML were out to corner them, and deprive them of their rightful share in the power structure. There was a palpable fear in the party leadership that supporting someone of G. P. Koirala's stature as the first President would lead to the emergence of a parallel power centre; that he would retain the loyalty of the NA, and traditional forces would rally around him. The spirit of a ceremonial presidency would be shattered when a man so used to exercising power occupied the position. The more ideological and dogmatic sections of the Maoists continued to perceive G. P. Koirala as a class enemy. They argued that the electoral victory had indicated a clear mandate for a reordering of class relations, and there was no reason to hand over the republican prize to a man who, until recently, had been supporting the monarchy.

After flirting with several names, and misleading the UML leader Madhav Kumar Nepal into believing that he could be the next President in a bid to increase the gulf between the NC and the UML, the Maoists proposed Ram Raja Prasad Singh as their candidate. Throwing up Singh's name was a masterstroke. He had been a republican for over four decades; he was a Madhesi; he had provided weapons training to early revolutionaries, including Prachanda, and had been broadly supportive of the People's War. With these credentials, he would appeal—or so the calculation went—to the Left, the republicans and the Madhesi parties.

The NC was now in a fix. G. P. Koirala did not wish to contest elections, but there was no question of giving the Maoists a free run. The UML, too, was bitter about its electoral rout, and the manner in which Madhav Nepal had been duped. The two parties agreed to put up a contest, even if the cards seemed heavily stacked in favour of the Maoists who appeared to have Madhesi support. But true to character, the unexpected occurred yet again in Nepali politics.

~

Ram Baran Yadav was in a curious position. A medical doctor who studied in Calcutta and Chandigarh and practised in his hometown of Janakpur before being selected as B. P. Koirala's personal physician in the early 1980s, Yadav was a Madhesi leader in the NC. But, unlike the other Madhesi leaders and activists of mainstream parties, he appeared to have little empathy for the Madhesi uprising of 2007 and 2008.

Instead, Yadav had called for an immediate end to the agitation for federalism, terming it anarchic; defended the NC-led interim government's actions; turned a blind eye to the police killings during the protests; and emerged as the ruling party's staunchest defender. This earned him considerable political capital with Prime Minister G. P. Koirala and gave him unprecedented popularity for a Madhesi in Kathmandu's hill-dominated media and opinion-making circles—they saw him as a man who stood for 'national integrity', one who did not succumb to 'populism' in the name of his community.

He was the archetypal Madhesi Mahendra's nationalism had sought to create—one who placed more emphasis on unity through uniformity rather than through expression of diversity, and one who was at home with the symbols of old Nepali nationhood, from daura-saluwar to the Nepali language. Like the Hindu extremists in India, whose favourite pastime is to ask Indian Muslims if they are Indians or Muslims first; like the Pakistanis who forced Bangla speakers to choose between the nation and their language, Nepal's hill chauvinists framed the question of identity in similar binary terms. The Madhesi political project was about contesting the very basis of the question, asserting how being a Nepali and being a Madhesi were not contradictory at all, and rejecting the need to prioritize loyalties. But Yadav played along, and his unvarying answer soothed the ears of the hill elite. 'I am a Nepali first.'

But it had also earned him the wrath of Madhesi activists who saw him as a sell-out; a leader who was willing to sacrifice the interests of his constituency for personal gain within the existing party structure; a man who would forget his roots and had reinforced the conservative narrative of seeing Madhesi assertion as a threat to national unity. Extremists from the armed groups had vandalized his house during the agitation. At a time when a majority of Madhesi leaders, including more senior figures like Mahant Thakur, quit national parties and plunged into the movement for identity, Yadav stuck to the NC. The kindest explanation was that he had firm convictions, that he was committed to the larger political-ideological project of the NC and saw identity as distracting from the goals of social democracy. The more accurate, though harsh, explanation was that with his astute political sense, Yadav had understood that being a minority within a national party would fetch handsome political dividends.

~

The Maoists set the terms by nominating Ram Raja Singh as their candidate. To dilute the 'Madhesi card', and prevent all Madhesi votes from gravitating towards Singh, the NC and the UML were forced to play the competitive game of inclusion. NC opted for Yadav while the UML fielded Ram Prit Paswan, a Madhesi Dalit leader, for the presidency. From being barely recognized as citizens, the fact that all three candidates for presidency were Madhesis was a testament to the success of the movement and its political impact. Irrespective of the result, what was certain was that a Madhesi would be the first citizen of the Federal Democratic Republic of Nepal.

But there was a twist. The three Madhesi parties—the MJF, the TMLP and the Sadbhavana—had agreed to back Ram Raja Singh for the presidency. But the question of the vice-presidency remained open. The Maoists put forward a Newar woman as their candidate, and expected Madhesi parties to reciprocate their support for the cause of larger unity between the forces fighting for inclusion and marginalized communities.

But the MJF had other plans. Upendra Yadav argued that since Singh was the candidate put forward by the Maoists, the MJF, too—as the largest Madhesi party—had a right to put up its own candidate for the vice-presidency. NC spotted an opportunity to capitalize on the rift between the Maoists and the MJF. Just before the elections, the NC, the UML and the MJF struck a deal in which Upendra Yadav agreed to support Ram Baran Yadav for President, and extracted a commitment from the two bigger parties that they would support his candidate for vice-president, Parmanand Jha, a former judge.

Upendra's decision to back Ram Baran created unease among sections of the Madhesi political class, given his doubtful commitment to the Madhesi agenda. Upendra was also castigated as being ungrateful, for there were reliable indications that Ram Raja Singh had lobbied with the BJP-led government in the early 2000s to get the MJF chairman released when he was arrested along with other Maoists. There was insinuation that Upendra had shifted camps to back a fellow Yadav, preferring caste over the larger agenda and the alliance of the marginalized. Kathmandu's grapevine even had it that influential Yadav leaders from Bihar and Uttar Pradesh had called up Upendra to lobby in favour of Ram Baran Yadav. But the MJF supporters countered this by suggesting that it was the upper-caste mafia of the TMLP and Sadbhavana that was supporting a fellow upper-caste leader, the Rajput, Ram Raja Prasad Singh. The MJF had an additional argument—by using the divisions between the three bigger parties, they were trying to get a Madhesi elected as vice-president as well.

In the first round of voting, the combined support of the NC, the UML and the three Madhesi parties allowed Parmanand Jha to sail through as the country's first-ever vice-president. The TMLP and Sadbhavana told their Maoist partners that they could not be seen as opposing a Madhesi candidate and broke ranks for this vote. But the polarization was more evident for the presidential poll. It was only with a second round of voting that Ram Baran Yadav managed to squeeze past Singh to become Nepal's first President.

~

Ram Baran Yadav and Parmanand Jha's election marked a historic turning point in contemporary Nepali politics.

Not only did it confirm the end of the monarchy, and the beginning of the institutionalization of the new republic, it also showed how identity movements, electoral success, and the vagaries of realpolitik often throw up surprising results.

The election was proof that the Madhesi parties would be the swing force in the fragmented CA, with each national party wooing them. The NC and the UML had no intention or desire to put up a Madhesi candidate but had to do so to wean the Madhesi Street away from the Maoists. It was a reflection of how the Madhesi parties would be ruthless in their quest to claim more than their share in the power structure to redress historical under-representation. This was demonstrated by the MJF's opportunistic, last-minute alliance to get a Madhesi vice-president elected—even though in a diverse land, the logic of inclusion suggested that the position should have gone to another social group.

Yadav's election also showed the kind of compromise all forces would have to make in the creation of a new Nepal—he was a Madhesi, a member of the numerically and politically influential Yadav sub-caste, but he was also a conformist who was keen to allay the concerns of the old establishment. His Madhesi background

helped him win the nomination; his caste helped tilt Upendra Yadav away from a rival candidate; but his opposition to the Madhes movement gave him credibility with the hill-dominated national parties. The limits of the moment soon became clear. President Yadav took his oath in Nepali. But Vice-President Jha took his oath of office in Hindi—the Madhesi political project had long pushed for Hindi as the link language in the Tarai, much to the chagrin of hill nationalists who saw it as an 'Indian language'. Jha's act outraged Kathmandu's hill leaders who mobilized their students' unions against him. The matter went up to the court which annulled the oath, and forced him to retake it in Nepali and Maithili. Getting elected to a ceremonial position was easier than using it to redraw the nation's social contract, a point Yadav intuitively understood, and one that Jha learnt after paying a price.

Yet, the symbolism of Ram Baran Yadav replacing the Shah monarchs cannot be overemphasized. A son of a farmer, from a community Nepal's rulers often saw as the fifth column, was now heading the Republic. It gave pride to the Madhesi population and opened up the doors for inclusion. The big question, however, remained—how would Madhesi leaders use the political power they had accessed?

2

'My family has been serving Nepal for 165 years.'

Abhishek Shah had many traits, but humility was not among them. As the youngest elected Member of the Constituent Assembly, the twenty-six-year-old Shah had reason to be proud. His father, Ajay Pratap Shah, was a member of the interim legislature from the Right-wing outfit, the Rastriya Prajatantra Party (RPP). Shah had died in 2007 and, in true South Asian political tradition, the party had nominated the son for the seat. Abhishek had fought elections on the MJF ticket and won from the traditional family constituency in central Tarai's Kapilbastu district.

Abhishek was conscious that his success was a result of an accident of birth, and spoke about his family 'legacy' at length when I met him in the middle of 2008. The battle for the presidency had ended, and the MJF had made up with the Maoists. They were now a part of the same coalition, with Upendra Yadav as the foreign minister. 'We came to Nepal in 1857. My ancestors had a state in India, but they supported the revolutionaries against the British in the Mutiny. When they won, the British expelled us from the country. The king in Nepal then was Rajendra Bikram Shah, whose wife Samrajya Devi—the most powerful queen in Nepal's history—was a relative of ours. She was from Gopalpur, near Gorakhpur. They requested the British to let us come to Nepal.' The regime granted the family land, and they established the town of Krishnanagar close to the border in Kapilbastu. 'We had a lot of land in the beginning, almost one lakh bighas. We used to collect tax all the way till Chitwan.' An old man who had served us tea and appeared to be a family retainer, chipped in, 'Sahib, Shahs were the biggest landlords of the Tarai.'

Abhishek said he was the fourth generation of his family in politics. 'My great-grandfather, Thakur Gaya Prasad Shah, was a minister in Mohan Shumsher Rana's government in 1951. My grandfather, Shiv Prasad Shah, was deputy minister for finance in B. P. Koirala-led first democratic government in 1960, and the most educated personality in the Cabinet. My grandfather's third brother, Raghvendra Pratap Shah, was a minister for agriculture and communication in the royal Panchayat government. Another grandfather, Pashupati Shah, was secretary of hydropower and the youngest of them, Birendra Shah, was secretary, roads and sewage. As you know, my father was an MP. And in twenty-five years, Prashantji, I will be the country's President or prime minister.'

'Sure,' I said, praising his ambition. But I could not resist pointing out how his family had allied with all political forces and parties, from the Ranas to the monarchists to the NC and, now, the MJF, irrespective of the nature of the regime.

He saw it as a badge of honour and replied, 'Dekhiye, jab ham public se attach rahenge, to government se attach rahenge. [Look, if we are attached to the public, we will be attached to the government.] It is a matter of dilemma and irony that now we are in the Maoist government also.' This was because they had always been oriented towards 'development'. 'Our great-grandfather donated 100 bighas and set up a school. My grandfather was roads secretary when the East-West Highway was constructed and our family donated land. Another grandfather fixed the exchange rate of Nepali and Indian currency to 1 and 1.6.' Democracy, he said, was in their blood. 'Only those who are greedy get affected by political changes. We have both Laxmi and Saraswati [the goddesses of money and brains, respectively] in our house.'

Politics, Abhishek claimed, had had a deep impact on him while growing up. He remembered how his father, late at night, had to go out regularly to sort out disputes whenever there was trouble in the area. On a visit to Kathmandu, he desperately wanted to meet the former prime minister and RPP leader, Surya Bahadur Thapa, but his father asked him to stay away from politics. He saw the Maoist conflict intensifying. Kapilbastu had been in the news for setting up vigilante anti-Maoist groups—called pratikar samiti—to whom the state outsourced its coercive authority, leading to human rights abuses. Abhishek's family supported these groups. 'During the Maoist time, there was a lot of exploitation and injustice. They used to enter people's homes, take away foodgrains, and use their land. People reacted. Wherever there was injustice, we opposed it.'

In 2006, his father, Abhishek said, had invited Upendra Yadav home for lunch after being impressed with his research on the under-representation of Madhesis in state services. When the Madhes movement began in the eastern Tarai, Abhishek pointed out, there was nothing in the west. 'I began the movement by taking out a masal julus [torchlit procession], supporting a bandh and then the Madhes pradesh demand.'

The story did not quite fit together, for Abhishek had become an MP from the RPP after the Madhes movement, once his father died of renal failure, and shifted to the MJF only later. I did not press the specific charge, but went back to the more generic question that had emerged about people like him.

Once the monarchy weakened after the Janandolan, many loyalists jumped ship, became a part of identity politics, and thus remained relevant. Bijay Gachhedar was in the NC, and had flirted with the monarchy. When he saw his prospects dim in the NC, he shifted to the MJF, after both the Madhes movements, a month before the elections. Sharad Singh Bhandari was a minister in the Panchayat autocracy in the late 1980s, became a Congress leader and, with Gachhedar, joined the MJF. Sarvendra Nath Shukla shifted from the royalist RPP to the TMLP. Did dozens of Madhesis die only to help rehabilitate discredited political leaders who had been an integral part of the structure that they held responsible for discrimination?

Many sought to delegitimize the entire Madhesi movement by pointing out such leaders even as they ignored the many people—the women, Dalits, intermediate caste leaders—who, for the first time, had access to political power.

I asked Abhishek what he felt about the perception of opportunism that marked their politics. 'I don't know about others. But if I had stood from RPP, if I had stood as an independent, even then I would have won. In our society, politics is not party-based but personality-based. We were always democrats. When people interacted with the king, we were with the king. Now, public is with the Maoists and we are with the Maoists in government.'

And could a man whose family owned over one lakh bighas of land represent the aspirations of the Madhes, where the problem of landlessness was most acute? 'We have less than 100 bighas in the family now. And there is no love for land anymore. One ropani in Kathmandu values more than the big plots in the Tarai.' Getting visibly agitated, Abhishek added, 'And is land reform about capture? It is about fertilizers, irrigation, diesel, equipment, and subsidy. And if it is about redistribution, you take all our land in Tarai and give us land in Kathmandu. Why should there be injustice?'

~

Back in his home district, Sanjeev Kumar scoffed at Abhishek Shah's logic. The party secretary of the Maoists for Kapilbastu neither saw an alliance with leaders like Shah as natural, nor bought his claims about the irrelevance of land reform.

I was meeting Sanjeev in the Maoist party's office in Taulihawa, a town so small that a traffic gridlock could occur if two rickshaws crossed each other in its narrow lanes. There was nothing here to indicate that Gautam Buddha was born just a few kilometres away over 2,500 years ago, and that this was a part of the greater Lumbini region. The district—with a mixed population of Muslims, Tharus, pahadis, Yadavs, Kurmis and Dalits—had witnessed the flaring up of communal riots in 2007 after the killing of a prominent Muslim leader which triggered clashes between pahadis and Madhesis, between the Maoists and regional leaders, and generated tensions between Hindus and Muslims.

Sanjeev believed that the problem was not identity as much as class, and people like Shah were the 'enemy'. 'These big zamindars have amassed land, 200 to 400 bighas, through exploitation. They have dual citizenship, both here and in India, for protection. The Maoists raised this issue during the war and, now, to ensure they do not get targeted when land reform measures are introduced, they are selling off land to convert into capital.'

Sanjeev's point was echoed by Baldev Ram in another corner of the Tarai.

A half-an-hour bus ride from Lahan, off the East-West Highway towards the town of Gaighat, Ram was sitting in a small community centre in Kadmaha village. A tiny figure, clad in dhoti-kurta, he was a legend among grassroots activists.

Ram had led a movement in Siraha in 1999. He was a Chamar, a Dalit sub-community, traditionally expected to dispose of cattle carcasses. But Ram and his fellow campaigners organized a resistance against the practice, and protested against their classification as untouchables. The district's land-owning upper- and intermediate-castes were infuriated by the challenge to the existing social hierarchy and the effort to reorder the division of labour. MPs of the time supported the upper castes and Dalits were prohibited entry into Lahan. A social boycott was enforced, and Chamars were refused loans, prohibited from using public resources and stopped from working in the market. The upper castes mobilized some Musahars, another Dalit sub-caste who were dependent on them for livelihoods, against the Chamars to prevent the Dalits from coming together.

But the movement continued, gaining much publicity in the national media and drawing the support of wider civil society. It eventually ended in a victory for the Dalit protestors, who insisted that they would continue the practice but only on more respectable, professional terms. The local administration had to mediate and engineer an agreement which clearly stated that no person could be forced to deal with carrion, and that the social boycott was inhuman and must end. The Dalit leaders had made a simple point—we serve a useful social function but are castigated as untouchables for that very reason; yet our legitimate protest was seen as 'disturbing social harmony'.

Ram shot to fame. He attended several international conferences, participated in the World Social Forum in Mumbai in 2004 and, when I met him, was the chairman of the Rashtriya Bhoomi Adhikar Manch, the National Land Rights Forum.

Ram said that the benefits of the Madhesi movement had not percolated down to the poor and the landless. 'Look, we supported the andolan. And we have even managed to send several representatives of the Landless Forum to the Constituent Assembly. But the promises to the landless have not been met.' I asked him whether the problem was their narrow agenda of land redistribution when the era of big landlords ended. 'This is not true. One MP in Saptari owns 300 bighas in his own name; another owns 500 bighas. They may have cleverly divided it in the names of their families. But Land Ceiling Act needs to be imposed more strictly.' An NC government in the 1990s had set a ceiling on land ownership at 10 bighas per household.

Ram also laid out their other demands—an end to absentee landlordism, the enforcement of tenancy rights, irrigation, subsidized agriculture, an increase in minimum wages, the use of waste land, and easier registration. 'Ours is a broad, not narrow agenda. The elites have a narrow agenda, of only saving their land.'

Could an Abhishek Shah represent the interests of Baldev Ram, for whom issues of caste and class starkly intersected? That would be the real test of Madhesi politics, and whether the electoral success and call for dignity had translated into benefits for the poorest constituents. Four years later, the answer was clear. Not a single land-reform measure had been implemented. The failure to re-examine land relations in the Tarai—which would include the more mundane tasks of updating land records, settling property disputes, returning property to rightful owners, rethinking links between agriculture and industry, besides redistribution—was to have tragic consequences, only a few of which came to public notice.

3

Uma Singh was a tough interviewer. It was 6 a.m. in Janakpur and, after a long drinking session at Navrang the previous evening, I was not really fit for the meeting. But Uma's questions woke me up from my haze.

A liberal radio licensing regime had revolutionized news in Nepal. Community stations had sprung up across the country and, with their regular news bulletins and chat shows, FM radio channels had done more to spread political awareness across the country than any other medium. The spread of the radio network also saw the emergence of a new generation of journalists, primarily male, in district towns. Janakpur alone had six FM stations.

Uma and I were sitting in the Radio Today studio that winter morning in late 2008. She was petite, wore a white kurta, and seemed to be in her early twenties. I was on a field assignment in the Tarai and a friend who worked in the media group which ran Radio Today had asked me to be a guest on Uma's popular show, *Garma Garam Chai*. Uma told me not to use English words and to stick to Maithili. I nodded, but said that I would not be able to match her fluency in the language. She responded, 'Try please. Use Hindi words if you must, but not English. People in villages are the audience.'

Uma Singh was inquisitive and comfortable with being live on-air. She asked me about the political machinations in the capital, the role of the Madhesi parties, the headlines in the national dailies that morning. We discussed the criminality of Madhesi armed groups. Unlike many Madhesi journalists, who instinctively supported their own representatives, Uma's line of questioning indicated that she had no such dilemmas—she felt that Madhesi leaders must answer for their use and abuse of power.

We chatted for a bit after the programme. Uma told me that she was originally from Siraha. 'But you know there are no opportunities in Lahan. Even in Janakpur, the media is limited. And for women, it is even tougher.' She said that she wanted to move to Kathmandu, and was looking for a good break. We exchanged numbers and promised to keep in touch.

Two months later, Uma was dead.

~

The media and human rights community in Janakpur were on the streets when I reached the town the day after Uma's murder.

A dozen men had barged in to her room on the evening of 11 January 2009 and had stabbed her repeatedly. Friends and fellow journalists took her first to the local hospital, where they realized that the only way of saving Uma was to immediately fly her to a better equipped hospital in Kathmandu. The president of the Federation of Nepalese Journalists (FNJ) happened to be Dharmendra Jha, who was originally from Janakpur. Jha spoke to the NA chief, General Rukmangad Katawal, to arrange for an air ambulance but it was already late at night, and the weather did not permit flight. Uma was then rushed in an ambulance to Kathmandu, an eight-hour drive away, but she succumbed to her injuries on the way.

When I arrived, tagging along with an FNJ fact-finding team from Kathmandu, Uma's body was in a jeep in the District Administration Office (DAO). Her mother was sitting next to it, quiet in her grief, while her sister-in-law sat some distance away. The FNJ's local chapter had decided that they would not cremate Uma till the state promised a thorough investigation into the killing, provided adequate compensation to the family, declared Uma a martyr, and strengthened security for journalists across the country.

People were huddled in small groups in the big open space inside the DAO. A debate was raging between officials of the FNJ on what strategy to pursue in order to push the government to meet their demands. Jha called up Information Minister Krishna Bahadur Mahara and warned him that the situation would get out of control if the government did not act quickly. A small group left to negotiate with the Chief District Officer (CDO). I approached some journalists from Janakpur, who were whispering amongst themselves, and met Ajay Anuragi, a bright reporter working for one of the FM stations.

Ajay took me aside and said, 'Bhaiji, this case is really tragic. Maoists had kidnapped and killed Uma's father and brother three years ago. Matrika Yadav's [the influential Maoist leader from the Tarai] group also confiscated her family property, and Uma was fighting against it. She had written one piece in a local magazine exposing the Maoists. The natural suspicion is towards them. But Rajesh will know more,' pointing to Rajesh Verma, a journalist from Siraha whom I knew from my travels in the district. Rajesh was sobbing inconsolably, surrounded by a group of people. He was the district reporter for *The Himalayan Times*.

A little later, I managed to have a quiet word with him. Rajesh told me that he had known Uma and her family for years, and that he had taught her journalism in a local campus in Siraha. 'I encouraged her to join the media, made her sub-editor in my local weekly. It's my fault. If she was not in this line, this may not have happened at all.' I asked him who he thought was behind the murder. Rajesh looked around and whispered quietly, 'There could be a family angle to this. I know that Uma and her bhabhi did not get along, especially after the brother's death. The bhabhi expected the property to be passed on to her, and Uma saw it as her father's land to which her mother and she had first claim. I am not suggesting anything, but it is one angle.' The family had property in Siraha's Maheshpur village, and in Mirchaiya bazaar.

Negotiations between the government and the activists had, meanwhile, concluded with the agreement that Uma would be cremated the next morning, and the CDO had privately assured the FNJ that their demands would be met. On 13 January, after a quick breakfast at Hotel Rama, we headed back to the DAO. Uma's body was taken across the town in a truck, with hundreds of people following in a procession. The bazaar was shut down as a mark of respect. Young people who had never participated in political demonstrations seemed to be on the streets this time. Curious onlookers climbed on to their terraces and looked out of their windows.

Ajit Tiwari, a journalist from Janakpur, said, 'If we do not get justice even now, there is no point in continuing with journalism. There is no hope for this country.' A town's conscience had been stirred, and the Madhesi-pahadi gulf seemed to have been forgotten. The media in Kathmandu had reached out across social boundaries and had helped carve out a new solidarity on issues that cut across geographies. That was perhaps the only silver lining of that dark moment.

Uma was cremated at the Ganga Sagar Ghat, less than two kilometres from the famous Janaki temple. Two days later, the information minister visited Janakpur and promised to speed up investigations. A Cabinet meeting declared Uma a martyr, awarded 1 million Nepali rupees to the family, and promised to guarantee press freedom. Prime Minister Prachanda made a public declaration that Uma's killers would not be spared, though many took it with a pinch of salt given that Maoist cadres were alleged to have been involved in the incident. But subsequent events were to show that accusing the Maoists for every crime, in a knee-jerk reaction, would not be right.

While individuals who, at some point had been associated with the party may have been implicated, there was no institutional decision taken by the Maoists to assassinate Uma. Her journalism, her willingness to assert and stand up for her rights, her questioning of the patriarchal order and carving out space in the almost completely male-dominated press of the Tarai, and her willingness to stake her claim both outside and inside her family made her vulnerable. But there was a definite personal element to the killing and the motives of different actors overlapped. Though some questions related to the murder remained unanswered, the police concluded that Uma's sister-in-law, Lalita Singh, had collaborated with people to engineer the killing for property. Lalita was convicted by a lower court in 2011.

Uma's murder brought together the various issues that were shaping lives in the Tarai—the proliferation of small arms; the intersection of the personal and the political; the rise in violence; the breakdown of relations over land and property; the presence of many, many young men ready to take life, and to do so brutally for a quick buck; the utter absence of the state and its inability or unwillingness to stamp out the culture of impunity that bred these killings; and the issues of gender justice and threats young professional women, balancing complex family lives and dangerous professions, had to face. On her way to Kathmandu in the ambulance, before she died, Uma's last words were questions—'Why? What crime did I commit?' Madhesi society is yet to conduct any serious soul-searching and find an answer to Uma's questions. And till it does so, there will be neither peace nor justice in the plains of Nepal.

~

Uma's murder shook me and, after the cremation, I began to reflect on the patterns of violence in the Tarai. Tula Sah, the Madhesi activist, had conducted an empirical survey of the killings in the plains and discovered that the violence essentially stemmed from disputes over property, caste-based discrimination and vendettas. But the antagonists, either to protect themselves or to further their goals, joined a political group, blurring the line between the private and the public realms. Armed groups, whose activities varied in intensity, continued to provide the most convenient cover for such rivalries to play out.

I had remained in touch with Rajeev Jha, who had taken me across to meet the armed group leader, Jwala Singh, in 2007. Jwala had tried to lure him to join the JTMM during our dinner in Darbhanga and, soon after we returned, Rajeev took the plunge. Before the elections, I went to meet him in Bihar's Sitamarhi town, across the Mahottari border.

Rajeev had replicated the modus operandi of other armed militants. He was now Chandrashekhar, the head of the JTMM's intellectual wing; he lived in small hotels under pseudonyms; he used three cellphones, one with a Nepali SIM which caught signals from across the border; and had a small radio set on which he could listen to news broadcast on Janakpur's FM stations. Another former student activist affiliated to the MJF, Mukesh Chaudhary a.k.a. Arjun Singh, was with him during the two days I spent in their hotel room in Sitamarhi.

Maoist literature was scattered around Rajeev's room, even though militants from the Tarai took great pains to distinguish themselves from the Maoists who, in their opinion, had betrayed the Madhesi agenda. But, subconsciously, the former rebels seemed to be their political role models. Rajeev used the same language of internal colonialism that the Maoists, and then other Madhesi activists, had adopted to describe the Tarai's relationship with Kathmandu. He insisted that violence was both necessary and effective, as demonstrated by the way in which the Maoists had occupied mainstream political space, and did not buy my argument that the former rebels had wrested that space only after forsaking violence. He told me that the CA would deliver nothing to the Madhesis, since Madhesi parties would never have a majority in the house. I overheard him give instructions on the phone to his cadres in Birgunj to step up the karabahi, physical action, against pahadis. We remained friendly, but I let it be known that I had faith that peaceful politics would deliver rights and justice to the Madhes.

With Uma's killing, I could not resist calling Rajeev and giving him unsolicited advice. He or his group may not have had anything to do with the incident, but there was little doubt that Uma was a victim of a larger political culture to which they, among many other groups and the state, were contributing. Not only was this delegitimizing the genuine Madhesi struggle—it was easy for hill chauvinists to use the reckless criminality to undermine the politics of the Tarai—but it was destroying an entire generation of young people, young Madhesis. Rajeev had split with Jwala Singh and set up his own armed outfit. He did not buy my theory, and persisted with his political line.

The state's approach only confirmed the most negative of the assumptions that Rajeev and other extremists had made about the Nepali regime.

In July 2009, late one evening, Rajeev called me up—his voice quivering, the panic apparent. He said that the chairman of his new party, Ram Narayan a.k.a. Manager Mahato, had been picked up by the Bihar police in Jainagar. 'They have handed him over to the Siraha district police in Nepal. We think they will kill him. Can you do something?' I was surprised by this rare instance of cross-border cooperation, for the Indian side had never handed Madhesi militants over to Nepal earlier. I told Rajeev that I would spread the word in Kathmandu's civil society and that he was perhaps being too fearful.

The next morning, Rajeev called again. This time, his voice was calm. 'They did it. The pahadi state killed him, and called it an encounter. Prashantji, you tell me to talk to such a government, such a state. We will extract revenge.' I was stunned. By afternoon, news reports trickled in of how the Siraha police had killed Mahato after he fired upon a police patrol late at night. The media had faithfully accepted the state's version, which was infuriating, for I knew that the truth was more complex, that Mahato had already been in police custody.

The next day, the same district police—led by a man hailed as a supercop by most of the Kathmandu media, Ramesh Kharel—was involved in yet another encounter and killed an alleged militant, Parshuram Yadav. That week, two other activists, suspected to be working for armed groups, were shot dead. Research conducted for The Tarai Human Rights Defenders' Alliance by the activist Dipendra Jha showed how over 100 Madhesi men had been killed by the state in extra-judicial executions, all under the cover of 'encounters'. Almost four years later, a report by the Bihar Human Rights Commission would slam personnel of the Bihar police for illegally handing over Mahato to Nepal.

With the structural violence, the Madhesis of the plains now had to confront other forms of violence—direct physical action by the armed extremists, the use of criminals to settle personal rivalries under political cover and, most dangerously, the unstated but clear policy adopted by the state to bump off inconvenient elements in the name of order and security, bypassing the due process of law and increasing the alienation of the Madhesi Street.

The government's ruthless policy, the long-term impact of which is yet to manifest itself, proved to be effective in the short run. The incentives for the militants suddenly changed.

Armed groups were once seen as a low-cost, high-return venture. The thrill, the economic windfall, and the sense that one was part of something larger, had attracted young men to these outfits—but the thrill, and the money, were worth the danger only when there was little chance that they would be caught or implicated, and when they had close enough ties with mainstream politicians and bureaucrats to get off the hook. But now the choice was starker. They could continue in an uncertain armed struggle, which had not been able to muster wide public support, whose relevance was increasingly questioned by the Madhesi Street after the success of the Madhesi parties in the elections, and where the risks of getting killed had increased. Or they could use the fig leaf of peace talks to emerge into open society, escape punishment, and adjust to the new political realities. Barring those who were truly ideologically committed, almost all members of the armed groups chose the second option.

In 2010 and 2011, as I continued to travel in the Tarai, I came across surrendered militants who, for a variety of reasons, had shifted course. Some cited pressure from their families to do something more acceptable, in an indication that violence did not have wider social sanction. Others, disillusioned about the prospects for change, picked up their passports and left the country. Some felt that they could create enough space within the ideological-political mainstream, inspired by the success of the Madhesi parties. They may have given up the gun, and the intensity of the armed activity may have dipped, but what still united these young people was what they called the Madhesvaadi sentiment which sought a Madhes pradesh and inclusion in state organs. Beneath the calm surface, discontent with the Nepali state simmered. Its strength may have become diluted, but the extremist pole of Madhesi politics—which stood for isolation from, as opposed to integration into Nepal—had not entirely faded away.

4

The stone hit its target; the windshield shattered and the jeep swerved right. The driver, in uniform, looked behind, while his co-passenger could be heard reporting the incident on his wireless phone. In seconds, the gate to Tundikhel—opposite the old bus park—opened, and the jeep sped inside. It was an army vehicle.

Tharu protestors had started from Maitighar Mandala, past

Tripureshwor and New Road, and had taken a round of the Khula Manch and Ratna Park to congregate right next to the army headquarters in the capital. The slogans were loud, the protestors were agitated, and the targets varied. The symbolism of an angry agitator from one of Nepal's poorest, most marginalized communities, which had suffered enormously at the hands of the security forces, pelting stones at an army vehicle in the heart of the capital, and the army choosing to make a quick retreat rather than confront the protest organizers, could not be missed.

But that afternoon in March 2009, Tharu political activists were on the streets opposing not the state as much as the Madhesi political class. It was the army which had suffered 'collateral damage'. The Joint Tharu Struggle Committee had shut down the Tarai for almost two weeks, and was now making its presence felt in Kathmandu. Raj Kumar Lekhi, the head of the Tharu Kalyankari Society, the oldest socio-cultural outfit of the community; Laxman Tharu, a former Maoist who had quit and quickly made his mark as a Tharu leader with a base in Kailali; Kishore Biswas, a former MJF leader from the highway town of Duhabi in the Sunsari district; and Gopal Dahit, a former royalist minister, were among those leading the march.

The trigger had been the draft of an Inclusion Bill in Parliament, which clubbed the Tharus with the Madhesis. As Ekraj Chaudhary had warned me in Nepalgunj in 2007, this would not be acceptable to the indigenous Tharu community—who saw both pahadis and Madhesis as aggressors, from the north and the south respectively, occupying land that was 'originally' the home of the Tharus.

The electoral success of the Madhesi parties, and their continued assertion that the Tharus were merely a sub-component of the broader Madhesi identity, had made Tharu leaders nervous. They ratcheted up their own rhetoric, denying that there was any region called the Madhes or a community called Madhesi, and insisting that the entire stretch in the plains, from the east to west, should be named Tharuhat. Their immediate demand was for the Tharus to be categorized as a distinct ethnic group in the Inclusion Bill, and not as Madhesis; and for the Tharus to be granted proportionate representation in state organs.

I had bumped into a young Tharu student during the Kathmandu march. He also worked as a part-time journalist at a radio station. I suggested to him that the Madhesi-Tharu battle was distracting both communities from the larger challenge, that of fighting the state. He agreed, but said something that stayed with me, 'Sir, if you think Madhesis are deprived, spare a thought for us. Our land was taken away. Our people became bonded labour. We are 6.75 per cent of the population, more than any other Tarai group, yet do you ever hear about Tharus of Nepal? And now when we have a chance to express ourselves and claim rights, the Madhesis seem to want to eat us up. How can we accept that?'

He had a point, but the Madhesi leaders—smug in their political success and their presence in the government—were too blind to notice the insecurities of others around them, in the same manner that the hill elites had dismissed the Madhesis' concerns earlier. It was a classic case of the oppressed seeking to turn into the oppressor.

But the bandh and the protests organized by the Tharus proved effective. The government was forced to sign a 6-point deal with the joint Tharu Struggle Committee, conceding that they were a distinct social group which would enjoy the special rights given to indigenous people and the plains, as a mark of respect to the various communities which lived there, would now be called the Tarai-Madhes. The Madhesis' effort to impose their hegemony over the Tharus failed, and the two groups would now have to deal with each other as equals.

5

The Tarai was in a ferment. Contradictions on the ground had sharpened after the elections. The issue of representation by the elite, and the questions of livelihood, land, violence, resistance and sub-identities had emerged as the primary concerns. But the Madhesi parties were too busy in the power politics of the capital to pay attention to any of them.

Two themes were to dominate the trajectory of the Madhesi politics in Kathmandu: their relationship with the Maoists, and the staggering, almost uninterrupted, fragmentation of the political landscape—the three Madhesi parties of 2008 eventually broke down into almost a dozen smaller outfits by 2012.

~

The MJF had joined the government led by the Maoists on more generous power-sharing terms than those which had been enjoyed by Madhesi leaders in the past. Upendra Yadav became the foreign minister, and Bijay Gachhedar got the lucrative Ministry for Physical Works and Planning. The Sadbhavana leader Rajendra Mahato stuck to his traditional, profitable, portfolio of supplies. For a force which had contested polls on an anti-Maoist plank, the Madhesis got along surprisingly well with the Maoists. Madhesi ministers used their portfolios to enhance their personal and political power while the Maoists used the presence of an erstwhile adversary to enhance their democratic legitimacy.

But there was an increasing sense of unease among a large section of the Madhesi political class, and opinion-makers, about the Maoists' intent and actions, which could be interpreted as an attack on existing 'values' or a bid to 'capture the state'. There was pressure on the Tarai parties to maintain their distinct identity. On a range of issues—when the Maoist minister for culture sought to change the age-old tradition of appointing Indian priests at Pashupatinath temple by replacing them with Nepali priests, when the Maoist defence minister took an increasingly confrontational position with the NA chief, when the integration and rehabilitation of Maoist combatants remained in the doldrums, and when the Maoists were alleged to have committed abuses in the Tarai—the Madhesi parties stuck a divergent note.

The break came when the Maoists sought to dismiss the army chief, General Rukmangad Katawal. Foreign Minister Upendra Yadav was in Cuba at the time, but had given the green signal to Prime Minister Prachanda and had assured him that the MJF would not have any objection to the move. But even as Yadav continued with his junket in Havana, the backlash against Prachanda's move within the non-Maoist political class only grew.

Egged on by India, the majority of members of Parliament belonging to the MJF, led by the late entrants into the party, Bijay Gachhedar and Sharad Singh Bhandari, opposed any move to 'play with the army'. By the time Yadav returned, the balance of power had shifted and he had a clear choice—go with India, the NA establishment and older democratic parties; or remain allied with the Maoists, at the cost of the party splitting and the MJF earning the wrath of the Indian establishment.

Prachanda had resigned after his attempt to dismiss Katawal was subverted by the President. Yadav saw an opportunity in the crisis, and calculated that this may well be his chance to become prime minister, with support from the Maoists, since there was little chance that the Maoists could get back the leadership of the government again. But he underestimated the consolidation of the non-Maoist forces. His initial support for the Maoists' move, his absence during critical weeks which allowed Gachhedar to consolidate his strength in the party and emerge as its 'democratic' face, and his untimely display of ambition eroded Yadav's credibility within his own party and with the non-Maoist forces.

Yadav then went along with the drift, with the MJF voting for the opposition candidate, Madhav Kumar Nepal. Through this period, tensions between Yadav and Gachhedar continued to sharpen, with things coming to a breaking point when Prime Minister Nepal appointed Gachhedar as his deputy prime minister as reward for his anti-Maoist campaign.

Yadav was stunned. The MJF was his party, he saw himself as the Madhesi 'messiah', he harboured prime ministerial ambitions, and here was Gachhedar—who had contributed little to the Madhesi movement and had joined just before the elections—hijacking the party and becoming its leader in government. Yadav threw Gachhedar and his followers out from the party the very next day and withdrew support from the government. But it was too late. Eventually, Yadav was left with twenty-five out of fifty-three MPs, with twenty-eight others forming a new MJF (Democratic) under Gachhedar.

~

The split of 2009 in the MJF was a significant milestone in Madhesi politics. It brought together all the elements that were to spark future splits—individual ambitions, ideological polarization, a crisis of leadership, and Indian policy preferences at a particular moment. The split was initially potrayed as having been caused by differences in principles. Bijay Gachhedar projected himself as fighting the good battle, in favour of democracy, resisting the Maoists' attempts to infiltrate the army and capture the state even as Yadav was portrayed as having compromised with his ideals.

But the ruthless political ambition underlying the split was obvious. Yadav thought that he could become prime minister, while Gachhedar saw in the split an opportunity to become the leader of the party. Yadav's working style had not helped either—he had become arrogant and was known to dismiss constituents who came to him for favours by telling them, 'I am the foreign minister, go to your district leader for this.' This is tantamount to hara-kiri in South Asian politics, where individual voters often demand a degree of respect and recognition in return for their support. This provided fertile enough ground for his rivals to consolidate support.

But domestic factors, in themselves, may not have been enough; the India hand, too, was visible in the split. Delhi had been uncomfortable with Upendra Yadav and had encouraged the formation of the TMLP before the polls. When it felt that Yadav was getting a bit too cosy with the Maoists, it backed Gachhedar to the hilt—persuading and cajoling MPs of the MJF to support him. When the split was imminent, Gachhedar told India that he needed money to bring MPs over to his side. Reliable sources—MJF MPs who received the cash, intermediaries who handled the transactions, and Indian officials serving in Kathmandu at the time—told me that millions were given to Gachhedar for the purpose.

I later asked a senior Indian diplomat why they had invested such capital, both political and financial, in splitting the party, 'We couldn't risk it. The stakes were very high. If Yadav had stuck to the Maoists, NC and UML would not have had the numbers to form the government. It was not an easy decision for us either. After all, we had kept telling Madhesis to unite and here we were encouraging a split. Yadav was utterly unreliable. The policy priority at the time was keeping the Maoists out and defeating their state-capture designs, and Gachhedar was an ally in that aim.'

The split in the MJF marked a new polarization in Madhesi politics. Like the rest of Nepali society, the question of how to view the Maoists—as a progressive force which would enable social change, or a force of evil which would wreck all democratic structures and leave society in ruins—had divided the Madhesi parties.

The MJF (D) led by Gachhedar was firmly in the anti-Maoist camp. The Mahant Thakur-led TMLP had not joined the Prachanda government, on the grounds that they were fighting for rights, not power. But under India's pressure to strengthen the legitimacy of the Madhav Nepal dispensation, TMLP joined the new government in 2009. Rajendra Mahato continued in his avatar as the minister for supplies. Their common position was that the Maoists had flouted the democratic rules of the game and, unless the party implemented its commitments to the peace process, renounced violence, gave up its army and returned confiscated property, the former rebels would not be allowed to come back to power.

Upendra Yadav now represented the other pole, and built up an understanding with the Maoists. He saw them as an ally in the battle for federalism, and told me at the end of 2009, 'Till we get a Madhes pradesh, we need to work with the Maoists. The NC and UML will never support Madhesi rights.'

Yadav also argued that the Maoists would never complete the peace process till they were accommodated in the power structure. His ire was also directed at the then Indian ambassador, Rakesh Sood, whom he blamed for the split in the MJF. 'Let Sood Sahib contest elections anywhere in Punjab, in Bihar, anywhere in India. And then let us see how many votes he gets. And here he comes to teach mass politicians like us politics.'

~

In the middle of 2010, Madhav Nepal resigned his prime ministership, after the CA's term was conditionally extended on the grounds that he would make way for a national unity government. To increase their bargaining position, Upendra Yadav became a part of the broader United Democratic Madhesi Front, popularly called the Morcha, along with the three other parties.

But the same tensions about relations with the Maoists emerged within the Morcha as well. Their common stated position was that they would support any candidate who would address the Madhesis' concerns on the issues of inclusion and federalism, and provide a roadmap to complete the peace process. The Maoists were more enthusiastic and sent a written response to the Morcha. In private negotiations, the Maoist chairman Prachanda was understood to have offered both Yadav and Gachhedar the position of deputy prime minister. A top Maoist leader was to tell me later, 'Prachandaji even gave millions to Bijay Gachhedar to get his support, yet he ditched us.'

Upendra Yadav wanted to back Prachanda as prime minister, but the rest of the Morcha wanted to remain neutral during the parliamentary vote between the NC candidate Ram Chandra Poudel and Prachanda. Seventeen rounds of voting in Parliament to elect a prime minister were held, though Prachanda withdrew after seven rounds. Neither candidate could command a majority. The UML, under the influence of Chairman Jhalanath Khanal, had decided to stay neutral in the contest, claiming that a majority government would not solve the political crisis. With the UML out, the Madhesi Morcha's support alone would not have seen Poudel home, so the Morcha stayed away as well. This was convenient, for it was difficult for the Madhesi outfits to side with the NC. It was their natural competitor in the Tarai, many Madhesi leaders had walked out of the NC and had projected it as being anti-Madhes, so political logic suggested that they would be on opposing sides.

But the Morcha did not support the Maoists, despite all the promises and inducements. Yadav was deeply unhappy at the decision. He got several of his MPs to break ranks with the Morcha and cross the floor to vote for Prachanda but, unless all Madhesi parties collectively voted for the Maoists, the numbers would not add up. Eventually, Yadav walked out of the broader Madhesi front again.

So why did the Morcha not back Prachanda? The answer, as we

saw earlier, was Delhi. India had strictly stuck to its decision to not allow the Maoists back into the power structure until they completed the peace process. Gachhedar bargained with the Maoists, but then turned to India and said he needed financial incentives to keep his MPs together and prevent them from walking over to the Maoists.

When the cash was not enough, and there was massive pressure from within the Madhesi ranks to support Prachanda, India sent Shyam Saran—the former foreign secretary and envoy to Nepal, who knew Madhesi leaders well—to Kathmandu. Over dinner at India House, Saran's clear indication to the Madhesi leaders was to stay away from the vote. Gachhedar, Mahant Thakur and Rajendra Mahato heeded the advice. Two Madhesi leaders who attended the meeting confirmed the tone and thrust of Saran's message to me.

In early 2011, there was a fresh round of voting in Parliament to elect a prime minister. Parties could not stay neutral perennially, and voting for a prime ministerial candidate could not exceed three rounds now. Politicians had realized that they had made a mockery of themselves by engaging in the farcical seventeen-round contest.

When Prachanda understood that the balance of power still remained the same, and that India would exert all its leverage to stop the Madhesi parties again, he played his ace. Withdrawing his own candidature, he supported UML leader Jhalanath Khanal for prime minister. A 'Left alliance' was born, with the stated commitment to nationalism which, in this context, meant resistance to India's political intervention. The Madhesi parties put up a token fight, with Gachhedar contesting as well, but with the Maoists and the UML on one side, Khanal sailed through. After Prachanda and Madhav Nepal, Khanal became the third prime minister—after the CA elections—in as many years.

Upendra Yadav had urged Prachanda to support Khanal soon after Madhav Nepal's resignation. While he stayed away from the vote officially, he was a natural political and ideological ally for the Left parties—it also helped Khanal give his government a more inclusive character. Yadav was appointed foreign minister, while Gachhedar, Thakur and Mahato now joined the opposition ranks along with the NC.

Yadav's return to power, however, came at the cost of yet another split in the MJF. J. P. Gupta, the co-chairman of the party and who had played a major role in building up its ideological platform, now walked away with eleven other MPs. India once again encouraged this split in order to weaken an ally of the Maoists. Gupta used the 'democrat-Maoist' binary, and said that he was choosing the former over the latter. He accused Yadav of selling out the Madhes's interests and insinuated that he was a casteist, and was promoting only Yadavs within the party structure. But like in the case of the Gachhedar-Yadav split, the political arguments only served as a cover for personal rivalries.

6

The Jhalanath Khanal government ended the political isolation imposed on the Maoists. But this was its sole achievement. The peace process, which had become synonymous with the integration and rehabilitation of former Maoist combatants living in cantonments, had not proceeded. If the Maoists had spoken firmly of a national unity government to oppose Madhav Nepal's 'democratic alliance' which excluded them, the NC and the Madhesi parties now spoke of the need for a unity government to oppose Khanal's 'Left alliance' which they projected as a threat to democracy. The similarities did not end there. The CA's term was to end on 28 May 2011 but, like in the previous year, when Madhav Nepal had to promise that he would quit and make way for a unity government to ensure that the Maoists supported an extension to the CA, in 2011, the NC said that it would support an extension only if Khanal resigned.

The internal dynamics among the Maoists also changed. Chairman Prachanda was the lynchpin of the Khanal government. But Vice-Chairman Baburam Bhattarai had opposed the Maoists' support for Khanal's elevation, and had insisted that only a unity government—which had both the Maoists and the NC—could break the impasse. He had also consistently reached out to the Madhesi parties in the opposition and argued that the Maoists and the Madhesis were the 'new forces', which were born out of political struggles and were committed to state restructuring, and must come together. He reiterated the party's earlier position that only a government led by the Maoists could resolve the issue of integration, and managed to convince his rival within the party, the dogmatic Mohan Vaidya 'Kiran' to pressurize Prachanda to change course.

All of this meant that by the time Jhalanath Khanal resigned in August 2011, the political dynamics had changed. The Maoists now nominated the more acceptable and less polarizing Bhattarai as their candidate, as Prachanda had assured RAW officials in their meeting in Kuala Lumpur. The party had swung back firmly to the peace-and-Constitution line after flirting with the idea of a People's Revolt, allaying fears about intent.

The NC put up its own parliamentary party leader, Ram Chandra Poudel, as the candidate—the same Poudel who had failed to get elected in 2010 even after contesting seventeen rounds of polls. Now, success in the battle depended on the support of the Madhesi parties. The UML pledged support to Poudel and, this time, Khanal had no grounds for objection because he felt betrayed by Prachanda and shared a hostile relationship with Bhattarai, who had opposed the Maoists' support for Khanal.

For the fourth time after the CA was elected in 2008, and within a period of three years, Nepal was to have a contest in Parliament to elect a prime minister. And the outcome would depend on the position of the Madhesi parties, the swing force in parliamentary arithmetic, and whether India would allow them the autonomy to pursue their own interests.

~

Mahant Thakur lived in Thimi in suburban Kathmandu, a five-minute drive from my house. I had got to know him well in my years of covering Madhesi politics, and went to see him as the elections approached.

Mahantji spoke of his dilemmas. He had quit the NC, after decades of serving the party and being a loyal G. P. Koirala aide, because he felt that the NC was not sensitive to the Madhesis' interests and felt that it was opposed to federalism and inclusion. Yet, his democratic schooling made him sceptical about the Maoists.

He told me, 'Madhesis, Janjatis, Dalits and women need the

Constitution the most in this country. For the ruling community, status quo is fine. To get to the Constitution, the peace process must be completed. And it is now clear that the peace process will not start unless the Maoists are in government.'

I agreed with Mahantji, and had consistently argued in my columns in the local press that it was politically counter-productive, undemocratic, and wrong to treat the Maoists as political untouchables. He added that there was enormous pressure on him from the second-rung within the party to back the Maoists. 'I know NC very well. They will never give us any rights.'

There was a strong element of realpolitik. If the three big parties—the NC, the UML and the Maoists—got together, Madhesi parties would get a minimum fraction in the power structure. If the Madhesi parties supported the NC candidate, the UML—as the second largest force—would walk away with the most lucrative portfolios. But Madhesis, as the swing force, would command the maximum space in a government led by the Maoists. Both Prachanda and Baburam Bhattarai had promised the home and defence ministries to the Morcha if their seventy-two MPs voted for the Maoists.

~

India clearly had a greater comfort level with Bhattarai, who had consistently—since 2003—stood in favour of democracy and engagement with India. He had been sceptical about the anti-India rhetoric of the party and had challenged the party leadership for having declared India the 'principal enemy' in 2009. He also enjoyed greater credibility with the rest of the political class, civil society and the national intelligentsia. India had let it be informally known that they would not have a problem with Bhattarai's name being proposed when Prachanda, in his meeting with RAW officials, had informed them of his intention to nominate the ideologue as the prime ministerial candidate.

Many saw this as India's ruse to split the Maoists, or proof that Bhattarai and Delhi had reached a private agreement. Delhi was indeed keen to encourage the more moderate lobby within the Maoists, but there is little evidence to show that it actively asked Bhattarai to walk away from the party.

Indeed, during his visit to Nepal in the middle of 2010, Shyam Saran, India's special envoy to Nepal, had met Bhattarai separately at The Dwarika Hotel in Kathmandu. A high-level source familiar with the conversation told me that Saran had asked Bhattarai if he was contemplating a split. Bhattarai had uttered a categorical no. And Saran had not pressed the matter at all. Contrary to the conspiracy theories that circulated in Kathmandu, India did not force the Maoists to nominate Bhattarai. The nomination was a result of the internal balancing of power within the Maoists' organization, wherein Prachanda had agreed to hand over key organizational responsibilities to the Kiran faction and nominate Bhattarai as prime minister in return for continuing as chairman after the two vice-chairmen had struck what was known as the 'Dhobighat alliance'.

The NC expected that India would use its substantial leverage with the Madhesi parties and get them to support Poudel. The UML's support to the NC was also premised on the understanding that India would get the Madhesis to support the 'democratic forces'. The problem was that these parties, in the traditional Nepali hill mindset, saw Madhesis as merely Indian 'agents', with little agency of their own.

On the other hand, the Maoists had been actively wooing Madhesi leaders, agreeing to support their substantive constitutional agenda and grant them a greater share in the power arrangements. Bhattarai had been developing close links with the energetic second-rung leaders of the regional parties ever since the Maoists quit the government way back in 2009.

A few days before the elections slated for 28 August, a Madhesi leader told me, 'We will go with Bhattarai.' I asked him if the Indians had given them the green signal. He asserted, 'No green signal and no red signal. They have said we can do what we want.'

~

The NC was now in panic mode. Ambassador Sood had completed his tenure in Kathmandu and had left a few months earlier. This had weakened the voice of the MEA within the establishment, which was more averse to giving the Maoists a chance. RAW, on the other hand, had veered towards allowing the Maoists another chance. They had not encouraged the Madhesi parties—but the 'agency', as Kathmandu politicians called RAW, had not discouraged them either. Left to domestic factors, the NC realized that there was little that would stop the Madhesi parties from choosing the more attractive option.

The NC now used all its political capital to get India involved on their side. The former party leader, and now President, Ram Baran Yadav, shared a personal equation with finance minister and old political warhorse Pranab Mukherjee—the only senior political leader in Delhi who really paid attention to Nepal. They spoke to each other in Bangla—Yadav had attended school in Calcutta. President Yadav warned Mukherjee that the Maoists' return to power would be dangerous, and they must help stop the Madhesis from voting for Bhattarai. An Indian embassy official, upset with the President's attempt to undercut the local mission and reach out directly to the political leadership, told me about this conversation and said that it had rattled Delhi. Surya Bahadur Thapa, the former prime minister who had excellent ties with Delhi's political and bureaucratic elite, called up his interlocutors with a similar warning. Thapa's grandson Siddhartha had become a close friend and, over coffee at Babar Mahal, Siddhartha expressed deep unease at the evolving Indian stance, as they saw it. Shekhar Koirala, G. P. Koirala's nephew who had played an active role in the run-up to the signing of the 12-point Understanding, shared cordial ties with National Security Advisor Shiv Shankar Menon. They had known each other since Menon's time as a joint secretary handling Nepal in the mid-1990s. Koirala called up his old friend, urging India to get the Madhesis to support Poudel. He warned India that having the Maoists in power at this time would ensure that they remained in office if the CA ended without a Constitution having been finalized and that would have adverse consequences for Delhi. I met Koirala in the CA compound a few days later, and he confirmed to me that he had reservations about India's position and felt that Delhi was making a mistake.

Delhi seems to have become worried by the multiple messages

from friendly interlocutors. The political section of the Indian embassy now got into the act. They warned the Madhesi parties that the Maoists would deceive them, that their commitment to federalism was opportunistic, and that the parties of the plains must reconsider their options. The pressure could either have been born out of a desire to show to the NC that India was doing its bit, or born out of a genuine policy line to block the Maoists once again. Delhi ordered RAW, which was more open to the Maoists, to step back from the process.

Madhesi leaders were confused, since they had assumed that India was fine with Bhattarai's candidature, and would stay out of the contest. Top leaders, including Bijay Gachhedar and J. P. Gupta, stopped taking calls from the embassy, fearing that India would pressure them to not vote for Bhattarai. Mahant Thakur, however, met the new Indian ambassador, Jayant Prasad, who had just arrived to take charge. Thakur conveyed to him that they had made up their minds and that there was pressure from the second-rung leadership within his party to support the Maoists. 'It is too late now to step back,' Thakur told Prasad. The next morning, right before he was headed to the Parliament for the vote, Thakur told me, 'It is impossible to understand the Indians. They have too many poles. Two weeks ago, an agency person was here and he did not indicate anything. Now, they are not happy with our decision it seems.'

When the contest had ended, I asked an Indian diplomat—a man who was in the thick of things—if they had indeed told Thakur not to support the Maoists. He responded emphatically, 'Look we did not say, do not go with the Maoists. He misunderstood us. Our worry was that the Madhesis were falling for the Maoist bait too easily. Our message to them was they must extract firmer assurances from the Maoists on peace-process issues, particularly integration. They must use their bargaining power to the hilt.'

Through those heady days in end August, I had been speaking with prospective prime ministerial candidate, Baburam Bhattarai, on the phone and could sense the shift in his mood. He had sounded confident a week before the polls but, as the vote approached, he felt that things were slipping out of their grasp. He told me that he had received information that sections in India who were belligerently anti-Maoist had once again become active. 'I don't understand what they hope to achieve. This is the final chance to take the peace and constitutional process forward.'

On 27 August, a day before the contest, Bhattarai had a quiet, private meeting with Ambassador Prasad in a room in Hotel Shangrila in Lazimpat, right next to the Indian embassy. The meeting was useful, for India assured the Maoist leader that they had no stakes in the battle and were only concerned about the completion of the peace process and the consolidation of democracy in Nepal. Bhattarai reiterated his commitment to take integration to an 'irreversible' point as soon as he took office.

The Maoist and Madhesi leaders hammered out a 4-point pact through the night of 27 August, which they announced inside the CA hall right before the vote. The Maoists pledged to complete the peace process and integrate and rehabilitate their former combatants; this allowed the Madhesi parties to claim credit for moderating the Maoists' ambitions. They also agreed to pass the Inclusion Bill in Parliament, and make the NA more inclusive, with a special provision

to recruit Madhesis. The clincher, however, was their joint commitment to federalism, and to autonomous provinces which would give rights to the marginalized communities of Nepal.

The NC and the UML were left stunned by the turn of events for, till the very end, they had hoped that Delhi would step in, like it had done during Prachanda's candidature in 2010, to stop the Madhesis.

With the support of all the Madhesi parties in Parliament, Baburam Bhattarai became Nepal's thirty-fifth prime minister.

~

The old ultra-nationalists, those who see Madhesis as Indians, and groups viscerally opposed to the Maoists, believe that the formation of the Bhattarai government was 'engineered' by India. But it was more complicated than that. India, as is clear, was engaged in the process, as it had been ever since the 12-point Understanding was signed. There had been a course correction in policymaking in Delhi, and the resistance to the Maoists had diminished when compared to 2010. This was as much a result of changes and introspection within the Indian government as the shift in the political line espoused by the Maoists themselves. There is also proof that the Indian establishment was divided on which approach they must adopt.

All of this had given the Madhesi parties enough space to operate autonomously in pursuing political choices that were more beneficial for them. The Maoists were giving the Madhesis a share in the power structure that was unprecedented in Nepali history; they had accepted the Madhesis' agenda; and, unlike the older parties who had great stake and ownership of the old state structure, both these new forces wished to reform and overhaul the state apparatus for their constituents. This was a natural political alliance which had earlier been blocked by India. But this time, inaction in the case of RAW, and partial opposition in the case of the MEA, allowed it to take root. To say that there would be active support for a Maoist government from an establishment as anti-Maoist as Delhi is naïve.

But, like in 2003 when Maoists reached out to India and it reciprocated cautiously, 2005 when their engagement intensified and there was a convergence of interests, 2008 when India supported elections to the CA and worked with the elected Maoist government of the day, the relationship between the region's pre-eminent power and Nepal's pre-eminent domestic political force was now coming back to an even keel after an extremely hostile phase. As was their democratic right as the largest party in the house, the Maoists were back to leading the government.

For its part, the Madhes movement had forced the Nepali political class to accept the principle of federalism. The elections had made the Madhesi parties the swing force in determining government formation in Kathmandu. The gulf between the Maoists and Madhesis—two forces fighting for change in Nepal—had only deepened the two-year-long national political deadlock. And the rapprochement between the Maoists and the Madhesis at a decisive moment had averted a conservative 'counter-revolution'. They now had to fulfill the two promises—that they would complete the peace process, and would help write the Constitution through the elected CA.

Together, the Maoists and the Madhesi parties prepared for the challenge of 27 May 2012, to frame a Federal Democratic Republican Constitution for before the term of the CA expired.

BOOK 4

POLITICS OF SHANTI-SAMBIDHAN

A Maoist fighter confided, his head lower, 'So this is what it has come down to. Our party is divided. We need the Nepali sena, the same army we fought against for so long, to save us from ourselves. Integration is a majaak [joke]. Most of us are taking cash and leaving.' And he raised the question that I had heard many former Maoist fighters ask, 'Our leaders have failed. Did we wage a war for this?'

—Interview, April 2012

'Did We Wage a War for This?'

Dahaban lies in the middle of the Maoist heartland, a few kilometres from the Holeri police station in the Rolpa district which was attacked by a core group of rebels to launch the People's War in 1996.

Fifteen years after the first shots were fired in its vicinity, a blue gate welcomed visitors to the Fifth Division headquarters of the People's Liberation Army (PLA) in Rolpa. A local bazaar had sprung up, with small shops selling items of daily use, tea-shops, a hair-cutting salon, and an eatery serving daal, bhaat, saag—lentils, rice and greens—the staple food of hill Nepalis.

A guard in combat fatigues checked our identity cards as we strolled up to the middle of the camp. It was an open space, surrounded on both sides by recently constructed structures. A few men had just finished their morning meal and were washing dishes. Some were exercising. But a large group had congregated around a single man, sitting on a chair, fielding what appeared to be aggressive questions. As we learnt later, he was Raj Bahadur Budhamagar 'Avinash', the vice-divisional commander and the de facto leader of the camp.

His presence was a reminder of a major transgression by the Maoists. The Rolpa divisional commander, Kali Bahadur Kham 'Bibidh', was in hiding, implicated in the murder of a businessman from Kathmandu in 2008, well after the Maoists had promised not to engage in violence. He had been promoted within the party hierarchy, even after strong evidence pointed to his involvement in the killing. When outsiders visited the cantonment, to avoid embarrassment and tough questions, Avinash was put forth as the visible face of the Fifth Division and fighters became cagey when asked about Bibidh's whereabouts.

But to be fair to the former rebels, this was an aberration. The ceasefire had held, and the Maoists had demonstrated enormous discipline, control and commitment in abiding by the new rules of the game.

It was the end of November in 2011. And that day in Rolpa—and in six other cantonments where the soldiers of the PLA had lived for the past five years—former fighters would finally get to choose their future in a process that came to be known as 'regrouping' in popular parlance. Earlier that month, after years of acrimonious negotiations and prolonged deadlock, the Maoists had finally signed a 7-point peace deal with the other major parties involved in the process, the Nepali Congress (NC), the Communist Party of Nepal (Unified Marxist Leninist) [UML], and the United Democratic Madhesi Front (UDMF).

1

The United Nations Mission in Nepal (UNMIN) had verified 19,602 former Maoist combatants. The Comprehensive Peace Agreement had declared that some could be possibly integrated into the state's security forces according to 'standard norms', while others would be rehabilitated. But the issue was closely linked to the nature of power politics and the political transition.

The future of the armies led to some of the fiercest political battles in post-republican Nepal. The UN's role and mandate would cause a deep rift between the Maoists and non-Maoist parties. Prime Minister Prachanda's attempted dismissal of General Katawal—which was to derail Nepali politics for over two-and-a-half years and displace the Maoists from power—had its roots in the existence of the PLA. The top brass of the Nepal Army (NA) was opposed to integrating any former combatant in their ranks at all, while the Maoists had hoped to ensure a pliable chain of command to enable relatively smooth integration on their terms. But precisely because they had a separate coercive structure, doubts about their intention had deepened and all anti-Maoist forces had stood against them.

The PLA's presence would once again become a stick to use against the Maoists when other parties insisted that until the question of integration was settled, the former rebels could not be allowed back into the government. The democratic parties also refused to discuss the Constitution as long as the Maoists maintained their army. Some openly suggested that the CA was the Maoists' agenda, a new Constitution was the Maoists' agenda, and if they wanted a Constitution to be written, they should give up the PLA to first create a level playing field.

For their part, the Maoists insisted that until they returned to power, they would neither detach themselves from the PLA, nor take steps that would lead to its disbandment. They were suspicious of the attempts to link the peace process with Constitution-writing, and argued that both processes must happen simultaneously. As Barshaman Pun 'Ananta'—a former deputy commander of the PLA, one of the men who had been a part of the first Maoist attack on Holeri, a key member of the Maoists' negotiating team, and a future finance minister—told me in 2010, 'They want us to surrender our strength, the PLA. But they will not write the Constitution after that because if a Federal Democratic Republican Constitution is written, Maoists will become even more powerful and NC and UML will get marginalized.' The Maoists were to argue that were it not for their army, the anti-Maoist forces would have succeeded in their plans to dissolve the CA in May 2010 or 2011—the presence of thousands of combatants deterred them from taking an action that would alienate the Maoists and irreversibly push them out of the political process.

The PLA's future was also inextricably linked to the future of the erstwhile Royal Nepalese Army (RNA). The peace accord had categorically stated that the 'democratization of the army' should happen simultaneously with the decision on the PLA. While many who wished to preserve the status quo argued that an army could not be 'democratic', since it runs on strong hierarchies, the issue was deeper, for the size of the NA, the nature of its composition, its role, its professionalism or the lack of it, and its human rights abuses had become apparent during the war.

The objective of the peace accord was to detach the NA from the Palace's control. It was strengthening the Ministry of Defence, instead of allowing the army to operate autonomously, and instituting civilian control. The army's strength had swelled from 45,000 in 2001 to 95,000 in 2006, and there was little doubt that an impoverished country like Nepal, with no major external or internal threats, could ill-afford an army of this size. Downsizing made political and economic sense, and would help reverse the militarization which had deepened over the course of the war.

The NA was also an exclusivist institution which did not reflect the country's diversity. Its leadership was primarily from the aristocratic Thakuri-Chhetri clan. Chhatraman Singh Gurung was the first member of the marginalized Janjati group to have risen up to become the army chief. But that was an aberration rather than a trend. The chain of command reverted to officers of the Hindu 'warrior' castes. There were less than 6,000 Madhesis in the entire force, less than 7 per cent, largely as technicians, engineers, doctors and barbers, people with no combat responsibilities. Making the NA inclusive and representative had become even more urgent in the wake of the rising aspirations of the under-represented ethnic groups. Tales of corruption in the NA, particularly during the war, were spoken of in hushed whispers in Kathmandu. Financial transparency, cleaner audit management and the investigation of past deals would help the NA function more professionally in the future.

The NC and the UML had suffered at the hands of the army when the monarch held sway, and were keen to detach it from the Palace. This was, in fact, one of the first major policy decisions taken by the reinstated Parliament in 2006. But beyond this, any demand for 'democratization' was interpreted by the older parliamentary parties as a move by the Maoists to enhance their control over the army. The NA had become an ally in the political struggle against the Maoists, and the army itself was reluctant—as expected—to institute fundamental changes in its functioning. Geopolitics, and the balance of power, favoured the NA's preference for status quo and the agenda for democratization would soon be lost.

~

But the twin, inter-related, issues were really at the heart of the transformation from war to peace, for no state could have two co-existing armies. The fact that neither army had won or lost, and that the war had ended in a stalemate, only complicated things. This made each of them prone to viewing any concession as surrender, and they stuck to maximalist positions.

Political and technical issues on integration took years to resolve. What was the nature and objective of integration to be? As the Maoists saw it, the aim ought to be to 'professionalize' the PLA and 'democratize' the NA, and merge them in order to create a new national army. In the Maoist worldview, the royal and feudal ideology which underpinned the NA needed to be corrected and this could be done only through mass integration. This position was rejected outright by the other forces, who even objected to the term 'two armies' for they saw in it a false equivalence between the NA and the guerillas. They referred to the rebels as 'former Maoist combatants'. The NA and non-Maoist forces had no faith that the combatants would detach themselves from the mother party, and saw it as a grand conspiracy to 'infiltrate ideologically indoctrinated workers, committed to one political force' into the state's forces. Their first priority was to ensure that the PLA was not integrated into the NA and, then, to see that the former Maoist combatants were accommodated into other security forces or reintegrated into society. While integration was essential to break the deadlock, they wished it to be minimal.

The numbers then became crucial. G. P. Koirala, the former prime minister and the original peace negotiator, had passed away in 2010. Non-Maoist parties said that the Maoists had promised in a private agreement with Koirala that '2,000-3,000' fighters would be integrated; the Maoists, however, said that the understanding had been for higher numbers, and demanded that over 10,000 be integrated.

If numbers were one issue, the 'modality' was even more vexing. Non-Maoist parties and the NA would have liked the process of integration to be as close to regular recruitment as possible, in which individual combatants would be hired and spread across existing battalions and divisions in such a manner that the structure of the institution would not be affected at all. The Maoists found this insulting. They reminded interlocutors that the war had ended in a military stalemate, and this was meant to be a process of integration, not routine recruitment. Instead, they asked for the group entry of combatants into either a specially created force or as a unit into an existing force.

The peace accord stated that the former combatants would have to meet the 'standard norms' of the security forces. The NA and non-Maoists interpreted this to mean the existing standard norms of age, marital status and educational qualifications, while the Maoists demanded that since this was a special process, new standard norms had to be created. This would have significant implications on numbers. In most cases, the combatants were older, and had lesser education than was required. Many women fighters—who comprised 40 per cent of the PLA at the peak of the war—were now married, and that made them ineligible for integration.

There were significant differences on the issue of rank. The non-Maoist forces were deeply suspicious of handing over any senior responsibilities to Maoist commanders. Officers of the NA were contemptuous of their Maoist counterparts; mid-level and junior officers felt that if the Maoists were given officer ranks, their own prospects would be compromised. The Maoists, for their part, felt that the PLA leadership had proved itself in the war, that integration meant it would happen at all levels, and if combatants were sent without any of their seniors, the NA could treat them in any manner and the Maoists would have no leverage.

Political negotiators had spent over six months in 2006 to arrive at an interim arrangement for the PLA, whereby combatants would remain in cantonments, their weapons locked away in containers. The interim Constitution had then stipulated that a Special Committee for Supervision, Integration and Rehabilitation of Former Combatants would determine their future. This was first established in mid-2007, but it was stillborn and was re-established in late October 2008. Its composition was affected by every change in government. The special committee then set up a secretariat to handle the technical aspects of the process.

Between 2008 and 2011, there were intense negotiations at the second-rung level of the parties over the thorny issues outlined above.

For the international community, integration was key to resolving the conflict and it funded think tanks, junkets, study trips and meetings on the issue generously, spawning an entire industry of security-sector experts. The returns were limited. India played a low-key but more effective role in pushing the political message on the need to expedite the peace process, but its specific position on integration was partisan and tilted strongly in favour of the NA's stance.

Incremental steps were taken. In February 2009, on the PLA anniversary in Nawalparasi which I covered, Prime Minister Prachanda told his fighters for the first time that they were now under the special committee, and not the Maoist party. In 2011, this was partially operationalized when the special committee formally stepped in to take charge of the Maoist cantonments at the end of the UNMIN's tenure. The secretariat then deployed monitoring teams to replace UNMIN monitors across the cantonments. UNMIN's end itself was an outcome of the NA's impatience with restrictions imposed on it under the CPA, and the agreement's provisions which equated the two armies. UNMIN had stayed true to the letter of the CPA, which endlessly annoyed the NA, its internal allies, and external backers like India.

About 4,000 individuals who were registered in the cantonments but were found to be ineligible because they were under-age, or had joined the PLA after the ceasefire, were disqualified by the UN. They were subsequently discharged in 2010 with options for rehabilitation. In May 2011, the Maoist leadership ended the system of 'dual security', under which they had both security personnel provided by the state and PLA combatants as personal guards. The personnel were sent back to the cantonments along with their weapons, in a move which signified that the Maoist leaders had come under the security umbrella provided by the state.

But the more substantive issues persisted. The Maoists had made it clear that until they returned to power, they would not push the peace process forward. And it was only with the election of the Baburam Bhattarai government in August 2011—enabled by an alliance with the Madhesis, and the quiet, though fractured, nod from India as we saw earlier—that the peace process would reach an 'irreversible stage'.

The day after Bhattarai became prime minister, the Maoist party handed over the keys to the containers in which their weapons were locked away to the special committee. This was a hugely symbolic move, for other parties had used the fact that the Maoists possessed weapons—rusted junk, stored for years together—to demonize the former rebels. It proved that the leadership's commitment to the peace process was beyond doubt. But this alienated the more dogmatic faction of the party, led by Mohan Vaidya 'Kiran'. Kiran and company had been publicly uncomfortable with the ideological shift towards peace and the Constitution-writing process, they had attempted to steer the party back to a confrontational path, and were now unhappy with the 'surrender' of the keys. But both Prachanda and Baburam Bhattarai had made up their minds, and pressed ahead.

On 1 November, the parties reached a new agreement after years of ardous negotiations, and a compromise was found on the most troublesome of issues. A maximum of 6,500 combatants would be integrated into a specially created general directorate under the command of the NA. This directorate would comprise a mix of NA soldiers, personnel from other security forces, and the Maoist fighters, and would be responsible for disaster relief, industrial security, development and protection. On the issue of 'standard norms', there were relaxations on age, education and marital status; on rank, the pact did not spell out the exact leadership level though it mentioned that it was the NA's standards which were to be complied with. Those who would not be integrated could either pick rehabilitation packages, or 'retire' with cash remuneration in two installments.

The next day, I spoke to Prime Minister Bhattarai. The relief palpable in his voice, and displaying uncharacteristic joy, he told me, 'The process is back on track now. We have given up many of our claims. I am now convinced that we will be able to write the Constitution.' It was an exhilarating moment. Those of us who had argued that the Maoists must be given their rightful share in the power structure felt vindicated. Nepal's peace process was finally reaching its 'logical conclusion'.

~

As we walked closer to the middle of the camp in Rolpa, it was clear that Vice-Commander Avinash was facing a barrage of questions around this deal, which was meant to ensure lasting peace, and what it meant for all those who had given their youth and middle age to the party and to the revolution.

He was also faced with a more practical concern. When combatants had first registered with the UN in 2007, they had stated their date of birth and their level of education. But, in the last five years, many of them had received new citizenship certificates with dates of birth that did not match the earlier one. They had also used the period to study and now had degrees and diplomas which they lacked earlier. Age and education would be important parameters in determining the eligibility for integration into the NA, and former fighters were unwilling to accept the 2007 data.

The controversy had already delayed the start of the integration process. Avinash called up the members of the Special Committee Secretariat—responsible for conducting the 'regrouping of combatants'—and a compromise was found whereby both sets of data would be included.

But others had more urgent concerns. Balwan Pun Magar 'Sandeep' was from Rolpa, and had joined the Maoists in 1997, in the early years of the war. But he had suffered severe limb injuries in a major battle against the RNA in Khara in 2002. His concern was regarding the provisions put in place for the differently abled and the wounded, and felt that the recent agreement lacked clarity. 'We want pension and life-long health treatment,' he said.

A day earlier, I had met Dipendra Basnet 'Sangarshashil' in the Shaktikhor cantonment in Chitwan in central Nepal. He had deserted the state security forces in 2003 and defected to the Maoists' ranks with a weapon in hand. The government had slapped a case against him and had frozen his provident fund. The case had not been withdrawn even though four governments had been formed with participation from the Maoists. And he would not be eligible to be reabsorbed into the NA. 'It is frustrating. I will take the cash and go,' he told me.

During that week, I travelled to five of the seven cantonments in the country along with two friends, Anagha Neelakantan of the

International Crisis Group and Thomas Mathew, a writer and editor. We were struck by how vulnerable these people, who had once shaken up the Nepali state, were in confronting the dilemmas of life. There was little empathy for their condition in the power circles of Kathmandu. The Maoist leadership had used them to access the power structure and viewed them as mere instruments. The anti-Maoist brigade had demonized the combatants as terrorists, representing the worst of Nepali society, and refused to grant them dignity and honour.

In Kailali district in western Nepal, in the middle of lush green hills, Deepak Chand was playing with his young daughter. A tall, somewhat chubby man, he had told us that while he would opt for integration into the army, his wife, Manju, would take the cash option. The two, like many other combatants, had used their years in the cantonment to get married and have a child. But Deepak was not sure if he would make it into the NA. 'I have some injuries from the war, and so I may not meet the physical standards. Then I will take the cash, too.'

The government was planning to offer anywhere between 500,000-700,000 Nepali rupees—between 7,000-9,000 US dollars—to each fighter depending on his or her rank. I teased Deepak, who had been a pharmacist before he joined the Maoists and was popularly called Doctor Saab by comrades, that two cash packages in the family would make them rich. He paused for a minute, and then responded thoughtfully, 'It is enough to run a household. But there are no avenues for investment. I don't want to go and set up a street-side shop. And the money is not enough to set up a big industry. So let's see.'

We asked Deepak why he or his wife had not chosen the rehabilitation option of 'vocational training', being forcefully endorsed by the international donor community in Nepal, which seemed to feel that by giving cash the government was rewarding violence and former combatants could not be trusted to be responsible with so much money. He scoffed, 'Who needs to learn how to make orange juice or rear goats?' Only six of the 17,000 plus who underwent the regrouping process eventually opted for rehabilitation.

In Surkhet's Dashratpur cantonment, Deepak Prakash Bhatt was the secretariat committee member who led the process of rehabilitation. He was a representative of the UML, but was also my senior from JNU, who had a PhD on the NA, and we had spent many evenings drinking together. His explanation for the lack of enthusiasm for rehabilitation was more nuanced. 'The Maoist leadership has not explained the option well. Plus the word rehabilitation appears to mean that the combatants have done something wrong, they are criminals who need to be reformed. Many find this insulting because they are committed to the cause they fought for. Also, taking this option is a lengthy process. You have to spend time on vocational training, depend on the state. People don't have faith that the government would run the programme on time; they may have to keep going back. Past experience has not been good.' After ten years of fighting, and five years in the cantonments, the combatants had little energy or patience left and wanted to start life afresh.

But the more serious problem was political.

Even as Avinash in Rolpa, at a press conference, said that they accepted the terms of the peace accord, his colleague, another vice-commander of the Fifth Division, Ram Lal Roka Magar 'Madan', sitting next to him, objected. Madan was loyal to the radical Kiran faction. They claimed that the PLA and the NA should have been merged to create a 'new national army' in the true spirit of the peace process; instead, what was happening was recruitment. Madan said, 'The agreement disregards the PLA's historic contribution, demeans and insults us. This is not what we fought for.' The two were sitting on the same sofa. They were addressing the same press conference, under the same party umbrella, but the distance between them was evident. It was indeed two parties within one, two organizations within one, two armies within one. The fact that this was happening in Rolpa could not be more ironic.

In the next few months, the tensions were to escalate. Kiran's loyalists tapped into the widespread sentiment in the PLA ranks that they deserved more dignity, and a better deal, after having brought about political change in Nepal. Many were to boycott the integration process and walk away with cash. The party establishment, led by Prachanda and Baburam Bhattarai, had pushed for the integration of the greatest possible numbers. In the first round of regrouping in November, when I had made the rounds of the cantonments, their efforts had paid off and over 9,000 people had initially opted for integration into the army.

But this number was to shrink rapidly over the next few months as an increasing number of combatants began to feel that they had been treated unfairly. The attraction of a cash package outweighed the uncertainty that integration would bring. And those who had doubts were convinced by an event no one could have foreseen, an event that forced them to question the very rationale for the war they had waged so bravely.

3

On the intervening night between 9 and 10 April 2012, the chain of command in the PLA broke. The Maoists had successfully kept the military structure under political control for the duration of the war and the peace process. This reflected the effective leadership skills of Prachanda and the PLA commanders, as well as the commitment and discipline of the cadres. Little did we know that beneath the surface, matters had reached breaking point.

As the second round of regrouping commenced, multiple tensions blew up. These had both to do with the ideological opposition to the process of the regrouping, as well as a backlash against the errors made by the party leadership.

Commanders had retained a part of the salary and the provident fund combatants had received from the state over the years. This had been done, ostensibly, for the welfare of the party. There had been no accountability, however, and suggestions that the leadership was misusing the money for personal benefit had gained traction. When the combatants demanded their money, it appears that the commanders refused to turn it over. Combatants rebelled and challenged their leaders, whose orders they had dutifully obeyed for years. The misappropriation of funds not only sharpened the trust deficit between warriors who had once fought shoulder to shoulder, but diluted the entire ideological claim of the Maoists that they were fighting for the public interest. They had become truly 'mainstreamed' in the corrupt ways of the existing political culture.

In the First Division cantonment in Ilam in far-eastern Nepal, it was reported that fights had broken out between commanders and combatants belonging to different ethnic groups and different regions. An official involved in the process in the camp said, 'Junior commanders want to know their ranks before they choose integration. They fear seniors will otherwise play favourites. No one is willing to accept the lack of transparency anymore.'

Deepak Prakash Bhatt, the secretariat member in charge of regrouping in Surkhet in western Nepal, told me over the phone that night, 'It has all broken down. Most combatants wanted to opt for retirement but, to save face, commanders have told them to take integration. If left to their free will, not more than a few thousand want to go into the army.' The agreement's silence on rank determination for commanders had also created trouble.

Kiran's loyalists, many of whom had retired voluntarily in the first round, had mobilized forces, congregated around the camps and incited further unrest. I had visited Kiran at his Gongabu residence on Kathmandu's Ring Road at the end of March. Over tea, early in the morning, he had criticized the leaders of his own party, 'On integration, the party's stand was that it should be collective and armed integration of combatants with the PLA chain of command intact. But what is now happening is disarmament. A national security policy should have been framed first, but we did not pay attention to that either.' If this situation continued, and integration was not 'respectable', Kiran warned that the Nepali people would have a 'right to revolt again'. He also allowed me a glimpse of the deep fissures within the organization when he admitted that it was an unusual situation, 'There is a party within a party, an organization within an organization.'

Several years earlier, Kiran had said that Prachanda was a young revolutionary talent he had recognized and appointed as the party's general secretary. Now, he looked up at the ceiling and said wistfully, 'In recent years, his revolutionary and communist spirit has been lacking.'

The radical ideologue's message had percolated down to the cadre. Discipline, and silence over intra-party differences, are the hallmarks of a communist—particularly Maoist—party. But if a top leader was willing to criticize the chairman of his own party, then dissent on the ground could not be quelled. The 'disqualified combatants' who had been discharged earlier from the camps were dissatisfied by how the party had treated them. They, too, were encouraging their comrades to oppose the party.

Back in Baluwatar, Prime Minister Bhattarai was alerted to the developments late at night. Party chairman Prachanda and Bhattarai conferred and, the next morning, they called in NC negotiators Krishna Prasad Sitaula and Amresh Kumar Singh to Prachanda's residence. Prachanda said that they had to act immediately, and he had only two choices.

The government would send the NA into the camps to enforce order and quell unrest, or he would, by that evening, be forced to withdraw from the peace agreements and walk away from the endeavours to maintain peace and write the Constitution. The Indian ambassador, Jayant Prasad, was in Delhi. Amresh Kumar Singh later told me he dialled Prasad's number and handed the phone over to Prachanda. The Maoist chairman conveyed to Prasad the gravity of the situation. Senior leader of the UML and former prime minister, Madhav Kumar Nepal, was contacted, and so was party chairman Jhalanath Khanal. The chief of the NA, General Chattraman Singh Gurung, confirmed that he was ready to abide by the directions of the political parties. Singh had spoken to both Lt General Nepal Bhushan Chand and Lt General Gaurav Rana, as well as the Director General of Military Operations.

Prachanda's choice was, in fact, no choice at all. Opposition parties and non-Maoist forces had always wanted to detach the cantonments, the combatants and the arms and ammunition from the Maoists—sending in the army would do that in concrete terms. They assented. This was exactly what they had wanted.

It was a decision laden with symbolism and irony. The Maoist leadership, which had created the PLA to fight the state army, had been forced to ask the very army they once battled to go into their camps to bring order and save the peace process—and to save the leadership itself.

~

A few days after the NA personnel were deployed, I went to the Ilam cantonment in far-eastern Nepal, where the tensions had been particularly acute. Combatants now had to show identity proofs to enter camps that had been their home, their territory, for the past five years. And they had to show it to the same men whom they had once fought against.

More and more fighters had now decided to choose retirement over integration. They felt stifled by the recent events, by how bonds that had been created over years of waging a war and living together had become fractured. Their motivation for joining the NA, to change it from within, now seemed hollow. The numbers of those opting for integration had shrunk to a little over 3,000 from 9,000 by the end of April. Eventually, less than 1,500 combatants—of the 19,602 eligible Maoist fighters—would get into the NA. The seniormost would receive the rank of a colonel. The rest would walk away with cash.

One fighter confided, his head bowed, 'So this is what it has come down to. The party is divided. We need the Nepali sena to save us from ourselves. Integration is a majaak [joke]. Most of us are taking cash and leaving.' And he raised the question that I had heard many former Maoist fighters ask, 'Our leaders have failed. Did we wage a war for this?'

The question shook me, and I felt that the man who had first convinced these young fighters to take up arms and to give their youth to the revolution owed an explanation to them—why had he sent the 'enemy' into the PLA camp?

I went to see the Maoist chairman, Prachanda, soon after his decision to ask for the deployment of the army. We were meeting at his new residence in Lazimpat. It had been a stressful week for him, but Prachanda looked relaxed and confident. I asked him how it felt to hand over the PLA to the NA, an army that they had fought a bitter war against. He said, 'The war was against the Royal Nepalese Army, now integration is happening with the Nepal Army. That was a royalist army, this is a republican army. That is a qualitative difference… The NA is also a national army, and the PLA which is going for integration is also going to get a chance to be a part of the national army. This is a matter of pride and a happy moment.' He paused, and added, 'The journey that had begun in Delhi with the 12-point Understanding has now come to a conclusion.'

But this answer hid more than it revealed. Had there been no trouble in the cantonments; had he not acted out of compulsion; had his colleagues not termed the process 'surrender'; and if he had to send the NA in, could he not have done so earlier and saved the country precious time?

Prachanda was emphatic that this situation could not have played out in any other way. He blamed the cantonment unrest on 'reactionary and royalist elements' who were seeking to derail the peace process, for that was the way to prevent a Constitution from being written and to re-establish their primacy. He denied that the Maoists had acted out of compulsion, and listed the steps taken by the party in the past year—from sending their own security personnel back to the camps to handing over the keys of the weapons containers—as proof of their committment.

Kiran had met Prachanda just before I saw him that afternoon. Both had excellent personal relations, despite their political differences, and Prachanda continued to look up to him as a guru figure, a man of integrity who was pursuing what he believed was right.

The Maoist chairman candidly recounted the conversation to me, 'Kiranji just said to me, "You have given up everything." I said, "I haven't left anything. This is transformation." We came to the peace process and competitive politics as a matter of commitment—not out of tactics. I told him taking your path would lead us towards the situation of either Myanmar's Karen rebels, or communists in Malaya, or those in Peru. There is a difference in our understanding of the world, the balance of power, the level of economic development, and the international communist movement. I said my outlook is more realistic, scientific and pragmatic while yours is classical.'

Prachanda was correct in standing up to the dogmatists. But this did not excuse his mismanagement of the issue of the future of the Maoist combatants. He had kept many of the genuine combatants within the party structure, while new recruits were picked up to inflate numbers in the cantonments. He then distorted the expectations of the soldiers of the PLA by promising its merger with the national army, even though this was not written in the peace accord and was impossible, given the balance of power.

Instead of sincerely trying to resolve the PLA issue and push through integration during his tenure as prime minister, I felt that Prachanda got too enmeshed in power games to expand control over the NA. Then, for years, he neglected the combatants—spending far more energy in the politics of manipulation in Kathmandu and making shabby compromises for space in the power structure. To appease the power centres in Kathmandu and Delhi, he completely ignored the democratization of the army. Prachanda seems to have felt that the balance of power did not permit the implementation of that agenda anymore. But if he had to accept the deal that he finally did—limited integration for some combatants and money for most—he could have done so a lot earlier, saving the country precious time. Young men and women who had spent their adolescence and youth in the most difficult of circumstances, fighting for the revolution and putting their lives on the line, had wasted productive years in their twenties and thirties waiting endlessly for a deal to be forged in Kathmandu.

Prachanda also did not spend adequate time in the cantonments, communicating with the former fighters and explaining his constraints to them. Instead, he turned a blind eye to the rampant corruption that allegedly occurred inside the camps. State-sanctioned money, meant for warriors who had helped usher in the political change, was widely reported in the national press to have been siphoned off by the Maoist party and its military's leadership. And now, instead of recognizing that combatants had genuine grievances, he was insulting them by calling their dissent a conspiracy.

To be fair to him, it was a big moment for the Maoist chairman. The army he had led for almost a decade as supreme commander, and which had helped him reach positions of political power in Kathmandu, no longer existed. He had to take on his political mentor, the man who made him the party chief two-and-a-half decades ago, to push the process forward. Prachanda lost old friends like Ram Bahadur Thapa 'Badal', with whom he had spent the initial years in Left politics in Chitwan. But he had done—through a mix of choice and compulsion—what he had promised to do when he entered open politics in 2006. He had detached the party from its coercive apparatus.

Would his gamble pay off? Would he accomplish his political objectives? Would it satisfy the cadres, who were already asking why they had fought the war?

There was only one way to know, one way to reignite the faith.

We were sitting in a makeshift hut in one of the cantonments, surrounded by greenery and hills, when I asked Prakash, a platoon commander, what he thought the PLA had contributed to Nepali history. He replied, 'We abolished the monarchy. And now we are giving up all that we built, all that we had, our army, our friends, our party, for one thing—a Federal Democratic Republican Constitution for Nepal, written by the Constituent Assembly.'

Death of a Dream

A political idea, once planted in the popular consciousness, does not die easily. The proof was the persistent demand for an elected CA where representatives of the Nepali people would draft a Constitution, determine how society would be organized and power distributed, and decide the structure of the Nepali state.

Kings betrayed the promise made in 1951. Democratic parties gave up, fatigued and desperate for a compromise with the Palace, in order to access formal power. In 1959, the veteran democratic leader, B. P. Koirala, chose to accept the king's Constitution in order to get to elections rather than insist on a CA which would have prolonged the almost decade-long transition. In 1990, democratic parties settled for a Constitution by a commission, which included royal representatives and the restoration of the multiparty system. The symbolism of King Birendra granting the Constitution to the people had significant political implications—it indicated that the king remained an integral part of the polity, albeit in a more limited role than the past.

When small regional and Left parties asked for a CA in 1990, it was deemed a loony, fringe demand. The Maoist revolution was dismissed as excessively 'romantic' and 'revolutionary' when they put forward elections to a CA—a perfectly democratic demand—in 2001. What was then blasphemous had become the mainstream agenda in less than five years. Across the political spectrum, no actor could afford to be perceived as being unsupportive of the idea that people had a democratic right to determine their own future.

But demanding a CA, and even getting it accepted, was easier than electing it and drafting a Constitution through a popularly elected mechanism, as Nepali politicians and the Nepali people were to learn over four agonizingly long years between 2008 and 2012.

1

The fate of Nepal's first CA was, in retrospect, sealed the day it was elected.

Elections in April 2008 had shaken Nepal's erstwhile power structure. The Maoists had emerged as the single-largest party. The Madhesi parties had become a swing force. A mixed electoral system, with proportional representation that guaranteed affirmative action, enabled 33 per cent representation of women. One Dalit had been elected in three Parliaments—1991, 1994 and 1999—under the old system. This time, forty-nine Dalits became members of the CA, though this was still less than their population share. One-third of the house consisted of Madhesi members, and Janjatis constituted one-third, with 218 MPs. There was, of course, an overlap between these categories described as Da-Ma-Ja-Ma—Dalit, Mahila, Janjati and Madhesi. But their unprecedented presence had made Nepal's legislature among the most inclusive not only in its history, but among the most diverse and representative in the region.

A vast swathe of forces in Kathmandu just did not know how to deal with the new political landscape.

Suddenly, Nepal's top businessmen, 'civil society' leaders, lawyers, editors and army generals, had to deal with a fresh set of faces. People they would contemptuously dismiss in the normal course of events were determining the country's fate.

One lawyer said to me after the polls, 'Take it from me. The CA will not write the Constitution. What do these these cooks, these cleaners, these sweepers, these vegetable-vendors, these women who have never got out of their houses, know about constitutionalism?' His perception of the CA was based on reports that, to fill their proportional representation quotas on inclusive lines, as mandated by election laws and the interim Constitution, political parties had chosen people with such backgrounds. He did not mention that Nepal's top businessmen—fourteen of them by one count—had also used the proportional representation quota to join the CA.

The elitist assumption about the political illiteracy of those who did not come from privileged professions and backgrounds, and the failure to understand that a Constitution is not about law but about forging a social contract between precisely such diverse social groups, had shocked me then.

I had met a senior army general, who was to later go on to occupy an even higher position in Nepal's military hierarchy, at his residence in central Kathmandu. It was early morning. He had just finished a workout and was enjoying a glass of fresh juice. The general exclaimed, 'This CA must not be allowed to write the Constitution. Otherwise, Nepal will break up. There will be a Limbuwan on one side, Madhes, Tamsaling, Newa ... all ethnic groups will fragment and national unity, which we in the army have nurtured, will get destroyed. This CA must fail.' This conversation happened in late 2008. Little did I know then how prophetic the general's words were, and how far those who thought like him would go to derail the constitutional project because they feared federalism.

But contests between groups who exercise power, and those who seek to shift it away, is a sign of deepening democracy. The CA was the site for these very battles.

~

Battles were indeed fought, but for Singha Durbar, the site of government, not Baneshwor, where the CA complex was located. The fact that the same house of 601 members operated both as the CA and the Legislature-Parliament meant that power-sharing could not be divorced from statute-drafting. The third element of this emerging triangle was the peace process.

As the analyst Anagha Neelakantan often said, parties saw the three processes as being interlinked. If they gave in on one front, they expected concessions on a second. Alternately, if they felt that they were getting a raw deal on any one of the indicators, they would harden positions in the other areas to enhance their bargaining strength and force a new deal.

The CA was able to decide its rules of procedure and the composition of the powerful Constitutional Council (CC) only eight months after elections, in November 2008. Through this period, the political leadership was busy wrangling with each other over the election of the President and vice-president, framing new parliamentary rules, forming a government, and making bilateral visits to neighbouring countries. After the politics of confrontation escalated with Prime Minister Prachanda's resignation in May 2009, the sole focus of the ruling Madhav Nepal-led UML-NC-Madhesi alliance was to preserve the government, while the Maoists sought to displace it through all possible means. This not only meant that the leaders thought little about the Constitution, but also that the acrimony and polarization spilled over and worsened disagreements in the CA committees. For over seven months after Madhav Nepal resigned, the meetings of the Legislature-Parliament resulted only in failed bids to elect a prime minister—the house rarely held a session in its capacity as the CA. When Jhalanath Khanal was elected, the incentives for the NC and Madhesis to cooperate over the writing of the Constitution dimmed.

Constitution-writing was also hostage to the seemingly intractable question of sequencing. The NC and the UML insisted that there would be no discussions on the draft as long as the Maoists had their army; the Maoists, as we saw earlier, wanted both processes to happen simultaneously.

The focus on the other elements of the politics—and not Constitution-writing which was the core of the political project— had a direct impact on the process.

Martin Chautari, a Kathmandu-based research institute, regularly tracked the CA's operations. In a policy brief, it recorded that the full CA, in four years, held 122 meetings, of which 101 happened between 2008 and 2010. For all its commitment to the new Constitution, the average attendance rate of the Maoist and Madhesi MPs was lower than that of the MPs of the NC and the UML. The no-show of top leaders was even more dismal for this 'undermined the authority of the CA and its importance', according to the report. Prachanda's attendance in the CA was 6.5 per cent, while NC's Sher Bahadur Deuba attended less than 3 per cent of the house meetings. But, in an interesting breakdown, Martin Chautari suggested that the participation of women and hill Dalits was consistently higher than that of the other groups, while Madhesi and Muslim participation declined as the years went by, perhaps signifying their diminishing faith in the process.

I had bumped into UML's Agni Kharel, a key negotiator on the Constitution, outside the CA secretariat and discussed Martin Chautari 's findings with him. Kharel's own attendance was over 95 per cent, but he told me that merely scanning the attendance register was not an accurate way to gauge participation as top leaders were involved in decisions on constitutional issues through other forums.

But, as the briefing pointed out, this was a parallel process initiated outside the CA, where senior leaders met and negotiated a range of issues. Many of these leaders—NC president Sushil Koirala and Krishna Prasad Sitaula, general secretary; K. P. Sharma Oli and Bamdev Gautam, both senior leaders of the UML—had lost elections. This was done in the name of the 'politics of consensus'. Given Nepal's top-heavy and centralized political culture, perhaps it was inevitable that decisions would be taken by the leaders and then instructions passed on to the members of the CA. But it did play a role in undermining the democratic processes within the house, and its sovereign authority.

The report issued by Martin Chautari also asserted that the rules and regulations were designed by the parties to 'maximise political party control over the members, maintain structured hierarchies and exclusion of the marginalised', and concluded, that the 'CA and the constitution-writing process operated in a non-democratic, non-transparent, non-inclusive and unaccountable manner'. The major procedural problem—of decision-making taken outside the CA under the garb of consensus—not only undermined the very rationale of having a diverse range of CA members, but would adversely shape the ultimate outcome of the CA.

~

If process, and the interplay of multiple issues, constituted one set of challenges, the substantive differences over the constitutional project represented another key hurdle for Nepali politicians.

The CA set up thematic committees on a range of issues—fundamental rights and directive principles, state restructuring, the protection of the national interest, the rights of the minorities, the distribution of natural resources and public finances, the nature of legislative bodies, the judicial system, the structure of constitutional bodies, cultural and social solidarity. Committee members met often, did their research and homework, and invited external experts and stakeholders. There was a major drive to survey public opinion in 2009; CA members went out in teams with a set of questions to solicit views. The questions were criticized later for being too technical, and the process itself a bit premature, but it did force the members of the CA to at least think about the issues that they had to grapple with. Some were delayed, but all thematic committees did eventually submit their reports to the CA.

The discussions and thematic report revealed the fundamental fault line in Nepali politics. As the author and analyst, Aditya Adhikari, argued in a piece explaining why the CA was taking more time than expected, 'On many issues, the viewpoints of the Maoists and non-Maoists were incommensurable ... it is fundamental differences over the interpretation of Nepali society and institutions required for it that have prevented the drafting of the constitution.'

The old democratic party, the NC, was wedded to a traditional Westminster system of governance and, since it believed that there was no problem with the political structure of the 1990s, there was no need to fix it. For them, the CA was little more than a sop offered to the Maoists to build peace, and the constitutional vision was to institutionalize similar precepts of liberal democracy. The Maoists' political vision went far beyond what it saw as a limited notion of democracy, catering only to 'certain classes and communities'. The Maoists had waged a war against precisely the system the NC idealized, and could not accept, or even be seen as accepting, it in full. They wished to create a structure which would address the concerns of those 'discriminated on the basis of region, ethnicity, gender and class', and enhance the party's power.

This played out in seemingly minor issues around semantics. The Maoists wanted to include terms like 'People's War' and 'People's Liberation Army' in the Constitution, as a validation of their rebellion, even as the other parties, precisely in order to register their ideological opposition to the People's War, pushed for terms like 'armed conflict' and 'Maoist combatants'.

For the NC, 'multiparty democracy' was non-negotiable. With the 12-point Understanding, engagement in open politics and participation in elections, the Maoists had accepted what they termed 'multiparty competition' but were hesitant to use the term 'multiparty democracy'. They were also reluctant to accept the term 'pluralism' for complex ideological and philosophical reasons—all so abstract that I could never quite comprehend them. Their refusal was even more incomprehensible because, in practice, they did accept the existence of multiple strands of thought, organizations, and practices, though with caveats. In a draft Constitution, the party proposed that 'pro-imperialist and feudal parties' should not be allowed to participate. This was read by sceptics as proof that the former rebels were still attached to the notion of a one-party, hegemonic, communist state.

The NC wanted a Supreme Court that was completely independent of the Parliament and the executive, in line with the doctrine of separation of powers. A Judicial Council would appoint judges; a judge of the Supreme Court would be appointed the chief justice, and it would be vested with the final authority to interpret the Constitution. But the Maoists, suspicious of the judiciary as a 'remnant of feudalism' and of the 'old regime', proposed that the Parliament should appoint judges, while people's representatives could interpret the Constitution. Madhesi parties, who had their own reasons to suspect the hill-dominated judiciary, supported elements of the Maoists' proposal. Their diagnosis of the problems with Nepal's justice system may have been correct, but their prescription pitched them against traditional democratic forces.

The NC also equated democracy with a parliamentary system. This is what it was accustomed to, and this is what the party's leaders had grown up seeing in India. But accepting it was out of question for the Maoists. The rebels viewed the Parliament as a talk shop. They felt that this system had weakened the state internally by leading to frequent changes in government and creating instability, and, externally, by allowing foreign powers to play within a fragmented landscape. Instead, they demanded a directly elected presidential system. This would create a degree of permanence and predictability. The Maoists argued that as Nepal would turn federal, the presidency would provide a much needed, strong central authority.

There was another realpolitik calculation here. Prachanda's personal ambition was to be Nepal's first directly elected executive. The experience of 2008-2012, when his government had been ousted and he had not been able to muster a majority to be re-elected as prime minister, made him feel even more strongly that he would never be able to exercise relatively unconstrained political authority. He was also confident that, in current politics, no one could match his charisma and popularity, which would give him an edge if there was ever a direct poll. This fed into the suspicions of the others that Prachanda wanted a presidential system in order to become an all-powerful, despotic leader.

There were other issues, too. In the initial stages, the Maoists sought a stronger, militarized state, and pushed for forced conscription for citizens above eighteen years of age. They also proposed in the National Interest Preservation Committee, headed by the more dogmatic leader Dev Gurung, that identity papers should be made compulsory for travel between Nepal and India. This reflected the ultra-Left's unease with and opposition to the special relationship between India and Nepal. But other parties, particularly from the Madhes, vocally opposed the provision.

In earlier proposals, the NC, the UML and Madhesi parties had pushed forward a bicameral legislature at the Centre and the voting age of eighteen even as the Maoists wanted a unicameral set-up and the reduction of the voting age to sixteen. There were complex debates on the electoral system, especially with regard to the share of the proportional representation system, and the categories which deserved affirmative action. The Maoists initially proposed 'revolutionary land reform', whereby those who possessed land above the ceiling would not be compensated while others suggested more moderate, 'scientific land reform'.

~

If the fault line between the Maoists and the non-Maoists defined Nepali politics on a range of issues, there was another fault line—between committed pro-federal forces versus the reluctant federalists—which would be even more central in determining the future of the Nepali state.

There were three key sources of support for the federal agenda.

The Maoists had promised 'autonomous' provinces with the 'right to self-determination' to Nepal's various 'nationalities', as they preferred to call distinct ethnicities. This had been a major tool for mobilization during the People's War. The party knew that backtracking from the agenda could cost it major political support and erode its base, as had happened in the Tarai. The Madhesi parties grew out of the movement for federalism and in opposition to the interim Constitution's silence on the issue. Federalism was central to their very existence and political construct. A wide constellation of Janjati groups—who had deep grievances over cultural discrimination and under-representation, and saw Nepal's history as not one of unification but of conquest—constituted the third pillar of support. These included groups within the CA, like a Janjati caucus across party lines. But powerful organizations like the Nepal Ethnic Federation of Indigenous Nationalities (NEFIN), Limbuwan groups in the far east, Tharu parties in the western Tarai, Newar cultural groups and figures in Kathmandu and the Janjati diaspora played a key role in mobilizing opinion and support for what came to be known as 'ethnic federalism'.

Even though they had arrived at it separately, through different ideological prisms, through different struggles, all three federal forces had a common understanding of the nature of the Nepali state and the need and rationale for federalism.

They agreed that the centralized, primarily hill-Hindu, upper caste-dominated state structure could only be democratized through federal restructuring. Federalism was not equal to decentralization and devolution—it went beyond merely granting administrative powers to local units and encompassed the constitutionally enshrined political rights given to provinces to decide on their finances, the language that they wanted to adopt, and the governance policies they wanted to put into place. For Madhesis and Janjatis, federalism was also a way to accord dignity to their constituents, who had felt alienated in their interactions with the state. All three forces also agreed that identity had to be the primary criteria in determining the state boundaries and names. Identity had been the basis for discrimination, and identity-based federalism—in which territory was carved out in a way which allowed erstwhile excluded groups to exercise a degree of power and gain political representation—was the solution.

But beyond this almost instinctive political overlap, based on viewing the old state structure as a common 'enemy', there were also wide-ranging differences between these forces at all levels, between the Maoists and the Madhesis, the Madhesis and the Janjatis, and the Maoists and the Janjatis.

Ethnic groups keenly suspected the Maoists' intent. They felt that the former rebels had only taken up the issue of ethnic liberation in order to increase their political strength, and the party's upper-caste leaders—both Prachanda and Baburam Bhattarai were Bahuns—could reject it at any time. For their part, the Maoists were supportive of federalism, but did not share the relatively extreme variant of 'ethnic federalism' favoured by many Janjati groups. And while using the rhetoric of 'autonomy', the Maoists were keen to establish a strong Centre. Within the ultra-Left, the orthodox leaders had, in any case, been uncomfortable with the category of identity overwhelming class. The Maoists also had a large constituency of Bahun and Chhetri supporters, and did not want to totally alienate the hill castes. So their support was moderated by various other factors, which made the marginalized social groups distrustful of them.

As we saw in Book 3, the Maoists and the Madhesis had shared a long, complex relationship with elements of both cooperation and competition. There was a strong element of chauvinistic nationalism within the Maoists' ranks and among the hill Janjati groups, who equated the Madhesis with Indians. The initial demand of the Madhesi parties was 'ek Madhes pradesh', an autonomous province across the plains from the east to the west. This was viewed as an India-sponsored conspiracy to weaken Nepal and was rejected outright by both the Maoists and the Janjatis.

The Madhesis also shared tense ties with the Tharus, who sought their own province in the western plains. There were disputes with the Limbus in the eastern hills, who sought three far-eastern Tarai districts as a part of greater Limbuwan, but which the Madhesis claimed ought to be a part of the plains.

If what united the Maoists, the Madhesis and the Janjatis was support for federalism, what united the NC and the UML was an instinctive aversion to the idea of state restructuring. This went back to their assessment of the 1990s and to the principle: if it isn't broken, why fix it? Since these parties had rarely articulated the identity-related grievances of the marginalized social groups, they could not see why federalism was so essential. And if at all federalism was necessary, why did it need to have a strong component of identity?

This partially stemmed from insecurity. If inclusive election rules could end up delivering a CA which included both Janjati and Madhesi MPs in such large numbers, federalism would shake up power structures even further. India was a compelling example. As federalism had become entrenched in the country, regional parties had grown stronger, marginalized social groups and castes had asserted power, and national parties had shrunk in size.

The Hindu upper castes of the hills of Nepal—Bahuns and Chhetris—together constituted almost 30 per cent of the population. While this segment was heterogeneous in terms of class, region, political orientation and beliefs, they had a strong sense of ownership of the existing Nepali state structure. They were fearful of the implications of restructuring, and what it would mean for the idea of the nation, and their own place in Nepal's political system. The NC and the UML represented, to a large extent, this strand in Nepali society.

Other important elements of what the writer C. K. Lal terms the Permanent Establishment of Nepal (PEON) were not enthusiastic about the idea either. The fact that the judiciary and the bureaucracy—conservative institutions in any setup—were almost entirely dominated by hill Brahmins deepened the resistance. I did not meet a single business leader who was supportive of federalism.

These formed a crucial support base for the older parties. One of Nepal's top industrialists told me, 'It will be a mess. There is already so much labour militancy. New parties will emerge in these new provinces and will now demand their share of the pie. Each state will have its own taxes, and transport costs will shoot up. Nepal will no longer be a unified market. Water is Nepal's biggest asset and sharing hydropower resources will become a point of conflict. This is not worth it.'

The army, which is institutionally oriented towards central rule anywhere in the world, too, was averse to federalism. The NC-UML and the NA had a tactical alliance against the Maoists, and shared a common worldview. The armed forces may have given up on the king, but the royalist ideological indoctrination, where the emphasis was on unity rather than on diversity, on assimilation and integration rather than on accommodation, on the homogenizing of symbols rather than allowing distinct practices to flourish, was strong. This was not surprising. An army general said, 'We have spent thirty years training to think like this. Don't expect us to be anarchists and critical of existing institutions. We will go for stability and order, nor for uncertainty and chaos.'

But given the overwhelming popular support for federalism, the fact that the interim Constitution had already promised it, and that these parties could not afford to neglect the sentiments of the substantial number of Madhesis and Janjatis in their own parties, the NC and the UML were slowly coming around to the idea. Krishna Hachhethu, a political scientist who would go on to become a key member of the State Restructuring Committee, called them 'reluctant federalists'. For them, federalism could be a way to 'decentralize' power, but the issue of how it was a tool for the marginalized to access power was not central in their imagination.

But the conservative parties remained concerned, and offered a set of principles to be kept in mind while determining the federal structure.

The first was 'national unity'. They projected alarmist scenarios of how the creation of provinces could potentially lead to the fragmentation of the country and to discord and conflict between communities. This was a bit of a red herring, since no force—except for the fringe armed groups from the Tarai—had ever sought secession. Maoist, Madhesi and Janjati leaders had clearly stated that in their imagination, the right to self-determination meant being able to exercise self-rule within the nation.

The second was economic rationale and 'capability'. Indeed, the CA concept paper on restructuring had suggested capability along with identity as the criteria for determining provincial boundaries. Some of the states proposed in the north-west and the north-east were too small and had little infrastructure to sustain themselves. In order to make provinces viable, the NC suggested a relatively fewer number of provinces. But Janjati groups viewed any effort to reduce the number of provinces with suspicion, for they felt that they could access political power only with a greater number of provinces. Given the spread of Bahuns and Chhetris across the country, lesser provinces would give these groups an electoral advantage, activists argued.

The third was administrative convenience. Nepal's hills are not easy to navigate. It is only recently that roads have reached all of the country's seventy-five district headquarters. Developmental priorities must take precedence over other factors. Ram Sharan Mahat, a former finance minister, often pointed out how territory carved out solely to give a particular ethnic group numerical dominance would make their lives more difficult, as many would have to travel longer distances to get to state capitals.

NC and UML leaders and their supporters asked, rhetorically, that if eight to ten big ethnic groups were given provinces of their own, would the country be divided into 101 pieces to ensure a small slice to all the ethnic groups listed in the census?

In their worldview, if federalism was to be introduced at all, the old development zones, or territories on the basis of old river basins, could be turned into provinces. These were carved out during the Panchayat regime, and went north to south. For the Madhesi parties, though, this would divide the Tarai in one stroke and weaken their identity and solidarity. It would also mean that Bahuns and Chhetris would enjoy a majority in each zone. The suggestion was greeted with outright hostility by the marginalized groups.

The missing link here was the Dalit community. As an excluded and under-represented group, its natural sympathies lay with the other marginalized communities. But the Dalits were ambivalent about federalism. They were spread out across the country, with no geographical concentration, and would thus not get a territory which they could call their own or where they could exercise power. Madhesi and Janjati groups often practised caste discrimination, and so Dalits did not quite see the rationale of supporting them. Yet, Dalit MPs knew that the existing structure—where Hindu hill castes dominated the government, society and the economy—was disastrous and maintaining the status quo would hurt them the most. Dalits voted on party lines for the most part and kept away from the federalism debate.

All these tensions played out in the CA Committee on Restructuring the State and Distribution of Power, headed by the Maoist member, Lokendra Bista Magar.

Maoists and Janjati members of the UML had come together to muster a majority and propose a fourteen-state model. These states would be named after the ethnic group dominant in that state. There would be agraadhikar, preferential rights, which meant that only members of that particular group—Limbu in Limbuwan, a Newar in Newa—could be eligible for chief ministership of the province for two terms in order to correct historical injustice, though the provision clearly went against the notion of individual rights. There would be autonomous regions within the provinces for smaller ethnic groups. The NC dissented, citing the lack of viability of these provinces, its consequences for 'national unity and social harmony', and objected to the way the proposal had been passed in the committee. The Madhesi parties put forth their maximalist demand for one province across the plains, disagreeing with both sides.

Even as power games and the peace process occupied the politicians, it was clear that issues such as these would be the hardest to resolve. As the committee chairman, Lokendra Bista, recalled later, 'I kept taking the committee discussions back to the leaders. I kept telling them that this was beyond us and their intervention was necessary. But they neglected the issue.'

True to form—like students who leave the tough questions for the end in an examination, only to realize that it had been a bad idea and that they were left with no time to think the answer through— Nepali parties left the difficult issues for the end, even as the CA's tenure kept ending, and getting extended, each time for a shorter period than the preceding occasion.

2

Over the years, though, progress did take place.

Tensions with India and other parties, as we saw earlier, had pushed Prachanda towards the more radical People's Revolt line. He had begun speaking of a People's Federal Republic as a result of pressure from the Kiran faction at a party conclave in Kharipati at the end of 2009. In a political culture where each word was weighed carefully, this was interpreted as a turn towards a more orthodox communist orientation, for he had signed up for a Federal Democratic Republic along with the other political parties.

But, by April 2011, after he had formally shifted back to the peace-and-Constitution line, I asked Prachanda about the implications of these terms, and whether it represented a shift in goalposts. He responded, 'It is true that we have agreed to institutionalize a Federal Democratic Republic. That is the bottom line. But we are communists—we believe in socialism, communism and people's democracy. Like the NC insists there should only be parliamentary democracy, we want the federal republic to be as pro-poor and as anti-feudal and anti-imperialist as possible and are pushing for this in the Constitution.' But he insisted that this was compatible with liberal democratic principles and argued, 'We have already accepted principles like freedom of press, independence of judiciary and human rights.'

As evidence, Prachanda displayed a remarkable degree of flexibility on constitutional issues, shedding positions which had been initially stated to reassure the other parties that a transformation was indeed taking place.

A CA committee had said in 2010 that there were 210 points of contention between parties in the thematic committees. But a Prachanda-led committee managed to resolve 127 of those issues. He was officially made the head of a Dispute Resolution Sub-Committee of the Constitutional Committee.

The parties agreed to call the statute the Constitution of Nepal. The debate over the usage of the term 'Maoist combatants' was deemed irrelevant as parties agreed to resolve the PLA issue before the promulgation of the Constitution. The Maoists had earlier argued for a simultaneous process.

The former rebels also gave up their insistence that no compensation be paid to those land owners from whom property—that was in excess of the stated ceiling—had been confiscated. This was an indication that they would respect the right to property even in circumstances where they felt that the property owner did not have a legitimate claim.

The Maoists accepted that there would be a bicameral legislature at the Centre, with a mix of first-past-the-post voting and proportional representation. There would be no restrictions on any parties, and multiparty democracy was a given.

The Maoists stepped back from their demand of parliamentary control over the judiciary, and accepted that an independent council would appoint judges. In turn, the other parties accepted that a new Constitutional Court would be created to interpret the Constitution, and to resolve disputes between the Centre and the states, as well as quarrels among the states.

~

The Maoists' flexibility had complex roots. They had become increasingly enmeshed in Kathmandu's existing political-economic mainstream, and the limits of their power had become clear.

I had publicly disagreed with the Indian policy of 'isolating and encircling' the Maoists, but it did have the effect of tiring out the former rebels. The ideological fervour among a large section of the cadres slowly dissipated, though a radical core remained. In political analysis, while discussing the big ideas, we often underrate the role of fatigue. Politicians get tired, their supporters get tired, rivals get tired, incentives change and it is only then that negotiations begin in full earnest and there is a willingness to let go of stated positions. From seeking the solution which would fetch them the best political returns, parties step down a notch to look for the second-best alternative; they then look for an acceptable solution and end up settling for any compromise that will break the stalemate without hurting their interests, even if they cannot win benefits.

There was also a realpolitik calculation. The Maoist leadership knew that there was no way that the party could impose any hegemonic system of governance on the country. The wisest political course of action would be to wrap up a Federal Democratic Republican Constitution, project it as their victory and a vindication of their political line, take credit, and aim to get a clear mandate in the next elections—for Prachanda as President, and for the Maoists as a party.

The Maoists' compromises on key ideological principles alienated radical, dogmatic members like Kiran.

Many months later, I asked Prachanda that if he had to give up certain precepts that were at the heart of their political ideology, why had he not done so earlier? 'These things take time,' he explained. 'We were attempting something unique and needed to get our cadre and machinery along. If I had acted earlier, the engine would have moved but the bogies would have got left behind.' This was a clear indication that like Prachanda's position vis-à-vis India, the party's initial red-lines on the integration of the PLA, steps like the dismissal of Katawal, their initial stance on constitutional issues which had made traditional democrats uncomfortable, had stemmed from internal pressure.

Looking back at the Kharipati meeting at the end of 2009—when Prachanda had allowed himself to be persuaded by Kiran and had adopted the People's Federal Republic line—the chairman explained, 'Look, both sides were evenly divided then. Baburamji and I had seventeen central committee members, and Kiranji's faction had seventeen. It would all have boiled down to Badalji's [Ram Bahadur Thapa] decision. If he had gone with Kiran, as was possible, then the entire peace-and-Constitution line would have got defeated. We would all have to go towards that, or they would have a majority in the party.' He admitted that he often had 'debates' with Baburam Bhattarai about that moment, since Bhattarai believed that Prachanda had then taken a wrong call. 'But I did not have a choice. The process would have collapsed.'

By compromising with Kiran then, Prachanda had to adopt a radical rhetoric. But, eventually, he felt that this had allowed him to show them the limits of their approach, weaken the dogmatic faction, make his own party machinery realize the need for compromise, and isolate the 'small faction' which was unwilling to shed its maximalist demands.

On another occasion, illustrating precisely this tactic, Prachanda had told me, 'Sometimes when you pick and eat a fruit that is not ripe, it is not good for health. If you take a decision without completing a certain phase of struggle, it can be negative. As a leader of the party, if I had not come through this path, I could not have taken this decision.' Reverting to military doctrine, he added, 'Launching a decisive attack when the time is not right can be counter-productive.' And referring to himself in the third person, he said, 'This is also Prachanda's working style. I took more than a year and a half before we decided to enter the peace process and accept competitive politics while the war was on. There is a need to create basis for any decision, that's my working style.' At the same time, he insisted that the Maoists had redefined the political mainstream through the constitutional project, which is why accusations of 'surrender' were flawed.

As he did during the end stages of the peace process, Prachanda was right in standing up to the dogmatists in his party. But this could not cover up his personal weaknesses and the political mistakes he made during the Constitution-writing exercise.

The fact was that for all their revolutionary rhetoric, the Maoist leadership had invested far more time in the games of government-formation than on the various elements of the new statute. They treated the house more as a regular Parliament, and less like a historic Constituent Assembly. Unlike the Indian CA, where the founding fathers of the nation had engaged in long debates on principles and specific provisions, barely any discussions took place in the full house in Nepal. As the largest party, the Maoists could not escape responsibility for this failure. The delay in settling the

PLA question stalled, and even delayed, substantive discussions on constitutional issues. The Maoists could have been far more proactive on this front.

The logic of having an elected CA draft the Constitution—according to the Maoists—was to ensure popular participation in the process. But the opposite happened. There was widespread disillusionment; people had little faith that the Constitution would ever be written due to the missed deadlines and repeated extensions; the euphoria of 2006 had all but dissipated and citizens were apathetic. The entire political class was at fault. But the Maoists, once again, must bear a disproportionate share of the blame as the largest party in the house. It was their responsibility to keep the focus on the Constitution and link it to the everyday concerns of citizens. Instead, they spent more time in closed-door negotiations, striking secret deals with other parties on a range of issues—which bred a culture of acute cynicism—rather than open up the Constitution-writing process and communicate with citizens about its importance.

But the substantial achievements could not be discounted, either. And the Maoists did deserve credit for it.

Nepal was now a republic. It was secular. It would become federal. The ambit of fundamental rights was exponentially expanded, and a rights-based regime, and welfare obligations, for the state were made binding. The electoral system would lead to greater inclusion and representation. Provisions against caste- and gender-based discrimination were institutionalized in law, though there was a huge gap regarding citizenship clauses where mothers were treated distinctly from fathers. A vision of a mixed economy—where the state, the private sector and cooperatives worked together—was envisaged. Local communities would have rights over natural resources. Provinces could choose their own languages, a provision which recognized the multilingual nature of the state.

Two major disputes remained—the form of government and the structure of federalism. These were integral to the Maoists' vision of a Nepali state and their prospects for political power. They had compromised on other constitutional matters. They had given up the PLA and had let the NA take over their cantonments. Their democratic commitment could not be doubted anymore. One could argue that these were steps the Maoists should have taken in the first place and they had not done anyone a favour. But, from their perspective, this represented a leap. And they now expected the other forces—particularly the NC—to demonstrate flexibility.

~

The parties had, after a great deal of acrimony, decided to set up a constitutionally mandated State Restructuring Commission (SRC) in late 2011. The four big forces, the Maoists, the NC, the UML and the Madhesi Front, nominated two members each and, subsequently, Madan Pariyar—a Dalit—was appointed chairman.

The nature of the nominees itself reflected the divide in political positions. The Maoists proposed the names of two Janjati activists, one of whom also worked on gender issues. The Madhesi parties proposed the name of a political scientist of Janjati background, Krishna Hachhethu, and a Madhesi lawyer. The NC nominated a historian who was a hill Brahmin, known for his scepticism about federalism, and one Janjati. The UML nominated a Madhesi economist from Janakpur and a Chhetri. In a context where the surname was a pretty good indicator of one's position on federalism, this was an interesting mix and it remained to be seen how representatives would cast their lot.

Eventually, the majority members of the SRC proposed a eleven-state identity-based federal model, including one non-territorial state for the Dalit community. Pariyar, the two Maoist and Madhesi nominees, and UML's Madhesi nominee voted for this model. The interim Constitution had clearly stated that the Nepali state had been discriminatory in the past, and marginalization on the basis of region, ethnicity, class and gender needed to be addressed. Federalism, according to the SRC, was one way to do it.

I knew Professor Hachhethu well and had often discussed the federal question with him. We had even attended some workshops on the issue in the Tarai. He had played a key role in drafting the eleven-state model, and explained its rationale to me, 'Look, the first thing is that this is not ethnic federalism. It is identity-based federalism.' The former would connote one ethnic group having a monopoly over political power in a province. But under the framework of identity-based federalism, the SRC members had sought to look at the question of 'demographic convenience and advantage'. Provinces would be named after particular identity groups in order to recognize their claims over their traditional territory, without giving them any political advantage.

In any case, exclusively 'ethnic provinces' were just not possible in Nepal, given its multi-ethnic mosaic, the migration of communities across the country from their 'traditional homelands' and the fact that not a single community had an outright majority, irrespective of how one carved out territory, especially in the hills.

Taking into account the factors of capability and economic viability, the SRC rejected three provinces proposed by the earlier CA committee—in the north-western and north-eastern upper reaches of the Himalayas, and one in the mid-eastern hills. It also merged two provinces in the far-western hills, bringing the numbers down.

The SRC suggested two provinces in the Tarai: Madhes in the east and Tharuhat in the west. The fact that nominees of the Madhesi parties were a part of the panel meant that the regional force had stepped down from its maximalist, and unreasonable, demand of a single province. It also paved the way for an agreement between the Madhesis and the Tharus, who had long been at loggerheads. In the hills, the SRC proposed carving out provinces in a way which would give a slight demographic advantage to the marginalized groups.

The SRC also dropped the contentious clause of agraadhikar, preferential rights, for the dominant ethnic group in a particular province. If the acceptance of two provinces represented the Madhesis' flexibility, letting go of preferential political rights symbolized an effort by the Janjatis to moderate their stance in response to criticism over how they had violated the idea of individual citizenship.

While the anti-federalists caricatured the SRC proposal as one backing 'ethnic federalism', and three members of the commission belonging to the NC and the UML submitted another proposal, it, in fact, represented the middle ground. It accepted the spirit of identity-based federalism, and not ethnic federalism, by suggesting that provinces be named after the dominant ethnic group and, as far as possible, efforts be made to give them a demographic advantage. But it was categorical in ensuring that all citizens, irrespective of ethnicity in the province, would be equal, and there would be no special rights for the titular community.

3

On 15 May 2012, I was sitting in a café opposite the UN House in Pulchowk in south Kathmandu. It was conveniently located, and I often used the space for meetings.

A month earlier, the NA had taken over the PLA camps. This had enabled a 5-point agreement between different parties in early May under which the NC and the UML agreed to join the Maoist-led government and give it the shape of a national unity government. In return, the Maoists agreed that once the Constitution was finalized, but before its promulgation, they would hand over power to the NC to lead the country towards the next elections. The NC had long argued that it was their 'turn' to lead the government, and the Maoists had let it be informally known that if the opposition party was flexible on the peace-and-Constitution process, they would be willing to hand over power and share credit for the success of the process.

India had actively backed the pact, and exercised its leverage with all sides to accept it. An official explained to me, 'This will revive the spirit of national unity and bring back the politics of consensus. It is inevitable that challenges will crop up during the final phase of the Constitution. But if all parties are together, they will be able to face it hopefully.'

India and the Maoists had, by now, reached a degree of accommodation. Delhi's low-key, but effective, diplomacy had helped prod and encourage the Maoists to move forward on the peace process. And without being over-bearing or intrusive or prescribing solutions, Delhi was keen to see Nepal forge a Constitution which would put it on the path to political stability.

At 4 p.m. that evening, as I sipped a black coffee, the Madhesi activist and friend, Tula Sah, who had given me a glimpse into his life as we travelled in the Tarai together, called up. A calm, sober and generally restrained person, Tulaji sounded angry. 'Did you hear?' I said I was not sure what he was talking about. He responded, 'They have come to a deal. Madhesi leaders have done what we had feared. They have sold out, given up on federalism, Prashantji. How could they do this?'

I immediately went online to check the news. The parties had just emerged from a meeting and declared that they had reached an agreement.

Nepal was to have a mixed form of government. Neither the Maoists' proposal for a directly elected, all-powerful President, nor the NC's insistence on the traditional parliamentary system was acceptable to the other side. A middle way was being discussed for months in Kathmandu's political circles, one which would have a directly elected President and a prime minister who would be elected by the Parliament. This was a terrible compromise, and would lead to constant paralysis and tensions between the two centres of power in a political culture where even a ceremonial President and an elected prime minister could not work together. Leaders knew that the solution was far from ideal, but they said that they were left with no choice. The President would be the supreme commander of the armed forces, and take charge of foreign policy, while the prime minister would be responsible for day-to-day administration. It was anyone's guess how this would work in practice, though the French and Finnish 'models' were casually thrown about in discussions as case studies.

An agreement on the electoral system had also been reached. The Centre would have two houses, and the lower house would have 171 directly elected seats to be contested through the first-past-the-post voting system, and another 140 seats would be filled via the proportional representation system. The upper house would have five members from each province.

News reports said that there had also been a 'breakthrough' on federalism. Parties had agreed to carve out eleven provinces. The boundaries would be decided by a Federal Commission, which would be constituted once the CA had promulgated the Constitution. The Parliament, in that case, would live on. (The interim Constitution stated that if the CA drafted a statute, it could continue to exist in the form of a Parliament till the next elections were announced.) The names of the provinces would be decided by the provincial assemblies once they were elected. Except the number, there was little by way of concrete detail on the content of the deal. Madhesi leaders Bijay Gachhedar and Mahant Thakur came out of the meeting and said that while they had reservations, they would not disrupt the Constitution-writing process.

But, as the news spread, information started trickling in that it was privately agreed to divide the Tarai into five provinces.

Tula continued, 'How can we accept this? One, they agree to a Constitution without full-fledged federalism. And then they go and divide up the Tarai into five parts.' Activist Dipendra Jha, Tula, members of the Madhesi Journalist Society and others were planning to torch a representative effigy of the Madhesi front in Baneshwor near the CA complex in a few hours. I said that I would visit them.

Within a few hours, I spoke to MPs, political activists, civil society leaders, and professionals in Tarai towns like Biratnagar, Janakpur, Birgunj and Nepalgunj. Tula's sentiment seemed to be representative of the mood in the Tarai, for no one celebrated the deal as a breakthrough and, instead, told me that it was a 'black day'. And as soon as Gachhedar and Mahant Thakur walked back to meet other Madhesi leaders in Singha Durbar, they faced severe recrimination for having betrayed the Madhesi agenda.

Prithvi Subba Gurung, the convener of the Janjati caucus in the CA, and an influential voice in the ethnic movement at that point, told me that evening, 'I see this as a conspiracy to maintain elite hegemony and counter the emerging alliance of the Madhesis and Janjatis. The provinces in the hills will be carved out it in a way that will make hill Brahmins and Chhetris the dominant groups. The Tarai will be divided into four or five parts, diluting its strength drastically.'

As I walked to Baneshwor's Masala Cottage restaurant, where Madhesi activists were making plans to register their protest, it became clear to me that this deal would not work.

The Kiran faction of the Maoist party had condemned the decision. This group was interested in undermining the entire constitutional project. It was on the verge of splitting away and was keen to tap into any anger against Prachanda and Baburam Bhattarai as a way to expand its own strength. It also believed that each crisis would expose the nature of the regime and help in fomenting a revolution. Had they been alone, Kiran and company could have been ignored or sidelined as they had been during the peace process.

But another Madhesi front, which was not in government, had also opposed the deal on federalism. Upendra Yadav was the leader of the Madhes movement in 2007, and a constitutional deal which alienated him would be difficult to sell in the Tarai. And then there were the Janjati MPs led by Prithvi Subba Gurung. Protests organized by the Tharus had already been underway in the western Tarai and they would not accept the merging of the Kailali and Kanchanpur districts of the western Tarai with the hills.

I stopped at a restaurant with free Wi-Fi and filed a column to be published in *The Kathmandu Post* the next day. The mood was eerily similar to the days before the interim Constitution was promulgated in 2007, when Kathmandu-centred parties had ignored the demand for federalism and, within days, the Tarai had gone up in flames.

I argued in my column, 'Marginalized communities have not waited for four years only to see their aspirations squashed or, in more polite terms, "postponed".' Recounting my conversations with the Janjati and Madhesi MPs, who smelled in the compromise an upper-caste conspiracy to delay the issue till the balance of power suited the upper castes in unelected commissions, I suggested that unless the deal was revised, it would only 'radicalise Janjati and Madhesi politics further'; and the best way would be to backtrack and engage in broader consultations on federalism with marginalized groups inside and outside the CA. If there was no time for discussion, given that the CA was meant to end on 27 May, another extension should be granted to the CA to focus purely on state restructuring.

~

The next morning, *Kantipur* and *The Kathmandu Post* published a map outlining what they claimed were the tentative boundaries of the eleven provinces. As many Madhesis had suspected, the map suggested that the Tarai would be divided into five provinces.

At 7 in the morning, I visited Mahant Thakur, the respected Madhesi leader, who was understood to have assented to the pact, though with reservations.

Looking at the *Kantipur* map, he said, 'Kahan maane hain hum log yeh? [We haven't accepted this!]' He said that they had exhibited flexibility because they did not want to 'disrupt the Constitution', which the marginalized groups needed most. 'But we will not give up the Madhesi interest either.' Events and reactions over the night seem to have shaken Thakur, who explained that any movement has costs, and he did not want to cause suffering, but it was now clear that they could not accept the earlier pact.

I later learnt why and how the Madhesi leaders had given in, defying their own stated positions that they would neither accept a Constitution without federalism, nor would they allow the Tarai to be divided into more than two provinces. A few days earlier, the RAW chief S. K. Tripathi had arrived in Kathmandu. India did not have any specific federal model to offer but it did want the Constitution to be written, and wished that the momentum created by the end of the PLA did not go waste. Tripathi met Gachhedar and Thakur and encouraged them to accept a deal, 'for the sake of the Constitution' as the struggle for federalism could continue even later. But if there was no Constitution, federalism itself would be lost. The Madhesi leaders were not comfortable, but accepted the RAW chief's advice. An Indian official source and one of the Madhesi leaders confirmed the meeting to me.

The backlash had stunned many, including India. A newspaper report claimed that a low-level embassy functionary in Birgunj had encouraged Madhesis to protest against the deal, but this seems to be a rogue officer acting on his own. The policy, as far as I could assess after speaking to officials in Kathmandu and Delhi, was to retreat. They felt that they had burnt their fingers with the 15 May deal and, as an official told me, 'The issues now are too internal and too divisive for us to offer advice. It is best for us to stay out.'

Several NC and UML politicians, and anti-federal commentators, saw pieces like mine as being deliberately provocative and I was accused of inciting communal discord and working against a compromise. I felt that this was unfair, since all I was doing was conveying and interpreting what I had seen on the ground. Like everything else, the mainstream Nepali media was dominated by the hill castes. They had made little effort to speak to leaders of excluded groups. They failed to read the mood and were now blaming the messenger. There could be legitimate questions about whether the pro-federal forces were making a mistake in not accepting a compromise for the sake of a Constitution, but to dismiss their grievances altogether was an insult.

That afternoon, Tula and others organized a joint Madhesi-Janjati meeting in Anam Nagar, next to the CA complex. The rhetoric was sharp, but the message was more coherent and radical.

There were three broad objections to the deal struck on 15 May. The interim Constitution had already declared an in-principle commitment to federalism, and it was the CA's task to specify it. A vague commitment, leaving everything else but the numbers for later, as-yet unelected commissions to sort out would not be acceptable. Two, if a deal had been forged to carve out five provinces in the Tarai, what was the basis of it? None of the constitutional mechanisms—either the CA committee or the SRC—had suggested this. And three, provinces must be named by the CA itself as it was a sovereign body. This concern about names emanated more from Janjati activists than from the Madhesis.

Health Minister Rajendra Mahato told his colleagues in the Madhesi Morcha that the status quo was not tenable and unless they would formally oppose the eleven-state deal, he would resign from the Cabinet. The pressure from second-rung leaders within the Morcha, Upendra Yadav from the outside, and Madhesi activists on the streets got too much for Gachhedar and Thakur, who were anyway reluctant partners in the deal. On 17 May, the Morcha formally backtracked from the 15 May pact.

In a meeting with Maoist chairman Prachanda, Madhesi ministers told him that they would resign and go back to the Tarai if it went through, and the Maoists could choose their course of action. Prachanda said that if the Madhesi leaders had objected as strongly earlier, his party would never have signed the agreement. The Maoists, too, would support the Madhesis and the Janjatis, and ask the NC and the UML to cooperate in revising the pact, and accept either fourteen states as suggested by the CA committee or ten states as proposed by the SRC.

Maoists, Madhesis, Janjatis, Muslims, Dalits and women's groups from across party lines had come together to sign a memorandum which opposed the pact and supported the recommendations of either the CA state restructuring committee or the SRC in favour of a 'constitution with federalism, and federalism with identity'. The collective strength of this group was over two-thirds of the house, the minimum number required to pass the Constitution if the issue was put to vote. There was no way that the 15 May deal could pass in the CA anymore.

The NC and the UML, however, refused to give in. Instead, they accused the Maoists and the Madhesi leaders of treachery, and insisted that either the eleven-state pact would stay or there would be no deal. To be fair, they had their own social base to worry about. Hill-caste communities, too, had stepped up the pressure. In the far west, Bahuns and Chhetris had launched a movement to oppose a unified Tharuhat province and had agitated for weeks for an akhanda sudur paschim, a unified far-west state. The Brahmin and Chhetri Samaj had just forced the government to recognize them as adivasi, indigenous, not only to dilute the claims made by the Janjati communities that they were the only original inhabitants of Nepal, but also to ensure that any benefit accruing from preferential reservation on the basis of caste and class would pass on to them. These groups were in no mood for compromise, and compelled their leaders across party lines to stay put.

Madhesi and Janjati members in the NC and the UML, too, told their leaders not to make any more compromises. Their motivation was somewhat different. Leaders of such communities from national parties would have to go back to their constituencies and compete with the Madhesi and Janjati leaders of ethnic parties and Maoists, and saw no reason to give them any additional political advantage by accepting their conditions. There was a genuine ideological divergence as well. Bimalendra Nidhi, a senior NC leader from the Tarai, had consistently maintained that having multiple provinces, instead of one or two provinces, would be more beneficial for the people of the plains. This would enhance their representation and get them access to more resources.

But the polarization only sharpened further. The umbrella Janjati organization, the Nepal Federation of Indigenous Nationalities (NEFIN), called a three-day strike to oppose the constitutional agreement. This was the most severe bandh that Kathmandu had seen in recent years. Usually, pedestrians, cyclists, bikers and press vehicles were allowed to move freely during such strikes. But NEFIN activists, who had divided up city corners and allotted them to different ethnic organizations, cracked down on everyone. Journalists who belonged to Hindu-caste backgrounds were selectively targeted and threatened, and the press was accused of being anti-Janjati. Vehicles were randomly vandalized and even pedestrians were beaten up.

The NEFIN bandh served the useful function of telling the Kathmandu establishment that the eleven-state deal was dead, and registering the strongest possible objection to it. But it also had other consequences. The intensity of the bandh, and its selective targeting along communal lines, alienated even those who had kept an open mind about the demands of the marginalized. Mainstream editors of hill-caste communities later confided that they decided after the bandh, 'Atti bhayo. [This had crossed all boundaries.'] The 'ethnic jargon and politics' had gone too far and they would oppose it.

Alienating progressives from the other camp at a moment like this, instead of explaining one's position to them reasonably, would turn out to be exceptionally, and irreversibly, damaging for the federal movement.

~

Nepal had never been as divided, and writing a Constitution at a moment like this seemed like an impossible task. While popular opinion had turned against the repeated extensions being granted to the CA, some of us had consistently argued that the CA deserved one final chance. It was only in April, with the end of the PLA, that serious discussions on federalism had started. Passions were at their peak and with time, tempers would cool, rational heads would prevail, and each side would step back.

At an all-party meeting on 22 May, parties decided to register an amendment to the Constitution to grant the CA a three-month extension. It was the Maoists who made the proposal, but this was accepted by the other forces as well. The parliamentary party leader of the NC, Ram Chandra Poudel, on his way out of the government secretariat, told an Indian diplomat, 'There is no choice but to extend it.' UML chairman Jhalanath Khanal expressed reservations, but did not object to it either. And it was the NC general secretary, and now law minister in the Baburam Bhattarai-led unity government, Krishna Prasad Sitaula, who went to the Parliament to register the amendment bill. But that very night, NC president Sushil Koirala called a press conference at his residence and said that the NC would oppose the extension to be granted to the CA.

In the preceding two years, cases related to the extension of the CA's term had gone up to the Supreme Court. The court had been inconsistent in the judgements that it had pronounced: it had given a green signal to one extension; at another time, it had declared that the CA would remain intact until the Constitution was written, and had thus granted the assembly a blank cheque; and, in November 2011, it had declared that the extension it was granting the CA would be the last. The court prescribed three courses of action if the Constitution was not written by 27 May 2012—there would be fresh polling to elect a new CA; a referendum might be taken; or, thirdly, any other 'appropriate arrangement' might be made according to the Constitution.

Sushil Koirala held up this judgement passed by the court, and claimed that in the spirit of respecting an independent judiciary, the NC would not support the extension. This was an incongruous situation, for it was his general secretary who had registered the CA extension bill. In the next two days, central committee members of the NC backed Koirala and Sitaula quit the government. In this period, the Kantipur Media Group also decided to oppose the proposed extension.

All of this gave confidence to the Supreme Court which, on 25 May, reiterated its earlier decision and disallowed a fifth extension to the CA. It hauled up the government for acting as if no order had been given by the highest court of the land and demanded that Prime Minister Bhattarai and former minister Sitaula explain why they should not be held in contempt.

Only the Maoists and, to some extent, the Madhesi parties dared challenge the judiciary and correctly termed the ruling an instance of judicial over-reach. The court had no business encroaching into the territory of the popular, sovereign body. If the political class had been united, and not as discredited as it had become because of its successive failures, they could have mounted a challenge to what was a violation of the principle of the separation of powers. Additionally, the court's judgement rested on shallow grounds. If four previous extensions were valid, why was this not? This was not a legal but a political judgement which, unfortunately, was not resisted.

The NC had been most unhelpful through the period. The party had first refused to take into account concerns raised by the Madhesi and the Janjati groups, or discuss them with a wider range of actors while forging the deal of 15 May. The opposition from social groups, and forces outside the CA, indicated that such a Constitution would not have the buy-in of a large section of the population. Yet, the NC and the UML refused to budge and revise the deal. And now that the end of the CA's term approached, they had contributed to foiling the government's attempt to extend tenure, which would have served as a breather and restored rationality to the discussions.

One could not help asking if the NC wanted a Constitution at all. A similar question could be asked of influential media groups.

I confronted a young NC leader who was at the forefront of the move to oppose the extension and he had a lame defence, 'We had been told by pro-NC lawyers that the SC was sure to strike down the government's move. So we thought it was better to be on the right side than be seen as violating the SC order.' He then paused, and admitted candidly, 'But in hindsight, our opposition would have helped the SC in taking the decision and given them confidence. It was a mistake.' Editors who opposed the extension said that they had hoped to generate pressure on the parties to strike a deal. One of them said, 'We really thought they would reach a compromise. It was not with any other intention. Only if we had known ...'

Irrespective of the motivations of the different players, the doors for any extension to the CA's term were now shut. There was now only one choice: either write the Constitution in two days, or witness the end of a dream which had been cherished by citizens for over six decades.

~

The judgement passed by the Supreme Court had opened up, as well as narrowed down, options.

The NC and the UML now said that it was not possible to draft a Constitution with federalism, given the deep differences in the polity. Instead, they recommended that parties promulgate a statute without going into the details of federalism. Once that was done, the house would survive in its capacity as a 'transformed Parliament'; there would be no legislative vacuum; and parties could decide on federalism in that forum.

For the Maoists, the Madhesis and the Janjatis, this was not acceptable at all. Prachanda had told me in April, 'We will not accept a Constitution without federalism, and federalism without identity. If the Maoists compromise on the issue of federalism or leave identity, then the identity of the Maoist party itself will finish.' There was a personal calculation as well. Prachanda knew that to become the directly elected President, he needed the support of the excluded groups. By giving up on federalism, there was a risk that he would irreversibly alienate them, a mistake he had committed in the Madhes in 2007 and still regretted.

Both sides now waited for the other to blink.

The NC and the UML had made a political choice to kill the CA rather than to accept identity-based federalism. This was shrewd, for it left the federal forces in a Catch-22 situation. If the Maoists and the Madhesis chose to have a Constitution, their only choice would be to drop federalism for now and wait for a Parliament where the party whip would not apply. Cross-party alliances on ethnic grounds could not be created, and the issue could be delayed indefinitely. If they chose to stick to their position, the CA—which was originally a plank for the Maoists and the most inclusive house Nepal had seen, one in which the marginalized groups had the greatest stake—would no longer exist. The conservatives would win either way.

To ensure that power did not remain in the Maoists' hands, even in the final hours of the Constitution-making process, certain NC and UML leaders decided to focus on filing a no-confidence motion, with the support of the Kiran faction of the Maoists who were furious with Prachanda and Baburam Bhattarai. The plan, however, collapsed because the Janjati and Madhesi members of the UML Parliamentary Board—focused on a federal Constitution—refused to support such a move and told the leadership that this was no time to play such games.

For the Maoists and the Madhesis, it was indeed a tricky situation. The only bargaining position they held was through control over the reins of the government, which they had already offered to the NC if it helped draft the Constitution. But both forces felt that giving up the issue of identity-based federalism, at this juncture, would be political suicide. Kiran would accuse the Maoist leadership of giving up on federalism and take away the Janjati and Madhesi support base of the party. For the Madhesi front, any compromise would translate into political dividends for Upendra Yadav and others sitting in the opposition in the Tarai.

More importantly, there was a strong feeling in the federal camp that if they gave in now—when they were the biggest forces in the CA, when they had over two-thirds of the members supporting their agenda—there would never be able to get federalism. Saving the agenda for the future, if not institutionalizing it immediately, became the primary goal.

It was with this mindset that both sides joined negotiations on the final day of the Constituent Assembly's term.

4

The meeting in Baluwatar got off to a cold and formal start.

On 27 May, as leaders congregated on either side of the prime minister in the meeting, they reiterated their formal stated positions. NC and UML leaders suggested that since there was no way that a full Constitution with federalism could be written, it would be best to come up with a draft and leave the contentious issues for Parliament to decide upon. The Maoists and the Madhesi parties said once again that this would not be acceptable, and asked the NC and the UML to pick either of the two models—ten states of the SRC, or fourteen states of the CA committee—as the federal structure.

These discussions continued in various forms—as bilateral, trilateral and multilateral exchanges.

Meanwhile, the Janjati caucus—an alliance of parliamentarians belonging to ethnic minorities across party lines—made their way to the prime minister's residence in the early afternoon.

The names of the provinces had been a contentious issue, with ethnic leaders insisting on what they called 'single-identity provinces', and others asking for 'multi-identity provinces'. These terms always seemed incorrect to me, as provinces would be multi-ethnic in any case. But they had come to be used in debates about the names of the provinces.

Janjati MPs suggested to the leaders that they had found a compromise formula to include both the geographic and the ethnic name in the province. So Kathmandu would be Newa-Bagmati-Bahujatiya Province—with Newa referring to the Newar ethnic group, Bagmati to the principal river of the city, and bahujatiya, multi-ethnic, would recognize the distinct social groups in the capital. Janjati leaders also emphasized that they did not wish to become the cause for the collapse of the CA, and were willing to exercise maximum flexibility. As an observer put it to me then, 'The SRC's ten-state model, with multi-ethnic names, was the simplest and least-complicated solution. But the NC and the UML did not relent.'

Madhesi leaders continued to push for the ten-state model of the SRC. But they were willing to offer basic concessions. Mahant Thakur had told me that morning, 'District boundaries are not sacrosanct. So in some parts of the Tarai, the northern belt which has dominant hill communities can be merged with the hill provinces.'

But this was not enough for many influential NC and UML leaders. They were, in particular, keen on carving out the three far-eastern Tarai districts—Morang, Sunsari and Jhapa—into a separate province. They argued that the demographic in this region was evenly divided between pahadis and Madhesis, and that their support base did not see why Jhapa—where Madhesi parties had failed to win a single seat—needed to be a part of Madhes with its capital in Janakpur. The fact that key negotiators—UML's K. P. Oli, NC's Sitaula and Minendra Rijal, and the entire Koirala family—came from the belt only made them more determined not to let their districts fall under a Madhes pradesh.

Even as negotiations were underway in Baluwatar, President Ram Baran Yadav called up the Indian ambassador Jayant Prasad. Yadav wanted India to use its leverage with the Madhesi parties to compel them to immediately give up their demand for federalism, leaving it for the transformed Parliament. Prasad had been subjected to similar pressure from the NC leaders in the past few days. In turn, Madhesi leaders wanted him to do the reverse—put pressure on the NC-UML combine to accept either the ten-state or the fourteen-state model.

India had made a conscious decision to stay away from the CA debate. But Yadav insisted that his message, 'as a request of the

President of Nepal', be conveyed to Delhi. Prasad spoke to National Security Advisor Menon, who authorized him to take the requisite steps. The Indian embassy in Kathmandu then called up leaders of the Madhesi Morcha and conveyed to them the wishes of the President, asserting that Delhi did not have any view on the matter as it was purely an internal issue, one which should be decided upon by the Nepalis themselves.

There are legitimate questions about whether India could have done more in mediating a pact between Nepal's political parties. After all, they had invested enormous capital in pushing the peace process and conveying the need to dismantle the PLA. Why were similar efforts not made with regard to the Constitution-writing project? Was it because while the peace process forced the Maoists to surrender a source of their power, a Constitution—written by a CA led by the Maoists—would only make them more powerful?

But while this may have been an underlying calculation for some in the Indian establishment, the facts on the ground suggest that India wanted to see the Constitution written. Delhi had come a long way from May 2010, when it sought to actively block the extension of the CA's term of operation. It wanted to wrap up the Nepali transition, but it chose not to use its leverage on either side since the 15 May episode, when its interference had revealed to it the depth of the passions involved in the process. Fundamental differences between Nepali politicians, social groups and communities were playing out. An external power, even one as influential as India is in Nepal, could perhaps do little.

I had gone over to the CA complex where MPs were waiting to hear about developments at the prime minister's residence in Baluwatar. Information was at a premium, and even the people's representatives did not know what to expect. A canteen was operational, where I sipped tea with a few MPs who were confident that a deal would happen. For a while, there was a sense of optimism in one corner. But the general mood was one of unease, impatience and restlessness. MPs were to begin demonstrating, chanting slogans, and protesting against their own leaders who had hijacked the entire CA process in a few hours.

Outside the complex, this was already happening. Reflecting the polarization in society, to the right of the entrance to the CA complex was the Brahmin and Chhetri Samaj. They had organized a fairly impressive demonstration, opposing what they called 'ethnic federalism'. And, to the left, Janjati, Madhesi and women's groups had congregated at the Baneshwor crossing. The roads had been taken over. There was nervousness and tension in the air, but there was also celebratory music and sporadic dances; everyone was anticipating the big moment, the breakthrough which would meet everyone's interests.

Leaders had now left Baluwatar. Prime Minister Baburam Bhattarai was to tell me a week later that they had planned to head to the CA complex, but the NC and UML leaders were 'scared' to face the CA members and, instead, headed to the chamber of the CA chairman, Subash Nemwang, in Singha Durbar, the government secretariat. To date there has never been a credible explanation of why the top leadership chose not to go to the CA at all on its last day.

This was a major omission, and brought into focus the implications of the procedural error in the CA's functioning. Even as a few hours remained for the term of the CA to end, leaders were busy attending closed-door meetings in a venue away from the legislature instead of giving a voice to the elected MPs, putting contentious issues to vote, and allowing the democratic process to take its own course, irrespective of the outcome. Prime Minister Bhattarai, in fact, claimed that they had proposed to put federal models to vote. If any model got two-thirds majority, 'well and good'; and if not, 'at least the CA members would be satisfied and we could find some other means'.

At 5 p.m., some leaders of the Madhesi Morcha called me up as I was strolling between the CA complex and the government secretariat, a few kilometres away from each other, witnessing the protests. The Morcha was meeting, and the leaders asked me to come over. I was a bit unsure since it did not seem correct to attend a political meeting as a journalist, but the temptation of having a ringside view to final negotiations prevailed.

The meeting was underway in an office of one of the bigger Madhesi outfits, and about two dozen MPs were present. I quietly took a seat at the back.

Madhesi civil society members had circulated a paper, and former ambassador Vijay Karna and activist Tula Sah were explaining it to the leaders. This was a document which laid out provisions for a possible compromise with the objective of saving the constitutional process. It suggested that since a full-fledged federal model could not be attained immediately, certain conditions could be imposed, as a mechanism of guarantee, if the discussions were to be taken to the transformed Parliament.

These would include a specific time period in which the federalism issue needed to be addressed; a prior commitment that there would not be more than a particular number of provinces in the Tarai; that the party whip would not apply to any vote and discussion on state restructuring in Parliament; that the names and the identities of the people living in the province would be taken into account when deciding on the name of the province.

The capital's media has often blamed Madhesi activists for inciting their leaders to take a more confrontational position in this period. But the fact is that independent intellectuals of the Tarai, till the last moment, were actually coming up with creative ideas which could serve as a political compromise.

The Madhesi leaders, however, were not keen on such details. They appeared to have made up their minds about either getting the federal structure as per the SRC's suggestions or letting the process collapse and allow a new reality to emerge.

Their focus was on the current state of play. In an indication of the trust deficit, even between allies, doubts had emerged in the Madhesi camp about whether the Maoists would stay the course with them or switch over to the NC and the UML. One party chairman asked, 'They are all one community after all. What should we do if that happens?' A loud cry came from the hall, with MPs shouting in one voice, 'Andolan!' But these concerns seemed to be misplaced for a few minutes later, a Maoist leader called and five Madhesi party chairmen went to another hall to meet other leaders.

I spoke with Hridayesh Tripathi, an influential minister, who was sitting in one corner of that hall. He said candidly, 'Now the game is power. NC and UML want the Parliament because as soon as there is a legislature tomorrow, they will file a no-confidence motion and, with Kiran's support, form the government. So we will be left with no federalism, no Constitution, and no government. What is the point of falling into that trap?'

That was the clearest indication of the power calculations on both sides and the fact that there was little hope that the Constitution-writing process could be saved that night. Only a few minutes later, news spread that the parties meeting in the CA chairman's chamber had concluded that a Constitution was no longer possible. It was 6 p.m. on 27 May. I had a sinking feeling. But the pace of events overwhelmed everything, and did not allow for introspection about what it all meant.

The debate was now about the next step in the political process. Maoist leaders initially floated the idea of declaring a state of emergency in order to extend the CA's term if others were willing to 'own the idea'. Prime Minister Bhattarai said that he was even willing to bear the kalank, the shame, of declaring an emergency if all parties agreed. But this was rejected by everyone except NC's former prime minister, Sher Bahadur Deuba, who said whatever had to be done, must be done to save the CA.

I was sitting with the minister for industries, Anil Jha, in his official chambers as we waited for news from the meeting hall. It was now 8.30 p.m., and rumours circulated that a Cabinet meeting was imminent. It appeared that Prime Minister Bhattarai, after his proposal of emergency was rejected, had come to his own office. Speculation was rife about what he would do, even as leaders of the NC and the UML were now slowly panicking, as the implications of the end of the CA—and the Parliament—sunk in. Their assumption that the forces supporting federalism would blink had fallen flat.

A Cabinet meeting was indeed called at 10 p.m. I went with Anilji in his car to the Prime Minister's Office (PMO), and waited downstairs with the rest of the reporters, when a string of NC and UML leaders, including several former prime ministers, could be seen walking briskly to the PMO. It appeared that they had changed their minds, and were now willing to support an emergency to extend the CA. Realization had struck that the end of the CA would also mean the end of the legislature and, once that happened, there would be no way to replace the Baburam Bhattarai-led government which could become all-powerful and answerable to no one.

But it was too late. Prachanda informed them that the Cabinet had been called. The Maoists and the Madhesi parties jointly decided to call for fresh polling to elect a new CA on 21 November. A minister made an announcement to news reporters, and then the prime minister rushed to the President's residence, Shital Niwas, to convey the Cabinet's decision to him before midnight.

I jumped into a press car to head to the prime minister's residence in Baluwatar and, around midnight, he announced at a press conference, beamed live across the country, that the 'anti-federal position' taken by the NC and the UML, despite the utmost flexibility exhibited by the Maoists and the Madhesis, had left the government with no choice. This would save the country from a constitutional crisis, and the experiences gained from the last CA would aid efforts to write the next Constitution.

The opposition parties were shocked. Their actions had contributed the most to this impasse, but they had not expected fresh elections to be announced and refused to accept the government's legitimacy. They had calculated, as an NC leader was to tell me a few weeks later, that the end of the CA would also mean the end of the government, and that the President would take over.

At midnight on 27 May, the chairman of the CA, Subash Nemwang, notified President Ram Baran Yadav that the working term of the Constituent Assembly of Nepal had ended without a Constitution having been drafted.

And just like that, it was gone.

16,000 people had died, 1,300 had disappeared, and thousands had been displaced. Millions had marched on the streets. The energies of thousands of men and women—from Maoist commanders and commissars to foot soldiers like Mahesh Arohi and Krishna KC, from Madhesi leaders to activists like Tula Sah and Rajeev Jha, from Gagan Thapa, the young NC politician who had first raised the cry for republicanism in his party, to civil society veterans of Kathmandu such as Devendra Raj Panday and Khagendra Sangroula—had been spent in bringing about peace, democracy and social justice, and in the hope that Nepalis would, sixty years after it was first promised, write their own Constitution.

It was not to be.

The dream was dead.

Postscript

'We are all stabdh.'

In a literal sense, stabdh translates into 'stunned'. But 'stunned' does not quite convey the numbness, the intensity of the shock, the emptiness, which is evoked by its Nepali equivalent.

It was the evening of 21 November 2013, forty-eight hours after elections to Nepal's second CA had concluded. Despite sporadic incidents of violence in the preceding few weeks, and a call for boycott by radical outfits, polling day had been remarkably peaceful, witnessing the highest-ever turnout in the country's democratic history. Results had begun trickling in the next morning. And, as preliminary speculative trends gave way to more certain seat projections, it became clear that Nepali voters had thrown up yet another surprise.

In 2008, they had elected the Communist Party of Nepal (Maoist) as the single-largest party in the first CA. In 2013, the same voters had decisively rejected the former rebels. From 240 seats in a house of 301, the Maoists shrunk to one-third of their original size, with only eighty members in the CA. The other progressive force—the Madhesi parties of the plains—would also see a dip in strength, from eighty-three to fifty seats.

The NC had emerged as the single-largest party with 196 seats, and the UML had come a close second with 175 seats. Together, the NC and the UML had close to a two-thirds majority in the house. The Rastriya Prajatantra Party Nepal, the ultra-conservative outfit, batting for the revival of the monarchy and a Hindu state, would also bag a respectable two dozen seats.

In five years, politics had come a full circle.

I had moved to India earlier in the year. After being immersed in covering the twists and turns of Nepali politics for six years, I felt that I needed to move on. I had developed strong and wide networks—which was good—but also strong alignments and opinions—which never bode well for a reporter. I needed distance. But I went back home to track the elections. After a quick run through the Tarai and Kathmandu, one could sense that the balance of power would shift, but I failed to read the extent of the anger against the Maoists and the regional forces. Two days after the polls, I got on the phone with Maoist chairman Pushpa Kamal Dahal 'Prachanda'.

'We are stabdh,' he told me. 'This is an unnatural, unbelievable, surprising result. There has been a conspiracy.' At 3 a.m. that morning, the Maoists had called an emergency party meeting, alleged systematic fraud, and walked out of the counting process. Prachanda was understandably numb and, on the phone, he repeated those allegations. When I pointed out that the Maoists were being seen as bad losers, and there did not appear to be tangible evidence to substantiate their conspiracy theory, the Maoist chairman responded, 'This has been done in a calculated, systematic way. Even votes from areas we know are our strongholds are missing. Ballot boxes were kept in the army barracks, and there has been some mischief.'

The larger issue, the man who had led the Maoists during the war and transformed them into a democratic, mainstream, political outfit said, was political. 'The CA was meant to draft a progressive, federal, democratic, secular, republican Constitution. But it has been hijacked by regressive forces. This CA cannot write a Constitution. We cannot enter the house and compromise on our agenda.'

This was striking, for the Maoists—since 2001—had argued that only a popularly elected CA could and should draft Nepal's Constitution. They agreed to end the People's War and enter a pact with other political parties only when the latter agreed to this demand for a CA.

After the first CA failed in May 2012, the Baburam Bhattarai-led government had called for a second CA election. Opposition parties were furious with the Maoists for having unilaterally declared polls, and had refused to recognize Prime Minister Bhattarai's government as legitimate. They demanded a change in guard. But the Maoists did not see any reason why they should allow a government led by the Nepali Congress to hold elections. For ten months, the political stalemate had paralysed the country. A compromise was eventually suggested by Prachanda himself, with India backing him. An interim election government led by the chief justice of the Supreme Court, Khila Raj Regmi, was constituted in March 2013, with the limited mandate of holding polls by the end of the year.

A party that had sacrificed so much for a CA seemed to be stepping back from its central political line. Would it return to its extremist roots? The Maoist chairman allayed my apprehensions and said, 'We are not walking out of the peace and democratic process. We are not walking out of the 12-point Understanding.'

Nepal had come a long way from the pact of 2005. But if it had to institutionalize its political gains in the new context, that framework remained crucial—for it was the bedrock of the partnership between the Maoists and the non-Maoists. Prachanda's reaction gave me a sense of the Maoists' anxieties about the fate of their political agenda and their role in the polity. But by reiterating his commitment to partnership with other democratic forces, the political strategist had left the door open for a compromise.

As the Maoists slowly came to terms with the result, and the shock turned to introspection, they recalibrated their initial position. By the end of December, Nepal's political parties arrived at a new agreement. To assure the Maoists of their commitment to progressive change, the NC and the UML reiterated that they would not step back from republicanism, secularism and federalism. A parliamentary committee would look into the charges of electoral fraud. And, in return, the Maoists would participate in Nepal's second elected Constituent Assembly.

In February 2014, the NC and the UML agreed upon a power-sharing deal. Sushil Koirala was elected the country's new prime minster, while UML's Bamdev Gautam took over as deputy prime minister. This happened after weeks of negotiations, indicating that the NC-UML relationship would not be free of acrimony. The

Maoists were keen on the chairmanship of the CA, but it was the UML's Subash Nemwang—who was the chairman of the first CA—who was re-elected. The parties promised to draft a Constitution in a year but, given their track record, few thought it likely that the statute would be written in such quick time.

~

What explained the rout of the progressive, federal forces, and the return of the traditional forces? What did it mean for inclusion and identity-based federalism, the issue over which the last CA had collapsed?

During the campaign, Prachanda admitted to three mistakes that he had made after entering open politics and winning the elections. The first was not supporting Girija Prasad Koirala for the post of the first President of the republic in 2008—this had ended the politics of consensus with the NC and had led to domestic polarization. The second was seeking to dismiss General Rukmangad Katawal in 2009—this had sharpened the Maoists' differences with India, led to their exit from government, and derailed the political process. And the third was not putting up the contentious constitutional issues to vote in the full CA—this had led to the collapse of the CA without elected representatives even getting a chance to resolve differences through democratic mechanisms.

Baburam Bhattarai, after the drubbing in the elections, declared in a post on Facebook that the biggest mistake of his life was not unilaterally declaring a state of emergency on the night of 27 May 2012 and extending the CA's term. He was to tell interlocutors that the party had also committed the blunder of handing over power to the chief justice of the Supreme Court and to former bureaucrats. They had also agreed to allow the Nepal Army to be deployed for security purposes during polling. These elements of the permanent establishment were the most viscerally opposed to the Maoists and Madhesis and to identity-based federalism. Even if there had been no fraud on the day of the election, the collective orientation of those holding polls—according to Bhattarai—had tilted the scales against the Maoists.

There is merit in the analysis made by both leaders, and it indicates that the party was politically and ideologically unclear at key moments in Nepal's recent history. They had flirted with extremism when the moment called for moderation, and had compromised too easily when they should have stood up for principles. But both Prachanda and Bhattarai's focus appeared to be on tactical elements rather than on the big picture.

The Maoists lost the elections because the people who had trusted the party to draft the Constitution in 2008 felt that it had failed in its fundamental task. As a taxi driver in Kathmandu told me two days before the polls, 'How does it matter to me why they could not write the Constitution? I had voted for a Maoist MP. He failed. Why should I repeat my mistake? What is the guarantee they will succeed now?' As incumbents, both Maoist and Madhesi MPs failed to answer this fundamental question. Their efforts to shift the blame for the collapse of the Constitution-writing process, too, did not work. The gamble made by the NC and the UML in May 2012 had worked. They had been rigid during the endgame of the Constitution-writing process because they knew that the Maoists would walk away with the credit if it was written. Now, the Maoists had to carry the burden of failure, and pay a price for it.

The more important factor was the Maoists' failure to govern in a manner which would improve livelihoods of citizens. In 2008, a key Maoist campaign slogan was, 'You have tried everyone else many times. Test us once.' By 2013, the same voters who had given Maoists the benefit of doubt turned. 'We have tested them, and they are even worse than the others,' said one voter in the capital's Baneshwor area.

The Maoists had been sucked into Nepal's degenerate political culture. Tales about Prachanda's wealth, his luxurious lifestyle, and his debauched son reminded citizens of the old king. 'Naya raja aayo. [We have a new king.],' was a popular refrain when the Maoist chairman's cavalcade passed through the streets of the capital. Maoist workers in districts were initially known, and admired, for their simplicity, their austere lives, their sacrifice and their willingness to put their lives on the line for the betterment of society. But now, the stereotypical image of the Maoist worker was that of a middle man or a contractor, using his access to power to earn a quick buck. The mainstream had truly co-opted the rebels before the rebels could change the mainstream.

To be fair to the party, the Maoists led the government for only eighteen months in the last Parliament's four-year term, between August 2008 and May 2009, and August 2011 and May 2012. But their failure to implement even basic welfare policies, make the government accessible to common citizens, embark on projects which would lead to rapid employment generation and manage inflation, would erode its popular support. 1,000 Nepalis were still leaving the country every day to work elsewhere. Their relationship with the Nepali state was reduced to seeking a passport. The Maoists were able to do little to reverse the tide and create conditions for people to remain home with their families, lead productive lives and earn their bread and butter. As Baburam Bhattarai was to admit to me at his Sanepa home in February 2014, the Maoists had lost the plot as far as their class base was concerned. 'We got disconnected from our own social base; the poor, the dispossessed and the marginalized, and could do little for them. And the other segment—the middle class—did not come to us. We were left with no core social group.'

The organizational disarray added to the popular disillusionment.

In June 2012, a month after the end of the Constituent Assembly, the party had suffered a vertical organizational split. Orthodox Maoists had never been able to internalize the peace-and-Constitution line taken by the party, its engagement with India, and remained wedded to the vision of a hegemonic political system. They tapped into the widespread disillusionment among the cadres, including in the PLA, at the compromises the party had made in its dealings with older traditional forces.

Mohan Vaidya 'Kiran', Ram Bahadur Thapa 'Badal', Dev Gurung, and C. P. Gajurel—influential leaders who had started the revolution in 1996 along with Prachanda and Baburam Bhattarai—led the new party. They were aided by a young militant leader, Netra Bikram Chand 'Biplab'. They claimed that the 'surrender' on the question of integration of Maoist combatants, and the CA's inability to draft a Constitution, signalled the failure of Prachanda and Bhattarai's peace-and-Constitution line. This faction boycotted the CA polls. Anecdotal evidence suggested that the extremist, Kiran-led Maoists had made it a point to vote for the NC and the UML to ensure the defeat of their former comrades.

The electoral debacle did not mean that the political line taken by the Maoists in 2005 was incorrect, and that the dogmatists were right. That would be like, in the words of Bhattarai, 'blaming the road if an accident occurs'. But the mismanagement of the peace process, particularly the integration and the rehabilitation of the combatants, gave enough ammunition to the hardliners to tap into the discontent within the party. If Prachanda had been more honest about the party's direction, and about the limits of what could be achieved, from the outset, they may have been able to inspire more faith among their own cadres.

In the plains, the Madhesi parties were routed for reasons similar to the ones which had affected the Maoists' performance.

In 2008, three parties—the Madhesi Janadhikar Forum, Sadbhavana and the Tarai Madhes Loktantrik Party—had contested the polls. In 2013, there were over a dozen Madhesi parties. The fragmentation was a result of personal animosities, ambitions and egos rather than principles. The consistent message conveyed by the Madhesi Street to its leaders was that they must unite for the larger cause, given that they all shared the same agenda. But the failure to do so would cost them heavily. There was a split in votes among the Madhesi parties, and the bigger national outfits only scraped through.

But while divisions damaged the Madhesis, so did their performance while in office. Madhesi ministers held some of the best portfolios, of direct relevance to their constituents. For most of the five years after 2008, a representative from the Tarai was in charge of the Ministry of Agriculture. There was not a single initiative to modernize farming, to ensure the easy availability of fertilizers at affordable prices, to re-engineer land relations, or to enhance productivity. Upendra Yadav was foreign minister twice.

But despite the fact that Madhesis constituted a huge segment of migrant workers, he did little to negotiate with governments in West Asia and Malaysia to improve working conditions for the Nepali working class. Madhesi ministers were responsible for the industries portfolio but they used it to dispense patronage among loyalists and appoint them as chairmen of sick public sector units. There was no initiative to either revive dysfunctional enterprises and provide employment, or to sell them and use the resources for other welfare projects. A Tarai leader had to step down as education minister after serious corruption charges were levelled against him, and his successors—mostly from Madhesi parties again—did little to improve the performance of the public education system, which was in tatters across the plains.

This is not an exhaustive list, but mere examples which reflect skewed priorities. People in the plains were watching and began asking if increased access to political power was meant to improve the lives of citizens or only the lives of the ministers and their families. The disillusionment turned to anger. The NC and the UML were smart in selecting Madhesi candidates in Tarai constituencies. This deprived the regional parties of the identity card, and voters were quick to choose alternatives.

The older parties succeeded because they made the 2013 elections a referendum on the performance of the Maoists and the Madhesi parties after 2008. The issue of development, local governance and corruption took precedence.

The debates around federalism, which had been central in the collapse of the last CA, did not figure prominently in the campaign. But it was clear that the pro-federal forces had failed to gauge the anxieties around the issue of state restructuring. There was a fear of the unknown, even among the marginalized social groups, and the traditional forces offered the promise of order, harmony and stability. After a decade and a half of turbulence, voters—it seemed—were not willing to experiment any longer.

Once the results trickled in, the NC and the UML interpreted the mandate as one which vindicated their position on state restructuring, which would prioritize principles of economic capability and resource allocation over the thorny questions of identity. Maoist, Madhesi and ethnic forces looked back at May 2012 with regret, wondering if they had made a mistake in not accepting the agreement on eleven provinces. But despite their depleted strength, they were determined not to let the federalism project fail.

Whether the Maoists and the Madhesi political formations would recover depended on how they cleaned up their acts, reconnected with their constituents, and re-articulated their demands.

As I close this book in the early spring of 2014, the signs for the progressive forces are not looking good. The Maoists are internally fractured, and Prachanda and Bhattarai are squabbling about who is to blame for the rout. There is also a lack of clarity about which ideological line the party should take in the future. Should it reach out to the Kiran faction and become more aggressive and confrontational with others? Should it be reconciled to being the UML's B-team as a junior Left party? Should it carve out a new ideological programme? Should it stick to its demand for identity-based federalism or revise its stance?

This disarray persists even as the permanent establishment is striking back. The Koirala Cabinet was marked by its exclusionary character—Dalits, women, Janjatis and Madhesis found little space in the fold. The UML instructed its MPs to take oath wearing a daura-saluwar, a symbol of the past. The NC and the UML opposed the creation of cross-party caucuses in the CA—which had enabled alliances among the excluded groups in the previous CA. Leaders of the NC were also ambivalent about their commitment to secularism. And there was a sense among political commentators of Kathmandu that politics had taken a Right-ward drift.

~

The process of political change takes generations.

In Nepal, the anti-Rana revolt of 1950 had led to the opening up of Nepali society and polity. It took thirty years of relentless struggle to restore democracy in 1990. The NC led the battle for freedom but, when it turned into the new establishment, there was resistance.

The political movement led by the Maoists created a popular new consciousness, shook up political structures and social relations, and ushered in a republic. Madhesi and ethnic politics forced open the doors of the polity to marginalized social groups. There were repeated setbacks and, at each stage, the forces of regression looked as powerful as those seeking to create a new society.

But the pattern is clear. Nepal is slowly moving towards creating a state that is more open, more democratic, more inclusive, more egalitarian and more just for its citizens. This is now an irreversible process, irrespective of electoral cycles.

The battles of the new republic—on questions of power-sharing, the nature of the army, the role of India and the principle of sovereignty, the structure of the state and the shape of federalism, the form of nationalism, and the use of violence—have defined Nepal's contemporary political journey. It is now up to the country's democratic political class to retain the fundamental political principles of republicanism, secularism, federalism, inclusion and democracy and find a middle way, a meeting point on the more specific contentious issues.

Few countries get a second chance to draft their own social contract. Nepal's Constituent Assembly provides precisely that opportunity. This time, we must not squander it.

Acknowledgements

To Aditya Adhikari—for helping me conceive this project at Jogbani Railway Station; all the alcohol-fuelled, politics-filled conversations over six years; being a partner in cynicism, hope and fury; for tempering my instincts with characteristic thoughtfulness; and for helping me frame the title for this book. Thanks man.

My greatest debt is to Nepali politicians, who have given me a glimpse of their worldviews, challenges, constraints, ambitions and vulnerabilities. I cannot possibly mention all of them here, but some stand out. Maoist leaders and former prime ministers, Pushpa Kamal Dahal 'Prachanda' and Baburam Bhattarai, opened their doors to me whenever I sought a meeting. In many ways, they are the central characters of the Nepali transition, and the story would have been incomplete without their perspectives.

At different points, President Ram Baran Yadav and former prime ministers—Sher Bahadur Deuba, Madhav Kumar Nepal, Jhalanath Khanal and Surya Bahadur Thapa—shared their insights about current Nepali politics.

Mahant Thakur, Upendra Yadav, Rajendra Mahato, J. P .Gupta, Hridayesh Tripathi, Sarvendra Nath Shukla, Rajkishore Yadav, Jitendra Dev and Jitendra Sonar from Madhesi parties; Barshaman Pun 'Ananta', Hisila Yami, Khimlal Devkota, Ram Karki and Bishwadeep Pandey of the Maoist party; Pradeep Giri, Shekhar Koirala, Bimalendra Nidhi, Ram Sharan Mahat, Minendra Rijal and Nabindra Raj Joshi of the Nepali Congress; Pradeep Gyawali, Raghuji Pant, Rajan Bhattarai and Deepak Prakash Bhatt of the Communist Party of Nepal (Unified Marxist Leninist) regularly spared time for conversations.

Four political activists—of different strains—grew to become friends. Gagan Thapa, Nepal's most popular young leader, gave me rare insights into the mind of a politician. Anil Jha, former minister for industries, told me about the struggles of a Madhesi activist. Amresh Kumar Singh, whose contribution to Nepal's peace process is often underrated, kept me informed about the latest twists and turns in the political drama. Manushi Yami Bhattarai introduced to me the idealism of a Left student activist, and the pragmatism which comes from belonging to a political family.

I continue to respect C. K. Lal—Nepal's bravest writer, who has consistently spoken truth to power at enormous personal cost—as much as I did when I was ten, when I first asked for his autograph. Devendra Raj Panday, Khagendra Sangroula, Vijay Kant Karna, Hari Roka, Dipendra Jha, Bimal Aryal and Anubhav Ajit were close comrades—all of them are involved in their own ways with Nepal's democracy and social justice movements. Tula Narayan Sah shared his life's trajectory with me, and made me understand how the political and the personal intersect. Rajeev Jha trusted me with secrets and gave me a glimpse of his life underground.

Anagha Neelakantan has been a rock and a sounding board 24/7. Yon Medina Vivanco must be the world's only honorary Peruvian-Nepali. Kathmandu would have been lonely, and the book a lot poorer, without them. Subel Bhandari, Kashish Das Shrestha, Bhaskar Gautam and Sujeev Shakya always went beyond the call of friendship. Rakesh Mishra in Biratnagar was my first port of call on any trip to the Madhes; he introduced me to life and society in the plains in new ways.

Manjushree Thapa is not only Nepal's finest English-language writer, she is also an extraordinarily generous friend—she pushed me to write, read the manuscript and gave me crucial feedback. At each of her last three book launches, she has said to me, 'You are next.' It took me a while Manju, but here it is. Thank you.

Amish Raj Mulmi was among the early readers of an initial draft and encouraged me to go ahead. Thomas Mathew is among South Asia's sharpest editors, and his perceptive feedback has enriched the book.

Ashok Gurung in New York has made extraordinary efforts to

ensure that the Nepal story figured in conversations among academics in the West, and has been a warm host on several occasions. Lt Gen. (retd.) C. B. Gurung introduced me to the unfamiliar world of military affairs. Vijay Kumar Panday shared memorable nuggets and insights from his illustrious career as Nepal's premier television anchor. Kanak Mani Dixit introduced me to long-form journalism, while I understood the art of crisp column-writing at Kunda Dixit's *Nepali Times*. Akhilesh Upadhyay stood up to enormous pressure to carry my writings, uncensored, in deeply polarized times in *The Kathmandu Post*. Conversations with Sudheer Sharma, Yubaraj Ghimire, Chandrakishore, Suman Pradhan, Ameet Dhakal, Narayan Wagle, Rajendra Dahal, Hari Sharma, Deepak Thapa, Seira Tamang, Pratyoush Onta, Lok Raj Baral, Krishna Hachhethu, Krishna Bhattachan, Deepak Gyawali, Bhekh Bahadur Thapa and Siddhartha Thapa have always been enriching.

In Delhi, Alka and Arun Chaudhary gave me a second home. Rumi and Ravi Tewari always checked to see how the book was faring, and have been kind and understanding. Ritika Sinha has always been a pillar for the family, while it was at Asha and Sanjay Jha's Patparganj home that we set up base for two years.

Sankarshan Thakur first opened up his office to give me a break in journalism and then his home to treat me as a family member. The idea of a 'gradual revolution'—the title of one section of the book—was born during a conversation with him several years ago. I have learnt more about journalism on my travels with him in Bihar and the Madhes than any textbook could have taught.

Siddharth Varadarajan recruited me at *The Hindu*, enabled the wonderful reporting opportunities which provided fodder for this book, shaped my political understanding, and always understood personal constraints. Professor S. D. Muni remains Nepal's closest friend in India, and I have learnt a lot about the bilateral relationship from him. Muni Sir spared time to read the manuscript and gave valuable inputs.

Many serving Indian officials, both in the foreign office and the intelligence apparatus, have been kind enough to share their views over the years on Nepal. They will, however, have to remain unnamed.

Conversations with some key figures in Indian diplomacy and public life—Shyam Saran, Jayant Prasad, Shiv Shanker Mukherjee, Deb Mukharji, Rakesh Sood, P. K. Hormis Tharakan, D. P. Tripathi, K. C. Tyagi, Bharat Bhushan, Harish Khare, C. Raja Mohan, C. Uday Bhaskar, Pratap Bhanu Mehta, Anuradha and Kamal Mitra Chenoy, Anand Swarup Verma and Achin Vanaik—have helped sharpen my own outlook about political developments. Menaka Guruswamy has always been a useful sounding board on matters related to the Constitution.

I have written parts of the book on a holiday with Moyukh Chatterjee in the vicinity of Shimla, discussed it in his apartment in Atlanta, and struggled with its end as we walked together in a park in Bangalore. Swara Bhaskar, Sambuddha Dutt, Ashis Roy, Uday Khare, Sukhleen Aneja, Vivek Roy and Samar Narayen have remained the SPV cushion. Aman Sethi has been a partner in ambition and crime ever since high school. Participating in politics in the Hindu College hostel, with an intimate set of friends, trained me in the ways of the world. I learnt the importance of 'structure', when debating, in Delhi University with Akash Banerjee and Rakesh Ankit. Shivam Vij brought me into kafila.org, India's best political blog. I often turned to Shruti Debi for advice on the ways of the publishing world.

I have benefited from the friendship of some leading experts on Nepal. General Sir Sam Cowan brought his military precision and thoroughness to the text. I have liberally borrowed insights and snippets of Maoist revolutionary songs from his authoritative work on the armed conflict. Ian Martin—UN diplomat par excellence and a committed peacemaker—corrected my mistakes on the technical elements of the arms management process. A. Peter Burleigh knows Nepal intimately ever since his days in the US Peace Corps in the western Tarai in the 1960s and gave perceptive feeback. John Bevan in London, David Gellner at Oxford, Sarah Levitt Shore in Brussels, Karin Landgren and Tamrat Samuel in Liberia, David Malone in Tokyo, Mark Turin and Sara Shneiderman at Yale, and Kai Bird in Lima have been helpful in many different ways.

A grant by the Norwegian Ministry of Foreign Affairs helped

sustain me over the years I worked on this book and enabled my research and travel. They tolerated my repeated requests for extensions. Ambassador Tore Toreng, Dag Nagoda and Kamla Bisht were remarkably supportive. Not once did they ask me for the manuscript or enquire about the content of the work, respecting the spirit of independent writing.

Bikas Rauniar, one of Nepal's veteran photo-journalists, and Dinesh Shrestha, who had access to the Maoists when few others did, have provided most of the pictures used in the book. Ammu Kannampilly of AFP also helped with photographs.

I first discussed *Battles of the New Republic* with Ravi Singh in 2009, and then disappeared. Four years later, when I got in touch, he still had faith in this book. His gentle nudges, precise advice, empathy for Nepal, and warmth and encouragement helped me refine the writing and enabled the book's publication. In the final stages, Anurag Basnet's meticulous copy-editing sharpened the text.

This book has been in my head for a very long time. But if it has got written, it is only because of one person. Ruhi Tewari forced me to sit down, checked what I was doing on the screen, cribbed about the distractions of the Internet, and told me, as only a journalist could, to write or I would miss the story. She also agreed to spend a year in Nepal to understand what it meant to me. Her presence in my life has given it meaning, made it fuller, more productive, and less debauched. There is more, and I am in debt. But some things are best left unsaid.

Chhotu, we are enormously proud of you and your work. Mummy, continue to be strong. Papa, I hope this brings back your smile. And Tatta, wherever you are, this is an outcome of the journey you made six-and-a-half decades ago. This book is for you.

Index